Payroll
Accounting 2016

Payroll Accounting 2016

Second Edition

Jeanette M. Landin
Landmark College

Paulette Schirmer
University of Phoenix

McGraw Hill Education

PAYROLL ACCOUNTING, SECOND EDITION

Published by McGraw-Hill Education, 2 Penn Plaza, New York, NY 10121. Copyright © 2016 by McGraw-Hill
Education. All rights reserved. Printed in the United States of America. Previous edition © 2015. No part of this
publication may be reproduced or distributed in any form or by any means, or stored in a database or retrieval
system, without the prior written consent of McGraw-Hill Education, including, but not limited to, in any
network or other electronic storage or transmission, or broadcast for distance learning.

Some ancillaries, including electronic and print components, may not be available to customers outside the
United States.

This book is printed on acid-free paper.

1 2 3 4 5 6 7 8 9 0 RMN/RMN 1 0 9 8 7 6 5

ISBN 978-1-259-57219-7

MHID 1-259-57219-6

ISSN 2373-2644

Senior Vice President, Products & Markets: *Kurt L. Strand*
Vice President, General Manager, Products & Markets: *Marty Lange*
Vice President, Content Design & Delivery: *Kimberly Meriwether David*
Managing Director: *Tim Vertovec*
Marketing Director: *Brad Parkins*
Brand Manager: *Steve Schuetz*
Director, Product Development: *Rose Koos*
Director of Digital Content: *Patricia Plumb*
Lead Product Developer: *Ann Torbert*
Product Developer: *Jonathan Thornton*
Marketing Manager: *Michelle Nolte*
Digital Product Developer: *Kevin Moran*
Digital Product Analyst: *Xin Lin*
Director, Content Design & Delivery: *Linda Avenarius*
Program Manager: *Daryl Horrocks*
Content Project Managers: *Dana M. Pauley/Brian Nacik*
Buyer: *Jennifer Pickel*
Design: *Srdjan Savanovic*
Content Licensing Specialists: *Melissa Homer/Lorraine Buczek*
Cover Image: *J.R. Bale/Alamy*
Compositor: *SPi Global*
Printer: *R. R. Donnelley*

The Internet addresses listed in the text were accurate at the time of publication. The inclusion of a website does
not indicate an endorsement by the authors or McGraw-Hill Education, and McGraw-Hill Education does not
guarantee the accuracy of the information presented at these sites.

Dedications

The authors dedicate this book to the following individuals:

For Chris, Kierstan, and Meaghan, who are the center of my universe.

—Jeanette Landin

For Royce and Elizabeth, who kept me grounded and reminded me to have fun.

—Paulette Schirmer

About the Authors

Jeanette Landin

Landmark College

Jeanette Landin is an Assistant Professor of Business and Accounting at Landmark College in Putney, Vermont, where she teaches undergraduate accounting and business courses to an at-risk student population. She is the faculty advisor for the college's Phi Beta Lambda chapter. Professor Landin is also a Certified Advanced Facilitator with the University of Phoenix, where she teaches composition and communications courses at the associate's level. Dr. Landin earned her B.A. degree from the University of California at Irvine before receiving her M.B.A. and Ed.D. from University of Phoenix, where she conducted research into college success strategies for at-risk students. She has earned Master's certificates in Accounting and Autism Spectrum Disorders.

She is an active member of the Institute for Management Accountants (IMA), Teachers of Accounting Curriculum at Two-Year Colleges (TACTYC), and Vermont Women in Higher Education (VWHE), and previously served as an active member of the California Business Educators Association and the Western Business Educators Association. Dr. Landin currently serves on the IMA's Committee for Academic Relations and as a peer reviewer for the American Accounting Association. She is a peer reviewer for the *Transnational Journal of Business* and a member of the Business Editorial Board with the Multimedia Educational Resource for Learning and Online Teaching (MERLOT).

Paulette Schirmer

University of Phoenix

Paulette Schirmer is an accountant with the Division of Finance for the State of Alaska and a Certified Advanced Facilitator for the University of Phoenix, where she teaches accounting courses at the bachelor's and master's level. Dr. Schirmer received her B.S. in Accounting from Metropolitan State College of Denver (now Metropolitan State University of Denver), her M.B.A. from Regis University, and her D.B.A. from University of Phoenix, where she conducted research on globalization strategies for small businesses.

Dr. Schirmer is active in the preparation of Alaska's Comprehensive Annual Financial Reports and that state's annual Compensation and Travel Report, as well as training state employees on the state's financial and reporting systems.

Businesses employ people, and part of employing people is compensating them for their labors. Labor costs often represent the largest company expenditure as well as the most complex one. Payroll accounting is very detailed, deadline driven, and of utmost importance for the successful functioning of a business. The changing, detailed nature of payroll accounting involves legal challenges, economic changes, technological advances, and—above all—governmental obligations. As we sought payroll accounting materials for study by our students, we realized that not many textbooks about the subject existed. We are passionate about college education. Our aim in *Payroll Accounting 2016* is to provide instructors with a payroll accounting text that allows them to teach students how to navigate this highly specialized and extremely necessary aspect of accounting.

When we began updating the materials for *Payroll Accounting 2016,* we noticed how quickly payroll information changes and how much it mirrors societal evolution. We continue to rely on the guidance of our colleagues, instructor feedback from the first edition, and the information gained from our peers. Additions to the second edition reflect industry and student needs, and we continue to follow these trends to inform future updates.

Our approach to payroll accounting is different from other existing texts because we have chosen to include both the financial and managerial accounting pieces so that students can understand both the techniques involved and the importance of their work in the broader scope of business. We have worked very hard to present content that is concise, thorough, and easy to follow. We are excited to produce this work through McGraw-Hill because of the top-quality teaching and learning resources that the company makes available. Teaching traditional payroll accounting and Internet-based financial accounting via McGraw-Hill's Connect platform for several years has been a wonderful experience for both our students and ourselves.

Our text features many interesting real-world connections throughout. We've drawn examples from many different disciplines to help make payroll accounting come alive for teachers and students alike. Two discussions are unique: (1) the content in Chapter 5 that explores labor planning (Learning Objectives 5-5 and 5-6) and (2) the discussion in Chapter 6 about the function of labor costs in business and employee benefit reports as strategic tools (Learning Objective 6-7). We believe that this information contributes to a comprehensive understanding of payroll accounting in the 21st century and that it will make accounting students more valuable to the organizations they work for in their careers.

Many payroll frauds and scandals occur in the real world. Payroll fraud continues to be a major source of loss for companies, and it is surprising to find how commonly it happens. We've included examples of the frauds that employees have perpetrated in recent years. One notable case that highlighted the scope of payroll fraud involved a $700 million scheme that resulted in hundreds of jobs lost and for which the perpetrators remain at large. Students are interested in these stories, which enliven and enrich class discussion. We've also included a section in each chapter about ethics and internal controls to teach students how to prevent payroll fraud and to identify potential data breaches. We believe that this information about internal controls will become increasingly important as sensitive personnel information becomes more readily accessible with the inclusion of cloud-based payroll systems.

Payroll accounting and the associated fields of economics and finance are continually evolving. As a result, the payroll industry contains an ever-changing array of rules and regulations, and the "Trends to Watch" box in each chapter will highlight the trends known at the time of publication. On the legal front, we are watching the ripple effects of the Supreme Court's legalization of same-sex marriages upon businesses and employees. The intersection of this legislation and the Affordable Care Act has affected employee benefits and tax reporting. Other trends we are watching include issues of cybersecurity that challenge the notion of secure electronic payroll deposits and cause internal control guidelines and new regulations to respond to the changing needs of the economy. In the "Internet Activities" sections at the end of each chapter, we provide Internet links for students who want to explore payroll topics in more depth.

In addition, we provide both a continuing problem, which is located at the end of each chapter, and a full-quarter additional comprehensive problem, located in Appendix A. Technological integration of the continuing problem and Appendix A within Connect provides a good tool for student learning. Smartbook, LearnSmart, and walk-through examples of tax forms are used to reinforce the questions and key terminology. A shortened version of Appendix A is another option for instructors who want a comprehensive problem with fewer payroll periods.

From our perspective, payroll accounting is complex enough to warrant specific attention in the curriculum.

Payroll Accounting 2016 is designed to fit the needs of terms as short as 3 weeks and as long as 15 weeks. The instructor may choose to assign the exercise sets found at the end of each chapter, the Continuing Payroll Project in each chapter, or the Comprehensive Project that encompasses an entire quarter of payroll accounting. We designed the content to give instructors curricular flexibility by offering many options for formative and summative assessments.

We are proud of what we have accomplished with this text and strongly believe that we have taken payroll accounting education to a higher level of rigor. The content of *Payroll Accounting 2016* is rich in its detail, yet readily understandable by students who may have little or no prior accounting information. We have included materials to show the integration of payroll in other aspects of both managerial and financial accounting as well as business operations. Within Appendix E, we have provided materials that allow readers to learn about payroll within the context of their own state's legal framework and links to each state's revenue department to facilitate specific learning. We hope that you enjoy reading and learning from this text as much as we enjoyed writing it.

Jeanette Landin
Paulette Schirmer

Changes to the Second Edition

Based on feedback from our reviewers and users, we have made several changes to this second edition of *Payroll Accounting*. We appreciate all the feedback we have received and user recommendations because they have helped us create a stronger, more complete text. The changes we have made have added clarity, updated information, and additional opportunities for students to demonstrate their understanding of the concepts presented. For instructors, we have revised our learning objectives to incorporate Bloom's taxonomy verbs and have correlated the learning objectives with End-of-Chapter exercises. The answers for the Stop & Check sections are now included at the end of the chapters.

The following are specific changes to each chapter.

Chapter 1

In Chapter 1, we updated payroll-related legislation to reflect as many changes as possible prior to publication. We have included specific information about the effects of the Affordable Care Act on payroll management with regards to reporting requirements. We addressed guidance from the U.S. Department of Labor about payroll treatment of same-sex marriages, a topic that is continuing to evolve. We incorporated information about the changing nature of exempt worker classification and discussed cloud-based payroll accounting practices.

Chapter 2

In Chapter 2, we included highlights of upcoming guidance about employees that will be issued by the Equal Employment Opportunity Commission. We included some payroll-specific items about the current debate about minimum wage. We added information about applications available via smartphones and tablets that foster improved accuracy and increased employee involvement in time tracking and payroll file maintenance. We discussed proposed paycard legislation that would both facilitate employee access to compensation and guard employees against fraud. We included a graphic to clarify document retention requirements.

Chapter 3

Chapter 3 opens with updated minimum wage and tipped minimum wage information. We added depth and clarity to the discussion of overtime calculations, especially for piece-rate workers. We included statistical information about Incentive Stock Options and executive pay, topics that are becoming discussed more frequently by government officials. We added information to the discussion of special pay situations and exercises to for students to apply their learning.

Chapter 4

We extended our discussion of insurance coverage with details about employer mandates under the Affordable Care Act. We created a chart to help students understand the differences among employer-sponsored retirement plans and clarification about Section 125 (cafeteria) items. We included step-by-step guidance about using the wage-bracket tables in Publication 15 to determine federal income tax withholding amounts. The discussion of post-tax deductions includes more detail about mandated post-tax deductions and limits on amounts that may be withheld. We offered a detailed explanation about the computation of grossed-up pay and figure with explicit details about paper paychecks.

Chapter 5

In Chapter 5, we have updated employer payroll tax information, especially as it pertains to FUTA and SUTA amounts. We have included guidance about employee compensation not subject to FUTA. All tax forms have been updated with the current year's editions. Figure 5-8 has been included to depict statistics about employer benefit costs to offer students a more complete picture of how payroll affects business profitability, reflecting payroll accounting's effect on managerial accounting. End-of-Chapter Exercise sections contain questions about Forms W-2 and W-3 so students may practice this skill.

Chapter 6

Chapter 6 opens with a discussion about employee retention and connects the payroll procedures discussed in the previous chapters to financial accounting concepts. We have updated the transactions to reflect current-year tax rates and have updated all accounting reports to match the presentation students will see in the End-of-Chapter Exercises.

Appendix A: Comprehensive Payroll Project

We have changed the location of Wayland Custom Wood-working to the state of Utah to facilitate computations of State Withholding Tax. We have included explicit instructions about the completion of employee paychecks.

Appendix D: State Income Tax Tables

We have included included tax rates for each state in Appendix D. This new information includes tax brackets, both married and single, and marginal tax rates.

Appendix F: Payroll Certification Information

We have included information from the American Payroll Association about its Fundamental Payroll Certification (FPC). Upon completion of their payroll course, students could consider obtaining this certification to add to their career portfolio.

Text Features

Chapter Opener

Each chapter opens by focusing on a payroll accounting topic related to a real-world company, to set the stage for the topic of the chapter.

Chapter

1

Payroll Practices and System Fundamentals

The payroll system of a company is the backbone of its employees' records and serves many functions. The most obvious and visible role for a company's payroll department is the employee pay and benefits management function. However, a well-designed payroll system can do so much more. Payroll systems are an integral part of job planning and strategic human resource management, cost management for products and services, and benefits analysis for a company. In this chapter, we will explore the need for a payroll system, legal requirements, ethical guidelines, best practices, and variations in payroll practices among different-sized companies.

LEARNING OBJECTIVES

After studying Chapter 1, you should be able to:

LO 1-1   Understand the Purpose of Studying Payroll Accounting

LO 1-2   Discuss the Legal Framework for Payroll Accounting

LO 1-3   Discuss the Ethical Guidelines for Payroll Accounting

LO 1-4   Identify Contemporary Payroll Practices

LO 1-5   Compare Payroll Processing Options for Different Businesses

Which Law?

STOP & CHECK

1. Requires employers to verify the employee's legal right to work in the United States?
2. Protects the rights of disabled workers?
3. Governs the management of retirement plans?
4. Protects discrimination of workers older than age 40?
5. Creates safe work environments for employees?
6. Mandates equal pay for equal work?
7. Extends medical benefits for terminated employees?
8. Ensures that child support obligations will be paid?
9. Protects workers and families with pre-existing medical conditions?
10. Enforces payment of monetary damages because of discrimination?

Stop & Check

The Stop & Check feature allows students to review their understanding of the content just read. It also enables instructors to conduct formative assessments at multiple points throughout each chapter, testing the students' understanding informally as well as offering opportunities to expand on the material.

Trends to Watch

Each chapter contains a feature box that connects payroll-related recent events with industry trends that shape the future of the profession. These trends offer instructors more opportunities to expand upon chapter topics, fostering discussion and application.

Trends to Watch

LEGAL ENVIRONMENT

To say that the legal environment of payroll is continually evolving is an understatement. During the early part of the 2010s, we have witnessed the following legal challenges:

- Modification of language in employee handbooks to refine terminology and remove offensive wording.
- Official revisions to define the term *supervisor* as it pertains to employee discrimination.
- Employer liability for accidents following alcohol consumption at employer functions.
- Repeal of the Defense of Marriage Act, which changed the definition of married couples to include same-sex unions.

End-of-Chapter Exercises

Students can demonstrate their understanding through exercises designed to complement the chapter's learning objectives. Each chapter has two alternative sets of exercises (A and B) to allow flexibility in classroom instruction and assessment.

Exercises Set A

1-1A.
LO 1-6

Anya is a candidate for the position of sales manager with the footwear department of a major retail outlet. She is going to be required to supervise several employees and can determine the direction in which she will complete the assignments given to her. What classification of employee should she be, exempt or nonexempt? Explain.

1-2A.
LO 1-6

John is the office manager for a small mortgage brokerage. Because it is a small office, he is required to keep track of all employee records

Critical Thinking Exercises

Want to challenge your students further? The Critical Thinking exercises require students to consider complex real-world situations that build confidence and turn learning into mastery. These exercises offer possibilities for team presentations or class debate.

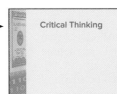

Critical Thinking	1-1. You have been hired as a consultant for a company facing accounting records. During your review, you notice and system involving overpayments of labor and payments to ees. What should you do?
	1-2. Lee Chen is the accountant for a local nonprofit organi tasked with managing the costs of the payroll so that staffi the same even if funding levels change. He considers ou to a payroll processing company. What are some factors sider in his decision? Why are these factors important?

In the Real World: Scenario for Discussion	The Brinker Restaurant Group, owners of restaurant franchises such as Chi and Bar and Maggiano's Little Italy, was sued by its employees for not pr adequate meal and rest breaks for employees. According to the Californi Code §512 and Wage Order no. 5, employees must be provided with re ods—specifically, a 30-minute meal break—every five hours that they wor 10 hours of consecutive work, the employee must be given a second mea The California Supreme Court ruled that the rest breaks had to be offered, employer did not have to ensure that the employee actually rested.
	What do you think? Should employers ensure that employees on breaks form any work? Why or why not?

In the Real World: Scenarios for Discussion

Each chapter contains a discussion scenario that is drawn from real-world events. These scenarios encourage the expansion of chapter content and allow students to apply their learning to real situations.

Internet Activities

The Internet Activities at the end of each chapter offer students the chance to use their Web navigation skills to expand on their learning. These exercises attract tech-savvy learners, allowing them to form their own understanding of payroll concepts on their own terms.

Internet Activities	1-1. Using the website www.jstor.org, search for articles about payroll-related laws or relevant employment legislation. Once you find an article, summarize the article, and explain how the legislation influenced contemporary payroll practices.
	1-2. Visit the website of the American Payroll Association at www.americanpayroll .org. On the right side of the Home page, you will find articles about recent developments in payroll practices and legislation. Choose an article and create a presentation to your class about how its content affects payroll practice.

Continuing Problem: Prevosti Farms and Sugarhouse

Starting with Chapter 1, each chapter has an integrated, continuing problem—about fictional company Prevosti Farms and Sugarhouse—that matches the chapter content and affords students a macro-level understanding of how each piece of payroll fits together.

Continuing Payroll Project: Prevosti Farms and Sugarhouse	Toni Prevosti is opening a new business, Prevosti Farms and Sugarhouse, which is a small company that will harvest, refine, and sell maple syrup products. In subsequent chapters, students will have the opportunity to establish payroll records and complete payroll information for Prevosti Farms and Sugarhouse.
	Toni has decided that she needs to hire employees for the business to grow. Complete the application for Prevosti Farms and Sugarhouse's Employer Identification Number (Form SS-4) with the following information:
	Prevosti Farms and Sugarhouse is located at 820 Westminster Road, Bridgewater, Vermont, 05520 (which is also Ms. Prevosti's home address), phone number 802-555-3456. Bridgewater is in Windsor County. Toni has decided that Prevosti Farms and Sugarhouse, the responsible party for a sole proprietorship, will pay its employees on a biw... Toni's Social Security number is 05... The

Appendix

Comprehensive Payroll Project: Wayland Custom Woodworking

Wayland Custom Woodworking is a firm that manufactures custom cabinets and woodwork for business and residential customers. Students will have the opportunity to establish payroll records and to complete and to complete all payroll information for Wayland.

Wayland Custom Woodworking is located at 1716 Nichol Street, Logan, UT 84321, phone number 435-555-9877. The owner is Mark Wayland. Wayland's EIN is 91-7444533, and the Utah Employer Account Number is 999-9290-1. Wayland has determined it will pay its employees on a semimonthly basis.

Students will complete the payroll for the final quarter of 2015 and will file fourth quarter and annual tax reports on the appropriate dates. When writing out the dollar amount for each check, write out all words and present cents as fractions of 100. For example, $1,250.50 would be One Thousand Two Hundred Fifty and 50/100.

At the instructor's discretion, students may complete a short version, which contains the payroll transactions beginning... number 1. Directions for completion of the short version follow the December 30...

Comprehensive Problem

The Comprehensive Problem (Appendix A) allows students to track a quarter's worth of payroll transactions for a company. This Comprehensive Problem offers instructors increased flexibility in teaching and assessment by offering a simulation equivalent to a full quarter of a fictitious company's payroll activities, including payroll transactions, pay processing, and tax form completion. The Comprehensive Problem may be presented in different lengths—as short as one month or in its three-month entirety—to meet curricular needs.

Required=Results

McGraw-Hill Connect®
Learn Without Limits

Connect is a teaching and learning platform that is proven to deliver better results for students and instructors.

Connect empowers students by continually adapting to deliver precisely what they need, when they need it, and how they need it, so your class time is more engaging and effective.

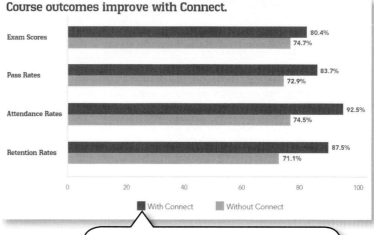

Course outcomes improve with Connect.

	With Connect	Without Connect
Exam Scores	80.4%	74.7%
Pass Rates	83.7%	72.9%
Attendance Rates	92.5%	74.5%
Retention Rates	87.5%	71.1%

Using **Connect** improves passing rates by **10.8%** and retention by **16.4%**.

88% of instructors who use **Connect** require it; instructor satisfaction **increases** by 38% when **Connect** is required.

Analytics

Connect Insight®

Connect Insight is Connect's new one-of-a-kind visual analytics dashboard—now available for both instructors and students—that provides at-a-glance information regarding student performance, which is immediately actionable. By presenting assignment, assessment, and topical performance results together with a time metric that is easily visible for aggregate or individual results, Connect Insight gives the user the ability to take a just-in-time approach to teaching and learning, which was never before available. Connect Insight presents data that empowers students and helps instructors improve class performance in a way that is efficient and effective.

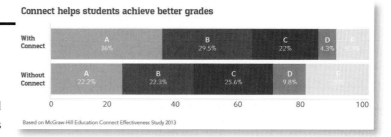

Connect helps students achieve better grades

	A	B	C	D	F
With Connect	36%	29.5%	22%	4.3%	
Without Connect	22.2%	22.3%	25.6%	9.8%	

Based on McGraw-Hill Education Connect Effectiveness Study 2013

Students can view their results for any **Connect** course.

Mobile

Connect's new, intuitive mobile interface gives students and instructors flexible and convenient, anytime–anywhere access to all components of the Connect platform.

Adaptive

THE FIRST AND ONLY **ADAPTIVE READING EXPERIENCE** DESIGNED TO TRANSFORM THE WAY STUDENTS READ

More students earn **A's** and **B's** when they use McGraw-Hill Education **Adaptive** products.

SmartBook®

Proven to help students improve grades and study more efficiently, SmartBook contains the same content within the print book, but actively tailors that content to the needs of the individual. SmartBook's adaptive technology provides precise, personalized instruction on what the student should do next, guiding the student to master and remember key concepts, targeting gaps in knowledge and offering customized feedback, and driving the student toward comprehension and retention of the subject matter. Available on smartphones and tablets, SmartBook puts learning at the student's fingertips—anywhere, anytime.

Over **4 billion questions** have been answered, making McGraw-Hill Education products more intelligent, reliable, and precise.

STUDENTS WANT

SMARTBOOK®

95% of students reported **SmartBook** to be a more effective way of reading material

100% of students want to use the Practice Quiz feature available within **SmartBook** to help them study

100% of students reported having reliable access to off-campus wifi

90% of students say they would purchase **SmartBook** over print alone

95% reported that **SmartBook** would impact their study skills in a positive way

Mc Graw Hill Education

*Findings based on a 2015 focus group survey at Pellissippi State Community College administered by McGraw-Hill Education

Technology Features

End-of-Chapter Content

End-of-Chapter Content is a robust offering of review and question material designed to aid and assess the student's retention of chapter content. The End-of-Chapter content is comprised of both static and algorithmic exercises, which are designed to challenge students using McGraw-Hill Education's state-of-the-art online homework technology. Instructors can also assign test bank questions to students in both static and algorithmic versions.

Payroll Form Problems

Templated payroll forms are integrated into *Connect* and are assignable. Students can complete the forms in these problems to gain a better understanding of how payroll forms are prepared in today's digital world.

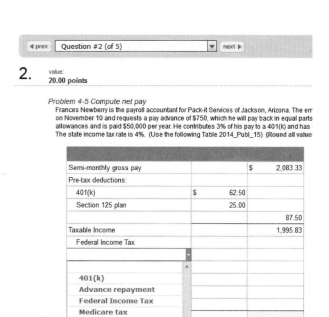

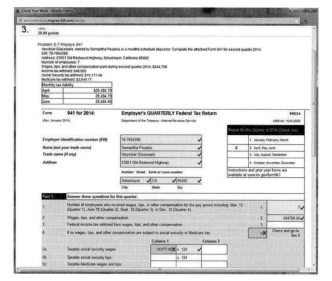

Acknowledgments

This second edition of *Payroll Accounting* would not have been possible without the patience, guidance, and encouragement of Steve Schuetz, Brand Manager; the diligence and commitment of Jonathan Thornton, Product Developer; the support and leadership of Dana Pauley and Brian Nacik, Content Project Managers; the incredible form templates designed by Kitty O'Donnell; and the amazing artwork of Srdjan Savanovic, Designer. We further want to thank Michelle Nolte, Marketing Manager; Melissa Homer and Lorraine Buczek, Content Licensing Specialists; Patricia Plumb, Director of Digital Content Development; Xin Lin, Digital Product Analyst; Kevin Moran, Digital Product Developer; and the compositing team at SPi Global. Special thanks goes to Anna Hoppmann, Digital Asset Librarian, and to Connie Schleisman and the Technical Support team for facilitating our online access and asset location needs. Thanks go to our project development team who handled every formatting request with professionalism.

A very special acknowledgment goes to the accounting students at Empire College who bravely tested and offered critical feedback on our comprehensive project during its early stages. We want to thank Allison LeBon for her assistance with the Benefit Analysis Report. Thank you also must go to Samantha Cox and Rick Street for the critical feedback and insights they offered to help us develop this second edition. We also wish to thank Samantha Cox, Paige Paulsen, and Rick Street, who helped us maintain the integrity of our work. We appreciate the patience and accommodations given by many of our colleagues, especially Tara Vrabec, Scot Arehart, and Roxanne Hamilton, who helped us balance our work and production schedules so that we could complete this textbook.

Countless other colleagues have offered their feedback, insights, and inspiration during various stages of this project. We want to extend sincere thanks to the reviewers and TACTYC session attendees who helped us shape the second edition:

Mark Bell
Maysville Community & Technical College

Michael Belleman
Saint Clair County Community College

William Brothers
Southwestern Community College

Gay Lynn Brown
Northwest Florida State College

Christine Crosby
York Technical College

Judy Daulton
Piedmont Technical College

Susan Davis
Green River Community College

Julie Dilling
Moraine Park Technical College

Lisa Gray
Valencia College

Steven Houston
Community College of Baltimore County

Anthony Newton
Highline Community College

Joseph Nicassio
Westmoreland County Community College

Paige Paulsen
Salt Lake Community College

Jamie Payton
Gadsden State Community College

Ronald Pearson
Bay de Noc Community College

M. Jeff Quinlan
Madison Area Technical College

Brian Schmoldt
Madison Area Technical College

Regina Shea
Community College of Baltimore County

Carolyn Strauch
Crowder College

Dominique Svarc
William Rainey Harper College

Melissa Youngerman
National Technical Institute for the Deaf

Our heart-felt thanks to all who have helped make this project a reality.

Jeanette Landin
Paulette Schirmer

Brief Contents

Contents

Chapter 6
The Payroll Register, Employees' Earning Records, and Accounting System Entries 204

Appendixes

Chapter 1

Payroll Practices and System Fundamentals

The payroll system of a company is the backbone of its employees' records and serves many functions. The most obvious and visible role for a company's payroll department is the employee pay and benefits management function. However, a well-designed payroll system can do so much more. Payroll systems are an integral part of job planning and strategic human resource management, cost management for products and services, and benefits analysis for a company. In this chapter, we will explore the need for a payroll system, legal requirements, ethical guidelines, best practices, and variations in payroll practices among different-sized companies.

LEARNING OBJECTIVES

After studying Chapter 1, you should be able to:

LO 1-1   Understand the Purpose of Studying Payroll Accounting

LO 1-2   Discuss the Legal Framework for Payroll Accounting

LO 1-3   Discuss the Ethical Guidelines for Payroll Accounting

LO 1-4   Identify Contemporary Payroll Practices

LO 1-5   Compare Payroll Processing Options for Different Businesses

LO 1-6   Differentiate between Exempt and Nonexempt Workers

Payroll Challenges for the World's Largest Employer

Walmart, based in Bentonville, Arkansas, is the largest American employer according to *24/7 Wall Street*. As of fiscal year 2014, Wal-Mart Stores, Inc., (d.b.a. Wal-Mart) employed 2.2 million workers, making it the largest private employer in the world. More than 1.4 million of Wal-Mart Stores' employees work in the United States. As of February 2015, Wal-Mart Stores announced that it would increase the minimum starting wage to $9.00 per hour for more than 500,000 employees due to long-standing pressure from labor organizations, and that the average wage for full-time workers will rise to $13.00 per hour. This wage increase represents an additional $1 billion in personnel costs to the company. As of 2014, Walmart retained its top spot in the Fortune 500 ranking of companies with the largest revenue, $476.3 billion, and more than $16 billion in profits. (Sources: *Reuters, Fortune Magazine, 24/7 Wall Street*)

The need for organized payroll practices grows in proportion to the business size. Companies have many options for their payroll management, depending on the firm's structure and size. In Chapter 1, we will explore the basics of payroll systems, including legal and ethical issues involved with employee pay.

LO 1-1   Understand the Purpose of Studying Payroll Accounting

Unlike many other types of accounting, payroll affects most (if not all) members of an organization. Payroll errors could lead to serious internal and external problems. Internal errors may cause a company to pay excessive wages for unneeded overtime, forego profits, or employ the wrong number of workers during seasonal or other workflow changes. Managers use internal reports about labor usage, staffing levels, and employee compensation trends to ensure operational effectiveness. Organizational decision makers use these reports to control labor costs, hire additional employees to meet surge demands, and manage the cost of goods sold. Payroll errors can result in governmental fines, taxes, or legal charges related to the violation of labor laws. External reports are provided to the Internal Revenue Service (IRS), state government tax departments, and many more agencies, depending upon the nature of the company.

According to the United States Bureau of Labor Statistics in 2015, the accounting industry is expected to increase 13% through 2022. Salaries can range between $34,960 for financial clerks and $63,550 for accountants with bachelor's degrees. (Source: www .bls.gov/ooh)

The legislative framework governing employers' payroll systems is very complex. These laws reflect societal evolution over time. Note how some of these laws have been challenged or changed since their inception.

The Equal Pay Act of 1963 mandated that males and females be paid equally for equal work. If an employee feels that they have been paid unequally and the only clear delineation is based upon gender, the employee has legal options to rectify the situation.

- First, they should gather documentation regarding the differential and determine if the other employee in question is willing to substantiate the difference.
- Second, they should speak with their supervisor to question the pay differential.
- Should the supervisor be unwilling to discuss or adjust, an attorney may become a necessary third step.

This Act was modified by the **Lilly Ledbetter Fair Pay Act of 2009,** which removed the 180-day statute of limitations on claims of unequal treatment.

> In 1979, Lilly Ledbetter, an employee of Goodyear Tire and Rubber Company, started at the same rate of pay as males in the same position. Over time, she was declined raises by management, which based its decisions on negative reviews that Ms. Ledbetter later claimed were discriminatory. Under the provisions of the 1963 Equal Pay Act, the claimant had 180 days to file a complaint. Although the U.S. Supreme Court agreed with her discrimination claims, it ruled in favor of Goodyear because of the lack of timeliness of Ms. Ledbetter's filing. This ruling ultimately led to the Lilly Ledbetter Fair Pay Act of 2009. (Source: www.govtrack.us)

The Civil Rights Act of 1964 prohibited discrimination based on race, creed, color, gender, or national origin. Since 1964, this Act has been extended by Executive Order 11478 to protect people with AIDS, pregnant workers, people with different sexual orientations, and people with disabilities. In 2015, discussions about LGBT employees' rights and workplace treatment have sparked debates about equal treatment based on sexual orientation and gender identity. (Source: www.eeoc.gov)

The Age Discrimination in Employment Act of 1967 (ADEA) prevents mandatory retirement of older employees (older than age 40) and prohibits age-based discrimination in hiring.

Several landmark cases followed ADEA enactment. Some of the most notable cases involved commercial airline pilots who were discriminated against based on their age, not their ability to pilot an airline. In the case of *Trans World Airlines v. Thurston* (1985), the defendant disputed the FAA's mandatory retirement age for pilots, claiming that older pilots should be given the same rights as disabled pilots, which involves reassigning these individuals as flight engineers. The U.S. Supreme Court upheld Thurston's claim but denied the double damages that Thurston sought. (Source: legal-dictionary.thefreedictionary.com)

The Occupational Safety and Health Act of 1970 (OSHA) defined and enforced healthy and safe working environments for employees. Employee safety programs and personal protective equipment represent an additional cost to the employer, but fines for noncompliance and payments made following workplace injuries are often far more costly.

© Martin Barraud/Caia Image/Glow Images, RF

The Employee Retirement Income Security Act of 1974 (ERISA) regulates the management of retirement and pension plans. ERISA has been extended by the Consolidated Omnibus Budget Reformation Act of 1986. During the recession of 2007–2009, the value of some employee retirement funds decreased, causing employees to postpone retirement. The Internal Revenue Service imposes limitations on retirement plan contributions, and those limits have shifted to reflect the need for employees to recoup losses sustained during the recession.

In *CIGNA v. Amara* (2011), the U.S. Supreme Court ruled on communications issued by retirement plan administrators. CIGNA was found in violation of ERISA because of its misleading and incomplete communications to plan participants that resulted in misunderstandings about the benefit level due to the participant. The Court ruled that the benefit level accrued under the plan needed to be commensurate with the benefits received upon the participant's retirement. (Source: www.nixonpeabody.com)

The Consolidated Omnibus Budget Reconciliation Act of 1985 (COBRA) extended medical benefits for terminated employees at the employee's expense. The federal government, in response to the high unemployment rates at the start of 2010, briefly subsidized COBRA insurance. The temporary reduction in COBRA remains available, but only for employees who were terminated between September 1, 2008, and March 31, 2010. The repeal of the Defense of Marriage Act (DOMA) in 2013 forced employers to offer COBRA coverage to same-sex spouses. (Sources: U.S. Department of Labor, SHRM)

The Immigration Reform and Control Act of 1986 (IRCA) requires employers to verify that employees are legally able to work in the United States. The form I-9 is the most common payroll-related application of this law. Immigration and citizenship laws require the collection of information within an I-9, and retention is three years from date of hire or one year from date of termination (whichever is longer).

© Image Source/PunchStock, RF

H.R. 399, Secure Our Borders First Act of 2015–2016, would strengthen immigration restrictions, affecting the number of immigrant workers available. Agribusiness is a $374 billion industry that is heavily dependent on immigrant workers. (Sources: www.congress.gov, immigrationimpact.com)

The Americans with Disabilities Act of 1990 (ADA) extended the provisions of the Civil Rights Act of 1964 by ensuring that people with disabilities have the same opportunities as those without mental or physical impairment. This law applies to employers with 15 or more employees on the payroll, including full-time and part-time workers.

The Civil Rights Act of 1991 granted employees who have been discriminated against the chance to be paid monetary damages through legal proceedings. This act applies to American employers and American-controlled employers with internationally based operations.

> In the case of *Pollard v. DuPont* (2000), Sharon Pollard sued DuPont for her managers' knowledge of a hostile work environment created by sexual harassment. Under Section VII of the Civil Rights Act of 1964, Ms. Pollard would not have received compensation for her complaint. However, the 1991 revision of the Civil Rights Act allowed her to receive $300,000 in compensation for damages. (Source: www.oyez.org)

The Family and Medical Leave Act of 1993 (FMLA) granted employees the right to take medical leave under reasonable circumstances without fear of job loss. The employee may have to take unpaid leave, but medical benefits must continue under FMLA provisions. Upon return from family leave, the employer must provide an equivalent position with equivalent pay, benefits, and terms of employment. The employer has many responsibilities under the FMLA that involve employee notification of benefits and processes while on leave. The repeal of DOMA provoked the need to clarify the term "family member." In 2015, the U.S. Department of Labor updated the definition of spouse to include same-sex marriages, regardless of where they live. (Source: U.S. Department of Labor)

> In the case of *Young v. Wackenhut,* the plaintiff was on unpaid leave according to FMLA provisions. Ms. Young had completed all forms provided by Wackenhut, her employer; however, Wackenhut neglected to issue a specific, individual notice about requirements involved with her return to work. The New Jersey District Court ruled in favor of Ms. Young because Wackenhut did not satisfy all stipulated notification requirements of FMLA. (Source: www.lexology.com)

© Hill Street Studios/Blend Images/ Alamy, RF

The Uniformed Services Employment and Reemployment Rights Act of 1994 (USERRA) governs the rights of military service members in terms of length of military service, return to work, and accommodations for injured veterans. USERRA was amended as to service members' rights in 2005. In 2011, USERRA was further amended by the Veterans Opportunity to Work, which allowed USERRA to recognize claims of a hostile work environment resulting from an individual's military status.

> The U.S. Department of Labor investigates many cases involving service members' rights. A notable case involved an Army reservist, Colonel Scott Harrison, who served multiple tours in the Middle East, during which he received many rank promotions for his military work. His civilian employer denied him promotions, stating that his military service detracted from his work performance. USERRA states that a service member must receive the same promotions and compensation that they would have received if they had not been absent for military purposes. Colonel Harrison received a promotion plus $96,000 in lost wages because of USERRA. (Source: U.S. Department of Labor)

The Personal Responsibility and Work Opportunity Reconciliation Act of 1996 (PRWOR) mandated that employers file a new hire reporting form within 20 days after an employee initially commences work. This act protected children and needy families by enforcing child support obligations. The child support provisions of PRWOR were strengthened by the passage of the **Personal Responsibility, Work and Family Promotion Act of 2002.**

The Health Insurance Portability and Accountability Act of 1996 (HIPAA) protects workers and their families who have pre-existing medical conditions from discrimination based on those conditions. The Ebola outbreak in 2014 led to additional guidance about HIPAA rights and notifications to interested parties, including employers, during emergency situations,

> In *Equal Employment Opportunity Commission v. Boston Market* (2004), the plaintiff claimed that Boston Market, an employer, sought access to employees' private psychological and medical records. Although the Supreme Court ultimately found that state law was more stringent than HIPAA legislation, Boston Market was found in violation of patient privacy law by seeking communication with medical professionals without prior specific authorization. (Source: www.americanbar.org)

The Sarbanes–Oxley Act of 2002 (SOX) provided criminal penalties for violations of ERISA. SOX provides protections for whistleblowers and mandates the rotation of auditors among publicly owned companies. Costs of SOX compliance have sparked discussion about the Act's effectiveness, especially following the 2008 financial crisis.

> An employee of Countrywide Mortgage, a Bank of America subsidiary, alerted OSHA officials to fraud in the company's financial records. This employee led internal investigations that revealed significant fraud in monetary transactions, as well as a history of retaliation against other whistleblowers. In 2011, the U.S. Department of Labor found Bank of America to be in violation of the Sarbanes–Oxley Act's whistleblower provision and awarded $930,000 to the employee. (Source: www.osha.gov)

The American Recovery and Reinvestment Act of 2009 (ARRA) provided tax credits for employers and employees through the Making Work Pay provisions. Changes in withholding allowances reduced the amount of taxes collected from workers, and unemployed individuals received between $400 and $800 on their tax return based upon specific qualifications within the act. Although ARRA's provisions have expired, parts of it were reinstated through the *American Taxpayer Relief Act of 2012 (ATRA)*. Many of the ATRA provisions were extended through 2015 by the extension of the Work Opportunity Tax Credit.

The Defense of Marriage Act of 1996 (DOMA) restricted payroll-related taxes and benefits to include only traditionally married couples, denying married status to people in same-sex unions. The U.S. Supreme Court overturned DOMA in its ruling in *U.S. v. Windsor* on September 6, 2013; the Internal Revenue Service subsequently mandated that all married same-sex couples must be treated as married for all tax purposes. The repeal of DOMA had a ripple effect throughout all phases of payroll because of the need to amend business and personal tax return filings back to 2011, owing to the three-year amendment rule. The effects of DOMA's repeal have had a ripple effect on employee rights, highlighting the need for additional legislative clarification.

> In *U.S. v. Windsor,* Ms. Windsor and her wife were recognized as a married couple by the State of New York and her compensation was taxed accordingly.
> *(continued)*

(concluded)

However, the IRS sued Windsor for unpaid taxes because her same-sex marriage violated DOMA. The U.S. Supreme Court found that DOMA violated Windsor's Fifth Amendment right to liberty and overturned DOMA. The IRS subsequently dropped its lawsuit. (Source: www.supremecourt.gov)

As times change, new legislation will be enacted, and existing laws are sometimes repealed and amended. For example, Vermont Governor Peter Shumlin proposed an additional 0.7% payroll tax effective in 2016 to offset employee healthcare costs related to the Affordable Care Act.

The payroll accountant's job is one of consistent and continual learning and research to ensure that the company is complying with all current regulations and reporting requirements. Many states, but not all, have additional payroll tax laws.

(See www.americanpayroll.org/weblink/statelocal-wider/ for more information)

Which Law?

STOP & CHECK

1. Requires employers to verify the employee's legal right to work in the United States?
2. Protects the rights of disabled workers?
3. Governs the management of retirement plans?
4. Protects discrimination of workers older than age 40?
5. Creates safe work environments for employees?
6. Mandates equal pay for equal work?
7. Extends medical benefits for terminated employees?
8. Ensures that child support obligations will be paid?
9. Protects workers and families with pre-existing medical conditions?
10. Enforces payment of monetary damages because of discrimination?

a. COBRA
b. ERISA
c. Civil Rights Act of 1991
d. PRWOR
e. IRCA
f. ADEA
g. HIPAA
h. ADA
i. OSHA
j. Equal Pay Act of 1963

LO 1-2   Discuss the Legal Framework for Payroll Accounting

© Michael A. Keller/Corbis Yellow/ Corbis, RF

Why did businesses start withholding taxes from people's paychecks? Federal income tax withholding was temporarily instituted in 1861 as a way to recover from the high costs of the Civil War; this tax was repealed in 1872. Throughout the 19th century, cities were growing in the wake of the Industrial Revolution, as factories and companies increased automation and institutionalized mass production. People were moving from rural to urban areas in unprecedented numbers, and the need for infrastructure and civil services grew. Roads needed to be built, law enforcement personnel needed to be increased, and outbreaks of disease prompted a need for sanitation systems. Therefore, the U.S. Congress formalized the permanent continuation of the federal income tax instituted during the Civil War as a means to fund the infrastructure improvements of the booming cities. After many failed attempts to reinstate a federal income tax, Congress passed the **Sixteenth Amendment to the U.S. Constitution** in 1913. This version incorporated a tiered income tax including exemptions and deductions to limit the tax imposed on wages earned (see Figure 1-1).

Payroll Regulations Timeline

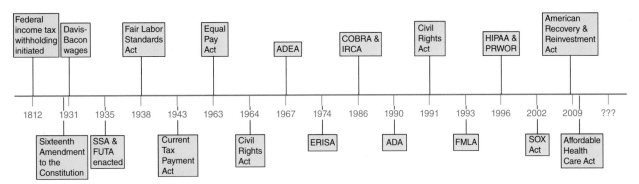

FIGURE 1-1
Timeline of Payroll Legislation.

During the Great Depression of the 1930s, the stock market collapsed, financial institutions went bankrupt, and companies released workers or ceased business operations. The government needed money to fund programs that would stimulate economic recovery. Additionally, the need for a social welfare system emerged as the number of displaced workers increased. The 1930s became a decade of landmark employment legislation that defined the legal environment for employers and employees, most of which remains enforced in 2015.

In 1931, Congress passed the *Davis-Bacon Act*, creating a standard of wages for governmental contracts more than $2,000. The higher standard wages created under the Davis-Bacon Act brought additional revenue to small businesses and the communities where the workers on the contracts lived, bought groceries, and purchased other services or goods. The Davis-Bacon Act combined more than 60 different federal statutes, providing a prevailing wage and wage classification strategy to guide employers and contractors.

In 1935, the **Social Security Act (SSA),** also known as the *Federal Insurance Contributions Act (FICA)*, established a contribution-driven fund that would help the average U.S. worker achieve a level of financial stability when he or she became too old or infirm to work. A contribution-driven fund's employees and employers pay a percentage of gross earnings into the Social Security fund. Originally, the fund was designed to be earmarked for a specific individual upon retirement, but it now also provides assistance for families who experience diminished wages and working situations because of infirmity of the worker or a family member. Social Security is synonymous with **Old-Age, Survivors, and Disability Insurance (OASDI).**

Medicare tax, a government-mandated health insurance program for individuals older than 62 years of age, was also included in the SSA legislation. The viability of the Social Security and Medicare system has been debated in recent years because of changes in eligible recipients that are beyond the scope of the program's original purpose.

The *Walsh-Healey Public Contracts Act* of 1936 affected governmental contractors providing goods or services exceeding $10,000. This act required companies to pay workers a minimum wage for all hours worked under 40 per week and time and a half (regular pay times 1.5) per hour for any hours over 40 per week. The Walsh-Healey Act also prohibited the employment of individuals younger than 16 years of age. Compliance with this act is enforced through the Employment Standards Administration Wage and Hour Division of the Department of Labor. These standards also apply to workers within the District of Columbia.

As another part of its social welfare legislation, the U.S. Congress passed the *Federal Unemployment Tax Act (FUTA)* along with the **Social Security Insurance (SSI) Act** as a way to help displaced workers, individuals from the workforce who find themselves unemployed and meet certain state or federal qualifications. FUTA and its state counterpart, *SUTA*, are based upon the wages earned by the employees. Unlike Social Security taxes, only employers pay FUTA. Some states require employers and employees to

contribute to SUTA. For example, Alaskan employees contribute up to an annual amount of $220.59 (2015 figure) to SUTA, which is collected at a rate of 0.57% of wages until the cap of $38,700 is met. Should an employee have more than one employer, the employee is allowed to request a return for the amounts over the annual cap in the following year.

The enactment of the *Fair Labor Standards Act (FLSA)* of 1938 required better record-keeping and worker protection. This act regulates the minimum wage, a topic that most workers are familiar with, stated as the lowest an individual under certain classifications can be paid. Less commonly known, minimum wage applies only to workers at businesses that conduct interstate commerce. Small businesses that conduct no interstate commerce, such as a restaurant that serves only locally obtained food from one state, are not subject to the minimum wage provisions of FLSA. Additionally, tipped employees, such as restaurant servers, are exempt from minimum wage standards under FLSA. In our modern business world, a business that does not conduct interstate commerce is rare, but the provision in FLSA remains in effect.

An important fact about FLSA wage guidelines is that no maximum wage cap exists. Securities and Exchanges Commission (SEC) regulations stipulate that the compensation packages of high-ranking employees of public companies must be published with the company's mandatory annual report.

One of the major provisions of FLSA is the classification of employees for overtime pay purposes. In 2015, the U.S. Department of Labor is clarifying and narrowing the guidelines for workers who are not subject to the FLSA overtime regulations. New guidance for employee classifications are scheduled to become effective in 2016. (Source: SHRM)

FLSA guidelines define maximum hours, minimum age, pay rates, and mandatory break times. This part of the FLSA is an outgrowth of the industrial environment of the early 20th century, when no such guidelines existed. Horror stories about working conditions and children working 12- to 14-hour days abounded during the 1930s. The FLSA created the classifications of exempt and nonexempt workers. Exempt workers are salaried workers who are not subject to the overtime provisions of FLSA. Overtime is the payment of wages at one-and-a-half times the normal rate for qualifying hours. Nonexempt workers are subject to overtime provisions.

Additionally, under FLSA, pay periods are not regulated, nor is the amount of paid time off given to employees. Those two items are at the discretion of the employer. Paid time off has become a topic of discussion since 2010, and companies such as McDonald's have begun offering it in 2015 as a regular part of employee benefit packages in response to pressure from labor leaders. (Source: *Bloomberg*)

A third class of workers, independent contractors, is not subject to the pay provisions of the FLSA. *Independent contractors* are typically treated as vendors of a business. According to the Internal Revenue Service, a person is an independent contractor when the payer directs only the result of the work, such as a prepared tax return or the finished remodeling of an office building. The payer does not control the process or provide tools to the contractor. Independent contractors are not employees of the business and are not reflected on payroll records.

To obtain the remittance of employers' withholding taxes, the federal government needed a way to standardize the collection of taxes from employers. Before the *Current Tax Payment Act (CTPA)* of 1943, no formalized guidelines for remittance of taxes existed. During the time before the CTPA, the remittance of taxes from employers was inconsistent and unreliable as a funding source for governmental projects. The CTPA was passed during World War II as a means of guaranteeing a source of funds to support the country's involvement in the war. The CTPA created the requirement for the submission of estimated taxes on wages earned during the year of earning instead of after the end of the year as previously required.

Another employer obligation is *worker's compensation*, commonly known as *worker's comp*. Unlike other payroll-specific laws, state laws govern worker's compensation laws. Worker's compensation is an insurance policy carried by employers to provide wage continuation and to pay for medical services for workers injured in the course of doing business. The amounts assigned to the policy vary by type of work being performed and associated risks for various professions. For example, heavy equipment operators would have a higher worker's comp rate than office secretaries because their exposure to injury is deemed higher

© Aabejon/E-plus/Getty Images, RF

by the insurance industry. Worker's compensation plans are subject to annual audits and are based upon payroll wages, less exempt employees (typically working owners). Employers must report all wages earned by the employee; however, only one-third of overtime hours are reported to the worker's compensation auditor. Each state has different requirements for coverage and eligibility. Because worker's compensation is an insurance program, it is not considered a tax, but it is a mandatory employer payroll expense.

Which Payroll Law?

STOP & CHECK

1. Established requirements for employer recordkeeping?
2. Provided government assistance for workers who are too old or infirm to work?
3. Established protection for displaced workers?
4. Required employers to file taxes collected in a timely manner?
5. Set aside funds for health insurance?
6. Regulated wages for employees whose employer engaged in governmental contracts?
7. Is governed on a state-to-state basis and protects employees injured during the course of work activities?

a. Social Security Act
b. Worker's compensation
c. Current Tax Payment Act
d. Fair Labor Standards Act
e. Davis-Bacon Act
f. Federal Unemployment Tax Act
g. Medicare

LO 1-3 Discuss the Ethical Guidelines for Payroll Accounting

© Comstock Images/Thinkstock Images/ Getty Images, RF

Professional *ethics* is critical in any accounting context, and especially so in payroll accounting. Remember that money belonging to the firm and owed to the government and employees is the responsibility of the payroll accountant. The American Institute of Certified Public Accountants (AICPA) defined a code of ethics that is commonly applied in the accounting profession. The basic guidelines of the AICPA Code of Ethics include the following tenets:

- Responsibilities
- The Public Interest
- Integrity
- Objectivity and Independence
- Due Care

> Ethisphere maintains an annual list of the most ethical companies in the world. In 2015, the list included many companies based in the United States such as Mattel, Inc., Texas Instruments, U.S. Bancorp, and several others. Although the companies on the list are in a wide variety of industries, certain ethical principles are common to all: integrity, social responsibility, care for all stakeholders, and honesty and transparency in all business dealings. (Source: Ethisphere)

Responsibilities

An accountant is responsible for maintaining confidences and exercising moral judgment in all actions. A payroll accountant deals with sensitive personnel information that must remain confidential. Social Security numbers, employee legal obligations, and an employer's tax liabilities are a few examples of information that a payroll accountant must protect.

> In 2009, DuPont sued a former employee who stole approximately 600 files by loading them onto a portable flash drive before leaving the company. These files contained confidential company information, and 550 of the 600 files were found on the former employee's home computer. The employee was sentenced to an 18-month prison term. (Source: Law360)

The Public Interest

Accountants must uphold the *public interest* by maintaining confidentiality and exhibiting professionalism in their practice. In terms of payroll accounting, the term *public interest* includes the needs of the firm, its employees, and associated governmental entities. A payroll accountant must complete all tasks and adhere to deadlines, despite any personal issues. Personal honesty and transparency of transactions are the core of acting in the public interest.

> One of the textbook's authors was at a very important conference during the end of her firm's pay period and had left her assistant in charge of the payroll's administration. During the conference, her firm's computer system encountered an issue that would have delayed the issuance of paychecks, which is an event that carries potential legal implications such as fines and the possibility of lawsuits. Protecting the best interests of her firm, the accountant spent the time needed to ensure that the computer issues were resolved to the best of her abilities and that the employees' paychecks were issued on time.

Integrity

In the workplace, integrity is the most important asset a professional can possess. *Integrity* involves doing the right thing despite any external pressure, personal temptations, or conflicts of interest. The main question when weighing the integrity of a decision is "Am I doing what is right and just for everyone concerned?" Any course of action that lacks integrity potentially restricts the rights of interested parties and compromises the best interests of the company.

> Payroll fraud can happen anywhere that pressures, opportunities, and rationalizations exist. In *Perrenod v. U.S.* (2013), the CEO of a company was held liable for the remittance of payroll taxes that the CFO (who had been fired) had embezzled. The CFO had issued the tax remittance checks to himself, which became apparent only when the IRS sent the company a notice of a tax default. The CEO, Perrenod, sued the United States, claiming that he had no knowledge of the liability and should be absolved of the late penalties. The Supreme Court ruled that Perrenod was liable for all penalties because, as CEO, he was responsible for all actions of the company's personnel. (Source: *Forbes*)

Objectivity and Independence

Accountants must take care to be free of any pressures that would compromise the integrity of their work. These pressures can come from business or personal relationships that may affect a payroll accountant's judgment concerning the best interests of all concerned in a given situation. *Objectivity* in accounting means that the accountant considers only facts relevant to the task at hand, independent of all other pressures.

> Social obligations may compromise a payroll accountant's objectivity. The AICPA Code of Ethics section 17 specifically addresses social club membership as a factor in the loss of an accountant's independence or objectivity. Such club membership could create a social debt that may cause an accountant to commit payroll fraud. (Source: AICPA)

Due Care

Due care revolves around an accountant's competence and assumes that the accounting professional is equally competent as other people in a similar role. According to the AICPA, an accountant must remain current with accounting practices and legal developments to comply with due care requirements. Payroll laws and tax guidelines change regularly. As a payroll accountant, it is extremely important to remain aware of annual changes that the IRS and other accounting bodies publish through participation in professional accounting organizations, subscriptions to accounting industry publications, and participation in discussions at accounting conferences.

> Staying current with payroll changes is an ongoing task. Some of the sources for this information include:
>
> - IRS (www.irs.gov)
> - AICPA (www.aicpa.org)
> - Financial Accounting Standards Board (FASB) (www.fasb.org)
> - American Payroll Association (www.apa.org)
> - Compliance Tools for HR Professionals (www.hr.blr.com)

STOP & CHECK

What's Ethical?

1. Giles is the payroll accountant for his company. His boss informs him that the company is considering switching payroll systems and asks for his input. What are some ethical concerns involved in changing accounting software?

2. Liza, the payroll manager, is in a sorority. At a social event, she discovers that one of her sorority sisters works for the same company. Her sorority sister asks Liza for confidential information about one of the employees in her department, claiming that the sorority oath requires Liza's compliance. What should Liza do?

LO 1-4   Identify Contemporary Payroll Practices

© Anatolii Babii/Alamy RF/Alamy, RF

Contemporary accounting practices reflect the effects of technology and electronic communications on business. Payroll practices have adapted to include modern tools that facilitate data transmission, and new challenges have emerged. Some examples include:

- Direct deposit regulations for employee pay and tax remittances
- Electronic filing requirements
- New timekeeping methods
- The availability of paycards as a method of wage and salary disbursement
- Government contract influences on payroll
- International employees
- Simultaneous in-house and outsourced payroll personnel
- Integration of payroll into other company functions

Payroll is no longer a standalone department. Integrated software packages such as QuickBooks and Sage 50 allow business owners to view data across departments and synthesize the information to make large-scale decisions. Contemporary payroll systems serve as a tool for strategic planning, performance measurement, and customer/vendor relations. Payroll accountants are a key element in the decision-making process and must remain educated about legal and compliance issues.

The payroll accountant plays a vital role in a company's structure, no matter how large or small. Payroll and other employee benefits often represent the largest category of a company's expenses. McDonald's Corporation reported more than $4.7 billion in payroll expense alone as of the end of 2014. The McDonald's Corporation operates more than 36,000 restaurants in more than 100 countries, and has more than 1.7 million employees worldwide.

OPERATING COSTS AND EXPENSES (in millions)			
Company-operated restaurant expenses	**2014**	2013	2012
Food & paper	**6,129.7**	6,361.3	6,318.2
Payroll & employee benefits	**4,756.0**	4,824.1	4,710.3
Occupancy & other operating expenses	**4,402.6**	4,393.2	4,195.2
Franchised restaurants-occupancy expenses	**1,697.3**	1,624.4	1,527.0
Selling, general & administrative expenses	**2,487.9**	2,385.6	2,455.2
Total Operating Costs	**19,492.1**	19,341.4	18,962.4
Net Income	**4,757.8**	5,585.9	5,464.8

Source: McDonald's Financial Highlights, 2015

Several options exist for payroll preparation. The most frequently used method for contemporary payroll preparation is electronic accounting programs. Other options available are manual calculation of payroll using spreadsheets, charts prepared by the Internal Revenue Service, and payroll preparation by outsourcing the process to a third party such as ADP, Paychex®, and myPay Solutions.

© Rob Daly/age fotostock, RF

Regardless of the payroll preparation method, it is important for the payroll accountant to understand how the process should work. During hardware failure, legislative, or tax changes, the accountant must ensure accurate payroll preparation. Companies can lose credibility as the result of flawed payroll, as well as be subject to substantial fines, IRS audits, and civil litigation. Cases in which companies have paid fines for improper payroll practices abound. Some companies have seriously shortchanged employees' paychecks, paying fines in addition to the standard payroll expenditures. Other tales of employee overpayment in the public sector highlight problems in payroll systems, such as computer glitches that have delayed payment of the company's wages. The volume of legislation and stories of problems involving payroll administration points to the need for a well-established payroll system. Despite the legislation concerning payroll practices, no legislation specifies the format and precise delivery of a payroll system.

The information contained in the personnel records is highly sensitive and must be protected against intrusion from unnecessary parties. The *Privacy Act of 1974* guaranteed the safeguarding of information contained in private personnel records and mandates information safekeeping as well as due process rights to individuals. Consider the implications of the legal requirements of information safekeeping:

- Personnel records contain information about an individual's marital status, children, other dependents, and legal residence—sensitive information that must be protected under the Privacy Act of 1974.

- Payroll records generally have information about the hourly rate and salary information for each employee—access to these records is protected by provisions of the *Equal Employment Opportunity Commission (EEOC)* and could provoke or inhibit discrimination lawsuits.

- The information contained in payroll records influences the accuracy and integrity of a company's accounting records—the recording of payroll expenses and liabilities affect the profitability of a company, which influences investor and customer relations.

- Companies engaging in business with the federal government must comply with the Davis-Bacon Act (for federal contracts) and potentially the *Copeland Anti-Kickback Act of 1934* (for construction projects—protecting taxpayers from unethical pay practices).

- The number of hours worked by an employee must comply with the provisions of the Fair Labor Standards Act (1935).

- Deductions for payroll, especially for retirement plans, must be documented and verified in accordance with the Sarbanes–Oxley Act of 2002.

Employers are required to file tax deposits for employee withholding, Social Security, Medicare, FUTA, and SUTA taxes according to an identified timeline depending upon the size of the company's payroll. Taxes may be remitted via telephone, Internet, mail, or the company's payroll software program. Additional reports are required from the employer on either a quarterly or an annual basis. A company has many responsibilities within its payroll system:

© Don Carstens/Brand X Pictures, RF

- Tax withholding must be done consistently, reflecting the requirements of federal, state, and local authorities.
- Employers must match amounts withheld from employee paychecks for certain payroll taxes.
- Withholding of deductions that the employee voluntarily elects, such as health care, insurance, and investments, must be correctly recorded and reported.
- Timely and accurate payment must be made to the employee, government agencies, and companies for which the employee has designated the voluntary deductions.
- Tax and other liabilities must be reported to governmental agencies in accordance with established deadlines.

An accurate payroll system allows managers to focus on the firm's business, not payroll administration. As such, a well-designed system benefits the employees and governmental agencies, and thus the firm. The timely forwarding of any monies withheld from employees, either by governmental regulation or voluntary election, is critical to a firm's success. If the establishment and implementation of a payroll system sounds complex, it is!

Besides administrating employee pay, a well-designed and accurately maintained payroll system is necessary during inevitable governmental audits. An audit is a process by which a third-party organization, either a public accounting firm or a government agency, inspects the accounting records of a firm for accuracy, integrity, and compliance with Federal rules and regulations. During a payroll audit, the auditor inspects the company's records of employee pay, tax remittance, and voluntary deduction maintenance. The thought of audits instills fear into the hearts of even the most seasoned accounting professionals. Their salvation, however, is to establish and maintain an accurate payroll system.

Consider the growth of some companies:

Tom's of Maine started in 1968 as a local organic personal care product company and is now a nationally recognized leader in environmental stewardship and sustainability. (Source: www.tomsofmaine.com)

Ben and Jerry's, which started as a $5 correspondence course in ice-cream making and a $12,000 investment in 1978, has become an icon of premium ice cream and environmental causes. (Source: www.benjerry.com)

McDonald's Corporation was started in 1955 by the McDonald brothers when they sold their hamburger business to Ray Kroc. The brand is now an international icon for fast food, serving approximately 68 million customers each day. (Sources: www.mcdonalds .com, *The Fiscal Times*)

All these companies share similar beginnings: one location, a few employees, and a relatively simple payroll. As each company has grown, so has the payroll complexity, including multiple departments and facilities in many states and countries. At the heart of each company is a well-run business model and a sound payroll system that has evolved with it.

Tracking and monitoring employee hours, locations, and applicable governmental requirements within various nations requires a knowledgeable payroll staff, willing to remain current with accounting trends and international regulations. Sophisticated payroll systems enable companies to create, populate, and file a multitude of documents using current software and Internet technology.

Privacy Protection

© Japser White/Image Source, RF

A company must make every reasonable effort to protect personnel information contained in payroll records. This is a critical part of any payroll accountant's job. Several privacy acts exist to protect the information contained in payroll and personnel records. Some of the privacy acts include (but are certainly not limited to):

- U.S. Department of Labor OCFO-1, which pertains to the privacy of information in payroll files
- U.S. Department of Health and Human Services Privacy Act 09-40-0006, which pertains to eligibility of public employees for pay, entitlements, raises, and benefits
- Common Law Privacy Act, which pertains to freedom from misuse or abuse of one's private affairs
- Privacy Act of 1974, pertaining to the use of information about private citizens
- Computer Fraud and Abuse Act (CFAA) of 1986, which addresses cybercrime, an issue that has grown in importance in recent years

The General Accounting Office of the federal government has been working to revise guidelines about records privacy and release of information as the Internet and e-business evolve. The Cyber Privacy Fortification Act of 2015 (H.R. 104) is an amendment to the CFAA that mandates notification to the U.S. Secret Service or FBI in the event of data breaches of records containing highly sensitive information. As proposed, H.R. 104 reinforces employer responsibility for the privacy of personnel records.

> Online privacy is a growing concern, and it affects the security of payroll data. In October 2013, the Internal Revenue Service used the first seven letters of employee last names and truncated Social Security numbers to verify employee information. Internet privacy concerns have prompted discussions about other potential encryption or truncation-of-data methods to foil hackers. (Source: Thomson Reuters)

The common element among these laws is the protection of sensitive employee information such as addresses, dependents, compensation amounts, and payroll deductions. The payroll accountant is also responsible for discretion in discussing pay rates, bonuses, or other compensation-related topics with employee and management. Sensitive topics should never be discussed with anyone other than the employee or appropriate managers. All employment-related items may be viewed during an audit of payroll records, and auditors must treat the information with absolute confidentiality.

One way that the federal government keeps track of employers is with Employer Identification Numbers (EINs). The EIN allows the IRS to know which companies may have employees, therefore generating employment tax revenue for the government and creating tax liabilities for employers. Form SS-4 (see Figure 1-2) reports the personal Social Security number, type of business, and existence of any prior EINs for a business owner. This number is required for all tax deposits, tax returns, and informational returns. It will appear on the company's Form W-2s, 940s, 941s, any state tax forms, and the annual tax return for the company.

Confidential Records

You are the payroll clerk of a company. A group of students approaches you to work on a class project and asks to see confidential personnel and payroll records. What would you do? What are the laws regarding the situation?

LO 1-5   Compare Payroll Processing Options for Different Businesses

Contemporary time-collection devices serve as more than simple time clocks. Although the old-fashioned punch clocks still exist, many companies have integrated different time collection systems as part of their office security and computer access procedures. Many

FIGURE 1-2
Example of Form SS-4

Form **SS-4** (Rev. January 2010) Department of the Treasury Internal Revenue Service	**Application for Employer Identification Number** (For use by employers, corporations, partnerships, trusts, estates, churches, government agencies, Indian tribal entities, certain individuals, and others.) See separate instructions for each line. Keep a copy for your records.	OMB No. 1545-0003 EIN 12-5555555

Type or print clearly.

1 Legal name of entity (or individual) for whom the EIN is being requested
  BD2 Enterprises

2 Trade name of business (if different from name on line 1) IC Snow Resort	**3** Executor, administrator, trustee, "care of" name
4a Mailing address (room, apt., suite no. and street, or P.O. box) 1234 Main Street	**5a** Street address (if different) (Do not enter a P.O. box.)
4b City, state, and ZIP code (if foreign, see instructions) Granite, NH 03942	**5b** City, state, and ZIP code (if foreign, see instructions)

6 County and state where principal business is located
  Winchester NH

7a Name of responsible party
  Kris King
	7b SSN, ITIN, or EIN
	  111-22-3333

8a Is this application for a limited liability company (LLC) (or a foreign equivalent)? ----------------------- ☐ Yes ☐ No   **8b** If 8a is "Yes," enter the number of LLC members ----------

8c If 8a is "Yes," was the LLC organized in the United States?   Yes   No

9a **Type of entity** (check only one box). **Caution.** If 8a is "Yes," see the instructions for the correct box to check.

Sole proprietor (SSN) 111   22   3333   Estate (SSN of decedent) _____
Partnership   Plan administrator (TIN) _____
Corporation (enter form number to be filed) _____   Trust (TIN of grantor) _____
Personal service corporation   National Guard   State/local government
Church or church-controlled organization   Farmers' cooperative   Federal government/military
Other nonprofit organization (specify) _____   REMIC   Indian tribal governments/enterprises
Other (specify)   Group Exemption Number (GEN) if any

9b If a corporation, name the state or foreign country (if applicable) where incorporated | State | Foreign country

10 **Reason for applying** (check only one box)
  Started new business (specify type) Ski Resort
                                Banking purpose (specify purpose) _____
                                Changed type of organization (specify new type) _____
                                Purchased going business
  Hired employees (Check the box and see line 13.)   Created a trust (specify type) _____
  Compliance with IRS withholding regulations   Created a pension plan (specify type) _____
  Other (specify)

11 Date business started or acquired (month, day, year). See instructions. 09/01/2014	**12** Closing month of accounting year December

14 If you expect your employment tax liability to be $1,000 or less in a full calendar year **and** want to file Form 944 annually instead of Forms 941 quarterly, check here. (Your employment tax liability generally will be $1,000 or less if you expect to pay $4,000 or less in total wages.) If you do not check this box, you must file Form 941 for every quarter.

13 Highest number of employees expected in the next 12 months (enter -0- if none). If no employees expected, skip line 14.

Agricultural	Household	Other
		25

15 First date wages or annuities were paid (month, day, year). **Note.** If applicant is a withholding agent, enter date income will first be paid to nonresident alien (month, day, year)   09/15/2014

16 Check **one** box that best describes the principal activity of your business.
  Construction   Rental & leasing   Transportation & warehousing   Health care & social assistance   Wholesale-agent/broker
  Real estate   Manufacturing   Finance & insurance   Accommodation & food service   Wholesale-other   Retail
                                            Other (specify) Recreation

17 Indicate principal line of merchandise sold, specific construction work done, products produced, or services provided.
  Downhill and cross-country skiing

18 Has the applicant entity shown on line 1 ever applied for and received an EIN?   Yes   No
  If "Yes," write previous EIN here

Third Party Designee	Complete this section **only** if you want to authorize the named individual to receive the entity's EIN and answer questions about the completion of this form. Designee's name	Designee's telephone number (include area code) ( )
	Address and ZIP code	Designee's fax number (include area code) ( )

Under penalties of perjury, I declare that I have examined this application, and to the best of my knowledge and belief, it is true, correct, and complete. | Applicant's telephone number (include area code)
Name and title (type or print clearly)   Kris M. King, Owner | (603) 555-4411
 | Applicant's fax number (include area code)

Source: Internal Revenue Service.

© D.Hurst/Alamy RF/Alamy, RF

companies now use biometric devices such as fingerprint readers to collect time for their hourly employees. Time clocks are used as part of a security system to log when people enter a building for work, which can yield analysis of simple on-site versus working-hour time. Other systems such as Kronos offer biometric badges and time-collection devices that connect with office telephones. Using computer access as another type of collection device serves a similar function, and can offer the additional functionality of specific task tracking and precise timekeeping. These practices relating to time collection affect and are integrated with payroll.

The basic elements of a payroll system are similar for all companies, but this is a case when size does matter. However, it is not only the size of the company but also the complexity of the laws that affect payroll procedures. Let's look at the differences between large and small company payrolls, and then explore certified payroll issues.

Large Businesses

Large companies present intricate problems for payroll accountants. Companies such as Apple, Google, and Microsoft have multiple divisions, many of which exist in different geographical locations. General Electric has different companies that operate as separate entities within GE's framework. Payroll procedures reflect the intricacy of the company's structure and may take many forms.

One of the major challenges in larger organizations is the existence of multiple departments in which an individual employee may work on any given day. Some companies can have shared employees, who will have allocable time to more than one department; for example, one employee may work for both the marketing and production departments. When this occurs, the payroll accountant will have to record the time worked for each department, and pay rates may differ based on the tasks that the employee performs for each department.

A common payroll procedure with large companies involves employee portals on company websites. On the company's payroll website, employees may enter vacation time, overtime, and address other issues that need to be entered into the payroll system. Through the same website, employees may change withholding allowances and voluntary deductions, and maintain certain other aspects of their employee files. Such web-based portals contain highly sensitive information, and security of the information is an obvious concern for the companies who use them. Multiple identity checks and security measures are in place to ensure privacy of employee data, such as SSL (secure sockets layer) encryption, *VPN* (virtual private network), and CAPTCHA programs that are designed to differentiate between humans and other computer programs.

Providing employees with Internet-based access to their personnel files is a challenging issue. Federal laws do not grant employees the right to access their personnel files, and companies must be aware of state laws before providing access. Questions of assigning access to other parties (such as union representatives), access to file artifacts, and the right of the employee to challenge items contained in their file are issues that a firm should address when creating a web portal through which employees may access payroll records. In addition, issues of cybersecurity must be addressed. (Source: SHRM)

To overcome some of the issues with payroll processing, large companies may rely heavily on payroll service vendors to assist with payroll preparation and human resources integration. Providers such as myPay Solutions work with the security needs of the company to offer websites that are secure and integrate multiple personnel functions seamlessly. Some larger firms will work with software engineers to develop independent systems specifically meeting unique company needs.

Large companies face other issues related to accurate timekeeping, such as the volume of employee records. Companies with computerized time-measurement systems may link employees' computer logins, telephone logins, or building access with the payroll system.

Companies working with radio frequency time cards and electronic payroll monitoring can properly allocate employee time to specific machines or production lines. With the computer software and services currently available, large companies have many options to maintain the accuracy and integrity of their payroll systems.

Small Businesses

© Comstock Images/Jupiter Images, RF

One apparent difference between large and small businesses is the volume and handling of payroll records. A small number of employees generally leads to fewer payroll-related transactions. Manual payroll systems may be maintained in very small businesses, including the use of handwritten time cards. Outsourcing of payroll activities may not be as prominent. With a small company, the amount of time to complete payroll-related tasks may be less than in a large company. For a small company, the task can be performed without disrupting the revenue-producing tasks of the business.

Small companies have the option of processing payroll in-house with a minimum of difficulty. However, small companies may lack specifically trained payroll personnel, which may place the responsibility for employee pay and benefits on other personnel and may increase the risk of pay or tax inaccuracies. The human resource director, office manager, and payroll professional may frequently be the same person. Using payroll software and a properly designed payroll system, the task of payroll for a small company is generally manageable by minimal company staff. Small companies may choose to explore outsourcing as the company grows. Outsourcing payroll may be a viable option if the task becomes unwieldy or legal obligations become unmanageable.

According to *Accounting Today,* common payroll mistakes made by small firms include:

- Misclassifying employees as independent contractors
- Omitting the value of gift cards awarded to employees as part of their taxable income
- Failure to make timely payroll tax deposits
- Improper treatment of expense reimbursements made to employees
- Incorrect treatment of taxable fringe benefits

Depending on the size of the company, number of employees, and complexity of the payroll process, the company may choose to purchase a computer-based accounting system, or it may continue to prepare worksheets and manual payroll checks, or it can decide to outsource the payroll preparation and associated tasks. Whichever decisions the company makes as it grows, the importance of understanding the mechanics of the payroll process is paramount. Following is an overview of the various computer-based systems available.

Large vs. Small

STOP & CHECK

What are some of the payroll processing methods available for large companies?

How does payroll processing differ for small companies?

Computer-Based Systems

Various accounting software packages exist to facilitate payroll-related accounting tasks, including QuickBooks, Sage50, and Microsoft Dynamics GP. According to the American

Payroll Association, computerized payroll systems eliminate approximately 80% of payroll processing time and errors. Computerized accounting systems foster the integration of payroll data with other company financial functions, which allows decision makers to develop a comprehensive understanding of the operational needs of the company. Although payroll professionals must verify employee data and update the software at regular intervals, computerized systems reduce the burdens of manual pay calculations, pay disbursement, and report compilation from the payroll accountant. (Source: *Inc.*)

When used properly, small companies may benefit from a computerized payroll system. Although concerns about confidentiality of personnel records exist, electronic access to records may streamline certain tasks like employee information updates and overtime reporting. Additionally, as year-end approaches, companies can deliver the employees' W-2 (see Figure 1-3) tax forms electronically, ensuring employees rapid access to their tax documents.

A trend in payroll processing involves the issuance of electronic paycards, much like preloaded credit cards, as opposed to paper checks. Paycards offer the employees the flexibility of not having to wait for their paycheck to be deposited at a bank. Companies that offer direct deposit as a pay option must offer paycards as an option to employees who do not have bank accounts. However, a paycard can be lost or stolen, and with it, the employee's paycheck, too. Additionally, employers may be charged fees for loading a paycard. When companies consider paycards as an option, it is important to communicate to employees an understanding that there may be costs associated from the provider of the card.

© Barry Gregg/Digital Stock/Royalty-Free/Corbis, RF

Manual Systems

With manual payroll systems, the payroll employee relies on deduction percentages that come presented in publications from the Internal Revenue Service. Publication 15 (also known as Circular E) is the manual payroll accountant's best friend, along with periodic updates and supplemental publications. (Source: www.irs.gov)

The largest challenges the manual payroll preparer faces are time constraints and updated tax tables. Companies can determine the length of time between the end of the payroll period and the employee payments with some degree of latitude. However, employees who do not receive accurate and timely pay for their labor are likely to become disenchanted with the organization.

Manual payroll accountants may use spreadsheet programs, such as Excel, in which the accountant can create lookup formulas or other connecting formulas to facilitate the accurate completion of the payroll process. Spreadsheets with formulas or macros should be used only if the accountant understands the formulas and can verify the linkage prior to finalizing payroll to ensure that calculations are correct.

FIGURE 1-3
Form W-2 Wage and Tax Statement

Source: Internal Revenue Service.

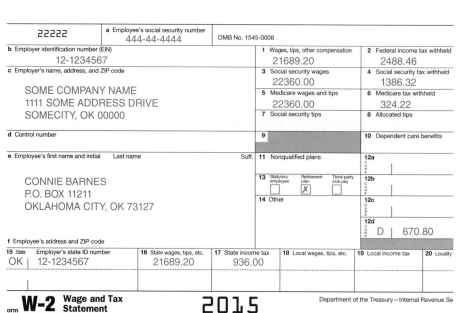

Outsourced Payroll Systems

Outsourced payroll processing has become rather popular as a way to ensure compliance with the changing legal structure and withholding requirements. When a company chooses to use an outsourcing firm for the completion of the payroll processes, there are several considerations: records retention, confidentiality, compliance, timeliness, and thoroughness. Managers should review the cost/benefits of outsourcing a firm's payroll processes prior to making the commitment.

External payroll providers offer flexibility and advanced data analysis that might be challenging for smaller internal departments. During a survey of more than 2,000 accounting professionals, an overwhelming margin stated that they would prefer to outsource payroll functions because of the time involved in the process. External payroll management providers such as ADP and Paychex® assist company owners and managers with strategic planning and related human resources issues. However, outsourcing is not a wise decision for all companies. For a small company, outsourcing may not be cost effective. For large or international companies, outsourcing may be the only option to manage the payroll complexity.

A recent trend in payroll accounting involves cloud-based computing, meaning that the data is housed on a server external to the firm that is accessible via an Internet connection. Companies such as ADP and Volt offer cloud-based payroll and human resource functions for businesses. These services reduce costs by allowing a company to avoid hardware and software costs associated with payroll. However, some issues have arisen with payroll vendor stability and information security. Before turning to a cloud-based service, a company needs to determine its needs to ensure that it makes the appropriate choice. (Source: www.payrolllab.com)

> ZenPayroll is a payroll service provider designed for small businesses. It combines a blend of cloud-based payroll and tax filing services that simplifies the process for small business owners. ZenPayroll has partnered with companies such as FreshBooks to provide integrated back office accounting services. (Source: *Forbes*, www.zenpayroll.com)

Certified Payroll

Companies who do business with the federal government under the Davis-Bacon Act are required to file a report (see Figure 1-4 for Form WH-347) delineating the payroll paid as part of the government contract with each payroll. *Certified payroll* is a way that the federal government keeps track of the money spent as part of government contracts. Davis-Bacon wages and the state versions of those regulations require special handling and knowledge. Certified payroll facilitates governmental internal accountability and verifies that Davis-Bacon related requirements are met.

FIGURE 1-4
Form WH-347 Certified Payroll

What Is the Difference?

STOP & CHECK

In a few words, compare the following:

a. Manual payroll systems

b. Computerized payroll systems

c. Outsourced payroll systems

d. Certified payroll

LO 1-6   Differentiate between Exempt and Nonexempt Workers

© Ariel Skelley/Blend Images LLC, RF

Company employees may be classified as either exempt or nonexempt workers. The distinction between the two terms is how the wage and hour provisions of FLSA apply to the worker. Exempt workers are not subject to the FLSA wage and hour provisions; wage and hour laws usually apply to nonexempt workers. For 2015, the Department of Labor is set to issue stricter guidelines for the classification of exempt "white collar" employees to prevent employers from foregoing overtime pay due to employees who should be classified as nonexempt.

Companies will typically classify highly skilled workers such as accountants, general managers, human resource managers, and upper management as exempt, salaried employees. When workers are employed under a salary basis, they are paid to perform a specific job regardless of the number of hours worked to accomplish that job. A recent Gallup Work and Education poll (see Figure 1-5) reflected that more than half of the salaried workers surveyed worked in excess of 40 hours per week; however, it should be noted the law currently provides that if salaried employees show up or are called by their employer for even an hour, the company may be required to pay them for the full eight-hour day.

FIGURE 1-5
Gallup Work and Education Poll Results

Average Hours Worked by Full-Time U.S. Workers, Aged 18+

Self-reported hours typically worked each week, based on pay structure

	Paid a salary	Paid hourly
	%	%
60+ hours	25	9
50 to 59 hours	25	17
41 to 49 hours	9	12
40 hours	37	56
Less than 40 hours	3	8
Weekly average	49 hours	44 hours

Based on Gallup's 2014 Work and Education poll, conducted Aug. 7-10, 2014

GALLUP

© Photodisc/Getty Images, RF

Salaried workers may be classified as either exempt or nonexempt. According to the FLSA, exempt employees must meet certain criteria: salary level, salary basis, and job duties. Exempt workers must meet all three tests to be considered exempt from FLSA wage and overtime requirements.

A primary difference is that nonexempt salaried individuals receive overtime pay for any hours exceeding 8 per day and 40 per week. We will discuss overtime calculations in depth later in the text. The difference between salaried and hourly workers in reference to overtime calculation is that the salaried workers will receive 8 hours of pay, even when not working the full 8 hours, and do not receive overtime when they work more than 40 hours per week.

Hourly (nonexempt) employees receive a predetermined amount per hour of work performed (or fraction thereof). Hourly employees must receive overtime pay for hours worked in excess of 8 per day and 40 per week. Some employers may make an election that permits four 10-hour shifts; should the election be made, the employee would be subject to overtime rates only after the 10 hours per day and 40 hours have been performed.

Certain individuals who work for a company are classified as independent contractors. These individuals may work for a firm, but the firm can control only the content and deliverables of the individual's work. The firm does not control the manner in which the work is done or provide the tools that the individual uses to complete the work. An independent contractor is not considered an employee of the firm and is not subject to any payroll-related laws.

Exempt vs. Nonexempt

STOP & CHECK

1. What is the difference between exempt and nonexempt workers?
2. What is the difference between an employee and an independent contractor?

Trends to Watch

LEGAL ENVIRONMENT

To say that the legal environment of payroll is continually evolving is an understatement. During the early part of the 2010s, we have witnessed the following legal challenges:

*   Modification of language in employee handbooks to refine terminology and remove offensive wording.
*   Official revisions to define the term *supervisor* as it pertains to employee discrimination.
*   Employer liability for accidents following alcohol consumption at employer functions.
*   Repeal of the Defense of Marriage Act, which changed the definition of married couples to include same-sex unions.

Some trends to watch include the following:

*   IRS revenue rulings about FICA refunds resulting from employee overpayment of taxes.
*   Increasing numbers of states legislating paycard use to protect employee rights and improve access to wages.
*   Enhanced enforcement of the Equal Pay Act by the EEOC to protect the rights of women and minorities.

Summary of Payroll Practices and System Fundamentals

Accounting practices have existed for centuries and a need continually exists for employers to compensate employees for the work they have performed. Once the United States began taxing personal income, payroll processing became increasingly complex. During the 20th century, payroll practices evolved to include provisions for withholding taxes from employees, remitting payroll taxes to government agencies, maintaining accurate and confidential records, and incorporating civil rights–related legislation. Payroll accounting is a field that, due to its changing nature, requires precision and attention to minute details. Additionally, because of the nature of their work, payroll accountants must adhere to ethical guidelines including due care, objectivity, independence, integrity, and the public interest.

The establishment of a payroll system involves careful, deliberate planning. The framework used for the payroll system must have ample room for company growth, structure to ensure system stability, and trained payroll personnel to ensure that company and government deadlines are met. Using the best practices outlined in this chapter may help a company implement a robust payroll system, whether the system is maintained by company personnel, outsourced, completed manually, or accomplished through the use of specifically designed software. Robust payroll system design may prevent problems with employees and governmental entities.

Key Points

- Legislation that has affected employees' working conditions has mandated many aspects of the workplace, including civil rights, retirement and health benefits, and reinvestment in American workers.

- Payroll-specific legislation has influenced working hours and employee wages.

- Employer and employee taxes have been enacted and the remittance of tax obligations has been mandated.

- Payroll accountants must adhere to ethical guidelines because of the nature of the work performed.

- Payroll practices have evolved to include the electronic transmission of employee pay and tax obligations.

- Security of employee information is an ongoing concern for companies, especially with electronic transmission of sensitive data.

- Payroll may be processed at a central corporate site or through an outsourced payroll processing company.

- Many companies use payroll accounting software such as QuickBooks and Sage 50, and cloud computing has become a new option for businesses.

- Employees are classified as either exempt or nonexempt from the FLSA provisions, based on the scope of their work and the job classification.

Vocabulary

ADA	ERISA	OSHA
ARRA	Ethics	Privacy Act of 1974
ATRA	FICA	PRWOR
Certified payroll	FLSA	Public interest
COBRA	FMLA	SOX
Copeland Anti-Kickback Act	FUTA	SUTA
Current Tax Payment Act	HIPAA	USERRA
Davis-Bacon Act	Independent contractor	VPN
DOMA	Integrity	Walsh-Healey Public Contracts Act
Due care	IRCA	Worker's compensation
EEOC	Medicare tax	
	Objectivity	

Review Questions

1. What is the purpose of a payroll system?

2. What are some differences between large- and small-company payroll practices?

3. What is certified payroll? Which companies must use it?

4. Why might it be a good idea to let employees manage their pay records? What are some of the pitfalls?

5. What are some ways that a payroll system may protect a company in the event of a visit from a government auditor?

6. What is payroll outsourcing? When might a company consider outsourcing its payroll?

7. Give three examples of federal laws that are essential to ensure legal, fair hiring practices.

8. What are the major types of payroll processing methods?

9. What are two laws governing the taxes that employers must withhold from employees?

10. What are two of the main provisions of FLSA?

11. Why was the Social Security Act of 1935 important? What did it provide?

12. What are the advantages of a computerized payroll system over a manual system?

Exercises Set A

1-1A.
LO 1-6
Anya is a candidate for the position of sales manager with the footwear department of a major retail outlet. She is going to be required to supervise several employees and can determine the direction in which she will complete the assignments given to her. What classification of employee should she be, exempt or nonexempt? Explain.

1-2A.
LO 1-6
John is the office manager for a small mortgage brokerage. Because it is a small office, he is required to keep track of all employee records and pay both employees and contractors. What differences exist between exempt and nonexempt employees?

1-3A.
LO 1-1, 1-2
Kristina is the accounting manager for a small, local firm that has full- and part-time staff. What are FLSA requirements as far as minimum wage is concerned?

1-4A.
LO 1-4, 1-5
Jeff is an accountant for his firm, a medium-sized company with 125 employees. The firm has traditionally maintained the administration of its payroll. His co-worker, the only other accountant in the firm, retires. Because of budget concerns, the firm chooses not to refill the position. What options does Jeff have regarding administration of the payroll?

1-5A.
LO 1-1, 1-2
Consolidated Construction obtained a job working for a nearby international airport, a project contracted with the federal government for $500,000, welding the support structures for the new extension of the terminal. What laws govern the wages Consolidated Construction pays to their welders for this project?

1-6A.
LO 1-1, 1-2
Juan is the office manager and payroll clerk for his company, which is composed of 12 employees. An employee, Joe, stops by Juan's office and wants to view his payroll record. What privacy regulations must Juan consider before granting his co-worker access?

1-7A. Roxie works as the payroll clerk for an agricultural firm that hires many
LO 1-1, 1-2 temporary and immigrant workers on an hourly basis. What law governs the hiring or documenting of these workers?

1-8A. A group of employees, who read on a website that income tax collection
LO 1-3 is illegal, approach Tarik, the controller for a large company. They request that he stop withholding income taxes from their pay unless he can explain what laws govern income tax collection. What should Tarik tell them?

1-9A. Kim-Ly is a member of the hiring board for her company. As they review
LO 1-4 candidates for a position, one of the other board members wants to exclude Eric, a man in his 50s, because his age might pose an insurance risk for the company. What law protects Eric against this practice?

1-10A. Sheri is a warehouse worker for a small grocery market. As she was
LO 1-1, 1-2 moving some merchandise, the loading dock door unexpectedly fell and injured her. What legal provisions does Sheri have for this type of injury?

1-11A. Ashlee is the new payroll accountant for a company. While she was
LO 1-3 exercising at the gym, she encountered Madison, the president of the company. Madison explained that he was under pressure to report certain levels of profit and asked her to meet with him about payroll expenses. What ethical guidelines should Ashlee consider before agreeing to meet?

1-12A. Kevin owns a new golf pro shop. As a small business owner, he has
LO 1-4, 1-5 several options for payroll processing. What are three options he should consider to facilitate his payroll accounting?

Match the following terms with their definitions:

1-13A. Manual payroll	a.	A pre-loaded credit card used to pay employees
1-14A. Time card	b.	The process of gathering information about hours worked for one or more employees
1-15A. Paycard	c.	A web-based application wherein employees can modify certain payroll-related information
1-16A. Employee Internet portal	d.	Governs accounting for firms with federal government contracts in excess of $2,000
1-17A. Certified payroll	e.	A record of the time worked during a period for an individual employee
1-18A. Outsourced payroll	f.	Examples of companies used for outsourcing payroll processing
1-19A. Auditor	g.	A way for governmental agencies to track the payroll associated with a government contract
1-20A. ADP and Paychex®	h.	Payroll administration using a paper payroll register
1-21A. Time collection	i.	The use of an external company to track time and benefits and pay employees
1-22A. Davis-Bacon Act	j.	A person or group who examines a company's accounting records for accuracy

Exercises Set B

1-1B.
LO 1-6

Hunter is a candidate for the position of marketing clerk with the promotions department of a film production company. He will work occasional overtime in his new position. What classification of employee should he be, exempt or nonexempt? Explain.

1-2B.
LO 1-6

Janet manages a regional office of a large multinational company. She maintains the records for all personnel in the region, including sales, administrative, and manufacturing workers. Which classification, exempt or nonexempt, should she apply to each of the classes of employees?

1-3B.
LO 1-1, 1-2

Bernie manages a ski resort that has year-round and seasonal employees. What are the FLSA requirements as far as minimum wage is concerned?

1-4B.
LO 1-4, 1-5

Roxie is the payroll administrator for a small company. Because of economic conditions, her boss has assigned her the additional duties of office management, and Roxie is considering outsourcing her payroll duties. What are the pros and cons of outsourcing the company's payroll?

1-5B.
LO 1-1, 1-2

Jim is the payroll clerk for a company in a state where same-sex marriage recently became legal. One of the company's employees informs Jim that he has been in a same-sex marriage since January 2011. What actions does Jim need to take regarding prior-year taxes?

1-6B.
LO 1-1, 1-2

Carl is a military veteran who requires many absences for medical reasons. His boss has demanded that he reduce the number of sick days unless he provides his medical history. Which laws govern this situation? Should Carl provide his medical records to his boss?

1-7B.
LO 1-1, 1-2

Valerie is a production worker at a large automobile manufacturing plant. After working there for 10 years, she discovers through conversations with a colleague with the same title and similar seniority that her wage is 20% lower than his wage. She feels that she has been a victim of discrimination. Which laws govern her situation? What action should she take?

1-8B.
LO 1-1, 1-2

Rob is a military reservist whose unit has been called to active duty. He informs his boss that his orders stipulate that he will serve for 12 months. What responsibilities does his employer have as far as Rob's current civilian employment is concerned?

1-9B.
LO 1-4, 1-5

Skylar is the new bookkeeper for a small company and was hired to replace a long-time employee who retired. Upon starting the position, Skylar notices that the prior bookkeeper used a purely manual system. The company owner has said that Skylar may update the payroll system. What options are available?

1-10B.
LO 1-6

Jeffrey is the accounting manager for a company that provides computer-consulting services. The computer-consulting company has a staff that includes five full-time employees and eight on-call consultants. The on-call consultants provide their own tools and decide which hours they will work. Are the consultants employees of the company? Explain.

1-11B.
LO 1-6

Paola is the payroll accountant for an import-export firm. Her most recent experience with accounting educational courses was when she was in college, which was eight years ago. What ethical guideline(s) govern her professional development?

1-12B.
LO 1-3

Nic is an accountant for a large, multinational firm. During payroll processing, he notices that the new state payroll tax updates have not been installed in the firm's software. What ethical guidelines govern his behavior in this situation?

Match the following terms with their definitions:

1-13B.	USERRA	a.	A provision of the Sarbanes–Oxley Act
1-14B.	*U.S. v. Windsor*	b.	Instituted a tiered income tax on workers
1-15B.	Mandatory auditor rotation	c.	Prohibited employment of individuals younger than 16 years of age
1-16B.	HIPAA	d.	Strengthened the child support provisions of PRWOR
1-17B.	Lilly Ledbetter Fair Pay Act	e.	Legislation that governs the treatment of military service personnel
1-18B.	Sixteenth Amendment	f.	A worker who is not subject to a company's direction or its payroll laws
1-19B.	Walsh-Healey Public Contracts Act	g.	Repealed the 180-day statute of limitations on equal pay complaints
1-20B.	Independent contractor	h.	Mandates completion of form I-9
1-21B.	Personal Responsibility, Work and Family Promotion Act of 2002	i.	The case responsible for the U.S. Supreme Court's repeal of DOMA
1-22B.	IRCA	j.	Protects the confidentiality of employee medical records

Critical Thinking

1-1.   You have been hired as a consultant for a company facing an IRS audit of their accounting records. During your review, you notice anomalies in the payroll system involving overpayments of labor and payments to terminated employees. What should you do?

1-2.   Lee Chen is the accountant for a local nonprofit organization. He has been tasked with managing the costs of the payroll so that staffing levels may remain the same even if funding levels change. He considers outsourcing the payroll to a payroll processing company. What are some factors that Lee should consider in his decision? Why are these factors important?

In the Real World: Scenario for Discussion

The Brinker Restaurant Group, owners of restaurant franchises such as Chili's Grill and Bar and Maggiano's Little Italy, was sued by its employees for not providing adequate meal and rest breaks for employees. According to the California Labor Code §512 and Wage Order no. 5, employees must be provided with rest periods—specifically, a 30-minute meal break—every five hours that they work. After 10 hours of consecutive work, the employee must be given a second meal break. The California Supreme Court ruled that the rest breaks had to be offered, but the employer did not have to ensure that the employee actually rested.

What do you think? Should employers ensure that employees on breaks not perform any work? Why or why not?

Internet Activities

1-1.   Using the website www.jstor.org, search for articles about payroll-related laws or relevant employment legislation. Once you find an article, summarize the article, and explain how the legislation influenced contemporary payroll practices.

1-2.   Visit the website of the American Payroll Association at www.americanpayroll.org. On the right side of the Home page, you will find articles about recent developments in payroll practices and legislation. Choose an article and create a presentation to your class about how its content affects payroll practice.

1-3. Want to know more about the specifics of some of the concepts in this chapter? Check out these websites:

www.dol.gov/esa/whd/regs/compliance/hrg.htm

www.taxhistory.com/1943.html

www.workerscompensationinsurance.com

www.Kronos.com

www.adp.com

www.paychex.com

Continuing Payroll Project: Prevosti Farms and Sugarhouse

© Api/Alamy, RF

Toni Prevosti is opening a new business, Prevosti Farms and Sugarhouse, which is a small company that will harvest, refine, and sell maple syrup products. In subsequent chapters, students will have the opportunity to establish payroll records and complete payroll information for Prevosti Farms and Sugarhouse.

Toni has decided that she needs to hire employees for the business to grow. Complete the application for Prevosti Farms and Sugarhouse's Employer Identification Number (Form SS-4) with the following information:

Prevosti Farms and Sugarhouse is located at 820 Westminster Road, Bridgewater, Vermont, 05520 (which is also Ms. Prevosti's home address), phone number 802-555-3456. Bridgewater is in Windsor County. Toni has decided that Prevosti Farms and Sugarhouse, the responsible party for a sole proprietorship, will pay its employees on a biweekly basis. Toni's Social Security number is 055-22-0443. The beginning date of the business is February 1, 2015. Prevosti Farms and Sugarhouse will use a calendar year as its accounting year. Toni anticipates that she will need to hire six employees initially for the business, three of whom will be agricultural and three who will be office workers. The first date of wages will be February 16, 2015. Toni has not had a prior EIN.

Answers to Stop & Check Exercises

Which Law?

1. e
2. h
3. b
4. f
5. i
6. j
7. a
8. d
9. g
10. c

Which Payroll Law?

1. d
2. a
3. f
4. c
5. g
6. e
7. b

What's Ethical?

1. Answers will vary. Some concerns include data privacy and integrity in the software switchover, tax and employee pay integrity on the new software, and employee pay methods.

2. Answers will vary. Liza could choose to ignore her sorority sister's request, claiming professional responsibility. She could also discontinue active participation in the sorority. In any case, Liza must not consent to her sorority sister's request for confidential information.

Continued on page 31.

Form **SS-4** (Rev. January 2010) Department of the Treasury Internal Revenue Service	**Application for Employer Identification Number** (For use by employers, corporations, partnerships, trusts, estates, churches, government agencies, Indian tribal entities, certain individuals, and others.) ▶ **See separate instructions for each line.** ▶ **Keep a copy for your records.**	OMB No. 1545-0003 EIN

Type or print clearly.

1	Legal name of entity (or individual) for whom the EIN is being requested		
2	Trade name of business (if different from name on line 1)	**3**	Executor, administrator, trustee, "care of" name
4a	Mailing address (room, apt., suite no. and street, or P.O. box)	**5a**	Street address (if different) (Do not enter a P.O. box.)
4b	City, state, and ZIP code (if foreign, see instructions)	**5b**	City, state, and ZIP code (if foreign, see instructions)
6	County and state where principal business is located		
7a	Name of responsible party	**7b**	SSN, ITIN, or EIN

8a	Is this application for a limited liability company (LLC) (or a foreign equivalent)? . . . . ☐ **Yes** ☐ **No**	**8b**	If 8a is "Yes," enter the number of LLC members . . . . ▶

8c If 8a is "Yes," was the LLC organized in the United States? . . . . ☐ **Yes**   ☐ **No**

9a **Type of entity** (check only one box). **Caution.** If 8a is "Yes," see the instructions for the correct box to check.

☐ Sole proprietor (SSN) _____

☐ Partnership

☐ Corporation (enter form number to be filed) ▶ _____

☐ Personal service corporation

☐ Church or church-controlled organization

☐ Other nonprofit organization (specify) ▶ _____

☐ Other (specify) ▶ _____

☐ Estate (SSN of decedent) _____

☐ Plan administrator (TIN) _____

☐ Trust (TIN of grantor) _____

☐ National Guard   ☐ State/local government

☐ Farmers' cooperative   ☐ Federal government/military

☐ REMIC   ☐ Indian tribal governments/enterprises

Group Exemption Number (GEN) if any ▶

9b	If a corporation, name the state or foreign country (if applicable) where incorporated	State	Foreign country

10 **Reason for applying** (check only one box)

☐ Started new business (specify type) ▶ _____

☐ Hired employees (Check the box and see line 13.)

☐ Compliance with IRS withholding regulations

☐ Other (specify) ▶

☐ Banking purpose (specify purpose) ▶ _____

☐ Changed type of organization (specify new type) ▶ _____

☐ Purchased going business

☐ Created a trust (specify type) ▶ _____

☐ Created a pension plan (specify type) ▶ _____

11	Date business started or acquired (month, day, year). See instructions.	**12**	Closing month of accounting year
13	Highest number of employees expected in the next 12 months (enter -0- if none). If no employees expected, skip line 14.	**14**	If you expect your employment tax liability to be $1,000 or less in a full calendar year **and** want to file Form 944 annually instead of Forms 941 quarterly, check here. (Your employment tax liability generally will be $1,000 or less if you expect to pay $4,000 or less in total wages.) If you do not check this box, you must file Form 941 for every quarter. ☐

Agricultural	Household	Other

15 First date wages or annuities were paid (month, day, year). **Note.** If applicant is a withholding agent, enter date income will first be paid to nonresident alien (month, day, year) . . . . ▶

16 Check **one** box that best describes the principal activity of your business.

☐ Construction   ☐ Rental & leasing   ☐ Transportation & warehousing

☐ Real estate   ☐ Manufacturing   ☐ Finance & insurance

☐ Health care & social assistance   ☐ Wholesale-agent/broker

☐ Accommodation & food service   ☐ Wholesale-other   ☐ Retail

☐ Other (specify)

17 Indicate principal line of merchandise sold, specific construction work done, products produced, or services provided.

18 Has the applicant entity shown on line 1 ever applied for and received an EIN? ☐ **Yes**   ☐ **No**

If "Yes," write previous EIN here ▶

Third Party Designee	Complete this section **only** if you want to authorize the named individual to receive the entity's EIN and answer questions about the completion of this form.	
	Designee's name	Designee's telephone number (include area code) ( )
	Address and ZIP code	Designee's fax number (include area code) ( )

Under penalties of perjury, I declare that I have examined this application, and to the best of my knowledge and belief, it is true, correct, and complete.

Name and title (type or print clearly) ▶

	Applicant's telephone number (include area code) ( )
Signature ▶ Date ▶	Applicant's fax number (include area code) ( )

For Privacy Act and Paperwork Reduction Act Notice, see separate instructions.   Cat. No. 16055N   Form **SS-4** (Rev. 1-2010)

Source: Internal Revenue Service.

Confidential Records

As a payroll clerk, your task is to protect the privacy and confidentiality of the information you maintain for the company. If a student group—or any personnel aside from the company's payroll employees and officers—wishes to review confidential records, you should deny their request. If needed, you should refer the group to your department's manager to discuss the matter in more depth. The laws that apply to this situation are the Privacy Act of 1974, the Freedom of Information Act, and potentially HIPAA.

Large vs. Small

Large companies have computer-based accounting packages such as QuickBooks, Sage 50, and Microsoft Dynamics GP available. Additionally, they may consider outsourcing their payroll functions to companies such as ADP and Paychex®, which provide companies with comprehensive payroll services and tax reporting.

For small companies, the cost of outsourcing the payroll function needs to be considered. On one hand, a small company may not have personnel who are proficient with payroll regulations and tax reporting requirements, which leaves a company vulnerable to legal actions and stringent fines. However, engaging a payroll service company may be cost prohibitive. The decision to outsource the payroll for a small company should take into account the number of personnel, locations, and types of operations in which the company engages.

What Is the Difference?

a. Manual payroll systems involve the use of paper and pencil recordkeeping or a spreadsheet program, such as Microsoft Excel. This is most appropriate for very small firms.

b. Computerized payroll systems can be used by any company, regardless of size. Examples of computerized systems include, QuickBooks, Sage 50, and Microsoft Dynamics GP. These computer packages range in price, depending on the company size and operational scope.

c. Outsourced payroll involves the engagement of a third party to manage a company's payroll data, issue employee compensation, and prepare tax forms.

d. Certified payroll pertains to companies with employees who work on federal government contracts. Certified payroll ensures that a company reports payroll expenditures of contractually allocated money.

Exempt vs. Nonexempt

1. Exempt workers are exempt from the overtime provisions of FLSA. Exempt workers tend to be employees in a company's managerial or other leadership functions, in which they may need to work more than 40 hours per week to complete their tasks. Exempt workers usually receive a fixed salary per period that is not based on the number of hours worked. Nonexempt workers tend to be compensated on an hourly basis and often do not have managerial or leadership responsibilities. It should be noted that some nonexempt workers do have managerial or leadership responsibilities and may receive a fixed salary; however, these particular employees are covered by the overtime provisions of FLSA.

2. An employee is defined as a person who works solely for one company. Most or all work-related materials are provided by the company. Employee payroll taxes are paid by the company, and the employee may be eligible for fringe benefits. In contrast, an independent contractor may have more than one company as a client. Independent contractors provide their own tools and materials, pay their own income taxes, and generally establish their working hours. An employee of a company is considered to be part of the payroll expense, whereas an independent contractor is a vendor of the company who submits invoices for payment.

2

Payroll System Procedures

Payroll procedures have a dual focus: (1) governmental rules and (2) the company's needs. The company must abide by the applicable governmental and industrial regulations or face potential fines, sanctions, or closure. To comply with regulations, a company must make several decisions: pay frequency, pay types (e.g., direct deposit, paycards, or paper checks), employee benefits, and handling of pay advances. The payroll accountant must prepare for the integration of new hires, transfer of employees among departments, and terminations that occur during the normal course of business. Employee benefits and government-required payroll deductions complicate the pay process.

Accountants handle documents that have varying levels of confidentiality. Some items include receipts for expenses, invoices from vendors, and other business-related documents that are not confidential. The employees' documents that payroll accountants handle are usually private and often contain highly sensitive personal information. Different regulations regarding the length of retention and storage procedures apply to payroll documents. A very important note about financial or personnel documentation is this: Any documents connected with fraudulent activity have no time limit for retention purposes. In the event of suspected fraud, investigators may request relevant fraud-related documents at any time.

LEARNING OBJECTIVES

After studying Chapter 2, you should be able to:

LO 2-1   Identify Important Payroll Procedures and Pay Cycles

LO 2-2   Prepare Required Employee Documentation

LO 2-3   Explain Pay Records and Employee File Maintenance

LO 2-4   Describe Internal Controls and Record Retention for a Payroll System

LO 2-5   Discuss Employee Termination and Document Destruction Procedures

© Steve Cole/Photodisc/Getty Images, RF

Document Destruction and Arthur Andersen's Downfall

In the late 1990s, Enron was one of the biggest names in the energy business. They leveraged contracts and used "mark-to-market" accounting to adjust energy contracts to fair market values and reported a pre-tax profit of $1.41 billion in 2000. However, irregularities in the firm's accounting practices led to a Congressional investigation into financial documents. During its probe, Congress found that Enron's auditing firm, Arthur Andersen, had destroyed many documents that would have contained information relevant to the investigation. Missing data included revenue transfers and payroll records. Although the U.S. Supreme Court ultimately overturned Arthur Andersen's conviction for obstruction of justice during the Enron investigation, the American Bar Association has delineated guidelines for document retention, including relevance, industry, compliance standards, and litigation needs. Congressional legislation regarding documentation is contained in 18 U.S.C. §1512(c) and 18 U.S.C. §1519. (Sources: American Bar Association, *Journal of Accountancy,* Greenberg Traurig LLP)

Personnel and payroll files are very closely related. In Chapter 2, we will explore payroll system procedures, including information about file security, legally required documents, and internal controls.

LO 2-1   Identify Important Payroll Procedures and Pay Cycles

© Sam Edwards/age fotostock, RF

The documentation required for paying employees starts before the first employee is hired. The EIN, obtained through Form SS-4, is the very first step in employer documentation, closely followed by the employee information files. Under FLSA, certain information is required in every employee file. According to the U.S. Department of Labor, the list of required information to be maintained in the employee file includes:

1. Employee's full name, as used for Social Security purposes, and the employee's identifying symbol or number, if such is used in place of their name on any time, work, or payroll records.
2. Address, including zip code.
3. Birth date, if younger than 19.
4. Sex and occupation.
5. Time and day of week when employee's workweek begins.
6. Hours worked each day and total hours worked each workweek.
7. Basis on which employee's wages are paid.
8. Regular hourly pay rate.
9. Total daily or weekly straight-time earnings.
10. Total overtime earnings for the workweek.
11. All additions to or deductions from the employee's wages.
12. Total wages paid each *pay period*.
13. Date of payment and the pay period covered by the payment.

Payroll documentation regulations protect employees by ensuring that they receive accurate paychecks. These regulations also keep employers in compliance with tax regulations and provide an audit trail for government bodies. *New hire reporting* requirements ensure that employees pay legal obligations such as child support and garnishments. Figure 2-1 shows an Employee Information Form, which contains elements of the information from the employee file. Note that the employee file is maintained by the firm's human resources department, and the employee information form shown in Figure 2-1 is maintained by the payroll department, so some FLSA elements may not appear on the form.

FIGURE 2-1
Sample Employee Information Form

EMPLOYEE EARNINGS RECORD

NAME   Jonathan A. Doe   Hire Date 1/1/2015
ADDRESS 100 Main Street   Date of Birth 4/16/1983
CITY/STATE/ZIP
Anytown, MD 21220   Position   Sales   PT/(FT)
TELEPHONE 202-555-4009   No. of exemptions   4   (M/S)
SOCIAL SECURITY
NUMBER   987-65-4321   Pay Rate $15.00   (Hr)/Wk/Mo

Period Ended	Hrs. Worked	Reg Pay	OT Pay	Gross Pay	Social Sec. Tax	Medicare	Fed Inc. Tax	State Inc. Tax	401(k)	Taxable income	Total Deduc	Net pay	YTD
1/7/15	40	600.00	0.00	600.00	37.20	8.70	14.00	12.00	25.00		96.90	503.10	600.00

> In 2015, the Equal Employment Opportunity Commission (EEOC) announced plans to enforce limits concerning the following issues:
>
> - Pregnant workers and employer obligations about maternity leave
> - Hiring barriers, specifically the legality of the use of credit and criminal background checks by employers
> - Reasonable accommodations for employees, as mandated by the Americans with Disabilities Act
> - Employer accommodations for employees' religious observations
> - Employee participation in employer-sponsored wellness programs, as legislated by the Affordable Care Act
> - Protections for lesbian, gay, bisexual, and transgender (LGBT) workers' rights under Title VII
>
> (Source: SHRM)

The EEOC's protection of employee rights, especially when it leads to a lawsuit, involves the firm's personnel documentation. Accurate and correctly maintained payroll records are especially important because they reflect the firm's treatment of its employees.

When a company develops or reviews its payroll system, the payroll accountant faces a multifaceted task. The employer must answer several questions:

- How will the company handle new hires?
- What will the procedure be when an employee transfers from one department to another?
- What is the procedure to follow upon employee termination?
- What processes should the company establish to ensure government compliance?
- How will employee time and attendance be tracked?

Pay Cycles

Let's start with a basic question: How often should the company pay its employees? Regardless of which accounting system the company is using, the determination of pay cycle, or pay periods, is the first thing a new company needs to establish. Some options for payroll cycles include the following:

Daily payroll is typically paid at the end of the day or by the end of the next business day. This method of payroll processing is typical in day labor situations; however, it should be noted that day labor could be treated as independent contractor work, and thus not be subject to payroll, payroll taxes, or a W-2.

Weekly payroll is typically used in a Monday through Friday workweek. The employees receive their paychecks the following Friday. Several types of companies use a weekly payroll system, including grocery stores, construction, and professional offices. This pay frequency may lead to 52 pay periods per year.

Biweekly payroll is typically processed based on a two-week period, and employees receive their paychecks approximately a week after the end of the pay period. Pay dates may be any weekday. This pay frequency generally has 26 pay periods per year.

Semimonthly payroll is paid twice a month. Examples of semimonthly payroll pay dates include (1) the 1st and 15th of the month and (2) the 15th and last day of the month. This is not the same as biweekly payroll, and taxation and hours paid are different. Employees receive 24 pay disbursements per year when using a semimonthly payroll system.

Monthly payroll is less frequently used than other methods. Some companies process payroll once per month and may allow a semimonthly draw to the employees. When employees are allowed to draw their wages at mid-month, the employer may or may not take payroll taxes out of the draw. If the mid-month draw does not have payroll taxes withheld, the month-end payroll will need to recover all taxes and withholdings for the month from the employee.

What's in the File?

STOP & CHECK

1. Which of the following artifacts must be included in the employee file?

   a. full name and address
   b. occupation
   c. mother's maiden name
   d. pay rate
   e. date of payment
   f. spouse's name

Match the pay frequencies:

2. Monthly
3. Semimonthly
4. Biweekly
5. Weekly

Number of pay periods:

a. 26
b. 12
c. 52
d. 24

LO 2-2   Prepare Required Employee Documentation

Employees versus Independent Contractors

People who work for a company may be classified as either employees or independent contractors depending on the nature of the work and the withholding of payroll-related taxes from the worker's compensation. According to the IRS, millions of workers have been misclassified, which has led to employers not depositing the full amount of taxes due and employees missing out on benefits. IRS form SS-8 (available at www.irs.gov) is a way that employers may receive official guidance about worker classification.

© Monty Rakusen/cultura/Corbis, RF

Employees

The determination of a worker as an employee has two primary criteria according to labor laws. The first is *work direction,* which means that the employer substantially directs the worker's performance. The employer provides the primary tools that an employee uses; for example, the employee may be given the use of a desk, computer, company car, or other items needed to complete the assigned work. The other criterion is *material contribution,* which means that the work that the employee completes must involve substantial effort. An employer withholds payroll taxes from an employee's compensation, provides company-specific benefits, and includes the worker on governmental reports.

Independent Contractors

Classification of a worker as an independent contractor means that the employer does not direct the worker's specific actions and does not provide the tools needed to complete the work. For example, if a worker performed accounting services for a company but used a privately owned computer and printer, as well as determined the number and timing of the hours worked for the company, the worker could be classified as an independent contractor. An independent contractor may or may not perform work that constitutes material contribution for the employer. The treatment of independent contractors (ICs) is important because cases in which independent contractors have been reclassified as employees have occurred and do contribute to fraud and potential tax avoidance by employers.

©Marc Romanelli/Blend Images LLC, RF

In two notable cases, *United States v. Silk* (1947) and *Bartels v. Birmingham* (1947), both of the employers reclassified ICs as employees for tax purposes, resulting in violations and fines under IRS section 530, which prevents such reclassification in situations where an IC is clearly working in a nonemployee capacity. According to the U.S. Department of Labor, investigations into employee misclassification usually involve examination of two years of employee records. In cases where intentional misclassification is suspected, the DOL will examine more years of employee records. (Source: American Payroll Association)

Payment records for ICs, although maintained separately from payroll records, are an instance in which payroll accountants must be aware of employee classification and record-keeping requirements to avoid fraudulent activity. Independent contractors are responsible for their own payroll taxes. They are paid through a company's accounts payable, not payroll. This subject has become increasingly important in the past decade as many employers sought to reduce liabilities through the incorrect classification of IC workers.

Reporting New Employees

Reporting newly hired employees is considered very important by governmental bodies. Why is this so?

- First, reporting employees creates a registry to monitor people who owe child support.
- Second, it helps immigration agencies track immigrants to ensure that they are still legally able to work in the United States.
- Third, for certain professions such as teaching, the new hire reporting system can be used to communicate issues such as ethical violations for which the professional has been censured by governmental or accrediting bodies.
- Finally, the new hire reporting system assists with the administration of COBRA medical benefits.

All newly hired employees must have certain specific documentation. For legal purposes, the minimum amount of documentation allowed is the *W-4* (see Figure 2-2) and *I-9* forms (see Figure 2-3). The W-4 is a publication of the Internal Revenue Service. The main purpose behind the W-4 is to help the employer determine the correct amount of federal income taxes to withhold from the employee's payroll. The I-9 form is published by the Department of Homeland Security, which stipulates that all new hires must be reported within 20 days of their start date. Registration of employees by using the I-9 form minimizes negative implications associated with monitoring legally authorized workers in the United States and tracking people with legal obligations such as child support and other garnishments.

As of the 2010 U.S. census, the estimated amount of child support transferred between custodial and noncustodial parents for children younger than the age of 21 in the United States exceeded $41.7 billion. (Source: U.S. Census Bureau)

Please refer to the following information for the Form W-4 shown in Figure 2-2 and the I-9 shown in Figure 2-3. The final page of the I-9 form contains the employee-provided documents needed to verify identity and eligibility to work in the United States. Employees must provide either one item from List A *or* one item from both List B *and* List C.

Jonathan A. Doe was born on 5/17/1981 and lives at 123 Main Street, Anytown, Kansas 54932. He is single. His Social Security number is 987-65-4321. His employer is Homestead Retreat at 9010 Old Manhattan Highway, Olathe, Kansas 59384. His email address is jonathandoe@anymail.com, and his phone number is (620)552-2299. When he filled out his new hire paperwork on January 2, 2015, Jessica Stolpp in Human Resources for Homestead Retreat verified his identity with both his Social Security card and his driver's license (G93847562), which expires on his birthday in 2017.

FIGURE 2-2
Form W-4 Employee Withholding Allowance Certificate

Form W-4 (2015)

Purpose. Complete Form W-4 so that your employer can withhold the correct federal income tax from your pay. Consider completing a new Form W-4 each year and when your personal or financial situation changes.

Exemption from withholding. If you are exempt, complete **only** lines 1, 2, 3, 4, and 7 and sign the form to validate it. Your exemption for 2015 expires February 16, 2016. See Pub. 505, Tax Withholding and Estimated Tax.

Note. If another person can claim you as a dependent on his or her tax return, you cannot claim exemption from withholding if your income exceeds $1,050 and includes more than $350 of unearned income (for example, interest and dividends).

Exceptions. An employee may be able to claim exemption from withholding even if the employee is a dependent, if the employee:

• Is age 65 or older,

• Is blind, or

• Will claim adjustments to income; tax credits; or itemized deductions, on his or her tax return.

The exceptions do not apply to supplemental wages greater than $1,000,000.

Basic instructions. If you are not exempt, complete the **Personal Allowances Worksheet** below. The worksheets on page 2 further adjust your withholding allowances based on itemized deductions, certain credits, adjustments to income, or two-earners/multiple jobs situations.

Complete all worksheets that apply. However, you may claim fewer (or zero) allowances. For regular wages, withholding must be based on allowances you claimed and may not be a flat amount or percentage of wages.

Head of household. Generally, you can claim head of household filing status on your tax return only if you are unmarried and pay more than 50% of the costs of keeping up a home for yourself and your dependent(s) or other qualifying individuals. See Pub. 501, Exemptions, Standard Deduction, and Filing Information, for information.

Tax credits. You can take projected tax credits into account in figuring your allowable number of withholding allowances. Credits for child or dependent care expenses and the child tax credit may be claimed using the **Personal Allowances Worksheet** below. See Pub. 505 for information on converting your other credits into withholding allowances.

Nonwage income. If you have a large amount of nonwage income, such as interest or dividends, consider making estimated tax payments using Form 1040-ES, Estimated Tax for Individuals. Otherwise, you may owe additional tax. If you have pension or annuity income, see Pub. 505 to find out if you should adjust your withholding on Form W-4 or W-4P.

Two earners or multiple jobs. If you have a working spouse or more than one job, figure the total number of allowances you are entitled to claim on all jobs using worksheets from only one Form W-4. Your withholding usually will be most accurate when all allowances are claimed on the Form W-4 for the highest paying job and zero allowances are claimed on the others. See Pub. 505 for details.

Nonresident alien. If you are a nonresident alien, see Notice 1392, Supplemental Form W-4 Instructions for Nonresident Aliens, before completing this form.

Check your withholding. After your Form W-4 takes effect, use Pub. 505 to see how the amount you are having withheld compares to your projected total tax for 2015. See Pub. 505, especially if your earnings exceed $130,000 (Single) or $180,000 (Married).

Future developments. Information about any future developments affecting Form W-4 (such as legislation enacted after we release it) will be posted at *www.irs.gov/w4*.

Personal Allowances Worksheet (Keep for your records.)

A	Enter "1" for **yourself** if no one else can claim you as a dependent	**A** ___1___
B	Enter "1" if: { • You are single and have only one job; or • You are married, have only one job, and your spouse does not work; or • Your wages from a second job or your spouse's wages (or the total of both) are $1,500 or less. } . . .	**B** ___1___
C	Enter "1" for your **spouse.** But, you may choose to enter "-0-" if you are married and have either a working spouse or more than one job. (Entering "-0-" may help you avoid having too little tax withheld.)	**C** _____
D	Enter number of **dependents** (other than your spouse or yourself) you will claim on your tax return	**D** _____
E	Enter "1" if you will file as **head of household** on your tax return (see conditions under **Head of household** above) . .	**E** _____
F	Enter "1" if you have at least $2,000 of **child or dependent care expenses** for which you plan to claim a credit . . . (**Note.** Do **not** include child support payments. See Pub. 503, Child and Dependent Care Expenses, for details.)	**F** _____
G	**Child Tax Credit** (including additional child tax credit). See Pub. 972, Child Tax Credit, for more information. • If your total income will be less than $65,000 ($100,000 if married), enter "2" for each eligible child; then **less** "1" if you have two to four eligible children or **less** "2" if you have five or more eligible children. • If your total income will be between $65,000 and $84,000 ($100,000 and $119,000 if married), enter "1" for each eligible child . . .	**G** _____
H	Add lines A through G and enter total here. (**Note.** This may be different from the number of exemptions you claim on your tax return.) ► **H**	___2___

For accuracy, complete all worksheets that apply.	{ • If you plan to **itemize** or **claim adjustments to income** and want to reduce your withholding, see the **Deductions and Adjustments Worksheet** on page 2. • If you are **single and have more than one job** or are **married and you and your spouse both work** and the combined earnings from all jobs exceed $50,000 ($20,000 if married), see the **Two-Earners/Multiple Jobs Worksheet** on page 2 to avoid having too little tax withheld. • If **neither** of the above situations applies, **stop here** and enter the number from line H on line 5 of Form W-4 below. }

--------------------- **Separate here and give Form W-4 to your employer. Keep the top part for your records.** ---------------------

Form **W-4** Department of the Treasury Internal Revenue Service	**Employee's Withholding Allowance Certificate** ► Whether you are entitled to claim a certain number of allowances or exemption from withholding is subject to review by the IRS. Your employer may be required to send a copy of this form to the IRS.	OMB No. 1545-0074 20**15**

1 Your first name and middle initial	Last name	**2** Your social security number
Jonathan A.	Doe	987-65-4321

Home address (number and street or rural route)	**3** ☑ Single ☐ Married ☐ Married, but withhold at higher Single rate.
123 Main Street	**Note.** If married, but legally separated, or spouse is a nonresident alien, check the "Single" box.
City or town, state, and ZIP code	**4** If your last name differs from that shown on your social security card, check here. You must call 1-800-772-1213 for a replacement card. ► ☐
Anytown, KS 54932	

5	Total number of allowances you are claiming (from line **H** above **or** from the applicable worksheet on page 2)	**5** | 2
6	Additional amount, if any, you want withheld from each paycheck	**6** | $
7	I claim exemption from withholding for 2015, and I certify that I meet **both** of the following conditions for exemption.	
	• Last year I had a right to a refund of **all** federal income tax withheld because I had **no** tax liability, **and**	
	• This year I expect a refund of **all** federal income tax withheld because I expect to have **no** tax liability.	
	If you meet both conditions, write "Exempt" here . . . . ► **7** |	

Under penalties of perjury, I declare that I have examined this certificate and, to the best of my knowledge and belief, it is true, correct, and complete.

Employee's signature
 (This form is not valid unless you sign it.) ► *Jonathan A. Doe*   **Date** ► 1/2/2015

8 Employer's name and address (Employer: Complete lines 8 and 10 only if sending to the IRS.)	**9** Office code (optional)	**10** Employer identification number (EIN)

For Privacy Act and Paperwork Reduction Act Notice, see page 2.   Cat. No. 10220Q   Form **W-4** (2015)

Source: Internal Revenue Service.

FIGURE 2-3
I-9 Employment Eligibility Verification Form

Employment Eligibility Verification

Department of Homeland Security
U.S. Citizenship and Immigration Services

**USCIS
Form I-9**
OMB No. 1615-0047
Expires 03/31/2016

▶**START HERE.** **Read instructions carefully before completing this form. The instructions must be available during completion of this form.**
ANTI-DISCRIMINATION NOTICE: It is illegal to discriminate against work-authorized individuals. Employers **CANNOT** specify which document(s) they will accept from an employee. The refusal to hire an individual because the documentation presented has a future expiration date may also constitute illegal discrimination.

Section 1. Employee Information and Attestation *(Employees must complete and sign Section 1 of Form I-9 no later than the first day of employment, but not before accepting a job offer.)*

Last Name *(Family Name)*	First Name *(Given Name)*	Middle Initial	Other Names Used *(if any)*
Doe	Jonathan	A	

Address *(Street Number and Name)*	Apt. Number	City or Town	State	Zip Code
123 Main Street		Anytown	KS	54932

Date of Birth *(mm/dd/yyyy)*	U.S. Social Security Number	E-mail Address	Telephone Number
05/17/1981	9 8 7 - 6 5 - 4 3 2 1	jonathandoe@anymail . com	(620) 552-2299

I am aware that federal law provides for imprisonment and/or fines for false statements or use of false documents in connection with the completion of this form.

I attest, under penalty of perjury, that I am (check one of the following):

[X] A citizen of the United States

[ ] A noncitizen national of the United States *(See instructions)*

[ ] A lawful permanent resident (Alien Registration Number/USCIS Number): _____

[ ] An alien authorized to work until (expiration date, if applicable, mm/dd/yyyy) _____ . Some aliens may write "N/A" in this field. *(See instructions)*

*For aliens authorized to work, provide your Alien Registration Number/USCIS Number **OR** Form I-94 Admission Number:*

1. Alien Registration Number/USCIS Number:_____

OR

2. Form I-94 Admission Number: _____

If you obtained your admission number from CBP in connection with your arrival in the United States, include the following:

Foreign Passport Number: _____

Country of Issuance: _____

Some aliens may write "N/A" on the Foreign Passport Number and Country of Issuance fields. *(See instructions)*

**3-D Barcode
Do Not Write in This Space**

Signature of Employee:	Date *(mm/dd/yyyy):* 01/02/2015

Preparer and/or Translator Certification *(To be completed and signed if Section 1 is prepared by a person other than the employee.)*

I attest, under penalty of perjury, that I have assisted in the completion of this form and that to the best of my knowledge the information is true and correct.

Signature of Preparer or Translator:	Date *(mm/dd/yyyy):*

Last Name *(Family Name)*	First Name *(Given Name)*

Address *(Street Number and Name)*	City or Town	State	Zip Code

🛑 *Employer Completes Next Page* 🛑

Source: United States Citizenship and Immigration Services

Section 2. Employer or Authorized Representative Review and Verification

(Employers or their authorized representative must complete and sign Section 2 within 3 business days of the employee's first day of employment. You must physically examine one document from List A OR examine a combination of one document from List B and one document from List C as listed on the "Lists of Acceptable Documents" on the next page of this form. For each document you review, record the following information: document title, issuing authority, document number, and expiration date, if any.)

Employee Last Name, First Name and Middle Initial from Section 1: Doe, Jonathan A,

List A Identity and Employment Authorization	**OR**	**List B** Identity	**AND**	**List C** Employment Authorization
Document Title:		Document Title: Driver's License		Document Title: Social Security Card
Issuing Authority:		Issuing Authority: State of Kansas		Issuing Authority: Social Security Administration
Document Number:		Document Number: G93847562		Document Number: 987-65-4321
Expiration Date *(if any)(mm/dd/yyyy)*:		Expiration Date *(if any)(mm/dd/yyyy)*: 05/17/2017		Expiration Date *(if any)(mm/dd/yyyy)*:
Document Title:				
Issuing Authority:				
Document Number:				
Expiration Date *(if any)(mm/dd/yyyy)*:				
Document Title:				**3-D Barcode** **Do Not Write in This Space**
Issuing Authority:				
Document Number:				
Expiration Date *(if any)(mm/dd/yyyy)*:				

Certification

I attest, under penalty of perjury, that (1) I have examined the document(s) presented by the above-named employee, (2) the above-listed document(s) appear to be genuine and to relate to the employee named, and (3) to the best of my knowledge the employee is authorized to work in the United States.

The employee's first day of employment *(mm/dd/yyyy)*: ___01/01/2015___ (*See instructions for exemptions.*)

Signature of Employer or Authorized Representative	Date *(mm/dd/yyyy)* 01/02/2015	Title of Employer or Authorized Representative Human Resources
Last Name *(Family Name)* Stolpp	First Name *(Given Name)* Jessica	Employer's Business or Organization Name Homestead Retreat

Employer's Business or Organization Address *(Street Number and Name)* 9010 Old Manhattan Highway	City or Town Olathe	State KS	Zip Code 59384

Section 3. Reverification and Rehires *(To be completed and signed by employer or authorized representative.)*

A. New Name *(if applicable)* Last Name *(Family Name)* First Name *(Given Name)*	Middle Initial	**B.** Date of Rehire *(if applicable) (mm/dd/yyyy)*:

C. If employee's previous grant of employment authorization has expired, provide the information for the document from List A or List C the employee presented that establishes current employment authorization in the space provided below.

Document Title:	Document Number:	Expiration Date *(if any)(mm/dd/yyyy)*:

I attest, under penalty of perjury, that to the best of my knowledge, this employee is authorized to work in the United States, and if the employee presented document(s), the document(s) I have examined appear to be genuine and to relate to the individual.

Signature of Employer or Authorized Representative:	Date *(mm/dd/yyyy)*:	Print Name of Employer or Authorized Representative:

LISTS OF ACCEPTABLE DOCUMENTS
All documents must be UNEXPIRED

Employees may present one selection from List A
or a combination of one selection from List B and one selection from List C.

LIST A		LIST B	LIST C
Documents that Establish Both Identity and Employment Authorization	**OR**	**Documents that Establish Identity** **AND**	**Documents that Establish Employment Authorization**
1. U.S. Passport or U.S. Passport Card		1. Driver's license or ID card issued by a State or outlying possession of the United States provided it contains a photograph or information such as name, date of birth, gender, height, eye color, and address	1. A Social Security Account Number card, unless the card includes one of the following restrictions: (1) NOT VALID FOR EMPLOYMENT (2) VALID FOR WORK ONLY WITH INS AUTHORIZATION (3) VALID FOR WORK ONLY WITH DHS AUTHORIZATION
2. Permanent Resident Card or Alien Registration Receipt Card (Form I-551)			
3. Foreign passport that contains a temporary I-551 stamp or temporary I-551 printed notation on a machine-readable immigrant visa		2. ID card issued by federal, state or local government agencies or entities, provided it contains a photograph or information such as name, date of birth, gender, height, eye color, and address	2. Certification of Birth Abroad issued by the Department of State (Form FS-545)
4. Employment Authorization Document that contains a photograph (Form I-766)		3. School ID card with a photograph	3. Certification of Report of Birth issued by the Department of State (Form DS-1350)
		4. Voter's registration card	
5. For a nonimmigrant alien authorized to work for a specific employer because of his or her status: **a.** Foreign passport; and **b.** Form I-94 or Form I-94A that has the following: (1) The same name as the passport; and (2) An endorsement of the alien's nonimmigrant status as long as that period of endorsement has not yet expired and the proposed employment is not in conflict with any restrictions or limitations identified on the form.		5. U.S. Military card or draft record	4. Original or certified copy of birth certificate issued by a State, county, municipal authority, or territory of the United States bearing an official seal
		6. Military dependent's ID card	
		7. U.S. Coast Guard Merchant Mariner Card	
		8. Native American tribal document	5. Native American tribal document
		9. Driver's license issued by a Canadian government authority	6. U.S. Citizen ID Card (Form I-197)
		For persons under age 18 who are unable to present a document listed above:	7. Identification Card for Use of Resident Citizen in the United States (Form I-179)
6. Passport from the Federated States of Micronesia (FSM) or the Republic of the Marshall Islands (RMI) with Form I-94 or Form I-94A indicating nonimmigrant admission under the Compact of Free Association Between the United States and the FSM or RMI		10. School record or report card	8. Employment authorization document issued by the Department of Homeland Security
		11. Clinic, doctor, or hospital record	
		12. Day-care or nursery school record	

Illustrations of many of these documents appear in Part 8 of the Handbook for Employers (M-274).

Refer to Section 2 of the instructions, titled "Employer or Authorized Representative Review and Verification," for more information about acceptable receipts.

The payroll accountant should retain a copy of the Employment Eligibility Verification Form (I-9) and a current Employee Withholding Allowance Certificate (W-4) in every employee's permanent file. The employer should request a new W-4 from employees annually to ensure that all addresses, life situations, and other information remain current. Because of the timing constraints on the release of annual tax documents such as the W-2 and W-3, employers should verify employees' W-4 information as close to January 1 as possible each year.

> The U.S. Congress is considering the e-Verify Act (H.R. 1147), which would mandate electronic verification of an employee's eligibility to work in the United States. If H.R. 1147 is signed into law, the paper I-9 form would be repealed in favor of the electronic verification system, which would improve communication among agencies such as the Department of Homeland Security and the Social Security Administration and reduce fraud. (Source: SHRM)

Hiring Packet Contents

© Ariel Skelley/Blend Images/Getty Images, RF

The *hiring packet* maintained by many companies may be as basic as a simple W-4 and I-9 form or may be incredibly complex if foreign workers and multiple types of voluntary deductions are involved. Common items in a hiring packet are items such as the federal forms mentioned above, state and local withholding allowance forms, elections for voluntary deductions, insurance paperwork, and the offer letter that specifies the pay rate and start date. Not all companies have the same items in the hiring packet and no legislative guidelines exist. The firm's management, after reviewing the needs of the company and the legal requirements for the position, determines the hiring packet contents. Many companies also are including diversity self-declaration papers to ensure compliance with equal opportunity legislation, requirements under federal contracts, or other special requirements.

Notification of New Hires to State Offices

The Immigration Reform and Control Act mandates that employers notify state offices within 20 days of an employee's start date. State forms for fulfilling this requirement vary and the reporting of new hires is a complex task with high potential for errors for companies with employees in multiple states.

The Office of Management and Budget (OMB) has designed a form (see Figure 2-4) for multistate employers to register and designate one state as the primary place to which they

FIGURE 2-4
Multistate Employer Notification Form

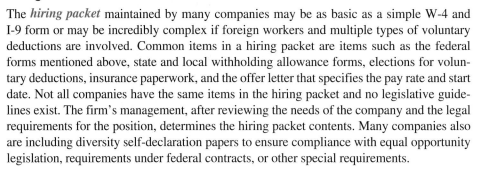

OMB Control No: 0970-0166
Expiration Date: 05-31-2016

MULTISTATE EMPLOYER NOTIFICATION FORM FOR NEW HIRE REPORTING

Employers who have employees working in two or more states may use this form to register to submit their new hire reports to one state or make changes to a previous registration. Multistate employers may also visit https://ocsp.acf.hhs.gov/OCSE/ to register or make changes electronically.

Federal law (42 USC 653A(b)(1)(A)) requires employers to supply the following information about newly hired employees to the State Directory of New Hires in the state where the employee works:

- Employee's name, address, Social Security number, and the date of hire (the date services for remuneration were first performed by the employee)

- Employer's name, address, and Federal Employer Identification Number (FEIN)

    If you are an employer with employees working in two or more states AND you will transmit the required information or reports magnetically or electronically, you may use this form to designate one state where any employee works to transmit ALL new hire reports to the State Directory of New Hires.

Source: United States Department of Health and Human Services.

will send new hire reports. They can designate on the form the other states in which they have employees. The use of the multistate registry helps employers ensure they remain in compliance with the law. The penalty for noncompliance is strictly enforced and ranges from $25 per unreported employee to $500 for intentional nonreporting.

Foreign Workers

Employers who hire non–U.S. citizens face additional challenges. The employer must verify that the employee is legally allowed to work in the United States. Generally, the I-9 form serves this purpose, but there may be occasions when the prospective employee does not have an appropriate government-issued visa for working in the United States. If no visa exists, the employer may file a petition with the U.S. Citizenship and Immigration Services office to gain permission for the foreign employee to work in the United States. Some exceptions exist to the rules for the visa. The fees for permanent workers not in the protected classes can range from $0 to $1,435, depending on the petitioner and the worker concerned. For information about the Permanent Worker Visa Preference Categories, please visit the U.S. Citizenship and Immigration Services website (www.uscis.gov).

Statutory Employees

Some personnel that would normally be classified as independent contractors must be treated as employees for tax purposes. The IRS classifies *statutory employees* as personnel who meet any of the following guidelines:

- A driver who distributes beverages (other than milk) or meat, vegetable, fruit, or bakery products; or who picks up and delivers laundry or dry cleaning, if the driver is a single company's agent or is paid on commission.
- A full-time life insurance sales agent whose principal business activity is selling life insurance or annuity contracts, or both, primarily for one life insurance company.
- An individual who works at home on materials or goods that a company supplies and that must be returned to that company or a designated agent in accordance with furnished specifications for the work to be done.
- A full-time traveling or city salesperson who works on a single company's behalf and turns in orders from wholesalers, retailers, contractors, or operators of hotels, restaurants, or other similar establishments. The goods sold must be merchandise for resale or supplies for use in the buyer's business operation. The work performed for that single company must be the salesperson's principal business activity.

Recall that the primary differences between an employee and an independent contractor are that the independent contractor sets his or her own hours and provides the tools necessary to complete the task. Statutory employees are a hybrid of employee and independent contractor. To ensure proper and timely remittance of employment taxes, the IRS has mandated that the employer withhold taxes from statutory employees in the same manner as other company personnel.

U.S. Workers in Foreign Subsidiaries

Many companies have foreign subsidiaries and divisions that employ U.S. expatriate workers. The *Foreign Account Tax Compliance Act (FATCA)* of 2010 requires employers to report the wages of employees who are permanent U.S. citizens that work in foreign locations to the IRS to facilitate appropriate taxation of such workers. Expatriate workers may exclude the first $100,800 of wages (2015 figure) from U.S. taxation, but must pay income tax on income above that level. Enforcement of FATCA has proven to be complex because the IRS often relies on intermediaries such as foreign financial institutions to keep track of expatriate wages.

© E. Audras/PhotoAlto, RF

Entering New Employees into the Database

The method of entering a new employee into the payroll system depends upon the system in place. A manual system would require minimal work, adding the employee to the

© John Flournoy/McGraw-Hill Education, RF

federal, state, and local lists for taxes withheld as well as adding the new hire to the list of employees to pay. Manual systems should have a checklist of all employees to ensure that no one is missed in the process.

Setting up a new employee in an automated system involves many more steps. The payroll employee enters in the pertinent data. Employee number, name, address, Social Security number, wage, pay frequency, withholding information from W-4, department, and contact information are typically included. The payroll employee must designate a worker's compensation classification, state of employment, and local jurisdiction (when local taxes are applicable). Depending on state requirements, additional location codes, job classification codes, and identifying characteristics may also be required.

Who Are You?

STOP & CHECK

1. Go to the website for the U.S. Citizenship and Immigration Services, located at www.uscis.gov, and type I-9 into the search box on the website. Click on the link for the PDF version of the I-9 form to obtain a digital copy. What are two different ways that you would be able to prove your eligibility for work in the United States?

2. Go to the IRS website, located at www.irs.gov, and type W-4 into the search box on the website. Click on the link for the PDF version of the W-4 to obtain a digital copy. Before you start, ask yourself how many exemptions you think you should claim. Complete the Personal Allowances Worksheet. How did the number of allowable exemptions compare with your estimate? Explain.

LO 2-3 Explain Pay Records and Employee File Maintenance

© Image Source/Corbis, RF

One of the most important parts of any payroll system is the maintenance of employee pay records. The maintenance of accurate and detailed records that reflect the pay period, pay date, pay rate, and deductions is critical not only because it is a legal requirement, but also for positive employee relations. Pay records may be manual, computerized through programs such as Sage 50 or QuickBooks, or maintained by external companies whose sole function is employee payroll implementation. Employers retain physical copies of employees' time records, pay advice, and any other documentation processed with the paycheck. Some other types of documentation include:

- Request for a day off
- Reports of tardiness or absenteeism
- Detailed records of work completed during that day's shift

Technological advances allow employers to scan and save this information digitally, such as using an Adobe Acrobat file, within the payroll accounting system. The availability of digital copies facilitates managerial, auditor, or authorized executives' review, approval, or commentary on the documentation attached to payroll documents. Digital copies also permit transparency of records between the employer and employee, reducing miscommunication and payroll discrepancies.

Pay Records

Employee wages involve far more than simple hourly rates or periodic salary payments. Employees can be subject to the Fair Labor Standards Act, and many provisions of that law affect employee pay. In this section, we will look at how different pay periods and methods influence the payment of employee wages.

The first payroll decision a company should make is the company's pay frequency (daily, weekly, biweekly, semimonthly, monthly). Choice of pay frequency affects the applicable amounts for employee income tax withholding. Separate schedules for federal income taxes are provided in *IRS Publication 15* (available at www.irs.gov), which is released in November for the following year (i.e., 2016 tax information is released in November 2015). Once the pay frequency has been determined, the payroll accountant can establish the payment schedule for federal and state payroll liabilities. Employers must submit government tax liabilities in a timely manner. Depending upon the level of payroll, more frequent tax deposits may be required.

Pay Rate

Pay rate is the amount per hour per pay period the company determines the employee should be compensated. The determination of pay rate depends upon many employee variables: experience, education, certifications, governmental regulations (minimum wage, Davis-Bacon, etc.), the hours worked, or a combination of all of the above. Employers may also pay specific rates for jobs performed. For example, employees working in a manufacturing environment may be subject to a different pay scale when cross-trained and working in a sales capacity. Minimum wage rates vary per state, and different parts of the same state may have different minimum wages.

> The idea of paying a living wage has become a prominent issue in 2015. Companies such as Walmart, Target, and McDonald's have all established minimum employee wages that are significantly higher than the federal minimum wage. Other smaller-scale employers such as Gravity Payments, a merchant services firm, have significantly increased the wages paid to all employees.

Classifying employee wages as salary versus hourly is a basic determination, linked to the type of work performed and the position within the company. **Salaried *exempt* employees** are not subject to overtime, are paid to do a specific job, and fulfill the FLSA requirement of self-direction; however, not all salaried employees are classified as exempt. Certain jobs such as nurses, police officers, and upper-level administrators may earn a fixed salary, but are classified as ***nonexempt*** because of the nature of management direction in their function. Nonexempt workers do not generally supervise other employees and generally work under the direction of a supervisor.

> The concept of a fluctuating workweek for salaried nonexempt employees has been a source of confusion for employers. Some salaried nonexempt employees work in industries that require them to be available at different times based on company needs. If an employee is nonexempt and salaried but has hours that are changeable due to the nature of their job, then they must receive overtime during periods when they work more than 40 hours in a given week. (Source: *Inside Counsel*)

Hourly employees are subject to both FLSA and overtime. When overtime pay is applied, hourly employees may earn more than their salaried counterparts. Overtime rules and rates are determined by FLSA; however, some states may have additional requirements for overtime pay. Overtime is calculated at one-and-a-half times the employee's hourly rate. For FLSA, overtime applies only to hours worked exceeding 40 in a week (with some exceptions). Some states may also require that employees receive overtime pay for any hours worked exceeding 8 per day in addition to the 40 hours per week, making it possible for an hourly employee to earn overtime pay without reaching the 40 hours in the week. For this book, all nonexempt employees work in a state with the over 8 hours per day and 40 hours in a week requirement for overtime calculations.

© Vladamir Godnik/Beyond Fotomedia
GmbH/Alamy, RF

Commissions and piece-rate compensation offer employees incentives for specific jobs. *Commissions* are a percentage of sales or services performed by an individual. An example of a commission would be a sales representative receiving 1% of all sales he or she initiates. *Piece rates* were widely used in the United States prior to industrialization and automated manufacturing. For example, when a shoe was being made, the person preparing the sole would receive a set rate per item.

Compensation structures can become complex if the employee is compensated using multiple pay types. A sales representative may receive a salary and commissions while working on the sales floor, but receive hourly and piece rates if filling in on the manufacturing floor. Proper classification of the various aspects of the employee's workday becomes exceptionally important for the correct processing of the payroll.

> • Juan is a manager for a textiles firm. He earns $52,000 per year, is classified as an exempt employee, and is paid biweekly. He normally works 40 hours per week. In June, he worked 85 hours during one pay period and 78 hours during the next. He would receive his salary of $2,000 (52,000/26) for each pay period no matter how many hours he worked because he is classified as an exempt employee.
>
> • Monique works as a maintenance worker at a busy hospital. She earns $52,000 annually, is paid weekly, and is classified as nonexempt. During one week, she worked 50 hours. She would earn her regular weekly wage of $1,000 (52,000/52) *plus* time-and-a-half for the overtime hours. Based on a 40-hour workweek, her hourly wage is $25 (52,000/(52 × 40)), so her overtime pay would be $375 (10 hours × 1.5 × $25). Thus, Monique's total gross pay for this week will be $1,375 ($1,000 regular pay + $375 overtime pay).

Entering Hours

When it is time to prepare the payroll, an automated system will provide the payroll employee with a simple form to complete; typically including wage type and number of hours worked. In complex organizations, an additional classification of job location may be required if the employee works in multiple departments or locations. The automated systems will complete the mathematics to obtain gross pay, and most automated systems will calculate overtime and shift differentials (i.e., higher pay for working during times not considered as "normal business hours").

> Many web-based applications exist to track employee attendance and calculate pay. TimeStation, FishBowl, and TimeDock use Quick-Read (QR) codes, employee PINs, and GPS location tagging to verify employee work. These apps may be useful tools for companies with employees at remote locations. Apps such as Weekly Hours allow employees to calculate their hours worked and to email the time sheet to a supervisor. Other apps such as iTookOff Paid Leave Tracker allows employees to manage their paid time off through a synchronized app.

Calculations of Weekly Regular Time and Overtime

Even with the use of automated systems, the payroll accountant must determine the breakdown of each employee's regular and overtime hours. Recall the discussion regarding the FLSA standard of 40 hours in a week and 8 hours in a day. This is where the calculation of overtime becomes important. The employee's hours are added up, daily overtime is separated from regular hours worked, and the total for the pay period is computed to determine if the employee worked more than 40 hours total for any given week. If the employee did not, the total regular and total overtime hours are noted on the timecard. If the employee did work more than 40 hours, the final day (or days) worked will be divided between the hours necessary to bring the employee to 40 hours and the remainder will be added to the overtime pay computation.

Depending upon company policy, the existence of paid holidays or sick days may alter payroll calculations. However, holiday hours, sick time taken, and vacation days are not usually included in the worked hours to determine overtime.

> According to the FLSA, employers are not required to pay for employee sick time; however, many states have either passed legislation or have pending bills that would mandate employer-paid sick time. For example, people who work in New York City for more than 80 hours per year are eligible to earn up to 40 hours of sick leave to care for their health or that of a family member. (Source: www.nyc.gov)

Worker Facts

STOP & CHECK

1. Which classification of workers is subject to the wage and hour provisions of the Fair Labor Standards Act?
2. What is the difference in tasks performed by exempt and nonexempt workers?
3. What are some examples of statutory employees?

LO 2-4 Describe Internal Controls and Record Retention for a Payroll System

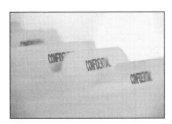

© Tetra Images/Corbis, RF

Should anyone in a company be allowed to sign payroll checks? Why or why not?

Internal controls are pervasive in the payroll system. Confidentiality of payroll information is one of the most important controls in establishing a payroll system. Pay records such as time records are considered confidential documents, and personnel who handle or maintain such records must ensure the privacy of the information they contain. Small firms may be able to maintain the confidentiality of handwritten time sheets; however, multifacility companies may need to use more secure time-collection methods to ensure information privacy.

Strategic planning of the payroll system prior to its inception can prevent data errors and losses related to inadequate *internal controls*. Most importantly, the payroll system design should be reviewed at regular intervals to determine its effectiveness and appropriateness for the company size and to correct errors before they become magnified.

A company with many departments and many employees will generally have a more complex *review process* than a small company will. In an organization that has one office and a dozen or fewer employees, certain steps of the verification process may be omitted and fewer people are required to conduct it. Conversely, a large organization with several departments and many employees could have several levels of verification in the *payroll review* process. Even outsourced payroll requires levels of the review process. The payroll executed by an external company is only as accurate as the data provided. For instance, a company could have a payroll review process such as the one shown in Figure 2-5.

An extremely important issue within internal controls is the determination of authorized signers. A common (and good!) practice in a company is to have at least one designated signatory for payroll checks. Often, these signers are different people than those involved in the review process. In many companies, more than one person signs the payroll checks as another level of review of the accuracy. Remember that the most important part of payroll is *accuracy*. The extra time it takes to review and obtain the necessary signatures is time well spent, as long as it prevents costly errors.

FIGURE 2-5
Payroll Review Process: Steps to Ensure Accurate Payroll

| Employee completes time card | Manager verifies the employee's time card | Payroll clerk computes the period wages for the employee | Payroll supervisor verifies the payroll clerk's math | Employee's check is presented with payroll register for verification and signatures |

Documentation of the payroll process is vital. As should be clear by now, execution of payroll is not merely writing checks to employees. Proper documentation of payroll entails a well-delineated procedure and properly trained personnel. Table 2-1 contains examples of different documentation controls, the activities involved in each, and the personnel who may be required.

Review of Time Collected

The time reported manually on time cards or electronically through other methods must be verified for accuracy prior to the completion of any payroll. Simple issues in employee underpayment (which can cause federal penalties) or overpayment (which can erode the company's available cash) can occur even with sophisticated systems. Time collection and employee payment errors can lead to reduced employee morale, lawsuits, and fines.

TABLE 2-1
Documentation Controls

Procedure	Example of Internal Control Activities	Could Be Performed by
Review and approval of time data from time cards or other time collection devices	Complete the time collection procedure Review of time collection for accuracy and approval	Employee Supervisor
Overtime approval	Approve the amount and type of overtime to be paid	Employee
Approval for leave of absence or other unpaid time off	Obtain all prior approvals for unpaid time away due to FMLA or other reasons	Employee
Timely entering of payroll data	Enter the payroll data into the payroll system in a timely manner, check for data integrity and accuracy	Payroll clerk
Payroll system security	Make sure that only designated employees or payroll vendors have access to payroll data	Payroll supervisor
Approval of the payroll prior to issuance	Obtain the approval from signatory prior to issuing checks	Authorized signer(s)
Maintenance of paid time off (i.e., vacation, sick, etc.)	Ensure that employees receive the exact amount agreed upon	Payroll clerk; employee; supervisor; other designee
Access to payroll data	Ensure that payroll data is confidential and secure	Payroll supervisor
Separation of duties	Make sure that different people verify data, enter data, verify checks	Payroll supervisor
Training of payroll staff	Ensure that payroll department employees and other department supervisors are aware of and follow company payroll policies	Payroll supervisor

Overtime Approval

Hourly employees are subject to federal overtime provisions, commonly known as time-and-a-half, but may include other pay bases such as double-time, and so forth. The Fair Labor Standards Act (FLSA) guarantees nonexempt employees' rights to appropriate pay for the hours worked; however, employees can misreport the overtime they work, costing the company money in the process. Therefore, a good practice is to obtain supervisor approval on all employee-reported overtime.

Computerized systems can also affect the reported overtime. The data is only as accurate as the person who entered it. One of the authors worked at a company that once paid her for 75 hours of overtime in one pay period—when she should have had only 7.5! This kind of error can cause chaos for both the employee, who must return the money, and the employer, who should not have paid it in the first place. Once again, improper pay can erode the morale of the employees. Overpayment on hours can create a myriad of other overpayments: federal withholding taxes, Medicare, Social Security taxes, and pension or 401(k) contributions that are driven by gross wages are just a few examples.

> A payroll specialist in Florida was HIV-positive and was afraid to reveal his illness to employers. Instead, he just took the money from his employer to pay for expensive medications. Despite a strong internal controls system, the employee found ways to circumvent the safeguards. He would memorize his co-workers' usernames and passwords to create "ghost" employees. These ghosts' pay would go to the payroll specialist's bank account. To cover his trail, he would falsify the payroll summaries he submitted for approval. The payroll specialist was found guilty of embezzling $112,000 before his termination. (Source: *Journal of Accountancy*)

Approval for Leave of Absence or Other Unpaid Time Off

The employee's supervisor is one level of oversight to ensure that the payroll data reaches the payroll department accurately and in a timely fashion. Supervisors work closely with their employees and should approve overtime and paid time off. Supervisors review individual timesheets for accuracy prior to delivery to the payroll department. Control of time away from work is the responsibility of the employee's supervisor, at the very minimum. The department supervisor should approve the time off. This approval needs to be tracked and maintained by the payroll department to ensure integrity in the payroll records. A suggested best practice is to keep requests for time away attached to the payroll stub for the affected pay period. The use of leave forms provides companies with a paper trail used to clarify perceived discrepancies in pay.

> Web-based services facilitate requests, approvals, and tracking for paid time off. Apps such as Zenefits allow managers to adjust paid time off, approve and track employee requests, synchronize calendars, and download reports detailing employee time away from work. (Source: www.zenefits.com)

File Security

According to many different pieces of federal and state legislation, all files pertaining to payroll, paper and/or electronic, must be kept secure from tampering. Another reason for *file security*, or restriction of personnel file access, is the firm's governmental payroll obligations. The tax information contained in the payroll records is required to prepare timely and accurate payment of payroll taxes, a factor that is nearly as important as paying the employees. Examples of methods to secure payroll records include multiple passwords for system access, locking file cabinets with controlled key disbursement, and encryption programs.

Because payroll data contains highly personal and private information, security of the information is important. To maintain file security, access to payroll records is restricted to a relatively small number of people. Paper-based payroll data is stored in a secure location; similarly, electronic payroll data is also securely backed up and encrypted. Many federal and state laws, including the Privacy Act of 1974, protect payroll information.

Paycard use for payroll disbursement is estimated to be nearly $57 billion in 2015, so data privacy and fund protection are a high priority for companies and legislators. Preventing breaches of payroll record security is a high priority and an evolving issue. The Electronic Fund Transfer Act of 1978, created to prevent problems with newly created ATM cards, has been expanded to address fraud and theft issues with *paycards*, a pre-loaded credit card that allows an employee to access his or her funds without needing a bank account.

> The Consumer Financial Protection Bureau (CFPB) has proposed legislation in 2015 that would include specific language on paycards, informing employees of their right to request another form of pay disbursement. Additionally, the CFPB is seeking legislation that would mandate the provision of paycard fee disclosures and additional terms and conditions of paycard use. (Source: American Payroll Association)

Alternating Duties and Cross-Training

The cross-training of payroll professionals can act as a safeguard of payroll information. One of the goals of the Sarbanes–Oxley Act of 2002 was to protect the integrity of accounting data by legislating document retention requirements and the rotation of duties by auditors. The same principle applies to payroll system workers. Cross-training and alternating the duties of the people in the payroll process may avoid or minimize errors and potential issues stemming from corruption. Furthermore, cross-training and rotation of duties foster professional development and proficiency with multiple tasks. This rotation of payroll duties refers only to personnel within the payroll department, not opening the payroll processing to nonaccounting departments.

Who Does Which Job?

Imagine that you have been approached to assist a business owner who is concerned about the security of his or her company's payroll. In a team of three or four people, decide how you would distribute payroll responsibilities to implement excellent internal control procedures. How did you divide the responsibilities? Explain.

Best Practices Involved in Employee File Maintenance

Maintenance of employee files is as important as the protection of employee information. IRS Regulation 26 CFR 1.6001 clearly states that the method of *file maintenance* is the responsibility of the employer. The Internal Revenue Code recommends record labeling, creation of backup copies, and secure record storage. An important note is that despite the choice of record maintenance, the employer retains all liability for auditor access to the information upon demand. Items such as time and work records, including time cards and electronic work records, must be maintained to be available for auditors because these items are vital components of a payroll system audit.

---

26 CFR 1.6001–1 Records.

(a) *In general.* Except as provided in paragraph (b) of this section, any person subject to tax under subtitle A of the Code (including a qualified State individual income tax which is treated pursuant to section 6361(a) as if it were imposed by chapter 1 of subtitle A), or any person required to file a return of information with respect to income, shall keep such permanent books of account or records, including inventories, as are sufficient to establish the amount of gross income, deductions, credits, or other matters required to be shown by such person in any return of such tax or information. (Source: www.gpo.gov)

Payroll record maintenance is important for employees at all levels of the organization. IRS Revenue Procedure 98-25, 1998-1 CB 689, was enacted in 1998 to govern the maintenance procedures and duration of recordkeeping for companies with employees. Some provisions of the law include payroll transaction details such as time worked, pay dates, employee status, record reconciliation, and correlation of IRS reports and employee records. With regard to executive-level pay, the company must keep records of how the executive's pay was derived, including benchmarks from similar companies, payout period, and scheduled increases. All pay disbursed must be justified according to the amount and type of work performed, regardless of employee level or classification. A company's payroll and legal department should work closely to determine and implement a maintenance and record destruction program that complies with IRS requirements but avoids the inaccessibility of data that occurs with information overload.

Electronic Records

© Danil Melekhin/E-plus/Getty Images, RF

Many companies have moved to electronic, scanned copies of payroll records that allow immediate access to employee files from a password-protected format. In remote locations, payroll accountants can send the managers and employees Adobe files requiring a password to access pay records. Several different data encryption programs are currently on the market allowing payroll managers to select the best fit for their individual company. All hard copies (i.e., paper versions) of payroll information must be in a locked file cabinet with limited access.

Computers have become a necessary part of business and offer significant benefits to the accounting department. Most accounting software for the preparation of payroll includes password requirements that the company can control, limiting access to electronic information about employees, pay, and personal information. Many regulatory agencies have addressed the issue of record security and safeguarding procedures; for example, the Food and Drug Administration enacted 21 CFR Part 11 that delineates electronic record security and safeguarding procedures.

Payroll accounting, according to the definition by the Internal Revenue Code, is a closed system because only certain employees are granted access to the information contained in the electronic records. All aspects of information security are the employer's responsibility, including access to, creation of, and maintenance of electronic personnel and pay records. Record identifiers would log who had accessed an electronic file, when, and from what location. Record logging provides an additional measure of security and protection against unauthorized access (also called "hacking") as well as tracking if unauthorized changes occur on records.

Like other payroll records, electronic records, especially those accessible over the Internet, must be safeguarded to prevent fraudulent activity and data corruption. Employers can provide access to information via a company's intranet (inside the organization) or via the Internet using encryption programs, passwords, and secured website locations. It is important to note that once a company has allowed Internet access to their payroll files, the company is opening itself up to additional risks from hacking or wrongful use of the payroll information. It is the payroll accountant's responsibility to report any suspicious activity to company managers or the information security department of the company.

Payroll as a Non-Solo Effort

One best practice is to have more than one person involved in the generation and maintenance of payroll records. Many errors can occur when the total payroll responsibility rests with one person. Errors that occur may be the result of a complex hacking effort or as simple as a mistake in failing to remove the system access from a former employee.

- Nonexistent or "ghost" employees could be created and paid via the payroll system. The person committing the fraud could circumvent the payroll system and divert the funds to themselves or an accomplice.
- Terminated employees could continue to be paid via the payroll system or the funds could be subverted to someone else perpetrating the fraud.
- Sales commission plans, employee bonus plans, incentive programs, and other arrangements intended to induce particular behaviors are all subject to employees' and management's manipulation.
- The payroll checks distributed to employees could be stolen individually or en masse prior to their distribution. In addition, check fraud could be perpetrated using actual checks or just the account information.
- The company's payroll system or payroll service provider could suffer a breach of the security protocols protecting the computer systems, which could allow any combination of fraud or theft to be perpetrated. (Source: *Houston Chronicle*)

Other instances of payroll fraud could have been avoided with a *separation of duties*, which involves the division of related tasks to prevent fraud.

- A payroll worker, disgruntled with his job, stole almost $300,000 from different companies by transferring the organizations' money into different bank accounts that he owned.
- A former bookkeeper forged $80,000 in payroll checks before the company owner discovered the discrepancy.
- In the Los Angeles Unified School District, internal inspectors found that the pay system was issuing paychecks to deceased employees.
- In a recent audit of Department of Transportation records in Florida, the auditors found that the paper files supporting the payroll system had been discarded to make room in the office. The audit revealed overpayments to employees caused by an incorrect calculation and a lack of payroll verifications. Of the employees who were overpaid, only one returned the money.

Internal controls promote improved accuracy when more than one person is involved in payroll preparation and disbursement. A division of record maintenance, employee verification, and the spread of pay disbursement responsibilities among different employees, depending upon the size of the company, would prevent many of the problems listed above. This protects not only the employer from complaints and potential legal issues stemming from payroll anomalies, but also provides a level of protection and verification to employees. Auditors look for well-defined internal controls within organizations to ensure legal compliance and file integrity.

Document Retention Requirements

According to the IRS Regulation 26 CFR 1.6001, records pertaining to any financial transaction must remain available for *payroll audit*, the inspection by regulating bodies, at all times. The purpose of the tax code is to maintain records for legal purposes in the event of the suspicion of fraudulent activity. IRS Regulation 26 CFR 1.6001 pertains to both manual and computerized records, including payroll records prepared by third-party sources. Both manual and electronic documents must be maintained in such a way that they maintain accessibility for the duration similar to tax record retention.

When a company institutes a retention schedule, the requirements of legislation and the IRS must be taken into consideration. The retention period does not begin until the disbursement of pay occurs or the employee terminates employment, whichever occurs last. Remember: In the event of fraudulent activity, retention requirements no longer apply and all company records can be requested by the courts.

Companies must abide by both state and federal law regarding document retention. Employee payroll records, consisting of all forms and payroll compensation statements, must be retained for a period of seven years following *termination* or separation.

In 2012, the U.S. Supreme Court issued specific guidelines to the IRS about the statute of limitations for audits. In *U.S. v. Home Concrete Supply, LLC,* the Court directed the following guidelines about records audits:

- Three years to assess a taxpayer's deficiency
- Six years if the taxpayer's gross assets were understated by more than 25%
- Unlimited time if intent to commit fraud exists (Source: www.supremecourt.gov)

The agencies that have the right to audit payroll records include:

- The Internal Revenue Service (IRS)
- Federal and State Departments of Labor
- Department of Homeland Security
- Other state and local agencies
- Labor unions

The following is a chart that explains federal record retention requirements, including relevant laws and types of documents. (Source: SHRM)

Payroll Records (time sheets, electronic records, etc.)	• 3 year retention period • An additional 5 year post-termination retention is recommended due to Lilly Ledbetter Act • Includes employee data, any pay records and all compensation, financial and non-financial
Employee Federal, State, and Local Tax Records	• 4 years from date the tax is due or paid • Includes all W-4s, state and local tax withholding forms, requests for additional tax withholding, and tax remittances
Form I-9 and Accompanying Employment Eligibility Documents	• 3 years after hire OR • 1 year after termination, whichever is longer
Employee Benefits and Contributions	• 6 years • All retirement plan contributions, plan changes, records pertaining to any other employee voluntary deductions
Health Plan Documentation	• No written guidelines, but a minimum of 6 years is recommended • All written notices about changes in health coverage, especially for health coverage after termination of employment

Even if your company outsources payroll activities, they are still accountable for all records and the information transmitted to the payroll service companies. The third-party payroll service provider attends only to the processing of company payroll but is not responsible for payroll tax payments. Tax remittance remains the liability of the company. Instances in which companies have diverted payroll tax liabilities for personal purposes have resulted in sizable fines and sanctions for companies.

Internal Controls and Audits

STOP & CHECK

1. Which of these is *not* a payroll internal control procedure?

   a. overtime approval
   b. removal of payroll oversight
   c. cross-training
   d. file security

2. Which of these records should be retained in the event of a payroll audit?

   a. employee medical records
   b. employee reviews
   c. employee time and work records
   d. employee nonpayroll correspondence

LO 2-5   Discuss Employee Termination and Document Destruction Procedures

Although many state and federal laws delineate the time requirement for document retention, there are also several methods for regulated *document destruction* of sensitive payroll data. According to the FLSA, Walsh-Healey, and Davis-Bacon Acts, employee pay records must be retained for two years after termination. Regarding immigration-related forms such as the I-9, the U.S. Department of Labor mandates a three-year retention or one year past the employee's termination. Personnel records with employee information must be maintained for three years and then destroyed. Any records pertaining to union employees must be retained for five years post-termination and then destroyed. Thus, it is important to understand the legal ramifications for retention prior to the destruction of records.

How must these confidential documents be destroyed? It is not as simple as throwing old payroll documents in the trash. Preferred destruction methods of confidential payroll documents include incineration, confidential shredding services, or pulping of the paper records. Electronic records must be purged from the server. Although specific destruction procedures and regulations vary among states and localities, the basic guidelines of confidential destruction after the required retention period are common to most areas. From small-scale record destruction using in-office paper shredders to large-scale operations such as ProShred, Iron Mountain, and many other companies, destruction of confidential business documents is a serious concern because of the federal privacy laws governing payroll documents.

Employee Termination

There are two different methods of separation of an employee from the company: termination and *resignation*. When an employee leaves a company, the payroll accountant must complete several steps with regard to the employee's and the firm's records. The employee's final paycheck will be a culmination of hours worked, and possibly, depending on the company policies, vacation earned and not taken, and sick time earned and not taken. Depending on the company's policies, if the employee's compensation is commission-based, there should be an agreement between management and the employee regarding sales and timing of the final paycheck to ensure payment of all earned commissions.

© John Lund/Drew Kelly/Blend Images LLC, RF

Final hours are calculated the same as for any normal pay period. The employee's daily hours are calculated to determine regular and overtime, and the week is added together to reach weekly hours and weekly overtime. If the employee earned any vacation or sick time, then those hours also need to be paid out on the final paycheck. Vacation and sick time are not included in the worked hours for the determination of overtime. No legislation exists that requires severance packages upon termination.

In terms of payroll accounting, the major difference between the termination and the resignation of an employee is the timing of the delivery of the final pay disbursement. When an employee quits, any compensation due will be processed and disbursed on the company's next scheduled pay date. However, when the employee is terminated, the company may be mandated to issue the final paycheck immediately or within a short time frame to comply with state labor laws. There is no federal regulation for the immediate issuance of the employee's final pay. Table 2-2 contains information about states' employee termination pay guidelines.

TABLE 2-2
States' Termination Pay Guidelines

State	Guideline	State	Guideline
AL	No termination pay guidelines	MO	On the day of discharge or within seven days if employee requests pay to be mailed
AK	Within three business days	MT	Next regular payday or 15 days from termination, whichever is soonest
AZ	Within seven working days or the end of the next pay period, whichever is sooner	NE	Next pay or within two weeks, whichever is soonest
AR	Within seven days of discharge	NV	Immediately upon discharge
CA	At time of discharge	NH	Within 72 hours
CO	Immediately upon discharge	NJ	By the next regular payday
CT	No later than the next business day	NM	Within five days when wages are definite, otherwise within 10 days if wages are indefinite
DE	Next regularly scheduled payday	NY	Next regular payday
DC	No later than the day following discharge	NC	Next regular payday
FL	Next pay period	OH	Next regular payday
GA	No termination pay guidelines	OK	Next regular payday for the pay period
HI	At time of discharge unless conditions render pay impossible; next business day in that case	OR	First business day after discharge or termination
ID	Within 10 days, excluding weekends and holidays	PA	Next regular payday
IL	No later than the next payday, immediately if possible	RI	Next regular payday
IN	Next regular payday	SC	Within 48 hours
IA	Next regular payday for the pay period	SD	Next regular payday or whenever the terminated employee returns all of the employer's property
KS	No later than the next regular payday	TN	Next regular payday or 21 days, whichever comes later
KY	Next regular payday or 14 days, whichever is sooner	TX	No later than six days after discharge
LA	Next regular payday or 15 days, whichever is sooner	UT	Within 24 hours
ME	Within a reasonable time after demand, either the next day or within two weeks	VT	Last regular payday or the following Friday if no regular payday exists

(continued)

TABLE 2-2   *(concluded)*

State	Guideline	State	Guideline
MD	Next regular payday	VA	On or before the next regular pay date
MA	Next regular payday or the following Saturday if no regular payday is scheduled	WA	Next regular payday
MI	Immediately upon severance after due diligence	WV	72 hours after demand or when wages become due under employment contract
MN	Within 24 hours of termination	WI	Next regular payday or monthly, whichever is sooner
MS	Next regular pay date	WY	Within five working days of termination date

(Source: www.bizfilings.com)

Destroy and Terminate

1. How should paper payroll records be destroyed? How about electronic records?

2. Charlie, a resident of Hawaii, is terminated without cause from his job on October 12. When must he receive his final pay? Is the employer required to pay him a severance package? Explain.

Trends to Watch

PAYROLL PROCEDURES

As we move further into the digital age, payroll procedures are changing to meet employer needs, technological availability, and employee accessibility. Some procedures that have changed during the early 2010s include the following:

- A growing use of electronic or Internet-based employment packets, including electronic delivery of employee manuals.
- An increase in the use of Internet-based employee files, which requires increasingly sophisticated security software and company protocols.
- Increased "job swapping" that requires employees to be cross-trained and employers to consider compensation needs of different positions.
- An increase in the "virtual marketplace," in which employers and employees will tele-commute or otherwise perform work from geographically dispersed locations.

Some trends to watch include the following:

- Cybersecurity is becoming an increasing priority for internal control and audit departments.
- Proper classification of employees as exempt and nonexempt under FLSA regulations.
- Employee reporting in terms of the provisions of the Affordable Care Act will require employers to complete additional governmental forms.
- Documentation of fringe benefits, specifically transit benefits, will require additional attention by employers.

Summary of Payroll System Procedures

The establishment of a payroll system involves careful planning and deliberation. The framework used for the payroll system needs to have enough room for company growth and enough structure to make sure that company and governmental deadlines are met. Using some of the best practices outlined in this chapter can help a company implement a robust payroll system, whether the system is maintained by company personnel or outsourced, completed manually or electronically with the use of specifically designed software. Adequate payroll system design can save a company from problems with employees and with governmental entities.

Although pay processes and methods vary among companies, the framework of internal review and the necessity for accuracy remain the fundamental aspects of any payroll system. Documentation of an employee's eligibility to work in the United States as well as compensation method, rates, tax liabilities, and voluntary withholdings are critical elements of employee files that the payroll accountant must maintain. The process of entering items into a payroll system varies depending on the type of work done and the compensation rates, for which the payroll accountant must have documentation. Depending on the company's preferences, anything from manual records to computerized records to external payroll vendors may be used to track the payroll. At employee termination, final pay must be issued, but the timing of that final pay depends on state legislation.

Payroll recordkeeping and maintenance are complex issues and subject to several federal and state regulations. Employee personal information must be safeguarded at all times and information privacy is paramount. Now that many companies are resorting to electronic pay records, information safeguarding is especially important, and encryption efforts are multidimensional, involving the accounting, legal, and information systems departments of an organization. Destruction of payroll-related documents after the required retention period is a serious concern, and an entire industry focuses on document retention and destruction.

Key Points

- Communication protocol varies among companies and departments within companies.
- Ethical payroll practices require protection of information and dissemination only to the employee or specifically relevant supervisory staff.
- Control of the payroll system involves regular system design review and delineation of specific tasks.
- Payroll, whether completed internally or by an *outsourced vendor* (a payroll service external to the company), is only as accurate as the information provided.
- Pay periods are at the discretion of the company. The IRS has developed *tax tables* (withholding amounts) for each pay interval that are contained in *Publication 15*, an annual IRS guide to payroll.
- File security is of utmost importance, especially when files are stored electronically and accessed via an Internet portal.
- Documentation for payroll exceptions such as time away from work should be maintained separately from regular work time documentation.
- Calculations of pay can involve many variables and require review of each employee prior to pay issuance.
- Final pay needs to reflect all earned compensation, paid time off, and all deductions up to the date of termination.
- The timing of final pay disbursement when an employee is terminated depends on state law.

Vocabulary

Biweekly payroll	Internal control	Resignation
Commission	Monthly payroll	Review process
Daily payroll	New hire reporting	Semimonthly payroll
Document destruction	Nonexempt	Separation of duties
Exempt	Outsourced vendor	Statutory employee
File maintenance	Pay period	Tax table
File security	Paycards	Termination
Foreign Account Tax	Payroll audit	W-4
Compliance Act	Payroll review	Weekly payroll
Hiring packet	Piece rate	
I-9	Publication 15	

Review Questions

1. What constitutes internal controls for a payroll department?

2. Why should more than one person prepare/verify payroll processing?

3. What documents should be included in all new-hire packets?

4. Why are new hires required to be reported to the state's employment department?

5. For the state in which you live, when must a terminated employee be paid his or her final paycheck?

6. What are the five main payroll frequencies?

7. What are some of the best practices in establishing a payroll system?

8. What are the important considerations in setting up a payroll system?

9. What are the different tasks involved in payroll accounting?

10. When does a payroll record retention period begin?

11. What agencies or organizations can audit a company's payroll records?

12. How long must employers keep terminated employee records?

13. Are independent contractors included in company payroll? Why or why not?

14. What is the difference between termination and resignation?

15. What is the difference among daily, weekly, biweekly, semimonthly, and monthly pay periods?

Exercises Set A

2-1A.
LO 2-1, 2-3

Amanda, a nonexempt employee at Old Tyme Soda Distributing, works a standard 8:00–5:00 schedule with an hour for lunch. Amanda works in a state requiring overtime for hours exceeding 8 per day and for those exceeding 40 in a week. During the week, she worked the following schedule:

Monday 8:00–11:00, 12:00–4:30
Tuesday 8:00–11:00, 12:00–5:15
Wednesday 8:00–11:00, 12:00–5:00
Thursday 8:30–5:00 (no lunch)
Friday 8:00–6:00 (no lunch)

Based on a 40-hour workweek, does she qualify for overtime under FLSA regulations? If so, how many hours of regular time and overtime did she work?

2-2A.

LO 2-1

Jason is a salaried employee earning $75,000 per year. Calculate the standard gross salary per pay period under each of the following payroll frequencies:
a. biweekly
b. semimonthly
c. weekly
d. monthly

2-3A.

LO 2-1, 2-3

Katherine quit her job after four years with Canvas Emporium on July 10. Canvas Emporium pays employees semimonthly on the 15th and last day of each month. Upon quitting, the company had a paid holiday for July 4th, Katherine had 16 hours of vacation accrued she had not used, and she had worked 52 hours, but was not eligible for overtime. Katherine earned an hourly wage of $16.50 at the time of her separation. Calculate Katherine's final gross (pre-tax and deductions) paycheck.

2-4A.

LO 2-4, 2-5

Angela, a resident of Texas, terminated her employment on December 11, 2015. By what date should she receive her final pay? Review your state's requirements for document retention (search the available resources for educational and governmental record retention). When will the company dispose of her payroll records?

2-5A.

LO 2-4

A company operating in California is required to hold their payroll records for three years. They work on governmental contracts that require the payroll record retention for two years. Additionally, the company has international contracts stipulating that payroll records must be maintained for six years. How should the company balance these requirements?

2-6A.

LO 2-3, 2-4

Jacob needs additional filing space at the end of the year in the company's offsite, secured storage. He sees several boxes marked for the current year's destruction. What methods can Jacob use to dispose of the payroll records? What steps should he take to ensure the company is not under obligation to retain these records further?

2-7A.

LO 2-3, 2-4

The controller has requested your assistance to price various accounting software programs available for document retention, payroll preparation, and financial reporting. What requirements should you ensure are present in the computer program?

2-8A.

LO 2-2, 2-3

Johan works for Noland Industries as an independent contractor. He has asked you to withhold Social Security and Medicare taxes from his fees. What advice should you offer Johan?

2-9A.

LO 2-2, 2-4

What are the forms of identification that establish identity for the I-9? How long does a company retain copies of an employee's I-9?

2-10A.

LO 2-2

Sue is a citizen of the Northern Pomo Indian Nation. She provides her Social Security card along with an official Northern Pomo Nation birth certificate as proof of employment eligibility for her I-9. Is this sufficient documentation?

2-11A.

LO 2-2, 2-3

Complete the W-4 for employment at Bernie's Bar and Grill

Kierstan Amber Winter-Casey
542 Sole Point Road
Sitka, Alaska 99835
SSN: 988-65-3124
Single, head of household
Two dependents

Form W-4 (2015)

Purpose. Complete Form W-4 so that your employer can withhold the correct federal income tax from your pay. Consider completing a new Form W-4 each year and when your personal or financial situation changes.

Exemption from withholding. If you are exempt, complete **only** lines 1, 2, 3, 4, and 7 and sign the form to validate it. Your exemption for 2015 expires February 16, 2016. See Pub. 505, Tax Withholding and Estimated Tax.

Note. If another person can claim you as a dependent on his or her tax return, you cannot claim exemption from withholding if your income exceeds $1,050 and includes more than $350 of unearned income (for example, interest and dividends).

Exceptions. An employee may be able to claim exemption from withholding even if the employee is a dependent, if the employee:

• Is age 65 or older,

• Is blind, or

• Will claim adjustments to income; tax credits; or itemized deductions, on his or her tax return.

The exceptions do not apply to supplemental wages greater than $1,000,000.

Basic instructions. If you are not exempt, complete the **Personal Allowances Worksheet** below. The worksheets on page 2 further adjust your withholding allowances based on itemized deductions, certain credits, adjustments to income, or two-earners/multiple jobs situations.

Complete all worksheets that apply. However, you may claim fewer (or zero) allowances. For regular wages, withholding must be based on allowances you claimed and may not be a flat amount or percentage of wages.

Head of household. Generally, you can claim head of household filing status on your tax return only if you are unmarried and pay more than 50% of the costs of keeping up a home for yourself and your dependent(s) or other qualifying individuals. See Pub. 501, Exemptions, Standard Deduction, and Filing Information, for information.

Tax credits. You can take projected tax credits into account in figuring your allowable number of withholding allowances. Credits for child or dependent care expenses and the child tax credit may be claimed using the **Personal Allowances Worksheet** below. See Pub. 505 for information on converting your other credits into withholding allowances.

Nonwage income. If you have a large amount of nonwage income, such as interest or dividends, consider making estimated tax payments using Form 1040-ES, Estimated Tax for Individuals. Otherwise, you may owe additional tax. If you have pension or annuity income, see Pub. 505 to find out if you should adjust your withholding on Form W-4 or W-4P.

Two earners or multiple jobs. If you have a working spouse or more than one job, figure the total number of allowances you are entitled to claim on all jobs using worksheets from only one Form W-4. Your withholding usually will be most accurate when all allowances are claimed on the Form W-4 for the highest paying job and zero allowances are claimed on the others. See Pub. 505 for details.

Nonresident alien. If you are a nonresident alien, see Notice 1392, Supplemental Form W-4 Instructions for Nonresident Aliens, before completing this form.

Check your withholding. After your Form W-4 takes effect, use Pub. 505 to see how the amount you are having withheld compares to your projected total tax for 2015. See Pub. 505, especially if your earnings exceed $130,000 (Single) or $180,000 (Married).

Future developments. Information about any future developments affecting Form W-4 (such as legislation enacted after we release it) will be posted at *www.irs.gov/w4*.

Personal Allowances Worksheet (Keep for your records.)

A   Enter "1" for **yourself** if no one else can claim you as a dependent . . . . **A** _____

B   Enter "1" if:
- You are single and have only one job; or
- You are married, have only one job, and your spouse does not work; or
- Your wages from a second job or your spouse's wages (or the total of both) are $1,500 or less.

    . . **B** _____

C   Enter "1" for your **spouse.** But, you may choose to enter "-0-" if you are married and have either a working spouse or more than one job. (Entering "-0-" may help you avoid having too little tax withheld.) . . . . **C** _____

D   Enter number of **dependents** (other than your spouse or yourself) you will claim on your tax return . . . . . **D** _____

E   Enter "1" if you will file as **head of household** on your tax return (see conditions under **Head of household** above) . . **E** _____

F   Enter "1" if you have at least $2,000 of **child or dependent care expenses** for which you plan to claim a credit . . . **F** _____
    (**Note.** Do **not** include child support payments. See Pub. 503, Child and Dependent Care Expenses, for details.)

G   **Child Tax Credit** (including additional child tax credit). See Pub. 972, Child Tax Credit, for more information.
- If your total income will be less than $65,000 ($100,000 if married), enter "2" for each eligible child; then **less "1"** if you have two to four eligible children or **less "2"** if you have five or more eligible children.
- If your total income will be between $65,000 and $84,000 ($100,000 and $119,000 if married), enter "1" for each eligible child . . . **G** _____

H   Add lines A through G and enter total here. (**Note.** This may be different from the number of exemptions you claim on your tax return.) ▶ **H** _____

For accuracy, complete all worksheets that apply.
- If you plan to **itemize** or **claim adjustments to income** and want to reduce your withholding, see the **Deductions and Adjustments Worksheet** on page 2.
- If you are **single and have more than one job** or are **married and you and your spouse both work** and the combined earnings from all jobs exceed $50,000 ($20,000 if married), see the **Two-Earners/Multiple Jobs Worksheet** on page 2 to avoid having too little tax withheld.
- If **neither** of the above situations applies, **stop here** and enter the number from line H on line 5 of Form W-4 below.

-------------------------------- **Separate here and give Form W-4 to your employer. Keep the top part for your records.** --------------------------------

Form **W-4**	**Employee's Withholding Allowance Certificate**	OMB No. 1545-0074
Department of the Treasury Internal Revenue Service	▶ Whether you are entitled to claim a certain number of allowances or exemption from withholding is subject to review by the IRS. Your employer may be required to send a copy of this form to the IRS.	2015

1 Your first name and middle initial	Last name		**2** Your social security number

Home address (number and street or rural route)	**3** ☐ Single ☐ Married ☐ Married, but withhold at higher Single rate.
	Note. If married, but legally separated, or spouse is a nonresident alien, check the "Single" box.
City or town, state, and ZIP code	**4** If your last name differs from that shown on your social security card, check here. You must call 1-800-772-1213 for a replacement card. ▶ ☐

5   Total number of allowances you are claiming (from line **H** above **or** from the applicable worksheet on page 2) . . . | **5** |

6   Additional amount, if any, you want withheld from each paycheck . . . . | **6** $ |

7   I claim exemption from withholding for 2015, and I certify that I meet **both** of the following conditions for exemption.
- Last year I had a right to a refund of **all** federal income tax withheld because I had **no** tax liability, **and**
- This year I expect a refund of **all** federal income tax withheld because I expect to have **no** tax liability.

If you meet both conditions, write "Exempt" here . . . . ▶ | **7** |

Under penalties of perjury, I declare that I have examined this certificate and, to the best of my knowledge and belief, it is true, correct, and complete.

Employee's signature
(This form is not valid unless you sign it.) ▶   **Date** ▶

8 Employer's name and address (Employer: Complete lines 8 and 10 only if sending to the IRS.)	**9** Office code (optional)	**10** Employer identification number (EIN)

For Privacy Act and Paperwork Reduction Act Notice, see page 2.   Cat. No. 10220Q   Form **W-4** (2015)

She is eligible for the child tax credit because of her two allowances. She is not claiming any additional amount to be withheld, nor is she claiming exemption from withholding. She has $1,500 annually in child care expenses

2-12A.
LO 2-2, 2-3

Complete the I-9 for employment at Excelsior College. Be sure to complete the "preparer" section.

Meaghan Ariel Lambert
Maiden name: Smith
Social Security number: 123-45-6789
Date of Birth: 7-1-1984
552 Coddington Road
Rio Nido, California 95555
U.S. Citizen
Passport number 5397816, issued by the United States State Department, expires 10/31/2018

Exercises Set B

2-1B.
LO 2-1, 2-3

Connie, a nonexempt employee of Westside Motel, works a standard 6:00–3:00 p.m. schedule with an hour for lunch. Connie works in a state requiring overtime for hours exceeding 8 per day and for those exceeding 40 in a week. During the week, she worked the following schedule:

Monday 6:00–10:30, 11:15–3:00
Tuesday 6:15–10:45, 11:45–3:15
Wednesday 5:45–10:00, 11:00–3:30
Thursday 7:00–12:00, 1:00–3:00
Friday 6:00–3:00 (no lunch)
Calculate her hours for the week. Based on a 40-hour workweek, does she qualify for overtime under FLSA regulations? If so, how many hours of regular and overtime did she work?

2-2B.
LO 2-1

Paolo is a salaried employee earning $84,000 per year. Calculate the standard gross salary per pay period under each of the following payroll frequencies:

a. biweekly
b. semimonthly
c. weekly
d. monthly

2-3B.
LO 2-3, 2-5

Terri quit her job after four years with Aspen Tree Service in Colorado on Friday, October 31. Aspen Tree Service pays employees weekly on Fridays. Upon quitting, Terri had 38.5 hours of vacation accrued that she had not used, and she had worked 45 hours, 5 hours of that was subject to overtime. Terri earned an hourly wage of $11.50 at the time of her separation. Calculate Terri's final gross (pre-tax and deductions) paycheck. When must she receive her final paycheck?

2-4B.
LO 2-4, 2-5

Brad terminated his employment on December 11, 2015. Review your state's requirements for document retention (search the available resources for educational and governmental record retention). When should the company dispose of his payroll records?

2-5B.
LO 2-4

A general contractor operating in Nebraska has in its company policy to retain its payroll records for four years. They work on interstate contracts with companies that require payroll record retention for three years. Additionally, the company has national contracts stipulating that payroll records must be maintained for five years. How should the company balance these requirements?

2-6B.
LO 2-4

Martin needs additional filing space at the end of the year in the company's office, and chooses to use offsite, secured storage. Upon arriving at the storage facility, he discovers that the unit is nearly full and sees several boxes marked for destruction at the end of the next calendar year. What are Martin's obligations regarding these payroll records? What steps should he take to ensure the company retains, stores, and disposes of payroll records properly?

2-7B.
LO 2-3, 2-4

Upon starting a new job in a company that has 70 employees, you notice that the company has been using manual accounting records and has retained every record since the business started 15 years ago. Your boss has asked you to recommend an accounting software system for accounting, payroll, and document destruction. Write your recommendations and rationale.

2-8B.
LO 2-2

Sandy is an independent contractor who is new to your company. Should you assign her compensation to the payroll clerk or to the accounts payable department? Explain.

2-9B.
LO 2-2

Quinn, a member of the Menominee Indian nation, is a new employee at Raven Enterprises. During the process of completing his I-9, his only means of identity is a Menominee Nation identification document. Is this document sufficient to verify his employment eligibility? Explain.

2-10B.
LO 2-3, 2-5

Frank was terminated for cause from Pineland Industries in Georgia. As of the date of his termination, he had accrued 24 hours of vacation and 15 hours of sick time. When must his final pay be issued? Will his accrued vacation and sick time be included in his final pay? Explain.

2-11B.
LO 2-2, 2-3

Complete the W-4 for employment at Dark Forest Ranch:

Madeline Emma Jenkins
203 County Road 4
Douglas, Wyoming 82036
SSN: 545-02-1987
Married filing jointly

Three dependents. She has no child care expenses, but is able to claim the child tax credit, and does not wish to withhold additional amounts.

She has a second job as a waitress at the Douglas Café, where she earns $12,000/year.

2-12B.
LO 2-2, 2-3

Complete the I-9 for employment with the Tennessee Department of Corrections. Be sure to complete the "preparer" section.

Martin Allan Davis
Social Security number: 987-65-4312
Date of Birth: 5-29-1975
5923 Bunker Hill Road
Clarksville, Tennessee 38205
U.S. Citizen
Tennessee Driver's License #U30290688, Expires, 5/29/2018

Employment Eligibility Verification
Department of Homeland Security
U.S. Citizenship and Immigration Services

USCIS
Form I-9
OMB No. 1615-0047
Expires 03/31/2016

▶**START HERE.** Read instructions carefully before completing this form. The instructions must be available during completion of this form.
ANTI-DISCRIMINATION NOTICE: It is illegal to discriminate against work-authorized individuals. Employers **CANNOT** specify which document(s) they will accept from an employee. The refusal to hire an individual because the documentation presented has a future expiration date may also constitute illegal discrimination.

Section 1. Employee Information and Attestation *(Employees must complete and sign Section 1 of Form I-9 no later than the first day of employment, but not before accepting a job offer.)*

Last Name (*Family Name*)	First Name (*Given Name*)	Middle Initial	Other Names Used (*if any*)

Address (*Street Number and Name*)	Apt. Number	City or Town	State	Zip Code

Date of Birth (*mm/dd/yyyy*)	U.S. Social Security Number	E-mail Address	Telephone Number
	☐☐☐-☐☐-☐☐☐☐		

I am aware that federal law provides for imprisonment and/or fines for false statements or use of false documents in connection with the completion of this form.

I attest, under penalty of perjury, that I am (check one of the following):

☐ A citizen of the United States

☐ A noncitizen national of the United States (*See instructions*)

☐ A lawful permanent resident (Alien Registration Number/USCIS Number): _____

☐ An alien authorized to work until (expiration date, if applicable, mm/dd/yyyy) _____ . Some aliens may write "N/A" in this field.
(*See instructions*)

For aliens authorized to work, provide your Alien Registration Number/USCIS Number **OR** *Form I-94 Admission Number:*

1. Alien Registration Number/USCIS Number: _____

OR

2. Form I-94 Admission Number: _____

If you obtained your admission number from CBP in connection with your arrival in the United States, include the following:

Foreign Passport Number: _____

Country of Issuance: _____

Some aliens may write "N/A" on the Foreign Passport Number and Country of Issuance fields. (*See instructions*)

3-D Barcode
Do Not Write in This Space

Signature of Employee:	Date (*mm/dd/yyyy*):

Preparer and/or Translator Certification *(To be completed and signed if Section 1 is prepared by a person other than the employee.)*

I attest, under penalty of perjury, that I have assisted in the completion of this form and that to the best of my knowledge the information is true and correct.

Signature of Preparer or Translator:	Date (*mm/dd/yyyy*):

Last Name (*Family Name*)	First Name (*Given Name*)		

Address (*Street Number and Name*)	City or Town	State	Zip Code

STOP *Employer Completes Next Page* **STOP**

Section 2. Employer or Authorized Representative Review and Verification

(Employers or their authorized representative must complete and sign Section 2 within 3 business days of the employee's first day of employment. You must physically examine one document from List A OR examine a combination of one document from List B and one document from List C as listed on the "Lists of Acceptable Documents" on the next page of this form. For each document you review, record the following information: document title, issuing authority, document number, and expiration date, if any.)

Employee Last Name, First Name and Middle Initial from Section 1:

List A	OR	List B	AND	List C
Identity and Employment Authorization		**Identity**		**Employment Authorization**

List A	List B	List C
Document Title:	Document Title:	Document Title:
Issuing Authority:	Issuing Authority:	Issuing Authority:
Document Number:	Document Number:	Document Number:
Expiration Date *(if any)(mm/dd/yyyy)*:	Expiration Date *(if any)(mm/dd/yyyy)*:	Expiration Date *(if any)(mm/dd/yyyy)*:
Document Title:		
Issuing Authority:		
Document Number:		
Expiration Date *(if any)(mm/dd/yyyy)*:		
Document Title:		
Issuing Authority:		**3-D Barcode**
Document Number:		**Do Not Write in This Space**
Expiration Date *(if any)(mm/dd/yyyy)*:		

Certification

I attest, under penalty of perjury, that (1) I have examined the document(s) presented by the above-named employee, (2) the above-listed document(s) appear to be genuine and to relate to the employee named, and (3) to the best of my knowledge the employee is authorized to work in the United States.

The employee's first day of employment *(mm/dd/yyyy)*: _____ **(See instructions for exemptions.)**

Signature of Employer or Authorized Representative	Date *(mm/dd/yyyy)*	Title of Employer or Authorized Representative
Last Name *(Family Name)*	First Name *(Given Name)*	Employer's Business or Organization Name
Employer's Business or Organization Address *(Street Number and Name)*	City or Town	State	Zip Code

Section 3. Reverification and Rehires *(To be completed and signed by employer or authorized representative.)*

A. New Name *(if applicable)* Last Name *(Family Name)* First Name *(Given Name)*	Middle Initial	B. Date of Rehire *(if applicable) (mm/dd/yyyy)*:

C. If employee's previous grant of employment authorization has expired, provide the information for the document from List A or List C the employee presented that establishes current employment authorization in the space provided below.

Document Title:	Document Number:	Expiration Date *(if any)(mm/dd/yyyy)*:

I attest, under penalty of perjury, that to the best of my knowledge, this employee is authorized to work in the United States, and if the employee presented document(s), the document(s) I have examined appear to be genuine and to relate to the individual.

Signature of Employer or Authorized Representative:	Date *(mm/dd/yyyy)*:	Print Name of Employer or Authorized Representative:

LISTS OF ACCEPTABLE DOCUMENTS
All documents must be UNEXPIRED

Employees may present one selection from List A
or a combination of one selection from List B and one selection from List C.

LIST A Documents that Establish Both Identity and Employment Authorization		LIST B Documents that Establish Identity	LIST C Documents that Establish Employment Authorization
1. U.S. Passport or U.S. Passport Card	OR	1. Driver's license or ID card issued by a State or outlying possession of the United States provided it contains a photograph or information such as name, date of birth, gender, height, eye color, and address	1. A Social Security Account Number card, unless the card includes one of the following restrictions: (1) NOT VALID FOR EMPLOYMENT (2) VALID FOR WORK ONLY WITH INS AUTHORIZATION (3) VALID FOR WORK ONLY WITH DHS AUTHORIZATION
2. Permanent Resident Card or Alien Registration Receipt Card (Form I-551)			
3. Foreign passport that contains a temporary I-551 stamp or temporary I-551 printed notation on a machine-readable immigrant visa		2. ID card issued by federal, state or local government agencies or entities, provided it contains a photograph or information such as name, date of birth, gender, height, eye color, and address	2. Certification of Birth Abroad issued by the Department of State (Form FS-545)
4. Employment Authorization Document that contains a photograph (Form I-766)		3. School ID card with a photograph	3. Certification of Report of Birth issued by the Department of State (Form DS-1350)
5. For a nonimmigrant alien authorized to work for a specific employer because of his or her status: a. Foreign passport; and b. Form I-94 or Form I-94A that has the following: (1) The same name as the passport; and (2) An endorsement of the alien's nonimmigrant status as long as that period of endorsement has not yet expired and the proposed employment is not in conflict with any restrictions or limitations identified on the form.		4. Voter's registration card 5. U.S. Military card or draft record 6. Military dependent's ID card 7. U.S. Coast Guard Merchant Mariner Card 8. Native American tribal document 9. Driver's license issued by a Canadian government authority **For persons under age 18 who are unable to present a document listed above:**	4. Original or certified copy of birth certificate issued by a State, county, municipal authority, or territory of the United States bearing an official seal 5. Native American tribal document 6. U.S. Citizen ID Card (Form I-197) 7. Identification Card for Use of Resident Citizen in the United States (Form I-179)
6. Passport from the Federated States of Micronesia (FSM) or the Republic of the Marshall Islands (RMI) with Form I-94 or Form I-94A indicating nonimmigrant admission under the Compact of Free Association Between the United States and the FSM or RMI		10. School record or report card 11. Clinic, doctor, or hospital record 12. Day-care or nursery school record	8. Employment authorization document issued by the Department of Homeland Security

Illustrations of many of these documents appear in Part 8 of the Handbook for Employers (M-274).

Refer to Section 2 of the instructions, titled "Employer or Authorized Representative Review and Verification," for more information about acceptable receipts.

Form W-4 (2015)

Purpose. Complete Form W-4 so that your employer can withhold the correct federal income tax from your pay. Consider completing a new Form W-4 each year and when your personal or financial situation changes.

Exemption from withholding. If you are exempt, complete **only** lines 1, 2, 3, 4, and 7 and sign the form to validate it. Your exemption for 2015 expires February 16, 2016. See Pub. 505, Tax Withholding and Estimated Tax.

Note. If another person can claim you as a dependent on his or her tax return, you cannot claim exemption from withholding if your income exceeds $1,050 and includes more than $350 of unearned income (for example, interest and dividends).

Exceptions. An employee may be able to claim exemption from withholding even if the employee is a dependent, if the employee:

• Is age 65 or older,

• Is blind, or

• Will claim adjustments to income; tax credits; or itemized deductions, on his or her tax return.

The exceptions do not apply to supplemental wages greater than $1,000,000.

Basic instructions. If you are not exempt, complete the **Personal Allowances Worksheet** below. The worksheets on page 2 further adjust your withholding allowances based on itemized deductions, certain credits, adjustments to income, or two-earners/multiple jobs situations.

Complete all worksheets that apply. However, you may claim fewer (or zero) allowances. For regular wages, withholding must be based on allowances you claimed and may not be a flat amount or percentage of wages.

Head of household. Generally, you can claim head of household filing status on your tax return only if you are unmarried and pay more than 50% of the costs of keeping up a home for yourself and your dependent(s) or other qualifying individuals. See Pub. 501, Exemptions, Standard Deduction, and Filing Information, for information.

Tax credits. You can take projected tax credits into account in figuring your allowable number of withholding allowances. Credits for child or dependent care expenses and the child tax credit may be claimed using the **Personal Allowances Worksheet** below. See Pub. 505 for information on converting your other credits into withholding allowances.

Nonwage income. If you have a large amount of nonwage income, such as interest or dividends, consider making estimated tax payments using Form 1040-ES, Estimated Tax for Individuals. Otherwise, you may owe additional tax. If you have pension or annuity income, see Pub. 505 to find out if you should adjust your withholding on Form W-4 or W-4P.

Two earners or multiple jobs. If you have a working spouse or more than one job, figure the total number of allowances you are entitled to claim on all jobs using worksheets from only one Form W-4. Your withholding usually will be most accurate when all allowances are claimed on the Form W-4 for the highest paying job and zero allowances are claimed on the others. See Pub. 505 for details.

Nonresident alien. If you are a nonresident alien, see Notice 1392, Supplemental Form W-4 Instructions for Nonresident Aliens, before completing this form.

Check your withholding. After your Form W-4 takes effect, use Pub. 505 to see how the amount you are having withheld compares to your projected total tax for 2015. See Pub. 505, especially if your earnings exceed $130,000 (Single) or $180,000 (Married).

Future developments. Information about any future developments affecting Form W-4 (such as legislation enacted after we release it) will be posted at *www.irs.gov/w4*.

Personal Allowances Worksheet (Keep for your records.)

A	Enter "1" for **yourself** if no one else can claim you as a dependent	A _____
B	Enter "1" if: { • You are single and have only one job; or • You are married, have only one job, and your spouse does not work; or • Your wages from a second job or your spouse's wages (or the total of both) are $1,500 or less. } . . .	B _____
C	Enter "1" for your **spouse**. But, you may choose to enter "-0-" if you are married and have either a working spouse or more than one job. (Entering "-0-" may help you avoid having too little tax withheld.)	C _____
D	Enter number of **dependents** (other than your spouse or yourself) you will claim on your tax return	D _____
E	Enter "1" if you will file as **head of household** on your tax return (see conditions under **Head of household** above) . .	E _____
F	Enter "1" if you have at least $2,000 of **child or dependent care expenses** for which you plan to claim a credit . . . **(Note.** Do **not** include child support payments. See Pub. 503, Child and Dependent Care Expenses, for details.)	F _____
G	**Child Tax Credit** (including additional child tax credit). See Pub. 972, Child Tax Credit, for more information. • If your total income will be less than $65,000 ($100,000 if married), enter "2" for each eligible child; then **less** "1" if you have two to four eligible children or **less** "2" if you have five or more eligible children. • If your total income will be between $65,000 and $84,000 ($100,000 and $119,000 if married), enter "1" for each eligible child . . .	G _____
H	Add lines A through G and enter total here. **(Note.** This may be different from the number of exemptions you claim on your tax return.) ▶	H _____

For accuracy, complete all worksheets that apply.	• If you plan to **itemize** or **claim adjustments to income** and want to reduce your withholding, see the **Deductions and Adjustments Worksheet** on page 2. • If you are **single and have more than one job** or are **married and you and your spouse both work** and the combined earnings from all jobs exceed $50,000 ($20,000 if married), see the **Two-Earners/Multiple Jobs Worksheet** on page 2 to avoid having too little tax withheld. • If **neither** of the above situations applies, **stop here** and enter the number from line H on line 5 of Form W-4 below.

---------------------------------- Separate here and give Form W-4 to your employer. Keep the top part for your records. ----------------------------------

Form W-4

Department of the Treasury
Internal Revenue Service

Employee's Withholding Allowance Certificate

▶ **Whether you are entitled to claim a certain number of allowances or exemption from withholding is subject to review by the IRS. Your employer may be required to send a copy of this form to the IRS.**

OMB No. 1545-0074

2015

1 Your first name and middle initial	Last name	2 **Your social security number**

Home address (number and street or rural route)	3 ☐ Single ☐ Married ☐ Married, but withhold at higher Single rate. **Note.** If married, but legally separated, or spouse is a nonresident alien, check the "Single" box.
City or town, state, and ZIP code	4 If your last name differs from that shown on your social security card, check here. You must call 1-800-772-1213 for a replacement card. ▶ ☐

5	Total number of allowances you are claiming (from line **H** above **or** from the applicable worksheet on page 2)	5	
6	Additional amount, if any, you want withheld from each paycheck	6	$
7	I claim exemption from withholding for 2015, and I certify that I meet **both** of the following conditions for exemption. • Last year I had a right to a refund of **all** federal income tax withheld because I had **no** tax liability, **and** • This year I expect a refund of **all** federal income tax withheld because I expect to have **no** tax liability. If you meet both conditions, write "Exempt" here . . . . ▶	7	

Under penalties of perjury, I declare that I have examined this certificate and, to the best of my knowledge and belief, it is true, correct, and complete.

Employee's signature
(This form is not valid unless you sign it.) ▶ _____ Date ▶ _____

8 Employer's name and address (Employer: Complete lines 8 and 10 only if sending to the IRS.)	9 Office code (optional)	10 Employer identification number (EIN)

For Privacy Act and Paperwork Reduction Act Notice, see page 2.   Cat. No. 10220Q   Form **W-4** (2015)

Employment Eligibility Verification

Department of Homeland Security
U.S. Citizenship and Immigration Services

USCIS
Form I-9
OMB No. 1615-0047
Expires 03/31/2016

▶**START HERE.** **Read instructions carefully before completing this form. The instructions must be available during completion of this form.**
ANTI-DISCRIMINATION NOTICE: It is illegal to discriminate against work-authorized individuals. Employers **CANNOT** specify which document(s) they will accept from an employee. The refusal to hire an individual because the documentation presented has a future expiration date may also constitute illegal discrimination.

Section 1. Employee Information and Attestation *(Employees must complete and sign Section 1 of Form I-9 no later than the **first day of employment**, but not before accepting a job offer.)*

Last Name *(Family Name)*	First Name *(Given Name)*	Middle Initial	Other Names Used *(if any)*
Address *(Street Number and Name)*	Apt. Number	City or Town	State	Zip Code

Date of Birth *(mm/dd/yyyy)*	U.S. Social Security Number	E-mail Address	Telephone Number

I am aware that federal law provides for imprisonment and/or fines for false statements or use of false documents in connection with the completion of this form.

I attest, under penalty of perjury, that I am (check one of the following):

☐ A citizen of the United States

☐ A noncitizen national of the United States *(See instructions)*

☐ A lawful permanent resident (Alien Registration Number/USCIS Number): _____

☐ An alien authorized to work until (expiration date, if applicable, mm/dd/yyyy) _____ . Some aliens may write "N/A" in this field. *(See instructions)*

*For aliens authorized to work, provide your Alien Registration Number/USCIS Number **OR** Form I-94 Admission Number:*

   1. Alien Registration Number/USCIS Number:_____

         OR

   2. Form I-94 Admission Number: _____

      If you obtained your admission number from CBP in connection with your arrival in the United States, include the following:

         Foreign Passport Number: _____

         Country of Issuance: _____

      Some aliens may write "N/A" on the Foreign Passport Number and Country of Issuance fields. *(See instructions)*

> **3-D Barcode**
> **Do Not Write in This Space**

Signature of Employee:	Date *(mm/dd/yyyy)*:

Preparer and/or Translator Certification *(To be completed and signed if Section 1 is prepared by a person other than the employee.)*

I attest, under penalty of perjury, that I have assisted in the completion of this form and that to the best of my knowledge the information is true and correct.

Signature of Preparer or Translator:	Date *(mm/dd/yyyy)*:
Last Name *(Family Name)*	First Name *(Given Name)*
Address *(Street Number and Name)*	City or Town	State	Zip Code

🛑 *Employer Completes Next Page* 🛑

LISTS OF ACCEPTABLE DOCUMENTS
All documents must be UNEXPIRED

Employees may present one selection from List A
or a combination of one selection from List B and one selection from List C.

LIST A		LIST B		LIST C
Documents that Establish Both Identity and Employment Authorization	**OR**	**Documents that Establish Identity**	**AND**	**Documents that Establish Employment Authorization**
1. U.S. Passport or U.S. Passport Card		1. Driver's license or ID card issued by a State or outlying possession of the United States provided it contains a photograph or information such as name, date of birth, gender, height, eye color, and address		1. A Social Security Account Number card, unless the card includes one of the following restrictions: (1) NOT VALID FOR EMPLOYMENT (2) VALID FOR WORK ONLY WITH INS AUTHORIZATION (3) VALID FOR WORK ONLY WITH DHS AUTHORIZATION
2. Permanent Resident Card or Alien Registration Receipt Card (Form I-551)				
3. Foreign passport that contains a temporary I-551 stamp or temporary I-551 printed notation on a machine-readable immigrant visa		2. ID card issued by federal, state or local government agencies or entities, provided it contains a photograph or information such as name, date of birth, gender, height, eye color, and address		2. Certification of Birth Abroad issued by the Department of State (Form FS-545)
4. Employment Authorization Document that contains a photograph (Form I-766)		3. School ID card with a photograph		3. Certification of Report of Birth issued by the Department of State (Form DS-1350)
5. For a nonimmigrant alien authorized to work for a specific employer because of his or her status: **a.** Foreign passport; and **b.** Form I-94 or Form I-94A that has the following: (1) The same name as the passport; and (2) An endorsement of the alien's nonimmigrant status as long as that period of endorsement has not yet expired and the proposed employment is not in conflict with any restrictions or limitations identified on the form.		4. Voter's registration card 5. U.S. Military card or draft record 6. Military dependent's ID card 7. U.S. Coast Guard Merchant Mariner Card 8. Native American tribal document 9. Driver's license issued by a Canadian government authority **For persons under age 18 who are unable to present a document listed above:**		4. Original or certified copy of birth certificate issued by a State, county, municipal authority, or territory of the United States bearing an official seal 5. Native American tribal document 6. U.S. Citizen ID Card (Form I-197) 7. Identification Card for Use of Resident Citizen in the United States (Form I-179)
6. Passport from the Federated States of Micronesia (FSM) or the Republic of the Marshall Islands (RMI) with Form I-94 or Form I-94A indicating nonimmigrant admission under the Compact of Free Association Between the United States and the FSM or RMI		10. School record or report card 11. Clinic, doctor, or hospital record 12. Day-care or nursery school record		8. Employment authorization document issued by the Department of Homeland Security

Illustrations of many of these documents appear in Part 8 of the Handbook for Employers (M-274).

Refer to Section 2 of the instructions, titled "Employer or Authorized Representative Review and Verification," for more information about acceptable receipts.

Critical Thinking

2-1. When BirMax was looking to implement a payroll accounting system, the manufacturing firm had several options. With only 40 employees, the manual preparation of payroll through spreadsheets and handwritten time cards was a comfortable option for the firm. Another option is to convince the senior management of BirMax to implement a software program for payroll processing. What are the key points to consider? If the company has more than one department, how can this transition be accomplished?

2-2. You have been hired as a consultant for a company facing an IRS audit of their accounting records. During your review, you notice anomalies in the payroll system involving overpayments of labor and payments to terminated employees. What would you do?

In the Real World: Scenario for Discussion

The Lilly Ledbetter Fair Pay Act of 2009 centered on a case in which Ms. Ledbetter discovered documents that revealed discrimination against her that resulted in unequal pay practices. The company argued that the documents were confidential and scheduled for destruction, and that Ms. Ledbetter should not have had access to the information. What are the issues in this case in terms of document privacy and retention? How could the situation have been prevented in the first place?

Internet Activities

2-1. Using a search engine such as Google, Yahoo, or Bing, search the Internet for the term "new hire packet contents." Compile a list of the different new hire packet items that you find in at least three companies. What are some unique items that you found on the companies' lists?

2-2. Go to www.irs.gov and search for IRS e-file security. List the facts that the IRS cites about why e-filing is secure. What about these practices makes the customer's information secure? How could the IRS improve e-filing security?

2-3. Want to know more about some of the concepts discussed in this chapter? Check out:

www.uscis.gov

www.irs.gov/businesses

www.archives.gov/federal-register/cfr/subject-title-26.html

www.proshred.com

www.ironmountain.com

Continuing Payroll Project: Prevosti Farms and Sugarhouse

Prevosti Farms and Sugarhouse pays its employees according to their job classification. The following employees make up Sugarhouse's staff:

Employee Number	Name and Address	Payroll information
A-Mille	Thomas Millen 1022 Forest School Rd Woodstock, VT 05001 802-478-5055 SSN: 031-11-3456 401(k) deduction: 3%	Hire Date: 2-1-2015 DOB: 12-16-1982 Position: Production Manager PT/FT: FT, nonexempt No. of Exemptions: 4 M/S: M Pay Rate: $35,000/year

Employee Number	Name and Address	Payroll information
A-Towle	Avery Towle 4011 Route 100 Plymouth, VT 05102 802-967-5873 SSN: 089-74-0974 401(k) deduction: 5%	Hire Date: 2-4-2015 DOB: 7-14-1991 Position: Production Worker PT/FT: FT, nonexempt No. of Exemptions: 1 M/S: S Pay Rate: $12.00/hour
A-Long	Charlie Long 242 Benedict Road S. Woodstock, VT 05002 802-429-3846 SSN: 056-23-4593 401(k) deduction: 2%	Hire Date: 2-7-2015 DOB: 3-16-1987 Position: Production Worker PT/FT: FT, nonexempt No. of Exemptions: 2 M/S: M Pay Rate: $12.50/hour
B-Shang	Mary Shangraw 1901 Main Street #2 Bridgewater, VT 05520 802-575-5423 SSN: 075-28-8945 401(k) deduction: 3%	Hire Date: 2-5-2015 DOB: 8-20-1994 Position: Administrative Assistant PT/FT: PT, nonexempt No. of Exemptions: 1 M/S: S Pay Rate: $10.50/hour
B-Lewis	Kristen Lewis 840 Daily Hollow Road Bridgewater, VT 05523 802-390-5572 SSN: 076-39-5673 401(k) deduction: 4%	Hire Date: 2-2-2015 DOB: 4-6-1950 Position: Office Manager PT/FT: FT, exempt No. of Exemptions: 3 M/S: M Pay Rate: $32,000/year
B-Schwa	Joel Schwartz 55 Maple Farm Way Woodstock, VT 05534 802-463-9985 SSN: 021-34-9876 401(k) deduction: 5%	Hire Date: 2-1-2015 DOB: 5-23-1985 Position: Sales PT/FT: FT, exempt No. of Exemptions: 2 M/S: M Pay Rate: $24,000/year base plus 3% commission per case sold
B-Prevo	Toni Prevosti 10520 Cox Hill Road Bridgewater, VT 05521 802-673-2636 SSN: 055-22-0443 401(k) deduction: 6%	Hire Date: 2-1-2015 DOB: 9-18-1967 Position: Owner/President PT/FT: FT, exempt No. of Exemptions: 5 M/S: M Pay Rate: $45,000/year

Form W-4 (2015)

Purpose. Complete Form W-4 so that your employer can withhold the correct federal income tax from your pay. Consider completing a new Form W-4 each year and when your personal or financial situation changes.

Exemption from withholding. If you are exempt, complete **only** lines 1, 2, 3, 4, and 7 and sign the form to validate it. Your exemption for 2015 expires February 16, 2016. See Pub. 505, Tax Withholding and Estimated Tax.

Note. If another person can claim you as a dependent on his or her tax return, you cannot claim exemption from withholding if your income exceeds $1,050 and includes more than $350 of unearned income (for example, interest and dividends).

Exceptions. An employee may be able to claim exemption from withholding even if the employee is a dependent, if the employee:

• Is age 65 or older,

• Is blind, or

• Will claim adjustments to income; tax credits; or itemized deductions, on his or her tax return.

The exceptions do not apply to supplemental wages greater than $1,000,000.

Basic instructions. If you are not exempt, complete the **Personal Allowances Worksheet** below. The worksheets on page 2 further adjust your withholding allowances based on itemized deductions, certain credits, adjustments to income, or two-earners/multiple jobs situations.

Complete all worksheets that apply. However, you may claim fewer (or zero) allowances. For regular wages, withholding must be based on allowances you claimed and may not be a flat amount or percentage of wages.

Head of household. Generally, you can claim head of household filing status on your tax return only if you are unmarried and pay more than 50% of the costs of keeping up a home for yourself and your dependent(s) or other qualifying individuals. See Pub. 501, Exemptions, Standard Deduction, and Filing Information, for information.

Tax credits. You can take projected tax credits into account in figuring your allowable number of withholding allowances. Credits for child or dependent care expenses and the child tax credit may be claimed using the **Personal Allowances Worksheet** below. See Pub. 505 for information on converting your other credits into withholding allowances.

Nonwage income. If you have a large amount of nonwage income, such as interest or dividends, consider making estimated tax payments using Form 1040-ES, Estimated Tax for Individuals. Otherwise, you may owe additional tax. If you have pension or annuity income, see Pub. 505 to find out if you should adjust your withholding on Form W-4 or W-4P.

Two earners or multiple jobs. If you have a working spouse or more than one job, figure the total number of allowances you are entitled to claim on all jobs using worksheets from only one Form W-4. Your withholding usually will be most accurate when all allowances are claimed on the Form W-4 for the highest paying job and zero allowances are claimed on the others. See Pub. 505 for details.

Nonresident alien. If you are a nonresident alien, see Notice 1392, Supplemental Form W-4 Instructions for Nonresident Aliens, before completing this form.

Check your withholding. After your Form W-4 takes effect, use Pub. 505 to see how the amount you are having withheld compares to your projected total tax for 2015. See Pub. 505, especially if your earnings exceed $130,000 (Single) or $180,000 (Married).

Future developments. Information about any future developments affecting Form W-4 (such as legislation enacted after we release it) will be posted at *www.irs.gov/w4*.

Personal Allowances Worksheet (Keep for your records.)

A   Enter "1" for **yourself** if no one else can claim you as a dependent . . . . **A** _____

B   Enter "1" if: {   • You are single and have only one job; or
         • You are married, have only one job, and your spouse does not work; or   } . .   **B** _____
         • Your wages from a second job or your spouse's wages (or the total of both) are $1,500 or less.

C   Enter "1" for your **spouse.** But, you may choose to enter "-0-" if you are married and have either a working spouse or more than one job. (Entering "-0-" may help you avoid having too little tax withheld.) . . . . **C** _____

D   Enter number of **dependents** (other than your spouse or yourself) you will claim on your tax return . . . . . . **D** _____

E   Enter "1" if you will file as **head of household** on your tax return (see conditions under **Head of household** above) . . **E** _____

F   Enter "1" if you have at least $2,000 of **child or dependent care expenses** for which you plan to claim a credit . . . **F** _____
      (**Note.** Do **not** include child support payments. See Pub. 503, Child and Dependent Care Expenses, for details.)

G   **Child Tax Credit** (including additional child tax credit). See Pub. 972, Child Tax Credit, for more information.
      • If your total income will be less than $65,000 ($100,000 if married), enter "2" for each eligible child; then **less** "1" if you have two to four eligible children or **less** "2" if you have five or more eligible children.
      • If your total income will be between $65,000 and $84,000 ($100,000 and $119,000 if married), enter "1" for each eligible child . . . . **G** _____

H   Add lines A through G and enter total here. (**Note.** This may be different from the number of exemptions you claim on your tax return.) ▶ **H** _____

For accuracy, **complete all worksheets that apply.**	• If you plan to **itemize** or **claim adjustments to income** and want to reduce your withholding, see the **Deductions and Adjustments Worksheet** on page 2.
	• If you are **single and have more than one job** or are **married and you and your spouse both work** and the combined earnings from all jobs exceed $50,000 ($20,000 if married), see the **Two-Earners/Multiple Jobs Worksheet** on page 2 to avoid having too little tax withheld.
	• If **neither** of the above situations applies, **stop here** and enter the number from line H on line 5 of Form W-4 below.

---- - - - - - - - - - - - **Separate here and give Form W-4 to your employer. Keep the top part for your records.** - - - - - - - - - - - - - - - -

Form **W-4**
Department of the Treasury Internal Revenue Service

Employee's Withholding Allowance Certificate

▶ **Whether you are entitled to claim a certain number of allowances or exemption from withholding is subject to review by the IRS. Your employer may be required to send a copy of this form to the IRS.**

OMB No. 1545-0074

2015

1 Your first name and middle initial Last name	2 Your social security number
Home address (number and street or rural route)	3 ☐ Single ☐ Married ☐ Married, but withhold at higher Single rate. **Note.** If married, but legally separated, or spouse is a nonresident alien, check the "Single" box.
City or town, state, and ZIP code	4 **If your last name differs from that shown on your social security card, check here. You must call 1-800-772-1213 for a replacement card.** ▶ ☐

5	Total number of allowances you are claiming (from line **H** above **or** from the applicable worksheet on page 2)	**5**
6	Additional amount, if any, you want withheld from each paycheck	**6** $
7	I claim exemption from withholding for 2015, and I certify that I meet **both** of the following conditions for exemption.	

     • Last year I had a right to a refund of **all** federal income tax withheld because I had **no** tax liability, **and**

     • This year I expect a refund of **all** federal income tax withheld because I expect to have **no** tax liability.

     If you meet both conditions, write "Exempt" here . . . . ▶ | **7** |

Under penalties of perjury, I declare that I have examined this certificate and, to the best of my knowledge and belief, it is true, correct, and complete.

Employee's signature
(This form is not valid unless you sign it.) ▶   **Date ▶**

8 Employer's name and address (Employer: Complete lines 8 and 10 only if sending to the IRS.)	9 Office code (optional)	10 Employer identification number (EIN)

For Privacy Act and Paperwork Reduction Act Notice, see page 2.   Cat. No. 10220Q   Form **W-4** (2015)

Employment Eligibility Verification

Department of Homeland Security
U.S. Citizenship and Immigration Services

USCIS
Form I-9
OMB No. 1615-0047
Expires 03/31/2016

▶**START HERE.** Read instructions carefully before completing this form. The instructions must be available during completion of this form.

ANTI-DISCRIMINATION NOTICE: It is illegal to discriminate against work-authorized individuals. Employers **CANNOT** specify which document(s) they will accept from an employee. The refusal to hire an individual because the documentation presented has a future expiration date may also constitute illegal discrimination.

Section 1. Employee Information and Attestation *(Employees must complete and sign Section 1 of Form I-9 no later than the **first day of employment**, but not before accepting a job offer.)*

Last Name *(Family Name)*	First Name *(Given Name)*	Middle Initial	Other Names Used *(if any)*

Address *(Street Number and Name)*	Apt. Number	City or Town	State	Zip Code

Date of Birth *(mm/dd/yyyy)*	U.S. Social Security Number	E-mail Address	Telephone Number

I am aware that federal law provides for imprisonment and/or fines for false statements or use of false documents in connection with the completion of this form.

I attest, under penalty of perjury, that I am (check one of the following):

☐ A citizen of the United States

☐ A noncitizen national of the United States *(See instructions)*

☐ A lawful permanent resident (Alien Registration Number/USCIS Number): _____

☐ An alien authorized to work until (expiration date, if applicable, mm/dd/yyyy) _____ . Some aliens may write "N/A" in this field. *(See instructions)*

For aliens authorized to work, provide your Alien Registration Number/USCIS Number **OR** Form I-94 Admission Number:

1. Alien Registration Number/USCIS Number: _____

OR

2. Form I-94 Admission Number: _____

If you obtained your admission number from CBP in connection with your arrival in the United States, include the following:

Foreign Passport Number: _____

Country of Issuance: _____

Some aliens may write "N/A" on the Foreign Passport Number and Country of Issuance fields. *(See instructions)*

3-D Barcode Do Not Write in This Space	

Signature of Employee:	Date *(mm/dd/yyyy):*

Preparer and/or Translator Certification *(To be completed and signed if Section 1 is prepared by a person other than the employee.)*

I attest, under penalty of perjury, that I have assisted in the completion of this form and that to the best of my knowledge the information is true and correct.

Signature of Preparer or Translator:	Date *(mm/dd/yyyy):*

Last Name *(Family Name)*	First Name *(Given Name)*

Address *(Street Number and Name)*	City or Town	State	Zip Code

STOP   *Employer Completes Next Page*   **STOP**

Form I-9   03/08/13 N   Page 7 of 9

Section 2. Employer or Authorized Representative Review and Verification

(Employers or their authorized representative must complete and sign Section 2 within 3 business days of the employee's first day of employment. You must physically examine one document from List A OR examine a combination of one document from List B and one document from List C as listed on the "Lists of Acceptable Documents" on the next page of this form. For each document you review, record the following information: document title, issuing authority, document number, and expiration date, if any.)

Employee Last Name, First Name and Middle Initial from Section 1:

List A **Identity and Employment Authorization**	OR	List B **Identity**	AND	List C **Employment Authorization**
Document Title:		Document Title:		Document Title:
Issuing Authority:		Issuing Authority:		Issuing Authority:
Document Number:		Document Number:		Document Number:
Expiration Date *(if any)(mm/dd/yyyy)*:		Expiration Date *(if any)(mm/dd/yyyy)*:		Expiration Date *(if any)(mm/dd/yyyy)*:
Document Title:				
Issuing Authority:				
Document Number:				
Expiration Date *(if any)(mm/dd/yyyy)*:				
Document Title:				**3-D Barcode** **Do Not Write in This Space**
Issuing Authority:				
Document Number:				
Expiration Date *(if any)(mm/dd/yyyy)*:				

Certification

I attest, under penalty of perjury, that (1) I have examined the document(s) presented by the above-named employee, (2) the above-listed document(s) appear to be genuine and to relate to the employee named, and (3) to the best of my knowledge the employee is authorized to work in the United States.

The employee's first day of employment *(mm/dd/yyyy)*: _____ **(See *instructions* for exemptions.)**

Signature of Employer or Authorized Representative	Date *(mm/dd/yyyy)*	Title of Employer or Authorized Representative	
Last Name *(Family Name)*	First Name *(Given Name)*	Employer's Business or Organization Name	
Employer's Business or Organization Address *(Street Number and Name)*	City or Town	State	Zip Code

Section 3. Reverification and Rehires *(To be completed and signed by employer or authorized representative.)*

A. New Name *(if applicable)* Last Name *(Family Name)* First Name *(Given Name)*	Middle Initial	**B.** Date of Rehire *(if applicable) (mm/dd/yyyy)*:

C. If employee's previous grant of employment authorization has expired, provide the information for the document from List A or List C the employee presented that establishes current employment authorization in the space provided below.

Document Title:	Document Number:	Expiration Date *(if any)(mm/dd/yyyy)*:

I attest, under penalty of perjury, that to the best of my knowledge, this employee is authorized to work in the United States, and if the employee presented document(s), the document(s) I have examined appear to be genuine and to relate to the individual.

Signature of Employer or Authorized Representative:	Date *(mm/dd/yyyy)*:	Print Name of Employer or Authorized Representative:

LISTS OF ACCEPTABLE DOCUMENTS
All documents must be UNEXPIRED

Employees may present one selection from List A
or a combination of one selection from List B and one selection from List C.

LIST A **Documents that Establish Both Identity and Employment Authorization**	**OR**	LIST B **Documents that Establish Identity**	**AND**	LIST C **Documents that Establish Employment Authorization**
1. U.S. Passport or U.S. Passport Card		1. Driver's license or ID card issued by a State or outlying possession of the United States provided it contains a photograph or information such as name, date of birth, gender, height, eye color, and address		1. A Social Security Account Number card, unless the card includes one of the following restrictions: (1) NOT VALID FOR EMPLOYMENT (2) VALID FOR WORK ONLY WITH INS AUTHORIZATION (3) VALID FOR WORK ONLY WITH DHS AUTHORIZATION
2. Permanent Resident Card or Alien Registration Receipt Card (Form I-551)				
3. Foreign passport that contains a temporary I-551 stamp or temporary I-551 printed notation on a machine-readable immigrant visa		2. ID card issued by federal, state or local government agencies or entities, provided it contains a photograph or information such as name, date of birth, gender, height, eye color, and address		
4. Employment Authorization Document that contains a photograph (Form I-766)				2. Certification of Birth Abroad issued by the Department of State (Form FS-545)
		3. School ID card with a photograph		
		4. Voter's registration card		3. Certification of Report of Birth issued by the Department of State (Form DS-1350)
5. For a nonimmigrant alien authorized to work for a specific employer because of his or her status: **a.** Foreign passport; and **b.** Form I-94 or Form I-94A that has the following: (1) The same name as the passport; and (2) An endorsement of the alien's nonimmigrant status as long as that period of endorsement has not yet expired and the proposed employment is not in conflict with any restrictions or limitations identified on the form.		5. U.S. Military card or draft record		
		6. Military dependent's ID card		4. Original or certified copy of birth certificate issued by a State, county, municipal authority, or territory of the United States bearing an official seal
		7. U.S. Coast Guard Merchant Mariner Card		
		8. Native American tribal document		5. Native American tribal document
		9. Driver's license issued by a Canadian government authority		6. U.S. Citizen ID Card (Form I-197)
		For persons under age 18 who are unable to present a document listed above:		7. Identification Card for Use of Resident Citizen in the United States (Form I-179)
6. Passport from the Federated States of Micronesia (FSM) or the Republic of the Marshall Islands (RMI) with Form I-94 or Form I-94A indicating nonimmigrant admission under the Compact of Free Association Between the United States and the FSM or RMI		10. School record or report card 11. Clinic, doctor, or hospital record 12. Day-care or nursery school record		8. Employment authorization document issued by the Department of Homeland Security

Illustrations of many of these documents appear in Part 8 of the Handbook for Employers (M-274).

Refer to Section 2 of the instructions, titled "Employer or Authorized Representative Review and Verification," for more information about acceptable receipts.

The departments are as follows:

Department A: Agricultural Workers

Department B: Office Workers

1. You have been hired to start on February 9, 2015, as the new accounting clerk. Your employee number is B-XXXXX, where "B" denotes that you are an office worker and "XXXXX" is the first five letters of your last name. If your last name is fewer than five letters, use the first few letters of your first name to complete the employee number. Your Social Security number is 555-55-5555, and you are full-time, nonexempt, and paid at a rate of $34,000 per year. You have elected to contribute 2% of your gross pay to your 401(k). Complete the W-4 and the I-9 to start your own employee file. You are single with only one job (claiming two exemptions). You live at 1644 Smitten Road, Woodstock, VT 05001. Your date of birth is 01/01/1991. You are a citizen of the United States and provide a Vermont driver's license #88110009 expiring 1/1/2017 in addition to your Social Security card for verification of your identity.

2. Complete the employee information form for each employee. Enter the pay rate earnings for each employee.

EMPLOYEE EARNINGS RECORD

NAME   Hire Date

ADDRESS   Date of Birth

CITY/STATE/ZIP   Position   PT/FT

TELEPHONE   No. of exemptions   M/S

SOCIAL SECURITY

NUMBER   Pay Rate   Hr/Wk/Mo

Period Ended	Hrs. Worked	Reg Pay	OT Pay	Gross Pay	Social Sec. Tax	Medicare	Fed Inc. Tax	State Inc. Tax	401(k)	Taxable Income	Total Deductions	Net pay	YTD

EMPLOYEE EARNINGS RECORD

NAME	Hire Date	
ADDRESS	Date of Birth	
CITY/STATE/ZIP	Position	PT/FT
TELEPHONE	No. of exemptions	M/S
SOCIAL SECURITY		
NUMBER	Pay Rate	Hr/Wk/Mo

Period Ended	Hrs. Worked	Reg Pay	OT Pay	Gross Pay	Social Sec. Tax	Medicare	Fed Inc. Tax	State Inc. Tax	401(k)	Total Deductions	Net pay	YTD

EMPLOYEE EARNINGS RECORD

NAME	Hire Date	
ADDRESS	Date of Birth	
CITY/STATE/ZIP	Position	PT/FT
TELEPHONE	No. of exemptions	M/S
SOCIAL SECURITY		
NUMBER	Pay Rate	Hr/Wk/Mo

Period Ended	Hrs. Worked	Reg Pay	OT Pay	Gross Pay	Social Sec. Tax	Medicare	Fed Inc. Tax	State Inc. Tax	401(k)	Total Deductions	Net pay	YTD

EMPLOYEE EARNINGS RECORD

NAME _____ Hire Date _____

ADDRESS _____ Date of Birth _____

CITY/STATE/ZIP _____ Position _____ PT/FT

TELEPHONE _____ No. of exemptions _____ M/S

SOCIAL SECURITY
NUMBER _____ Pay Rate _____ Hr/Wk/Mo

Period Ended	Hrs. Worked	Reg Pay	OT Pay	Gross Pay	Social Sec. Tax	Medicare	Fed Inc. Tax	State Inc. Tax	401(k)	Total Deductions	Net pay	YTD

EMPLOYEE EARNINGS RECORD

NAME _____ Hire Date _____

ADDRESS _____ Date of Birth _____

CITY/STATE/ZIP _____ Position _____ PT/FT

TELEPHONE _____ No. of exemptions _____ M/S

SOCIAL SECURITY
NUMBER _____ Pay Rate _____ Hr/Wk/Mo

Period Ended	Hrs. Worked	Reg Pay	OT Pay	Gross Pay	Social Sec. Tax	Medicare	Fed Inc. Tax	State Inc. Tax	401(k)	Total Deductions	Net pay	YTD

EMPLOYEE EARNINGS RECORD

NAME	Hire Date	
ADDRESS	Date of Birth	
CITY/STATE/ZIP	Position	PT/FT
TELEPHONE	No. of exemptions	M/S
SOCIAL SECURITY NUMBER	Pay Rate	Hr/Wk/Mo

Period Ended	Hrs. Worked	Reg Pay	OT Pay	Gross Pay	Social Sec. Tax	Medicare	Fed Inc. Tax	State Inc. Tax	401(k)	Total Deductions	Net pay	YTD

EMPLOYEE EARNINGS RECORD

NAME	Hire Date	
ADDRESS	Date of Birth	
CITY/STATE/ZIP	Position	PT/FT
TELEPHONE	No. of exemptions	M/S
SOCIAL SECURITY NUMBER	Pay Rate	Hr/Wk/Mo

Period Ended	Hrs. Worked	Reg Pay	OT Pay	Gross Pay	Social Sec. Tax	Medicare	Fed Inc. Tax	State Inc. Tax	401(k)	Total Deductions	Net pay	YTD

EMPLOYEE EARNINGS RECORD

NAME	Hire Date	
ADDRESS	Date of Birth	
CITY/STATE/ZIP	Position	PT/FT
TELEPHONE	No. of exemptions	M/S
SOCIAL SECURITY		
NUMBER	Pay Rate	Hr/Wk/Mo

Period Ended	Hrs. Worked	Reg Pay	OT Pay	Gross Pay	Social Sec. Tax	Medicare	Fed Inc. Tax	State Inc. Tax	401(k)	Total Deductions	Net pay	YTD

Answers to Stop & Check Exercises

What's in the File?

1. a,b,d,e
2. b
3. d
4. a
5. c

Who Are You?

1. Student answers will vary. One possible way to prove both identity and employment is a current U.S. passport. Alternatively, a current state-issued driver's license and a Social Security card will work for the purposes of the I-9.
2. Student answers will vary. Many students may underestimate their estimated exemptions.

Worker Facts

1. Nonexempt
2. Exempt workers receive a fixed amount of money and generally direct the actions of other employees; nonexempt workers are eligible for overtime, and generally have their work directed by a manager.
3. A beverage distribution driver, full-time life insurance agents for a single life-insurance company, home workers that use furnished materials, traveling salespersons who work on a single employer's behalf.

Who Does Which Job?
Student answers will vary. The answer should reflect a clear separation of duties, cross-training, rotation of tasks, and security protocols.

Internal Controls and Audits

1. b
2. c

Destroy and Terminate

1. Paper payroll records should be shredded or burned. Computer records should be purged from the server and all other storage devices.

2. Charlie should receive his final pay on October 12, and not later than October 13. His employer is not required to provide him with a severance package, although he may be eligible for his accrued vacation pay.

Gross Pay Computation

Two important terms in payroll accounting are gross pay and net pay. *Gross pay* is the amount of wages earned before deducting amounts for taxes or other deductions. *Net pay* is the amount of money the employee actually receives in a paycheck, after all taxes and other deductions have been subtracted. In this chapter, we will focus on computing gross pay.

The calculation of an employee's gross pay is the first step for payroll processing. Employee pay may be calculated in different ways. *Hourly* employees are paid for each hour, or fraction thereof, that they work in a given day. Salaried employees are broken into two classifications: *exempt* and *nonexempt*. Salaried exempt employees receive pay based on the job they perform, regardless of the number of hours it takes. Salaried non-exempt employees may receive both *salary* and *overtime*. Another class of employees work on a *commission* basis, which means that some or all of their wages are based on sales revenue. Commission-based employees receive wages only when they complete sales or perform duties, outlined in their employment contract, that qualify them for a commission. A final classification is *piece-rate* employees. Typically found in manufacturing environments, employees are paid based upon the number of pieces completed during a work shift. Production reports are required and authorized by a supervisor as accurate, and the compensation per piece is calculated based in part on the labor dedicated to a specific job.

LEARNING OBJECTIVES

After studying Chapter 3, you should be able to:

LO 3-1   Analyze Minimum Wage Pay for Nonexempt Workers

LO 3-2   Compute Gross Pay for Different Pay Bases

LO 3-3   Calculate Pay Based on Hours and Fractions of Hours

LO 3-4   Apply Combination Pay Methods

LO 3-5   Explain Special Pay Situations

© Ryan McVay/Photodisc/Getty Images, RF

The Minimum-Wage Controversy: What Constitutes a Living Wage?

The idea of establishing a minimum wage for workers began in New Zealand in 1896. In the United States, minimum wage laws existed in various states but were not federally mandated until the passing of the Fair Labor Standards Act of 1938, which set the minimum wage at 40 cents per hour. The minimum wage has been raised over time, but many parties, including labor unions, contend that the current federal minimum wage of $7.25 is too low for workers to support their families. Opponents of the minimum wage laws maintain that legislation of a mandatory minimum wage leads to overpayment of workers for the level of service they provide a company. As of 2015, more than 1.25 million wage-based workers earn the federal minimum wage. (Source: U.S. Department of Labor, *Opposing Viewpoints in Context*)

Employee pay is the focus of Chapter 3. We will examine different bases for gross pay computations and how these compensation bases differ.

LO 3-1   Analyze Minimum Wage Pay for Nonexempt Workers

© Danita Delimont/Alamy, RF

Two primary classifications of employees exist: exempt and nonexempt. These classifications refer to the provisions of the Fair Labor Standards Act (FLSA). The FLSA provisions protect nonexempt employees but not exempt workers. Exempt employees include employees who meet U.S. Department of Labor guidelines for exempt classification, which includes job titles such as Department Supervisor or Warehouse Manager. Nonexempt employees are operative workers whose workdays may vary in duration, whose tasks do not meet the U.S. Department of Labor guidelines for exempt employees, and who do not generally have supervisory or managerial duties.

For hourly workers, FLSA contains wage provisions that stipulate the *minimum wage* an employer may pay an employee. However, the law exempts some employers from the minimum-wage requirements. According to the U.S. Department of Labor, the following conditions exempt an employer from paying the federal minimum wage:

- Firms that do not engage in interstate commerce as part of their business production.
- Firms with less than $500,000 of annual business volume.

Certain firms are covered by the FLSA, regardless of their interstate commerce or annual business volume. These businesses include hospitals, schools for mentally or physically disabled or gifted children, preschools, schools of any level, and governmental agencies. Additionally, FLSA minimum-wage provisions cover domestic service workers, such as nannies and chauffeurs, who earn more than $1,700 in wages annually. Note that occasional babysitters generally do not meet this requirement.

Minimum Wage

An important consideration with the minimum-wage provision of the FLSA is the existence of separate tiers of minimum wage. Wages for *tipped employees* are lower than those of nontipped employees. Federal wage and hour laws, as of 2015, stipulate a federal minimum wage of $7.25 and a minimum hourly wage of $2.13 for tipped employees. States may enact additional minimum wage laws in light of the economic differences among states. The District of Columbia declared the minimum wage to be $1.00 more than the federal minimum wage. This minimizes the legislative need to continually revisit the minimum wage. As of 2015, there are 10 states (AZ, CO, FL, MO, MT, NJ, NV, OH, OR, and WA) that have tied their minimum wage to the consumer price index. A map depicting minimum wage for 2015 is shown in Figure 3-1, and the details of specific minimum-wage rates are shown in Table 3-1. Some examples involving different minimum wages follow. Note that a few states have a minimum wage that is less than the FLSA minimum wage. These lower minimum wages may be paid by employers who are not subject to FLSA provisions because they do not conduct interstate commerce.

> **Examples:**
>
> - Don works for a Georgia employer who conducts no interstate commerce, and whose annual business volume is less than $300,000. He earns the minimum wage for Georgia, which is $5.15 per hour. During a 40-hour pay period, he would earn $206.00 (40 hours × $5.15/hour).
>
> - Wendy is a minimum-wage worker in the state of Washington. During a 75-hour, two-week pay period, she would earn $710.25 (75 hours × $9.47/hour).
>
> - Karin is a minimum-wage employee in Washington D.C., who worked 37.5 hours during a one-week period. She would earn $356.25 (37.5 hours × $9.50/hour).

Tipped Employees

Workers in professions such as waiters, waitresses, bartenders, food-service workers, and some hotel service personnel may receive an hourly wage less than the minimum wage rates listed in Table 3-1. The rationale for the decreased minimum wage is that these employees have the opportunity to earn tips from patrons of the establishments as a regular

FIGURE 3-1
Minimum-Wage Hourly Rates for 2015

Source: U.S. Department of Labor, 2015

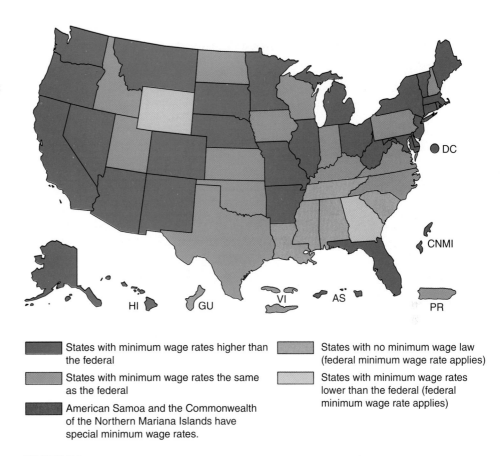

States with minimum wage rates higher than the federal

States with minimum wage rates the same as the federal

American Samoa and the Commonwealth of the Northern Mariana Islands have special minimum wage rates.

States with no minimum wage law (federal minimum wage rate applies)

States with minimum wage rates lower than the federal (federal minimum wage rate applies)

TABLE 3-1
Minimum Wage Hourly Rates by State

AK	$8.75	IA	$7.25	MS	$7.25	PA	$7.25
AL	$7.25	ID	$7.25	MT	$8.05	RI	$9.00
AR	$7.50	IL	$8.25	NC	$7.25	SC	$7.25
AZ	$8.05	IN	$7.25	ND	$7.25	SD	$8.50
CA	$9.00	KS	$7.25	NE	$8.00	TN	$7.25
CO	$8.23	KY	$7.25	NH	$7.25	TX	$7.25
CT	$9.15	LA	$7.25	NJ	$8.38	UT	$7.25
DC	$9.50	MA	$9.00	NM	$7.50	VA	$7.25
DE	$7.75	MD	$8.00	NV	$8.25	VT	$9.15
FL	$8.05	ME	$7.50	NY	$8.75	WA	$9.47
GA	$5.15	MI	$8.15	OH	$8.10	WI	$7.25
HI	$7.75	MN	$8.00	OK	$7.25	WV	$7.25
		MO	$7.65	OR	$9.25	WY	$5.15

Source: U.S. Department of Labor, 2015

part of their employment. The federal minimum wage for tipped employees is $2.13 per hour; however, each state has different regulations about how much the employee must earn in tips to meet federal wage and hour laws.

The difference between the tipped employee minimum wage and the federal minimum wage is known as the *tip credit*. Federal wage and hour laws mandate that the tip credit is $5.12 per hour. Note that the tip credit is the difference between the minimum wage and the tipped employee minimum wage ($7.25 − $2.13 = $5.12). Some states, such as Alaska, California, and Montana, do not allow tip credit; instead, all workers receive minimum wage. Table 3-2 contains the details about tip credit for each state.

TABLE 3-2

Table of 2015 Minimum Hourly Wages for Tipped Employees, by State

Jurisdiction	Basic Combined Cash and Tip Minimum Wage Rate	Maximum Tip Credit against Minimum Wage	Minimum Cash Wage	Definition of Tipped Employee by Minimum Tips Received (monthly unless otherwise specified)
Federal: Fair Labor Standards Act (FLSA)	$7.25	$5.12	$2.13	More than $30
State Law Does Not Allow Tip Credit				
Minimum rate same for tipped and nontipped employees				
Alaska			$8.75	
California			$9.00	
Minnesota:				No tip credit allowed
Large employer *Annual receipts > $625,000 per year*			$8.00	
Small employer *Annual receipts < $625,000 per year*			$6.50	
Montana:				
Business with gross annual sales exceeding $110,000			$8.05	
Business with gross annual sales of $110,000 or less			$4.00	
Nevada			$8.25	With no health insurance benefits provided by employer and received by employee
			$7.25	With health insurance benefits provided by employer and received by employee
Oregon			$9.25	
Washington			$9.47	
State Law Allows Tip Credit				
Arizona	$8.00	$3.00	$5.05	Not specified
Arkansas	$7.50	$4.87	$2.63	More than $20
Colorado	$8.23	$3.02	$5.21	More than $30
Connecticut:	$9.15			At least $10 weekly for full-time employees or $2.00 daily for part-time in hotels and restaurants. Not specified for other industries.
Hotel, restaurant		34.8% ($3.37)	$5.78	
Bartenders who customarily receive tips		18.5% ($1.69)	$7.46	
Delaware	$7.75	$5.52	$2.23	More than $30
District of Columbia	$9.50	$6.73	$2.77	Not specified
Florida	$8.05	$3.02	$5.03	
Hawaii	$7.75	$0.50	$7.25	More than $20
Idaho	$7.25	$3.90	$3.35	More than $30
Illinois	$8.25	40%	$4.95	$20

(continued)

TABLE 2-2   *(concluded)*

Jurisdiction	Basic Combined Cash and Tip Minimum Wage Rate	Maximum Tip Credit against Minimum Wage	Minimum Cash Wage	Definition of Tipped Employee by Minimum Tips Received (monthly unless otherwise specified)
Indiana	$7.25	$5.12	$2.13	Not specified
Iowa	$7.25	$2.90	$4.35	More than $30
Kansas	$7.25	$5.12	$2.13	More than $20
Kentucky	$7.25	$5.12	$2.13	More than $30
Maine	$7.50	50%	$3.75	More than $30
Maryland	$8.50	$4.37	$3.63	More than $30
Massachusetts	$9.00	$6.00	$3.00	More than $20
Michigan	$8.15	$5.05	$3.10	Not specified
Missouri	$7.65	50% ($3.825)	$3.825	Not specified
Nebraska	$8.00	$5.87	$2.13	Not specified
New Hampshire	$7.25	55%	45%	More than $30
New Jersey	$8.38	$6.25	$2.13	Not specified
New Mexico	$7.50	$5.37	$2.13	More than $30
New York:	$8.75			Not specified
Food service workers		$3.75	$5.00	
Service employees		$3.10	$5.65	
Service employees in resort hotels if tips average at least $4.90 per hour		$3.85	$4.90	
North Carolina	$7.25	$5.12	$2.13	More than $20
North Dakota	$7.25	33%	$4.86	More than $30
Ohio: The increased minimum wage will apply to employees of businesses with annual gross receipts of more than $297,000 per year.	$8.10	$4.05	$4.05	More than $30
Oklahoma	$7.25	$3.625	$3.625	Not specified
Pennsylvania	$7.25	$4.42	$2.83	More than $30
Rhode Island	$9.00	$6.11	$2.89	Not specified
South Dakota	$8.50	(50%) $4.25	$4.25	More than $35
Texas	$7.25	$5.12	$2.13	More than $20
Utah	$7.25	$5.12	$2.13	More than $30
Vermont: Employees in hotels, motels, tourist places, and restaurants who customarily and regularly receive tips for direct and personal customer service	$9.15	50% ($4.575)	$4.575	More than $120
Virginia	$7.25	$5.12	$2.13	Not specified
West Virginia	$8.00	70% ($5.60)	$2.40	Not specified
Wisconsin	$7.25	$4.92	$2.33	Not specified
Wyoming	$5.15	$3.02	$2.13	More than $30

Source: U.S. Department of Labor, 2015

Pay Your Employees Correctly

STOP & CHECK

1. Heather works as a clerk receiving minimum wage for a pharmaceutical company in North Carolina that pays its employees on a biweekly basis. She is classified as nonexempt and her standard workweek is 40 hours. During a two-week period, she worked 88 hours and received $638.00. Was Heather's pay correct? Explain.

2. Tony works as a publisher's representative receiving minimum wage in New York. He works 39.5 hours during a one-week period. How much should he receive?

3. Mary is an intern for a popular radio station, which is a large employer in Minnesota. She receives minimum wage and works 32 hours per week. How much should she receive for two weeks of work?

LO 3-2   Compute Gross Pay for Different Pay Bases

Salaried Workers

© PhotosIndia.com/Glow Images, RF

Employees in highly technical, qualification-driven positions within a company are generally classified as exempt from FLSA regulations. Accountants, engineers, lawyers, managers, and supervisors are included in this classification. Section 13(a)(1) of the FLSA defines the eligible exempt employees in the following job descriptions: executives, administrative personnel, professionals, and outside sales representatives. Section 13(a)(17) of the FLSA also allows specific computer-related employees to be included in the classification of salaried workers. The FLSA also provides a minimum wage for salaried workers of not less than $455 per week.

The division of salaried workers into exempt and nonexempt statuses has historically correlated with company policy more than legal requirements. However, in 2015 the U.S. Department of Labor has begun to investigate employee classifications to ensure compliance with FLSA stipulations. For nonexempt salaried workers, the employment contract entered into between the employee and the employer determines at what level of hourly work they would receive overtime pay. Overtime pay is the payment of wages at one-and-a-half times the employee's normal wage rate. Many salaried nonexempt worker contracts, when specified, are for approximately 45 hours per week.

Examples:

- If a salaried, nonexempt employee were earning $1,000/week for 45 hours, the hourly compensation would be $22.22 per hour ($1,000/45 hours) and the overtime rate would be $33.33 per hour ($22.22 × 1.5).

- For the same salaried, nonexempt employee, if the contract between employee and employer stated that all hours exceeding 45 were considered for overtime, then the individual would need to work 45.25 hours or more in the week to qualify for overtime. However, if the contract stated that 40 hours were required before overtime rates applied, then the 5 hours would be paid at overtime rates.

- NOTE: A salaried exempt worker would be paid $1,000 regardless of the number of hours worked.

Employers may not prorate a salaried worker's pay when the number of hours worked is fewer than the contractual hour requirement. An exception to this would be time away from work in accordance with the employer's sick or vacation policy. The company would allow employees to take paid time off under either of these programs to supplement their missed wages. Companies may also offer salaried employees the option of leave without pay for missed days; however, contractual hours covered under leave without pay must be documented and signed by both a manager and the employee.

Salary Translation to Hourly Rates

The calculation of gross pay for salaried employees depends on the firm's choice of pay periods. An employee's gross pay is determined by dividing the annual pay by the number of pay periods in a year. For instance, if a firm paid employees on a monthly basis, then the salary calculation would be $\frac{1}{12}$ of the yearly amount. It is occasionally necessary to determine the hourly rate for salaried employees. To get the hourly rate, you would use the following equation:

$$\text{Hourly rate} = \frac{\text{Annual amount}}{\text{Total hours worked per year}}$$

To arrive at the total number of hours worked per year, multiply the number of weeks in a year (52) by the number of hours worked in a standard week without overtime.

Jackie earns a salary of $60,000 per year for ABD Industries. ABD Industries pays its employees on a monthly basis. Her gross pay would be $60,000/12 or $5,000. If she were a nonexempt employee, it becomes necessary to calculate her hourly rate. When calculating the hourly rate, using the correct number of hours in a regular workweek is critical in determining the overtime pay rate.

Number of hours in the regular workweek	Annual salary # of hours × 52 weeks	Hourly rate
40	$\dfrac{60{,}000}{(40 \times 52)}$	$28.85
37.5	$\dfrac{60{,}000}{(37.5 \times 52)}$	$30.77
35	$\dfrac{60{,}000}{(35 \times 52)}$	$32.97

What happens if the salaried employee decides to take unpaid leave during a pay period? That amount must be deducted from the gross pay amount. In the case of unpaid leave, the amount of time taken and the number of regular hours in the pay period are the major factors.

Example:
Jackie wants to take two extra days off around a holiday but has no paid time off remaining for the year. The company is paying Jackie on a biweekly basis, and there are 80 hours in a pay period. At 8 hours per day, she will be taking 16 hours of unpaid leave (8 hours × 2 days). Using the previous example for Jackie's work with ABD Industries with her regular working hours as 40 hours per week, her normal salary is $2,307.69 per pay period.

To calculate her pay, including the unpaid leave, we need the proportion of her paycheck that will be unpaid. We calculate the proportion of the total paycheck she will be taking as unpaid leave by dividing 16 by 80, which is 0.20. That means she will receive 0.80 (or 80%) of her normal gross pay. She will, therefore, receive $2,307.69 × 0.80 or $1,846.15, as her gross pay for the period.

In many instances, nonexempt employees are paid on a salary basis to avoid paperwork such as *time cards* or pay sheets if they consistently work a fixed number of hours per week. According to 29 CFR 778.113(a), the employer and employee must agree on the standard number of hours to be worked each week for which the employee shall receive fixed pay. If the employee is classified as a nonexempt worker, however, the FLSA requires that these salaried workers are eligible for overtime. For a nonexempt salaried worker, the hourly rate is necessary to compute pay beyond the agreed-upon weekly hours per 29 CFR 778.113(a).

If the employee works less than the agreed-upon number of hours during the week, some states have provisions by which the employee's salary may be reduced. In this case, the hourly rate is again necessary to make sure the gross pay is correctly calculated.

Salaried Workers and Minimum-Wage Comparisons

In the case of a salaried nonexempt worker for whom FLSA provisions apply, the fixed weekly salary must adhere to minimum-wage guidelines.

> **Example:**
> Sally is a receptionist for KTC Incorporated, located in California. She works 40 hours per week, but is nonexempt because her job classification is nonmanagerial. If she were to be paid $275 per week for her work, her hourly wage would be $275/40, or $6.88/hour, which is below the minimum wage of $9.00 per hour. She would need to be paid a minimum of $360 per week for her work to meet FLSA minimum-wage requirements because of her weekly salary agreement with her employer.

Hourly Workers

Hourly workers are paid for any hour or fraction of an hour they work. These employees may be either skilled or unskilled. Hourly employees must receive overtime for hours worked in excess of 40 per week, according to FLSA. Overtime is the same for hourly workers as it is for the salaried nonexempt workers. Hourly workers are paid for each minute worked, and the computation of those minutes depends upon company policy. Companies may offer different work shifts and workday lengths, such as four 10-hour shifts or five 8-hour shifts, to reach the 40 hours needed. State regulations may require the company with the 10-hour shifts to file an election to avoid overtime regulations for the two additional hours per day. The reason stated should not be overtime avoidance, but a deemed economic benefit to the longer schedules. For example, in a manufacturing environment set-up time can eliminate anywhere from half an hour to an hour of productive time. By working the longer schedules, manufacturing efficiency can be improved.

An employee working for an hourly wage may work in more than one job classification. When this occurs, the employee's pay per classification may vary. For example, a manufacturing employee may work on the sales counter where the pay differential provides an additional $1.50 per hour. When situations like this occur, the payroll accountant must be informed of hours performed for each of the job classifications to provide accurate pay, classification, and reporting. Methods used to communicate this include notes on the time card, schedules provided to the payroll clerk, or job duty notification forms.

© Liam Bailey/Image Source, RF

> **Example:**
> Merrill is an hourly worker for a fast-food establishment and earns $7.25 per hour. He occasionally is the crew chief, during which he receives a $2.00/hour differential. During a 40-hour workweek, he worked 16 hours as a crew chief and 24 hours as a regular employee. His pay would be calculated as follows:
>
> Regular pay: 24 hours × $7.25/hour = $174.00
>
> Crew chief pay: 16 hours × $9.25/hour = $148.00
>
> Gross pay = $174.00 + $148.00 = $322.00

Commission Work

Commissions are compensation based on a set percentage of the sales revenue for a product or service that the company provides. Commission-based compensation is appropriate in the following types of situations:

- Retail sales personnel
- Automotive sales personnel
- Media databases or monitoring that pertains to media relations
- Marketing sales agents

Example:

An ice machine company may have sales representatives earning 5% commission on all sales made. If sales representative A sells $100,000 worth of ice machines in the month, the commission due to that employee would be $5,000, calculated as the sales price $100,000 × 5%.

Commissions may be contingent upon the company's return/warranty policy. If the same sales representative had returns in the following month of $7,500, the commission for that month could be reduced by $375 (5% of $7,500), depending upon the sales contract between the company and representative.

An important classification of a sales representative's job is the difference between inside and outside sales. An inside sales representative is one who conducts business via telephone, email, or other electronic means. An inside sales representative does not travel to customer sites. An outside sales representative meets with customers either at the customer's facility or another agreed-upon location. Some inside sales representatives are covered under the FLSA and must receive at least minimum wage for their labors. Outside sales representatives are excluded from minimum-wage requirements under FLSA. In a 2010 circuit court decision, the judge ruled that inside sales representatives are nonexempt from FLSA wage and hour provisions, whereas outside sales and retail sales representatives are exempt.

Example:

Sally works as an inside sales representative in the company store and receives 5% commission for all sales she makes during her shift. During the week, she made 15 sales via telephone for a total dollar value of $1,500. Her commissions for the week are $1,500 × 5%, or $75. Based upon a 40-hour workweek, she would have constructively earned $1.88 per hour; thus, the employer would be responsible for meeting the minimum-wage requirements under FLSA.

Samantha works as an outside sales representative for the company. She made sales this week of $2,000 and has an agreed commission percentage of 10% of her total sales revenue. Her commission for $2,000 of sales equals 2,000 × 10%, or $200, divided by 40 hours per week, which equals $5.00 hour. Because she is an outside sales representative, she is exempt from minimum-wage regulations under FLSA.

Gross Pay for Commission-Based Employees

In situations where the employee is principally engaged in the sale of a product or service but in no way engaged in the manufacturing of the item, a commission pay basis is appropriate. In some states, the commission-based employee may receive commissions for work even after termination if the sale was completed prior to termination. In many ways, commission-based pay is a contract between the employer and employee to sell a product. The payment for such a contract may not be reneged upon, even after termination of employment. It should be noted that many states prohibit deductions pertaining to the cost of doing business from an employee's commission. In other words, if a customer received a product that was damaged, lost, or otherwise destroyed, the employee's commission will not be affected.

Example:
Sonja works as a salesperson with Bayfront Watercraft. Her whole function with Bayfront is to sell the company's products, for which she receives a commission of 5% on the retail price of all sales she makes. If she makes $20,000 in sales during a week, her commission is $20,000 × 0.05, or $1,000.

Pamela is also a salesperson for Bayfront and makes a 5% commission on her weekly sales. If Pamela made $35,000 in sales during a week, her commission would be $35,000 × 0.05, or $1,750.

© David Planchet/McGraw-Hill Education, RF

Commission pay can vary by employer, by client, by sales volume, and by employee based on his or her seniority or experience with the company. For instance, sales made by an employee to Client A may have a different commission rate than sales made to Client B, as well as be different for all other clients. Different products may also have varying commission rates, and changes in sales volume can alter commission rates. A sample of a commission-tracking sheet follows.

Salesperson	Client	Product or Service	Total Sales Price	Rate	Commission
Anthony B	Thompson Milbourne	RR-223	$1,245	2%	$ 24.90
Anthony B	Kockran Heights	RS-447	$2,016	5%	$100.80
Anthony B	Hoptop Ranges	RT-11	$892	3.5%	$ 31.22

It is important that commissions earned be tracked closely for a variety of reasons:

- Employee pay accuracy
- Sales employee performance
- Sales tracking
- Job order tracking

Commission pay must still meet FLSA minimum-wage standards unless the employee is classified as an exempt worker. Similar to salaried nonexempt employees, commission-based employees are subject to the 40-hour workweek as a basis for FLSA minimum-wage computations.

In the example concerning Sonja and Pamela at Bayfront, Sonja's pay was $1,000 for 40 hours of work, whereas Pamela's was $1,750 for the same time. Sonja effectively made $25 per hour ($1,000/40 hours) and Pamela made $43.75 per hour ($1,750/40 hours).

However, suppose that Anita, another commission-based employee, made only $250 in commission for the week. Her effective hourly rate would be $6.25/hour, which is below the minimum wage in California. It is the employer's responsibility to compensate the employee at the minimum wage, so Bayfront would have to adjust Anita's compensation to meet FLSA requirements.

Piece-Rate Work

© Ronnie Kaufman/Larry Hirshowitz/
Blend Images, RF

Piece-rate work involves paying employees for each unit that they manufacture or each action they perform. This type of pay, based on task completion, is one of the oldest forms of performance-based pay. Dating back to the 16th century, piece-rate pay is thought to have evolved from journeyman artisans whose masters paid them per unit they completed. Prior to computations of hourly wages, piece rate was an accurate measure of how productive an employee was. Frederick Taylor wrote about a piece-rate system in 1896, citing that it placed an emphasis on efficiency and production. A criticism of Taylor's analysis, however, is that the piece-rate system overemphasizes production and may create an adversarial relationship between workers and managers.

FLSA requirements subjected the piece-rate system to minimum-wage requirements. Piece-rate workers must be paid no less than the minimum wage for their location, forcing employers to track their work hours accurately. In many ways, piece-rate pay is more difficult to track and to administer than other types of pay. Not only must the employees be compensated for the work they complete, but they are also subject to FLSA minimum and daily break provisions, including lunch and other breaks.

> **Example:**
> John is a piece-rate worker in Tennessee who receives $15 per completed piece of work. During a week, he completes 30 pieces. His pay would be $15 × 30, or $450. Based on a 40-hour workweek, his hourly rate equivalent is $11.25/hour. John's pay exceeds the FLSA minimum wage for his location, so the employer does not have to adjust John's compensation.
>
> Sarah works for the same employer as John and receives the same rate of pay. She completes 15 pieces during the week. Her pay would be $15 × 15, or $225. Based on a 40-hour workweek, her hourly rate equivalent is $5.63/hour. She does not meet the minimum-wage requirement, so the employer would have to examine Sarah's work and pay rates to ensure that she meets the FLSA minimum-wage requirements.

Gross Pay for Piece-Rate Workers

Unlike commission-based pay, piece-rate worker compensation connects the amount of the work completed during a process linked with manufacturing. It links the worker's effort to the number of units produced as a means of rewarding the worker, as well as benchmarking productivity and fostering a basis for job cost analysis. Calculation of the wages under the piece-rate method is done by multiplying the completed number of units by the amount specified per unit.

> **Example:**
> Pat is a fabrication worker who creates hulls at Bayfront Watercraft, and his pay is based on the number of hulls he completes during a specific period multiplied by the piece rate per hull. If he completed 30 hulls in a two-week period and earned $100 per hull, his gross pay for that period would be 30 × $100, or $3,000.

A wide variety of occupations benefit from piece-rate pay systems. Some of these occupations include:

Vineyard workers	Inspectors
Installers	Customer service agents
Machinists/fabricators	Production workers
Sheep shearers	Forest workers

The common thread is that each position has output that is quantifiable and linked to some aspect of a manufacturing or service industry. The important part of piece-rate work is that a quantifiable base must be linked with a specified standard rate per amount of work.

>Vineyard workers: Tons of grapes harvested
>
>Inspectors: Number of items inspected
>
>Installers: Number of items installed
>
>Customer service agents: Number of customers assisted
>
>Machinists/ Fabricators: Number of items produced
>
>Sheep shearers: Pounds of wool gathered
>
>Forest workers: Amount of wood cut

At Bayfront Watercraft, the manufacturing department has different types of fabricators, installers, and other production workers in addition to Pat (our hull maker). Let us assume that Joanna works in the upholstery department where she constructs vinyl covers for seats. Rick is in the assembly department and assembles steering mechanisms for the boats.

Worker	Number of Items	Rate per Item	Gross Pay
Pat	30 hulls	$100	$3,000
Joanna	100 seat covers	$ 25	$2,500
Rick	25 steering mechanisms	$ 40	$1,000

Each worker is compensated based on the work he or she completes. In some companies, workers may work on multiple items for which different rates exist. In cases where one worker completes multiple pieces at different rates, the rates for each different piece must be computed:

Worker	Item	Number of Items	Pay per Item	Total Pay
John	Motor installation	10 motors	$50 per motor	$500
	Rudder installation	15 rudders	$20 per rudder	$300
			Total pay for John:	$800

A separate record for each employee is important in the case of piece-rate pay, especially when the employee works with multiple production items at different rates. Overtime rates for piece-rate workers are computed differently than for hourly workers. Once the standard number of pieces per hour is determined, the amount per hour per piece can be computed.

Example:
Bayfront determines that 50 ignition assemblies can reasonably be completed in a 40-hour workweek by one worker and ignition assemblies are paid at a rate of $25 per assembly. Thus, the standard amount paid per 40-hour workweek is $1,250 (50 assemblies × $25). The amount per hour is $1,250/40, or $31.25. If the employee worked overtime, the rate would be one-and-a-half times the regular hourly rate, or $46.875. If the employee worked a 45-hour workweek, the pay would be computed as $1,250 + (5 × 46.88) *or* $1,484.38 (rounded).

According to FLSA provisions, piece-rate workers must have a standard number of items that can be reasonably completed each day that allows for breaks and rest periods. To increase compensation, it could be very easy for an employee to engage in overwork so that he or she could complete more items. According to 29 CFR 525.12(h)(2)(ii), piece-rate employees must have a standard number of items per period and most are subject to minimum-wage provisions.

Like the overtime rate calculation, the piece-rate calculation can be used to determine if the minimum-wage rate provisions are met. In the example above, Rick is installing steering mechanisms. His pay for a two-week period is $1,000 for 25 mechanisms completed.

According to the job analysis, he can reasonably complete 13 mechanisms per 40-hour workweek. Suppose Rick was paid only $10 per completed mechanism. His weekly pay would be $130. Dividing $130 by 40 hours, we arrive at $3.25 per hour, well below the FLSA minimum wage. In this instance, Bayfront would have to adjust the piece rate for Rick's work to meet the FLSA minimum wage.

Pay Computations for Different Bases

STOP & CHECK

1. Tony is a tipped minimum-wage worker for a Minnesota company with $615,000 in annual revenues. He worked 75 hours during a biweekly pay period, in which he earned $1,000 in tips. What is his gross pay (excluding tips)?

2. Natasha is a marketing representative who earns a 3% commission based on the revenue earned from the marketing campaigns she completes. During the current pay period, she completed a marketing campaign with $224,800 revenue. How much commission will she receive from this campaign?

3. Jeremy is a specialty artisan for a luxury car maker based in South Carolina. He makes handcrafted dashboards and receives $550.00 per completed assembly. During a semi-monthly pay period, he completes two dashboard assemblies and works 90 hours. How much does he receive for the completion of the assemblies? Does this amount comply with minimum-wage requirements? Explain.

LO 3-3 Calculate Pay Based on Hours and Fractions of Hours

Employees, both salaried nonexempt and hourly, are paid based upon the number of hours or fractions thereof. The payroll accountant must learn how to convert a fraction of a 60-minute clock into a fraction of 100. Very few accounting software packages are able to convert minutes into payable units; typically, the payroll accountant does this math. Fortunately, the math for this calculation is fairly straightforward.

> **Example:**
> If an employee works 30 minutes, then the computation for pay purposes is 30 minutes ÷ 60 minutes/hour = 0.5 hour, or 50/100.
> If an employee works 33 minutes, then the payroll computation is 33 minutes ÷ 60 minutes/hour = 0.55 hour, or 55/100.

Calculations of employee wages are broken down by the hour or fraction thereof. Regardless of the classification of employee, a determination of pay per pay period causes the payroll accountant to break down all wages. Salaries are determined based upon a yearly salary, and therefore need to be broken down per pay period (monthly, bimonthly, weekly, or biweekly). Companies may pay employees by fractions of an hour (hundredth-hour basis) or by the quarter hour (rounded to the nearest 15-minute interval), depending upon company policy. The next section will walk you through the calculations of both the hundredth and quarterly processes.

Hourly Calculations

Depending on the company's policy, time payments can be paid either by the individual minute or rounded to the nearest designated interval. Hourly calculations are a combination of minutes and hours. Hours are broken into two categories, regular and overtime. When determining the hourly wage for a salaried individual, the number of average hours required under the salary must be known.

Example:

1. If a manager is expected to work 45 hours per week for $75,000, her effective hourly wage would be $75,000/(45 × 52 weeks) for $32.05 per hour.

2. Jason worked four days during the payroll week. He worked 7.5 hours the first day, 8.75 hours the second day, 7 hours the third day, and 9.5 hours the fourth day. He called in sick once, using 8 hours of his paid sick time. His employer pays overtime wages for any time worked in excess of 8 hours per day.

   To determine his regular hours: 7.5 + 8 + 7 + 8 = <u>30.5 hours</u>

   To determine his overtime hours: 0.75 + 1.5 = <u>2.25 hours</u>

   He will also receive 8 hours sick time.

   Jason's gross pay will have 38.5 hours regular pay (30.5 + 8) and 2.25 hours overtime pay.

3. Karen worked four days during the week with a holiday on Monday. Her hours worked were 8.25 hours the first day, 9 hours the second day, 7.75 hours the third day, and 8.5 hours the fourth day. The company pays 8 hours for the holiday. Her employer pays overtime wages for any time worked in excess of 8 hours per day.

   To calculate her regular hours: 8 + 8 + 7.75 + 8 = <u>31.75 hours</u>

   To calculate her overtime hours: 0.25 + 1 + 0.5 = <u>1.75 hours</u>

   She will also be paid 8 hours regular pay for the holiday.

   Karen's gross pay will contain 39.75 hours regular pay and 1.75 hours overtime.

Quarter-Hour System

Some employers compensate employees based upon rounding working hours to the nearest 15 minutes, a system widely known as the *quarter-hour system*. The payroll accountant becomes responsible for rounding the time either up or down consistently across all individuals and pay periods. If an individual worked 8 hours and 6 minutes, he would be paid for 8 hours. However, if that same individual were to work for 8 hours and 10 minutes, he would be paid for 8 hours plus 15 minutes of overtime.

Example:
Amanda worked from 8 a.m. until noon. She took one hour for lunch and returned to work at 1 p.m. At the end of the day, Amanda ended up leaving work at 4:20 p.m. Because her employer uses the quarter-hour system, she would be paid for the 7.25 hours worked:

   From 8 a.m. to noon: 4 hours
   From 1 p.m. to 4:20 p.m.: 3.25 hours, because
   4:20 p.m. rounds to 4:15 p.m. under the quarter-hour system.

Justin worked from 8 a.m. until 12:30 before taking a half-hour lunch. He returned at 1 p.m. and worked until 4:10 p.m. His employer also pays on the quarter-hour system, so Justin would be paid for 7.75 hours:

   From 8 a.m. to 12:30 p.m.: 4 hours, 30 minutes, or 4.5 hours
   From 1 p.m. to 4:10 p.m.: 3.25 hours, because 4:10 p.m. rounds to 4:15 p.m. under the quarter-hour system.

Hundredth-Hour System

The *hundredth-hour system* is similar to the quarter-hour system in that it calculates partial hours of work performed. Instead of rounding the employee's time to 15-minute intervals, the hundredth-hour system divides the hour into 100 increments. The calculation of partial minutes is simple: Minutes worked divided by 60. If an employee worked 4 hours and 16 minutes, she would receive 4 hours plus 16/60, totaling 4.27 hours (rounded) on the payroll. An employee working an 8-hour shift with 15 minutes of overtime would have the following calculation (employee earns $10 per hour):

8 hours × $10 per hour = $80 regular and 15/60 minutes × $10 × 1.5 (remember the calculation for overtime is one-and-a-half times normal rate) for 0.25 × $15 = $3.75 overtime pay for a total of $83.75 for that week.

Below is a list of how the time may appear on an individual's time card. Note that an employer should choose only one method of computing partial hours, quarter-hour or hundredth-hour, and apply it to all situations.

Amanda Parker: Employee Number 1776M				
Clock In	Clock Out	Clock In	Clock Out	Hours Worked
08:00	11:00	12:00	16:54	7 hours 54 minutes 7.90 (hundredth)
08:00	11:00	12:00	16:54	7 hours 54 minutes 8.00 (quarter)
07:00	12:08	13:15	17:30	9 hours 23 minutes 9.38 (hundredth)
07:00	12:08	13:15	17:30	9 hours 23 minutes 9.50 (quarter)

Quarter-hour vs. Hundredth-hour

1. Blue Sky Manufacturing has historically paid its employees according to the quarter-hour system. Software changes have caused them to change to the hundredth-hour system. What is the number of hours worked under the quarter-hour system? What is the time worked under the hundredth-hour system?

Employee	Time In	Time Out	Time In	Time Out	Total
Ann	8:06 a.m.	12:25 p.m.	1:20 p.m.	4:57 p.m.	Quarter hour: Hundredth:
Nevada	7:58 a.m.	12:02 p.m.	1:02 p.m.	5:05 p.m.	Quarter hour: Hundredth:
Pat	8:32 a.m.	11:54 a.m.	1:05 p.m.	5:32 p.m.	Quarter hour: Hundredth:

2. Why do discrepancies exist between the quarter-hour time and the hundredth-hour time totals?

3. Why would it be worthwhile for Blue Sky Manufacturing to switch to the hundredth-hour system?

LO 3-4 Apply Combination Pay Methods

Employers often offer their employees *combination pay* methods. Sometimes the employee performs two different jobs for the same employer, and those two tasks have different compensation bases. Other situations involve payroll-based incentives that link to company productivity.

Base Salary Plus Commission

A very common method includes a base salary plus a commission or piece rate, depending on the nature of the work performed. Another method is a combination of salary plus hourly compensation that reflects a standard set of work hours plus additional hours that are paid only when worked. The purpose of the combination pay method is to meet minimum-wage requirements and encourage employees to achieve sales or production goals. The base salary offers both the employer and employee a level of stability in pay amounts because they will know the minimum amount of compensation for each pay period. Whatever the employees earn above the base salary may vary from pay period to pay period, depending on the employee's capabilities, production needs, and customer needs.

Many types of jobs have a combination pay method because it has been found to boost employee productivity and maintain FLSA compliance. Some jobs that use combination pay methods include:

© Josh Rinehults/iStock/Getty Images, RF

District managers	Account executives
Recruiters	Retail sales workers
Farm workers	College instructors

To compute combination pay methods, knowledge of the employee's base salary plus variable rate is essential.

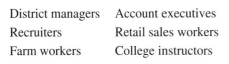

> Todd is an account executive for Bayfront Watercraft. He earns a base salary of $36,000 plus a commission of 0.5% on each sale he makes. Suppose that Todd sold $100,000 of boats during a two-week pay period. His base salary for biweekly pay is $36,000/26, or $1,384.62. His commission is $100,000 × 0.5%, or $500. Todd's total gross pay for the period is:
>
> | Base: | $1,384.62 |
> |---|---|
> | Commission: | 500.00 |
> | Total pay: | $1,884.62 |
>
> Maria installs the seating in the boats. In her position, she earns a base salary of $26,000 per year plus a piece rate of $100 for each boat completed during the pay period. During the pay period, Maria installed the seating for 8 boats. Her biweekly base salary is $26,000/26, or $1,000. Her piece rate pay is $100 × 8, or $800. Maria's total gross pay for the period is:
>
> | Base: | $1,000.00 |
> |---|---|
> | Piece rate: | 800.00 |
> | Total pay: | $1,800.00 |

Like any other type of pay method, the important element in computing combination pay is accurate maintenance of the base salary, the variable rate, and the amount of items or sales for which the variable rate must apply.

Payroll Draw

A special situation in commission-based pay is a situation called a *draw*. A draw generally involves an employee whose regular compensation is little more than the minimum wage, such as a retail sales position. Employees have sales goals they must meet and receive compensation on a commission basis once they meet or exceed those sales goals. If the sales goal is not met, the employee may draw salary against future commissions. The expectation with a draw is that the employee will eventually generate enough sales to cover any draws during pay periods when sales revenues were lower than expected.

A draw is generally associated with a commission-only job in which the employer allows new employees to receive money for expected future commissions. For example, an employee's starting base salary may be $1,000 per month with an expected $2,000 in commissions, totaling $3,000 per month. If the employee earned only $1,000 in commissions, the employee would receive only $2,000 and may draw $1,000 against future earnings. With a draw, it is implied that the draw may occur on a regular basis.

Another example where the company may allow individuals to draw on their payroll exists when the pay period is monthly. In this situation, many employers allow their employees to draw up to 30–40% of their wages at mid-month. Some organizations may not withhold taxes from the draw, and the employee will have the full amount of taxes withdrawn upon their next payroll.

Employers must be careful when allowing employees to draw against future wages. A written and signed authorization must be obtained from the employee that specifies when the draw will be deducted from the employee's future wages to avoid legal issues with deductions, such as wage garnishments, that could be affected by the draw.

Scott is a new salesperson with Bayfront Watercraft. He receives a base salary of $19,500 per year, paid biweekly, plus a 5% commission on sales once he achieves his sales quota of $20,000 during a pay period. During his first pay period, he closed $10,000 in sales, making him ineligible for a commission. His base pay is $19,500/26, or $750 biweekly. He is eligible for a draw up to the minimum commission of $20,000 × 5%, or $1,000. He takes this draw, so his compensation for the first two weeks is

Base:	$ 750
Draw:	1,000
Total pay:	$1,750

Incentive Stock Options (ISOs)

Other employee compensation plans, known as *incentive stock options (ISOs)*, allow an employee to report a small base salary for tax purposes and to be issued company stock that must be held for a certain period before being sold. The purpose of ISO stock option plans is a deferral of taxes and salary liabilities for the employer and employee. This type of compensation is often found in executive pay packages.

According to the National Bureau of Economic Research in 2015, chief executive officers (CEOs) in the United States receive more than half of their annual compensation in the form of incentive stock options. In contrast, CEOs received less than 20 percent of their annual compensation as stock options in 1980. The current ISOs are designed as multi-year plans that allow executives to exercise the stock option at a later date, preferably when the market price of the stock is favorable. (Source: National Bureau of Economic Research)

© Digital Stock/Corbis, RF

LO 3-5 Explain Special Pay Situations

Compensation laws have many exceptions. According to the FLSA, every aspect of labor legislation, including minimum wage and overtime provisions, has its less-common applications. The introduction of new types of knowledge-based employment during the 21st century, as well as the continuance of more traditional agricultural tasks, necessitates an examination of these special pay situations.

Combination Pay Methods

STOP & CHECK

1. Shelly, a service administrator, receives a base salary of $42,000 per year paid semi-monthly, plus $100 commission for each service contract she sells to her customers. During a pay period, she sells five contracts. What is her gross pay for the period?

2. Adam is a new salesperson with S&D Music. He receives a base salary of $36,000 paid monthly. Company policy allows him to draw 35% of his salary on the 15th of each month. How much will Adam receive at mid-month if he elects to take a draw? How much will he receive at the end of the month if he takes the 35% draw?

3. Joy, an executive for Adarma Chemicals, receives an annual salary of $75,000 plus an additional 3% in an ISO. What amount of stock does she receive annually? What is her total annual compensation?

© Tetra Images/Alamy, RF

Compensatory Time

The FLSA allows public employees to receive *compensatory time*, often called "comp time," in lieu of overtime. According to section 3(s)(1)(c) of the FLSA, exempt public employees must receive comp time equal to 1.5 times the overtime hours worked. Therefore, if a public employee worked five hours of overtime, the comp time awarded must be 7.5 hours.

Comp time is often misconstrued by the private sector. FLSA provisions for comp time are only for public-sector employees, such as government workers, law enforcement, and seasonally hired laborers. Unless specifically designated by a firm's policies, a private-sector employer is not required to offer comp time. Additionally, many private-sector employers offer comp time on a straight-line basis, meaning that they offer the same number of compensatory hours as the number of overtime hours worked.

When calculating an employee's gross pay, it is prudent to be aware of any effects that a comp time award may have on overtime pay to ensure that the employee's compensation is accurate.

> **Example:**
> David works as an exempt employee of the federal government. In the course of his work, he accrues eight hours of overtime during a pay period when he completes additional work for an absent co-worker. According to FLSA regulations, David must receive 12 hours of comp time because he is not eligible for paid overtime as an exempt government employee.

On-Call Time

Some professions require employees to be available for work outside of normal working hours. This availability is known as *on-call time*, and two classes of on-call time exist: on-call at the employer's premises and on-call away from the employer's premises.

- If the employee is required to remain at the employer's premises, the employee's freedom is restricted and he or she must be compensated for the on-call time.
- If the employee is not restricted to the employer's premises for the on-call time, compensation is not required.

In either case, company policy must be specific regarding the conditions of the on-call time. The number of hours specified for on-call compensation must be added to the employee's gross pay.

Example:
Kevin works as a service representative for an equipment manufacturer. The employer requires that each service representative rotate on-call duties in one-week increments in which they remain available for service calls outside of working hours, but may otherwise engage in personal activities. During this on-call time, company policy stipulates that on-call service representatives receive two hours of regular pay for each on-call day. Kevin would receive 14 hours of additional straight-time pay for his on-call time.

Travel Time, Wait Time, and Sleeping Time

Employees have traditionally commuted to and from work, although a growing trend toward telecommuting exists in the 21st century. Travel to and from an office is not compensable time; however, many employees do not work at a single location. Additionally, many employees travel for their employer's benefit for training or other business requirements. Similarly, employees may be required to wait by their employer, as in the case of a chauffeur or a bus driver. Other employees such as firefighters or medical personnel may be required to work 24-hour shifts, and must be given at least five hours of paid *sleeping time* during that 24-hour period. An agreement between the employer and employee may exist to exclude up to eight hours if the employer provides furnished facilities for uninterrupted sleep.

© Alloy/Big Cheese Photo/Corbis, RF

According to FLSA, the guideline that assists in the determination of compensable activity in these three situations is if the activity is for the employer's benefit. Travel among customer or business-related sites is compensable as *travel time* because it directly benefits the employer. Requiring a driver to wait as part of the job description also benefits the employer and is compensated as *wait time*. Travel from the employee's home to the office in the morning and returning home in the evening benefits the employee, and is not compensable.

Example:
Daniel is a surgical resident at a busy inner-city hospital. He works 24-hour shifts in the regular course of his employment. His employer provides him a quiet sleeping area, per FLSA requirements. During a single 24-hour shift, he sleeps seven hours. According to FLSA guidelines, his pay may not be reduced for the first five hours that he sleeps. Daniel's gross pay will reflect a two-hour reduction for the additional sleep over the five-hour requirement.

Sub-Minimum Wage Situations

Tipped employees are not the only workers that may legally receive compensation lower than the minimum wage. Other specific classes of employees may receive an hourly wage that is less than the FLSA minimum wage:

- A 1996 amendment to the FLSA allows workers younger than the age of 20 to be paid a minimum wage of $4.25 per hour, but only for the first 90 calendar days of employment.
- An employer may obtain a certificate to pay a worker with disabilities related to the work performed an amount less than the minimum wage.
- Full-time students in the employ of retail establishments, agriculture, colleges, and universities may receive a wage that is 85% of the federal minimum wage.
- Student learners in vocational education programs may be paid at a rate of 75% of the federal minimum wage.

Katie works in the café at a university. She is a student of the university and is 20 years old. According to the FLSA, she may receive 85% of the minimum wage. If the minimum wage for the location is $7.25 per hour, Katie may legally be paid $6.16 per hour while she is a full-time student.

EMPLOYEE COMPENSATION

Employee compensation tends to be a hot topic because of the way it affects people on a personal level. Some developments since 2010 in employee compensation include:

- Increased diligence in overtime tracking and compensation following a lawsuit involving large companies.
- New types of incentive pay to increase employee engagement, including merchandise rewards, additional company benefits, and other nonmonetary awards.
- Discussions of the legality of differential pay levels for travel time by nonexempt employees.
- Discussions about gaps in wages between people with and without a college education.

Some trends to watch in employee compensation include the following:

- Wage inequality debates will continue as lawmakers strive for gender-based wage equality.
- Investigation into pay disparity among different levels within a company and the effect of the disparity on job satisfaction.
- Discussions about wage growth and economic recovery.
- Grass-roots pressure in the form of strikes and public demonstrations about the concept of minimum wage versus a living wage.

What Is the Correct Pay?

STOP & CHECK

1. Alex is a nonexempt employee of The Silver Club. He works 10 hours of overtime during a pay period and requests that he receive compensatory time instead of overtime pay. His employer grants his request and offers him 10 hours of compensatory time. Alex claims he should receive 15 hours. How much comp time should Alex receive? Explain.

2. Stacy is a student in a vocational program at a cosmetology school. She accepts employment as a shampooer at Cuts & Styles Hair Salon in Alabama. The agreement between the school and the salon is that students receive the student-learner minimum wage. How much should Stacy be paid per hour?

Summary of Gross Pay Computation

Gross pay is the employee's compensation before taxes and other withholdings are deducted; net pay is the amount of money an employee receives after taxes and other deductions are subtracted. We discussed the different types of methods for pay computation, including salary, hourly, commission, and piece-rate pay. We looked at the effect of FLSA provisions and applicability of different compensation methods and offered examples of some job classifications that could be compensated using different methods. We concluded with a discussion of special compensation situations, especially on-call time, time spent unoccupied for the employer's benefit, and situations in which an employee may receive less than the FLSA minimum wage.

Key Points

- Gross pay is the total amount earned by an employee prior to the deductions for taxes or other withholdings.
- Employees may be subject to the wage and hour provisions of the FLSA (nonexempt) or they may not (exempt), depending on the type of job and employee duties.
- Nonexempt hourly employees are compensated on a basis that recognizes an economic connection between work performed and wages paid.
- Nonexempt salaried employees work a fixed number of working hours per week and receive overtime compensation.
- Exempt employees receive a fixed salary and may work more hours than their nonexempt colleagues.
- Commission-based pay connects employee compensation with sales revenue.
- Piece-rate pay compensates employees based on the manufacturing or completion of goods or services.
- Employees may have the option to draw against future earnings.
- ISOs are a means of offering compensation that is connected to company profitability.
- Compensatory time is legally required for public-sector exempt employees, and may be offered to private-sector employees at the employer's discretion.
- Employees may be compensated for time that they are unoccupied if they are required to be available for the employer's benefit.
- In certain circumstances, employees may receive less than the FLSA minimum wage.

Vocabulary

Combination pay	Incentive Stock Option	Salary
Commission	(ISO)	Sleeping time
Compensatory (comp)	Minimum wage	Time card
time	Net pay	Tipped Employee
Draw	Nonexempt	Tipped wages
Exempt	On-call time	Travel time
Gross pay	Overtime	Wait time
Hourly	Piece rate	
Hundredth-hour	Quarter-hour	

Review Questions

1. How is overtime pay computed for nonexempt salaried workers?

2. When do overtime rates apply?

3. How does minimum wage affect commission employees?

4. How does the tipped minimum wage differ from the FLSA minimum wage?

5. What types of occupations are typically salaried?

6. What is an ISO and how does it affect employee pay?

7. What is the difference between a salary and a draw?

8. How is overtime computed for piece-rate employees?

9. In what situations could a salaried employee receive overtime pay?

10. What is the primary difference between commission work and piece-rate work?

11. In what situations might an employee draw money against his or her future pay?

12. What is the difference between quarter-hour and hundredth-hour pay?

13. Why are companies moving toward the hundredth-hour system?

14. What is comp time?

15. Under what circumstances may an employee receive compensation for on-call time?

16. When are wait time, travel time, and sleep time compensable?

17. Aside from tipped employees, under what circumstances may an employee receive less than the FLSA minimum wage?

Exercises Set A

3-1A.
LO 3-3

Amanda M. worked the following schedule: Monday, 8 hours; Tuesday, 9 hours; Wednesday, 7 hours 48 minutes; Thursday, 8 hours; Friday, 8 hours. The employer pays overtime for all time worked in excess of 40 hours per week. Compute the following:

	Total Time	Regular Time	Overtime	Quarter-Hour Time	Hundredth-Hour Time
Amanda M.					

Which pay is more favorable for Amanda, quarter-hour or hundredth-hour?

3-2A.
LO 3-2

Justin is a salaried exempt worker with a contract that stipulates 40 hours per week at $60,000 per year. This week there was a company paid holiday for two days. Calculate Justin's pay:

Regular pay: _____

Holiday pay: _____

Gross pay: _____

3-3A.
LO 3-2

Tessa completed 17 pieces on her 15-piece contract for the company. There is a bonus earned if the individual exceeds 2% of their piece contract. How many pieces must Tessa complete in the remainder of the week to receive the bonus?

3-4A.
LO 3-4

Aaron is a shared employee: He works in the manufacturing department and has been trained to work the sales counter in times of need. During other employees' vacations, he was asked to work in the sales department two days for six hours each day. When he works in the manufacturing department, he earns $11.50 per hour. Aaron earns a $2.50 pay differential for working the sales counter. He worked a total of 39.58 hours during the week.

Compute:

Aaron's regular pay for the manufacturing department _____

Aaron's regular pay for the sales department _____

3-5A.
LO 3-3

Enrique submitted a pay card reflecting the following hours. He earns $13.98 per hour. Compute his pay under both the hundredth-hour and quarter-hour systems. The company pays overtime only on hours worked exceeding 40 per week.

In	Out	In	Out	Total Hours with Hundredth-Hour	Total Hours with Quarter-Hour
8:00	11:22	12:17	5:22		
7:29	12:30	1:45	4:10		
9:12	11:45	12:28	3:36		
8:00	11:00	12:02	5:00		

Enrique's total pay in a hundredth-hour system: _____

Enrique's total pay in a quarter-hour system: _____

3-6A.
LO 3-4
Daniel is paid $10 per hour and receives commission on net sales. He does not receive commission until his net sales exceed $150,000. Once the minimum sales volume is reached, he receives 2% commission on all of his sales at Carl's Canopies. This week he sold $163,000 of canopies; however, he had $1,500 of returns from last week's sales. Company policy requires he return commissions on sale returns. What is his gross pay for the week?

Daniel's regular pay for 40 hours _____

Commission for $163,000 of sales _____

Less: returned commission for $1,500 sales returns _____

Gross pay _____

3-7A.
LO 3-1, 3-2
Cathy, an outside sales representative for a magazine company, receives 10% commission on all new subscriptions she receives in her sales territory. This week she sold $5,000 of new subscriptions and worked 40 hours.

What is her gross pay? _____

Is she subject to minimum-wage laws? _____

Why or why not? _____

3-8A.
LO 3-1, 3-2
Telemarketers receive $15 commission on all new customers they sign up for phone service through Birch Phones. Each telemarketer works 40 hours. The company ran a competition this week to see who could sign up the most new people and the winner would get a bonus of $50. Because these employees are paid solely on commission, the employer must ensure that they earn the federal minimum wage for 40 hours each week. Compute the gross pay for each of the following outbound sales representatives.

Employee	Number of New Customers Signed	Total Commission	Difference between Commission and Minimum Pay	Total Gross Pay
Kenny	22			
Charles	18			
Laurie	29			
Phyllis	16			

3-9A.
LO 3-1, 3-2
For each of the piece-rate workers below, determine gross pay. If the employees have a standard 40-hour workweek, what is their affected hourly wage (Reminder: gross pay divided by 40 hours equals hourly wage)? Based on the FLSA minimum wage, calculate each employee's minimum weekly pay. What is the difference the employer must pay between their calculated gross pay and the calculated FLSA minimum pay?

Worker	Number of Items	Rate per Item	Gross Pay	Gross Pay/ 40 Hours	Minimum Pay	Difference to Be Paid by the Employer
Mark	25 hulls	$10				
Richie	70 seat covers	$15				
Tony	45 steering mechanisms	$ 4				

3-10A.
LO 3-1, 3-2
Rick is a waiter at Palace Eats in Delaware. He receives the standard tipped hourly wage. During a 40-hour week, he received $160 in tips. Calculate the following:

Rick's wages for the week (hourly rate × hours) _____

Rick's gross pay (wages + tips) _____

Minimum wage for Delaware (minimum-wage rate × 40 hours) _____

How much does Palace Eats need to contribute to Rick's wages to meet FLSA requirements? _____

3-11A.
LO 3-4

Grace is a salaried, nonexempt administrator for her company and is paid biweekly. Her annual salary is $48,000, and her standard work-week is 35 hours. During a pay period, she worked 8 hours overtime.

What is her regular wage for the pay period? _____

What are her overtime earnings? _____

What is her gross pay? _____

3-12A.
LO 3-5

Nadine is an administrative assistant for her employer. At the end of her shift one day, her employer requires her to deliver a package to a customer before traveling home. She spends two hours driving to the customer site, and then three hours driving home. How much of Nadine's travel time is compensable?

3-13A.
LO 3-5

Colin is an 18-year-old worker in the receiving department of a company. On his first paycheck, he notices that he received $170.00 gross pay for 40 hours of work. Did his employer pay him correctly? Explain.

Exercises Set B

3-1B.
LO 3-3

Nick B. worked the following schedule: Monday, 8 hours, 24 minutes; Tuesday, 7 hours, 44 minutes; Wednesday, 9 hours, 8 minutes; Thursday, 8 hours, 2 minutes; Friday, 8 hours, 36 minutes. The employer pays overtime for all time worked in excess of 40 hours per week. Compute the following:

	Total Time	Regular Time	Overtime	Quarter-Hour Time	Hundredth-Hour Time
Nick B.					

Which pay is more favorable for Nick, quarter-hour or hundredth-hour?

3-2B.
LO 3-2

Shawn is a salaried exempt worker with a contract that stipulates 37.5 hours per week at $75,000 per year. This pay period there was a company-paid holiday for three days. Calculate Shawn's biweekly pay (Hint: Determine how many hours Shawn is required to work per day to determine holiday pay, assume five-day workweeks.)

Regular pay: _____

Holiday pay: _____

Gross pay: _____

3-3B.
LO 3-2

Janet completed 1,200 pieces on her 1,400-piece contract for the company. There is a bonus earned if the individual exceeds 15% of their piece contract. How many pieces must Janet complete in the remainder of the week to receive the bonus?

3-4B.
LO 3-4

Paris is a shared employee: She works in the accounting department and has been trained to work at the front desk in times of need. During other employees' vacations, she was asked to work at the front desk four days for five hours each day. When she works in the accounting department, she earns $13.62 per hour. Paris earns $12.98/hour for working at the front desk. She worked a total of 38.75 hours during the week.

Compute:

Paris's regular pay for the accounting department _____

Paris's regular pay for the front desk _____

3-5B.

LO 3-3

Jasper submitted a pay card reflecting the following hours. He earns $16.45 per hour. Compute his pay under both the hundredth-hour and quarter-hour systems. There is no overtime in the calculations.

In	Out	In	Out	Total Hours with Hundredth-Hour	Total Hours with Quarter-Hour
8:08	11:57	12:59	4:57		
9:04	12:17	1:28	5:18		
7:45	11:45	12:43	4:01		
7:57	12:04	1:03	5:06		

Jasper's total pay in the hundredth-hour system _____

Jasper's total pay in a quarter-hour system _____

3-6B.

LO 3-4

Priscilla is paid $16.50 per hour and receives commission on net sales. She does not receive commissions until her net sales exceed $5,500 during a weekly period at TLA Medicinals. Once the minimum sales volume is reached, she receives 4% commission on all of her sales. This week she sold $6,700 of medicinals, but had $900 of returns from last week's sales. Company policy requires that she return commissions on sale returns. What is her gross pay for the week?

Priscilla's regular pay for 40 hours _____

Commission for $6,700 of sales _____

Less: Returned commission for $900 of sales returns _____

Gross pay _____

3-7B.

LO 3-1, 3-2

Mareka, an outside sales representative for an insurance company, receives 3% commission on all new policies she receives in her sales territory. This week she sold $150,000 of new policies and worked 40 hours.

What is her gross pay? _____

Is she subject to minimum-wage laws? _____

Why or why not? _____

3-8B.

LO 3-1, 3-2

Outbound sales representatives receive a $20 commission on all new customers they sign up for new magazine subscriptions. Each outbound sales representative works 40 hours. During a weekly competition, the outbound sales representative who sold the most subscriptions was awarded a $125 bonus. Because these employees are paid solely on commission, the employer must ensure that they earn the federal minimum wage for 40 hours each week. Compute the gross pay for each of the following outbound sales representatives.

Employee	Number of New Customers Signed	Total Commission	Difference between Commission and Minimum Pay	Total Gross Pay
Angela	35			
Catherine	22			
Tom	42			
Frank	29			

3-9B.

LO 3-1, 3-2

For each of the piece-rate workers below, determine gross pay. If the employees have a standard 37.5-hour workweek, what is their effective hourly rate (the gross pay/37.5 hours)? Based on FLSA minimum wages, what is the minimum wage they must receive each week? If they are not receiving the FLSA minimum wage for the pay period, what is the difference that must be paid by the employer? If not, what is the difference between gross pay and minimum that the employer must pay?

Worker	Number of Items	Rate per Item	Gross Pay	Gross Pay/ 37.5 Hours	Minimum Pay	Difference to Be Paid by the Employer
Brenda	25 snowboards	$9				
Mike	30 helmets	$7.75				
Bruce	80 bindings	$4.50				

3-10B.

LO 3-1, 3-2

Maddie is a waitress at Quick Lunch in Vermont. She receives the standard tipped hourly wage. During a 40-hour week, she received $105 in tips. Calculate the following:

Maddie's wages for the week (hourly rate × hours) _____

Maddie's gross pay (wages + tips) _____

Minimum wage for Vermont (minimum-wage rate × 40 hours)

_____

How much does Quick Lunch need to contribute to Maddie's wages to meet FLSA requirements? _____

3-11B.

LO 3-4

Eric is a salaried, nonexempt accountant for his company and is paid semi-monthly. His annual salary is $39,000, and his standard workweek is 37.5 hours. During a pay period, he worked 10 hours overtime.

What is his regular wage for the pay period? _____

What are his overtime earnings? _____

What is his gross pay? _____

3-12B.

LO 3-5

Marshawn is a sales assistant whose normal commute time is 30 minutes in each direction. At the beginning of his shift one day, his employer requires him to pick up a package from a customer before arriving at work. He spends 1 hour driving to the customer site, and then 1.5 hours driving to the office. How much of Marshawn's travel time is compensable?

3-13B.

LO 3-5

Olivia is a 19-year-old accounting clerk. During the first month of her employment with a firm, she noticed that she received $369.75 for her first semi-monthly pay covering 87 regular hours. Did the employer pay her correctly? Explain.

Critical Thinking

3-1. West Virginia State University has a policy of hiring students to work in its bookstores and cafeterias. Assuming that 138 students work for the university at minimum wage rates, what is the amount of pay they will receive for a biweekly pay period, assuming they each work 30 hours per week?

3-2. Daniel owns Veiled Wonders, a firm that makes window treatments. Some merchandise is custom-made to customer specifications, and some is mass-produced in standardized measurements. He has production workers who work primarily on standardized blinds and some employees who additionally work on custom products on an as-needed basis. How should he structure his pay methods for his production workers?

In the Real World: Scenario for Discussion

Motor vehicle service technicians usually must provide their own tools as part of their employment. These tools are the property of the technician, and service technicians generally receive an hourly wage. Some automobile dealerships split service technician wages into classifications such as tool reimbursements and wages.

The result of this practice is that the worker's hours are taxed and the tool reimbursements are not because they are classified as a business expense.

Should the tool reimbursement be treated as income on the service technician's W-2? Why or why not? What are some implications of this practice?

Internet Activities

3-1. Using a search engine such as Google, Yahoo, or Bing, search "Commission-based pay." Sites such as the Society for Human Resource Management (www.shrm.com) have a large volume of articles about commission-based pay and workplace cases. Choose a case and find out as much as you can about the company involved. Why do you think that commission-based pay is such a popular topic among human resource professionals?

3-2. Go to www.accountingtools.com/podcasts and look for payroll-related podcasts. Once you have listened to one or more podcasts, what do you feel was the most interesting information you learned?

3-3. Want to learn more about the concepts in this chapter? Check out:

> www.dol.gov/whd/minwage/america.htm
>
> www.flsa.com/coverage.html
>
> www.finance.ohiou.edu/financials/100thHourTable.htm
>
> www.fairmark.com/execcomp/iso.htm

Continuing Payroll Project: Prevosti Farms and Sugarhouse

February 16 is the first pay date for Prevosti Farms and Sugarhouse and includes work completed during the week of February 9–13. Compute the employee gross pay, using 35 hours as the standard workweek for all employees except Mary Shangraw who works 20 hours per week and receives overtime for any time worked past that point. The other hourly employees receive overtime pay when they work more than 35 hours in one week. Joel Schwartz has made $5,000 in case sales at a 3% commission rate during this pay period. Remember that the employees are paid biweekly. The first day of work for Prevosti Farms and Sugarhouse for all employees is February 9, 2015. Note that the first pay period comprises only one week of work, but the pay frequency for Federal income tax purposes is biweekly.

The hours for the nonexempt employees are as follows:

Name	Hourly Rate	Hours Worked 2/9–2/13	Regular Time Pay	Overtime Pay	Gross Pay
Towle	$12.00	35 hours			
Long	$12.50	40 hours			
Shangraw	$10.50	21 hours			
Success (You)	$34,000/year	35 hours			

Update the Employee Earning record for the period's pay and the new YTD amount. Pay will be disbursed on February 16, 2015.

February 27, 2015, is the end of the final pay period for the month. Compute the employee gross pay and update the Employee Earning Record with the February 27 pay and the new YTD amount. Schwartz has sold $7,500 of product during this pay period at a 3% commission. Pay will be disbursed on March 2, 2015.

The hours for the nonexempt employees are as follows:

Name	Hourly Rate	Hours Worked 2/14–2/27	Regular Time Pay	Overtime Pay	Gross Pay
Towle	$12.00	80 hours			
Long	$12.50	70 hours			
Shangraw	$10.50	42 hours			
Success (You)	$34,000/year	71 hours			

Answers to Stop & Check Exercises

Pay Your Employees Correctly

1. No. Heather should have received time-and-a-half for the additional 8 hours. Her pay should have been $667.00 ((80 × 7.25) + (8 × 1.5 × 7.25))
2. $345.63 (39.5 × 8.75)
3. $512.00 (32 × 2 × 8.00)

Pay Computations for Different Bases

1. Ann:
   Quarter-hour: 8.25 hours
   Hundredth-hour: 7.93 hours
   Nevada:
   Quarter-hour: 8 hours
   Hundredth-hour: 8.12 hours

   Pat:
   Quarter-hour: 8 hours
   Hundredth-hour: 7.82 hours

2. The difference exists because the time worked during a quarter-hour system is rounded to the nearest quarter hour. In a hundredth-hour system, the worker is paid for the exact number of minutes worked.

3. It would be beneficial to adopt a hundredth-hour system to reduce payroll inaccuracies that may affect both employees and company profits.

Combination Pay Methods

1. Base pay = $42,000 ÷ 24 = $1,750
   Commission = $100 × 5 = $500
   Gross pay = $2,250
2. $36,000 ÷ 12 = $3,000 per month
   $3,000 × 0.35 = $1,050 mid-month draw
   $3,000 − $1,050 draw = $1,950 received at the end of the month
3. $75,000 × 0.03 = $2,250 received in stock.
   Annual compensation = $75,000 + $2,250 = $77,250

What Is the Correct Pay?

1. 15 hours because comp time must be awarded at 1.5 times regular hours.
2. $5.44 per hour ($7.25 × 75%)

Chapter 4

Employee Net Pay and Pay Methods

Death and taxes are the two certainties in life. Taxes are withheld from the employees' earnings and remitted to the governing body. Companies operate as the collector and depositor of income taxes, garnishments, and other deductions on behalf of the employee. The tax code permits certain qualifying deductions to be taken out of an employee's pay prior to the income taxes being calculated. These deductions are called pre-tax deductions. Other deductions come out of the employee's pay after income taxes have been calculated; these are called post-tax deductions. Circular E, also known as Publication 15 (and all supplemental materials), from the Internal Revenue Service provides a comprehensive list of employee taxes, employer responsibilities, and guidance for special situations.

The pre-tax deductions reduce the current taxable income of the employee and may be taxed at a later time; for example, contributions to a qualifying retirement program would be a pre-tax deduction. Some pre-tax deductions will not be taxed later. The IRS refers to these pre-tax items as *fringe benefits* and clearly differentiates between taxable and nontaxable fringe benefits.

LEARNING OBJECTIVES

After studying Chapter 4, you should be able to:

LO 4-1   Identify Pre-Tax Deductions

LO 4-2   Determine Federal Income Tax Withholding Amounts

LO 4-3   Compute Social Security and Medicare Tax Withholding

LO 4-4   Apply State and Local Income Taxes

LO 4-5   Explain Post-Tax Deductions

LO 4-6   Analyze Employee Net Pay

LO 4-7   Discuss Employee Pay Methods

© Ryan McVay/Photodisc/Getty Images, RF

The Pros and Cons of Paycards

Payroll debit cards or "paycards" are used widely by employers. More than 26 million paycards are issued annually, containing nearly $150 billion in employee compensation. Paycards offer employees instant access to their funds and do not require them to maintain a bank account. They also facilitate secure payments to certain types of workers who earn daily cash wages by offering a secure method of tracking and disbursing pay.

Nearly 30% of all paycards issued do not contain access to an ATM network, forcing the employee to incur fees to access their wages. The bank-related fees for transactions and other restrictions related to paycard use have prompted legislative proposals in many states. Proposed legislation includes a seven-day period during which an employee may elect to have direct deposit to a bank account instead of the paycard, fee disclosure regulations, and prohibitions on employers requiring employees to accept paycards as part of their employment. (Sources: APA, 24/7WallSt)

The convenience and low cost of paycards are balanced by the need for increased vigilance and disclosure about employee fees to access their wages. In Chapter 4, we will explore computations of employee net pay and the methods used to transmit that pay to the employees.

Deductions from Gross Pay

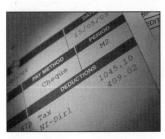

© Powered by Light RF/Alamy R/ Alamy, RF

An employer deducts mandatory and voluntary deductions from an employee's gross pay. These deductions include federal income tax, Medicare, and Social Security taxes which are the primary mandatory deductions. Other mandatory deductions that the employee may be subject to include *state income taxes*, city or county income taxes, and regional taxes. For example, Denver has a "head tax" for those employees working within the city and county. Federal Unemployment Tax is the single purely employer-only tax. Some states require employees to contribute for the State Unemployment Tax, whereas other states consider it an employer-only tax.

Another class of amounts withheld from employee pay are voluntary deductions. Employees may choose to contribute to retirement programs, additional health or life insurance, or medical insurance through amounts withheld from their pay. Some of these voluntary deductions are pre-tax deductions and some are post-tax deductions.

A third class of deductions are mandated deductions, which are required by court order. These include child support or student loan repayment. These items are post-tax deductions and are subject to minimal income requirements typically stipulated within the court order. Employers are provided documentation by the state regulatory office responsible for the redistribution of the withheld amounts to the appropriate parties. Union employees are also required to pay union dues out of each payroll in a mandated deduction.

LO 4-1   Identify Pre-Tax Deductions

Two classes of deductions exist: pre-tax and post-tax. Pre-tax deductions are those deductions that are withheld from an employee's *gross pay*, which is the amount of compensation prior to computing any tax liability or applying any deductions. The effect of pre-tax deductions is that they reduce the taxable income of the employee. Pre-tax deductions are *voluntary deductions* that have been mandated by the federal government as eligible for pre-tax withholding status, including certain types of insurance, retirement plans, and cafeteria plans.

Insurance

Employers may provide subsidized health insurance coverage for their employees. The employees pay a portion of these health insurance expenses out of their paycheck and the company makes up the difference. How much a company pays is determined by the company and could vary greatly, depending on the costs of health insurance and the policy selected by the employee. For health insurance policies to qualify for pre-tax status, they must meet the IRS Code for a qualified cafeteria program.

In 2010, the Affordable Care Act was passed, providing small businesses a tax credit when their employees are at low- and moderate-income levels for providing health insurance coverage. The act extended coverage of children until the age of 27 to be included as an option to employees on a pre-tax basis. This is only for employees covered under a qualifying cafeteria plan. IRS Code 6056 changed the reporting requirements for health insurance programs provided to employees. Employers with more than 50 employees are required to file an information return with the IRS and must provide a detailed summary of health coverage to employees. The value of the insurance coverage contributed by the employer must be reported on the employee's W-2 year-end tax statement within box 12 using code DD, and should reflect the amounts contributed by both the employee and the employer. It is important to remember that the amounts reported for the employer's contribution to health insurance do not add to the taxable wages of the employee.

According to the Internal Revenue Service, the Affordable Care Act mandates that individuals must have "minimum essential coverage." Examples of minimum essential coverage include:

- Employer-provided health insurance
- Health insurance purchased through an approved health insurance exchange
- Coverage provided under federal auspices such as Medicare and Medicaid
- Privately purchased health insurance

Minimum essential coverage does not include the following limited benefit or limited term coverage plans:

- Vision and dental insurance issued on a standalone basis (i.e., not grouped with a medical insurance policy)
- Worker's compensation insurance
- Accidental death and disability plans maintained by the employer

(Source: IRS)

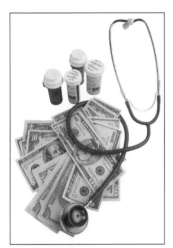

© Comstock Images/Jupiter Images, RF

© Jim Arbogast/Digital Vision/Getty Images, RF

Supplemental Health and Disability Insurance

Another option many employers are offering is a flow-through (i.e., the company does not cover any of the costs) of supplemental health and disability insurance. One of the largest providers of this type of insurance is American Family Life Assurance Company of Columbus (AFLAC). There are a variety of policies under AFLAC with separate treatment for taxation purposes (whether pre- or post-tax). The IRS Revision Ruling 2004-55 dealt specifically with the tax treatment of short- and long-term disability, and IRS Code Sections 104(a)(3) and 105(a) deal with the exclusion of short- and long-term disability benefits from employees' gross wages. Long-term disability is excluded from taxable income under the ruling. If an employer pays for long-term disability, these amounts may be excluded from or included in gross pay, depending upon the election of the company. When determining the tax treatment for the supplemental health insurance, the IRS guidance provides the following: If the income derived will be estimated to be tax-free, then the cost associated will also be tax-exempt. Note: These are not tax-exempt for Social Security and Medicare taxes.

Retirement Plans

Retirement plans were covered under the Employee Retirement Income Security Act (ERISA) of 1974 in conjunction with the Internal Revenue Code. There are two basic types of retirement plans: *defined benefit* and *defined contribution*. In a defined benefit plan, the employer guarantees the employee a specific level of income once retirement has been reached. As an example, under a defined benefit plan, the employer may guarantee 1% of average salary earned in the final five years of employment.

In a defined contribution plan, the individual places money from his or her payroll, pre-tax, into a retirement plan and the company may or may not match to a percentage. There are several different types of defined contribution plans such as *401(k)*, *SIMPLE 401(k)*, *403(b)*, *IRA*, *SIMPLE IRA*, *SEP*, *ESOP*, and profit sharing. Note: These are not tax-exempt from Social Security and Medicare taxes. See Table 4.1 for an explanation of Retirement Plan Types.

Cafeteria Plans

Cafeteria plans, also known as health plans or Section 125 plans, are offered by the employer and are usually pre-tax deductions. A cafeteria plan is health insurance coverage that allows employees to make selections from a variety of tax-free, cash, and taxable benefits options. There are many different varieties of health plans. One type of health plan includes a *Health Savings Account (HSA)* that can be used to pay long-term care costs. Another benefit that can be included in the cafeteria plan is a *Flexible Spending Account (FSA)*. FSAs are available to assist in the payment of medical expenses,

TABLE 4-1
Retirement Plan Types

Type of Plan	Description
401(k)	A group of investments, typically invested in stock mark–based or mutual fun–based plans
403(b)	Similar to a 401(k), but offered by nonprofit employers such as hospitals and schools
Savings Incentive Match Plan for Employees (SIMPLE)	The major limitation is employers may not have more than 100 employees. Funds are specifically set aside for the individual employee in a bank, mutual fund account, or into a stock market SIMPLE 401(k)
Individual Retirement Account (IRA)	Funds are specifically set aside for the individual employee in a bank or mutual fund account.
Employee Stock Ownership Plan (ESOP)	The company offers employees the ability to earn company stock for the duration of their employment.
Simplified Employee Pension (SEP)	A tax-favorable IRA is set up by or for the employee and the employer contributes the funds into the account. The SEP is tax-favorable because it reduces the employee's income tax liability.

including copayments and prescriptions, transportation, and certain child-care expenses. Not all HSAs can be considered tax-exempt. Only those included as part of the company's qualifying Section 125 cafeteria plan are deemed exempt from Social Security, Medicare, and federal income taxes.

Although several items are included in the health insurance cafeteria plan, there are also several items that cannot be included in the company's cafeteria plan per IRS regulations. Examples of non-allowed deductions are employee tuition assistance, employee discounts, meals, moving expenses, and transportation benefits (for a full list, view IRS Publication 15B).

What Counts as Pre-Taxable?

STOP & CHECK

1. What are some examples of pre-tax deductions?
2. Which act offered a small-business tax credit for employees' health insurance premiums?
3. What are examples of different retirement plans that qualify as pre-tax withdrawals?

LO 4-2 Determine Federal Income Tax Withholding Amounts

Now let us shift our focus to *mandatory deductions* that must be withheld from employee pay. The first class of mandatory deductions is the federal income tax. This is an employee-only tax, meaning that the employer does not contribute a matching amount for the federal income tax withheld from an employee's pay.

Federal Income Taxes

The first tax we will cover is the federal income tax. The federal income tax amounts to be withheld are calculated using the information reported by the employee on form W-4. The withheld tax is the employee's deposit against income taxes. The employee's federal income tax is determined by four factors:

- Gross pay
- Pay frequency (weekly, biweekly, semi-monthly, etc.)
- Marital status
- Number of withholding allowances claimed on Form W-4

The highest taxed federal income tax bracket is single with zero dependents. Employees who work more than one job or have additional income for which no income tax is withheld may request additional amounts as either percentages or dollars to be withheld and submitted to the IRS on their behalf. The employee makes these requests on form W-4.

The employer acts as a collector and depositor for these funds. When an individual files the income tax return, the amounts withheld from his or her pay during the year reduces the amount he or she may have to pay with the return. Federal taxable income is reduced by pre-tax deductions discussed previously.

Examples:

Amanda's gross wages are $950, she has subscribed to the company's cafeteria plan, and she has agreed to a 10% investment of her gross wages to a qualified 401(k) plan. Her portion of the health insurance is $56.90 per pay period. To calculate her taxable pay we must first determine the 401(k) deduction: $950 × 10% for $95. Therefore, her taxable pay is:

$950.00	gross pay
−95.00	401(k) deduction
−56.90	health insurance
$ 798.10	Taxable income

Daniel has gross wages of $1,125, participates in the company's 401(k) program at $100 per pay period, has health insurance and AFLAC (all pre-tax) totaling $113.80. The calculation of Daniel's taxable income is:

$1,125.00	gross pay
−100.00	401(k) deduction
−113.80	health insurance and AFLAC
$ 911.20	Taxable income

Had Daniel participated in the company's 401(k) as a percentage instead of a fixed dollar, the percent would be calculated prior to other deductions. For instance, if he elected to invest 3% of his gross pay, his taxable income is:

$1,125.00	
× 0.03	
33.75	401(k) contribution

$1,125.00	gross pay
−33.75	401(k) contribution
−113.80	health insurance and AFLAC
$ 977.45	Taxable income

Regardless of the method used for calculating federal income taxes, the reduction for pre-tax items will remain the same. In manual systems, there are two commonly used methods to calculate the employee's federal income tax: wage-bracket and percentage.

Wage-Bracket Method

Using the wage-bracket method, the payroll clerk identifies the individual's marital status, number of exemptions, and taxable income level, and then follows the chart located in Publication 15 for the amount to be withheld. If manually calculating the wage-bracket method, it is important to apply the appropriate withholdings prior to calculating the tax amounts. The wage-bracket method may be programmed into an automated payroll system. The wage-bracket method is useful for manual payroll preparation because the process of federal tax withholding is an estimate for the year-end amount of taxes due. Figure 4-1 contains an example of the wage-bracket table that Publication 15 contains.

To determine taxes to withhold using the *wage-bracket method*, see Figure 4-1, which is for married persons who are paid on a biweekly basis. A single person with three

FIGURE 4-1

Biweekly Payroll Period–Married Persons, Wage-Bracket Method

Example:

Employee A is Married and has three withholding allowances. The employee is paid biweekly and earned $1,639. What is the Federal income tax for Employee A?

Wage Bracket Method Tables for Income Tax Withholding

MARRIED Persons – BIWEEKLY Payroll Period

(For Wages Paid through December 31, 2015)

And the wages are–		And the number of withholding allowances claimed is—										
At least	But less than	0	1	2	3	4	5	6	7	8	9	10
		The amount of income tax to be withheld is—										
$1,500	$1,520	$141	$118	$95	$72	$56	$41	$26	$10	$0	$0	$0
1,520	1,540	144	121	98	75	58	43	28	12	0	0	0
1,540	1,560	147	124	101	78	60	45	30	14	0	0	0
1,560	1,580	150	127	104	81	62	47	32	16	1	0	0
1,580	1,600	153	130	107	84	64	49	34	18	3	0	0
1,600	1,620	156	133	110	87	66	51	36	20	5	0	0
1,620	1,640	159	136	113	90	68	53	38	22	7	0	0
1,640	1,660	162	139	116	93	70	55	40	24	9	0	0
1,660	1,680	165	142	119	96	73	57	42	26	11	0	0
1,680	1,700	168	145	122	99	76	59	44	28	13	0	0
1,700	1,720	171	148	125	102	79	61	46	30	15	0	0
1,720	1,740	174	151	128	105	82	63	48	32	17	1	0
1,740	1,760	177	154	131	108	85	65	50	34	19	3	0
1,760	1,780	180	157	134	111	88	67	52	36	21	5	0
1,780	1,800	183	160	137	114	91	69	54	38	23	7	0

Important facts:

- The employee is Married.
- Has 3 withholding allowances
- Pay frequency is biweekly.
- Earned $1,639

The page of the table is for **Married** employees with **biweekly** pay.

Go to the row that contains the bracket containing the employee's pay. In this example, the pay is $1,639, which is in the **$1,620–1,640** row.

Go to the column that contains the number of withholding allowances. In this case, the employee has **three** withholding allowances.

The intersection of the **row and column of the table is the **withholding tax,** which is **$90.***

withholding allowances and with $1,639 in biweekly earnings will have $90 of federal income tax withheld. Note that the amount of tax withheld decreases as the number of withholding allowances increases.

The process of using wage-bracket tables for employees' claiming single status is similar. Figure 4-2 is a sample of the wage-bracket table for a single person with semi-monthly wages.

Using the table in Figure 4-2, a single person earning a semi-monthly wage of $1,188 with one withholding allowance will have a federal income tax of $120.

Percentage Method

There are many tables in Publication 15 from the IRS to assist employers with the correct amount of withholding given the variety of pay period, marital status, and exemption

FIGURE 4-2
Semi-Monthly Payroll Period–Single Persons

Employee B is Single and has one withholding allowance. The employee is paid semimonthly and earned $1,188. What is the Federal income tax for Employee B?

Wage Bracket Method Tables for Income Tax Withholding

SINGLE Persons—SEMIMONTHLY Payroll Period

(For Wages Paid through December 31, 2015)

And the wages are—		And the number of withholding allowances claimed is—										
At least	But less than	0	1	2	3	4	5	6	7	8	9	10
		The amount of income tax to be withheld is—										
$800	$820	$88	$63	$38	$21	$5	$0	$0	$0	$0	$0	$0
820	840	91	66	41	23	7	0	0	0	0	0	0
840	860	94	69	44	25	9	0	0	0	0	0	0
860	880	97	72	47	27	11	0	0	0	0	0	0
880	900	100	75	50	29	13	0	0	0	0	0	0
900	920	103	78	53	31	15	0	0	0	0	0	0
920	940	106	81	56	33	17	0	0	0	0	0	0
940	960	109	84	59	35	19	2	0	0	0	0	0
960	980	112	87	62	37	21	4	0	0	0	0	0
980	1,000	115	90	65	40	23	6	0	0	0	0	0
1,000	1,020	118	93	68	43	25	8	0	0	0	0	0
1,020	1,040	121	96	71	46	27	10	0	0	0	0	0
1,040	1,060	124	99	74	49	29	12	0	0	0	0	0
1,060	1,080	127	102	77	52	31	14	0	0	0	0	0
1,080	1,100	130	105	80	55	33	16	0	0	0	0	0
1,100	1,120	133	108	83	58	35	18	1	0	0	0	0
1,120	1,140	136	111	86	61	37	20	3	0	0	0	0
1,140	1,160	139	114	89	64	39	22	5	0	0	0	0
1,160	1,180	142	117	92	67	42	24	7	0	0	0	0
1,180	1,200	145	120	95	70	45	26	9	0	0	0	0
1,200	1,220	148	123	98	73	48	28	11	0	0	0	0
1,220	1,240	151	126	101	76	51	30	13	0	0	0	0
1,240	1,260	154	129	104	79	54	32	15	0	0	0	0

Important facts:

- The employee is Single.
- Has 1 withholding allowance
- Pay frequency is semimonthly.
- Earned $1,188

The page of the table is for **Single** employees with **semimonthly** pay.

Go to the row that contains the bracket containing the employee's pay. In this example, the pay is $1,188, which is in the **$1,180–1,200** row.

Go to the column that contains the number of withholding allowances. In this case, the employee has **one** withholding allowance.

The intersection of the **row and column of the table is the **withholding tax,** which is **$120.****

options that can be available. The *percentage method* for calculating employee withholding is tiered, with each layer building upon the previous layer. The table for the amounts for one withholding allowance using the percentage method is contained in Figure 4-3. Note that if the employee has more than one withholding allowance, the amount in the table

FIGURE 4-3
Percentage Method for One
Withholding Allowance—2015

Payroll Period	One Withholding Allowance
Weekly	$ 76.90
Biweekly	153.80
Semimonthly	166.70
Monthly	333.30
Quarterly	1,000.00
Semiannually	2,000.00
Annually	4,000.00
Daily or miscellaneous (each day of the payroll period)	15.40

should be multiplied by the number of withholding allowances claimed on the employee's Form W-4.

When using the percentage method, the deduction for each withholding allowance is subtracted prior to computing the taxes. Note that the wage-bracket and percentage methods will yield similar results as to income tax withholding; the percentage method shown in Figure 4-4 allows more flexibility for calculations involving high-wage earners or uncommon pay periods.

Using the percentage method tables can be confusing, so let's look at a step-by-step example.

How to calculate federal income tax using the percentage method: Caroline is single and claims two withholding allowances on her Form W-4. She is paid semi-monthly and earns $48,000 per year.

Step 1: Total wage payment	$48,000 ÷ 24 = $2,000
Step 2: One withholding allowance for semi-monthly pay (Figure 4-3)	$ 166.70
Step 3: Allowances claimed on W-4	2
Step 4: Multiply Step 2 by Step 3	$ 333.40
Step 5: Amount subject to withholding	$2,000 − 333.40 = $1,666.60
Step 6: See Table 3a in Figure 4-4 (Semi-monthly wages for single person). Look at the column labeled "of excess over" and choose line 3 "$1,656.00"	−$1,656.00
Step 7: Subtract Step 6 from Step 5	= $ 10.60
Step 8: Multiply Step 7 by 25% (from line 3 in Table 3a)	$10.60 × 0.25 = $ 2.65
Step 9: Add Step 8 plus $214.80 (from line 3 in Table 3a) to compute the Federal income tax to withhold	$2.65 + 214.80 = $ 217.45

The amount of federal income tax withholding may differ slightly between the wage-bracket and percentage methods. Going back to our married employee earning $1,639 biweekly, with three withholding allowances, using the percentage table, the taxes to be withheld will be calculated as follows: $1,639 (gross) − $461.40 (withholding allowances) = $1,177.60 taxable − $1,040 = $137.60 × 15% = $20.64 + $70.90 = $91.54 total tax (the wage-bracket method yielded a result of $90).

The single taxpayer earning $1,188 semi-monthly will move into the second tier of taxes, and therefore will have taxes calculated as $38.40 plus 15% of amounts exceeding $480. Calculated out: $1,188 − $166.70 = $1,021.30 − $480 = $541.30 × 15% = $81.20 + $38.40 = $119.60 (the wage-bracket method yielded a result of $120).

FIGURE 4-4
Percentage Method Tables for Income Tax

Percentage Method Tables for Income Tax Withholding

(For Wages Paid in 2015)

TABLE 1—WEEKLY Payroll Period

(a) SINGLE person (including head of household)—

If the amount of wages (after subtracting withholding allowances) is: The amount of income tax to withhold is:

Not over $44 . . . . $0

Over—	But not over—		of excess over—
$44	—$222 . .	$0.00 plus 10%	—$44
$222	—$764 . .	$17.80 plus 15%	—$222
$764	—$1,789 . .	$99.10 plus 25%	—$764
$1,789	—$3,685 . .	$355.35 plus 28%	—$1,789
$3,685	—$7,958 . .	$886.23 plus 33%	—$3,685
$7,958	—$7,990 . .	$2,296.32 plus 35%	—$7,958
$7,990	. . . .	$2,307.52 plus 39.6%	—$7,990

(b) MARRIED person—

If the amount of wages (after subtracting withholding allowances) is: The amount of income tax to withhold is:

Not over $165 . . . . $0

Over—	But not over—		of excess over—
$165	—$520 . .	$0.00 plus 10%	—$165
$520	—$1,606 . .	$35.50 plus 15%	—$520
$1,606	—$3,073 . .	$198.40 plus 25%	—$1,606
$3,073	—$4,597 . .	$565.15 plus 28%	—$3,073
$4,597	—$8,079 . .	$991.87 plus 33%	—$4,597
$8,079	—$9,105 . .	$2,140.93 plus 35%	—$8,079
$9,105	. . . .	$2,500.03 plus 39.6%	—$9,105

TABLE 2—BIWEEKLY Payroll Period

(a) SINGLE person (including head of household)—

If the amount of wages (after subtracting withholding allowances) is: The amount of income tax to withhold is:

Not over $88 . . . . $0

Over—	But not over—		of excess over—
$88	—$443 . .	$0.00 plus 10%	—$88
$443	—$1,529 . .	$35.50 plus 15%	—$443
$1,529	—$3,579 . .	$198.40 plus 25%	—$1,529
$3,579	—$7,369 . .	$710.90 plus 28%	—$3,579
$7,369	—$15,915 . .	$1,772.10 plus 33%	—$7,369
$15,915	—$15,981 . .	$4,592.28 plus 35%	—$15,915
$15,981	. . . .	$4,615.38 plus 39.6%	—$15,981

(b) MARRIED person—

If the amount of wages (after subtracting withholding allowances) is: The amount of income tax to withhold is:

Not over $331 . . . . $0

Over—	But not over—		of excess over—
$331	—$1,040 . .	$0.00 plus 10%	—$331
$1,040	—$3,212 . .	$70.90 plus 15%	—$1,040
$3,212	—$6,146 . .	$396.70 plus 25%	—$3,212
$6,146	—$9,194 . .	$1,130.20 plus 28%	—$6,146
$9,194	—$16,158 . .	$1,983.64 plus 33%	—$9,194
$16,158	—$18,210 . .	$4,281.76 plus 35%	—$16,158
$18,210	. . . .	$4,999.96 plus 39.6%	—$18,210

TABLE 3—SEMIMONTHLY Payroll Period

(a) SINGLE person (including head of household)—

If the amount of wages (after subtracting withholding allowances) is: The amount of income tax to withhold is:

Not over $96 . . . . $0

Over—	But not over—		of excess over—
$96	—$480 . .	$0.00 plus 10%	—$96
$480	—$1,656 . .	$38.40 plus 15%	—$480
$1,656	—$3,877 . .	$214.80 plus 25%	—$1,656
$3,877	—$7,983 . .	$770.05 plus 28%	—$3,877
$7,983	—$17,242 . .	$1,919.73 plus 33%	—$7,983
$17,242	—$17,313 . .	$4,975.20 plus 35%	—$17,242
$17,313	. . . .	$5,000.05 plus 39.6%	—$17,313

(b) MARRIED person—

If the amount of wages (after subtracting withholding allowances) is: The amount of income tax to withhold is:

Not over $358 . . . . $0

Over—	But not over—		of excess over—
$358	—$1,127 . .	$0.00 plus 10%	—$358
$1,127	—$3,479 . .	$76.90 plus 15%	—$1,127
$3,479	—$6,658 . .	$429.70 plus 25%	—$3,479
$6,658	—$9,960 . .	$1,224.45 plus 28%	—$6,658
$9,960	—$17,504 . .	$2,149.01 plus 33%	—$9,960
$17,504	—$19,727 . .	$4,638.53 plus 35%	—$17,504
$19,727	. . . .	$5,416.58 plus 39.6%	—$19,727

TABLE 4—MONTHLY Payroll Period

(a) SINGLE person (including head of household)—

If the amount of wages (after subtracting withholding allowances) is: The amount of income tax to withhold is:

Not over $192 . . . . $0

Over—	But not over—		of excess over—
$192	—$960 . .	$0.00 plus 10%	—$192
$960	—$3,313 . .	$76.80 plus 15%	—$960
$3,313	—$7,754 . .	$429.75 plus 25%	—$3,313
$7,754	—$15,967 . .	$1,540.00 plus 28%	—$7,754
$15,967	—$34,483 . .	$3,839.64 plus 33%	—$15,967
$34,483	—$34,625 . .	$9,949.92 plus 35%	—$34,483
$34,625	. . . .	$9,999.62 plus 39.6%	—$34,625

(b) MARRIED person—

If the amount of wages (after subtracting withholding allowances) is: The amount of income tax to withhold is:

Not over $717 . . . . $0

Over—	But not over—		of excess over—
$717	—$2,254 . .	$0.00 plus 10%	—$717
$2,254	—$6,958 . .	$153.70 plus 15%	—$2,254
$6,958	—$13,317 . .	$859.30 plus 25%	—$6,958
$13,317	—$19,921 . .	$2,449.05 plus 28%	—$13,317
$19,921	—$35,008 . .	$4,298.17 plus 33%	—$19,921
$35,008	—$39,454 . .	$9,276.88 plus 35%	—$35,008
$39,454	. . . .	$10,832.98 plus 39.6%	—$39,454

Percentage Method Tables for Income Tax Withholding (continued)

(For Wages Paid in 2015)

TABLE 5—QUARTERLY Payroll Period

(a) SINGLE person (including head of household)—

If the amount of wages (after subtracting withholding allowances) is:

Not over $575 . . . . $0

Over—	But not over—	The amount of income tax to withhold is:	of excess over—
$575	—$2,881	$0.00 plus 10%	—$575
$2,881	—$9,938	$230.60 plus 15%	—$2,881
$9,938	—$23,263	$1,289.15 plus 25%	—$9,938
$23,263	—$47,900	$4,620.40 plus 28%	—$23,263
$47,900	—$103,450	$11,518.76 plus 33%	—$47,900
$103,450	—$103,875	$29,850.26 plus 35%	—$103,450
$103,875	. . . .	$29,999.01 plus 39.6%	—$103,875

(b) MARRIED person—

If the amount of wages (after subtracting withholding allowances) is:

Not over $2,150 . . . . $0

Over—	But not over—	The amount of income tax to withhold is:	of excess over—
$2,150	—$6,763	$0.00 plus 10%	—$2,150
$6,763	—$20,875	$461.30 plus 15%	—$6,763
$20,875	—$39,950	$2,578.10 plus 25%	—$20,875
$39,950	—$59,763	$7,346.85 plus 28%	—$39,950
$59,763	—$105,025	$12,894.49 plus 33%	—$59,763
$105,025	—$118,363	$27,830.95 plus 35%	—$105,025
$118,363	. . . .	$32,499.25 plus 39.6%	—$118,363

TABLE 6—SEMIANNUAL Payroll Period

(a) SINGLE person (including head of household)—

Not over $1,150 . . . . $0

Over—	But not over—	The amount of income tax to withhold is:	of excess over—
$1,150	—$5,763	$0.00 plus 10%	—$1,150
$5,763	—$19,875	$461.30 plus 15%	—$5,763
$19,875	—$46,525	$2,578.10 plus 25%	—$19,875
$46,525	—$95,800	$9,240.60 plus 28%	—$46,525
$95,800	—$206,900	$23,037.60 plus 33%	—$95,800
$206,900	—$207,750	$59,700.60 plus 35%	—$206,900
$207,750	. . . .	$59,998.10 plus 39.6%	—$207,750

(b) MARRIED person—

Not over $4,300 . . . . $0

Over—	But not over—	The amount of income tax to withhold is:	of excess over—
$4,300	—$13,525	$0.00 plus 10%	—$4,300
$13,525	—$41,750	$922.50 plus 15%	—$13,525
$41,750	—$79,900	$5,156.25 plus 25%	—$41,750
$79,900	—$119,525	$14,693.75 plus 28%	—$79,900
$119,525	—$210,050	$25,788.75 plus 33%	—$119,525
$210,050	—$236,725	$55,662.00 plus 35%	—$210,050
$236,725	. . . .	$64,998.25 plus 39.6%	—$236,725

TABLE 7—ANNUAL Payroll Period

(a) SINGLE person (including head of household)—

Not over $2,300 . . . . $0

Over—	But not over—	The amount of income tax to withhold is:	of excess over—
$2,300	—$11,525	$0.00 plus 10%	—$2,300
$11,525	—$39,750	$922.50 plus 15%	—$11,525
$39,750	—$93,050	$5,156.25 plus 25%	—$39,750
$93,050	—$191,600	$18,481.25 plus 28%	—$93,050
$191,600	—$413,800	$46,075.25 plus 33%	—$191,600
$413,800	—$415,500	$119,401.25 plus 35%	—$413,800
$415,500	. . . .	$119,996.25 plus 39.6%	—$415,500

(b) MARRIED person—

Not over $8,600 . . . . $0

Over—	But not over—	The amount of income tax to withhold is:	of excess over—
$8,600	—$27,050	$0.00 plus 10%	—$8,600
$27,050	—$83,500	$1,845.00 plus 15%	—$27,050
$83,500	—$159,800	$10,312.50 plus 25%	—$83,500
$159,800	—$239,050	$29,387.50 plus 28%	—$159,800
$239,050	—$420,100	$51,577.50 plus 33%	—$239,050
$420,100	—$473,450	$111,324.00 plus 35%	—$420,100
$473,450	. . . .	$129,996.50 plus 39.6%	—$473,450

TABLE 8—DAILY or MISCELLANEOUS Payroll Period

(a) SINGLE person (including head of household)—

If the amount of wages (after subtracting withholding allowances) divided by the number of days in the payroll period is:

Not over $8.80 . . . . $0

Over—	But not over—	The amount of income tax to withhold per day is:	of excess over—
$8.80	—$44.30	$0.00 plus 10%	—$8.80
$44.30	—$152.90	$3.55 plus 15%	—$44.30
$152.90	—$357.90	$19.84 plus 25%	—$152.90
$357.90	—$736.90	$71.09 plus 28%	—$357.90
$736.90	—$1,591.50	$177.21 plus 33%	—$736.90
$1,591.50	—$1,598.10	$459.23 plus 35%	—$1,591.50
$1,598.10	. . . .	$461.54 plus 39.6%	—$1,598.10

(b) MARRIED person—

Not over $33.10 . . . . $0

Over—	But not over—	The amount of income tax to withhold per day is:	of excess over—
$33.10	—$104.00	$0.00 plus 10%	—$33.10
$104.00	—$321.20	$7.09 plus 15%	—$104.00
$321.20	—$614.60	$39.67 plus 25%	—$321.20
$614.60	—$919.40	$113.02 plus 28%	—$614.60
$919.40	—$1,615.80	$198.36 plus 33%	—$919.40
$1,615.80	—$1,821.00	$428.17 plus 35%	—$1,615.80
$1,821.00	. . . .	$499.99 plus 39.6%	—$1,821.00

Source: Internal Revenue Service.

How Much Tax to Withhold?

STOP & CHECK

1. Jennifer earns $52,000 annually. She is married with two allowances and is paid semi-monthly.

   Calculate the amount to be withheld using (a) the wage-bracket method and (b) the percentage method.

2. If Jennifer elected to deduct $100 per pay period for her 401(k), how much would that change the tax withheld from her paycheck? (Use the wage-bracket method.)

3. How much would Jennifer's Federal income tax be if her $75 health insurance and $55 AFLAC premiums were deducted each pay period pre-tax? (Use the wage-bracket method, independent of question 2.)

LO 4-3 Compute Social Security and Medicare Tax Withholding

The Social Security Act of 1935 mandated the withholding of certain taxes in addition to federal income tax. Two different taxes were part of the Social Security Act legislation: Social Security tax and Medicare tax. Employers collect only federal income taxes on employees without making a corresponding contribution. Social Security and Medicare, collectively known as FICA (Federal Insurance Contributions Act) taxes, contain both the employer's and employee's portion. When the employer deposits the federal withholding tax, they deposit the Social Security and Medicare amounts at the same time. The deposits are usually done online, but may be made by standard mail in certain circumstances. The report provided to the IRS does not provide a breakdown of tax amounts for individual employees.

Social Security Tax

Social Security tax, formerly known as OASDI, was designed to cover people for illness, retirement, disability, and old age. As a method of social insurance by which communities will help provide for people who are unable to work, Social Security has evolved into a tax that is levied upon all employees until their annual income reaches a specified level. The maximum income, known as the *wage base*, for the Social Security tax changes annually. In 2015, the amount is $118,500. The tax rate on employee pay is 6.2% of eligible wages. Remember that eligible wages can be different from gross pay because of pre-tax deductions and the wage base maximum.

Examples of Social Security Tax Computations

Employee	Period Wages	YTD Salary at End of Previous Pay Period	Social Security Tax Computation	Social Security Tax Amount to Be Withheld
1	$ 1,700	$ 55,600	$1,700 × 6.2%	$105.40
2	$ 2,850	$ 90,000	$2,850 × 6.2%	$176.70
3	$ 7,200	$112,600	$5,900 × 6.2%*	$365.80
4	$ 6,200	$118,000	$ 500 × 6.2%*	$31
5	$10,500	$195,000	$0**	$0

* The employee's wage base reaches the maximum during this pay period; thus, only the amount under the $117,000 is taxed for Social Security: $117,000 − $112,600 = $4,400 so only the $4,400 is taxed.
** The employee's wage base maximum was met prior to the current pay period, so no Social Security taxes are withheld.

The employee earnings record is especially important in computing and tracking the Social Security taxes due for each employee. Current records allow payroll accountants to keep track of annual salaries for each employee to avoid exceeding the maximum wage base, preventing excess deductions from employees' pay.

The employer and employee pay the same amount for the Social Security tax. Remember that the Social Security tax has a maximum withholding per year based on the employee's salary. After reaching that maximum, neither the employee nor the employer pay any more Social Security tax.

Medicare Tax

Medicare taxes differ from Social Security taxes in a couple of significant ways. *Medicare taxes* were levied on American employees to help provide basic health coverage for all people older than age 62. The Medicare tax amount for employee wages is 1.45% on all wages earned; there is no maximum wage base for Medicare taxes. The Affordable Care Act of 2010 levied an *additional Medicare tax* of 0.9% on workers with annual wages exceeding $200,000. This made the simple computations and tracking for Medicare taxes a little more challenging for payroll accountants and increased the need for accuracy on the employee earnings report. Note that the Medicare tax is levied only on the employees, so there is no employer match.

Examples of Medicare Tax Computations

Employee	Period Wages	YTD Salary at End of Previous Pay Period	Medicare Tax Computation	Total Medicare Tax Liability (Employee and Employer)
1	$ 1,700	$ 55,600	$1,700 × 1.45%	$ 24.65 × 2 = $49.30
2	$ 2,850	$ 90,000	$2,850 × 1.45%	$ 41.33 × 2 = $82.66
3	$ 7,200	$112,600	$7,200 × 1.45%	$104.40 × 2 = $208.80
4	$ 6,200	$118,000	$6,200 × 1.45%	$ 89.90 × 2 = $179.80
5	$10,500	$195,000	Employee: (10,500 × 0.145) + (5,500 × 0.009) = $201.75	Employee: $201.75 + Employer: $152.25 Total = $354.00

Remember that the applicable wages may have pre-tax deductions. Social Security and Medicare taxes apply to the employee's gross pay if an employee elects to have a 401(k) deduction. However, qualified Section 125 (cafeteria) plans are exempt from FICA taxes. When computing employee taxes, understanding the tax effect of the pre-tax deductions is important in computing accurate FICA deductions.

Maintaining accurate records of taxes withheld through payroll registers and employee earnings records is a critical part of calculating proper FICA tax deductions. Whether a company uses a manual system, an automated system, or outsources the payroll duties, it remains responsible for the accuracy of the deductions and maintenance of associated records.

FICA Taxes

1. Trent is an employee whose annual salary prior to the current pay period is $63,500. His current pay is $5,280. What amount must be withheld for Social Security tax? For Medicare tax?

2. For Trent's FICA taxes, what is the total tax liability including employee and employer share?

3. Sarah is the CEO of a company making $250,000 per year. Her year-to-date salary for the 19th pay period of the year was $197,916.73. She contributes 5% of her pay to her 401(k) and has a qualified Section 125 deduction of $75 per semi-monthly pay period.

   a. For the 20th pay period, what is her Social Security tax liability? Medicare tax liability?

   b. For the 21st pay period, what is her Medicare tax liability?

LO 4-4 Apply State and Local Income Taxes

Many states and localities apply taxes in addition to the federal income tax, Social Security, and Medicare. According to the IRS, all but nine states withhold income taxes. Those states are:

Alaska	Texas
Florida	Tennessee
Nevada	Washington
New Hampshire	Wyoming
South Dakota	

State-Specific Taxes

All other states (except the nine above) withhold income tax from their employees, and many apply other taxes as well. For instance, employees in the state of California have State Disability Insurance (SDI) of 0.9% of gross pay (up to a maximum wage of $104,378), in addition to the Personal Income Tax (PIT) that the state levies. Like federal income tax, California's PIT amounts vary by income level, pay frequency, and marital status. California, like many other states, offers both the wage-bracket and the percentage method of determining the PIT amount due. In contrast, Illinois charges a flat rate of 5% on all employees for its state withholding tax (see Appendix D for State Income Tax Information).

If a firm operates only in one state, deciphering state income tax requirements is reasonably simple but becomes increasingly complex as the firm does business in more locations. State income tax information is readily available through each state's department of revenue as well as through most computerized payroll software programs (see Appendix E for State Revenue Department List.)

Some states require the collection and remittance of income taxes based upon all wages earned within their state. This could result in the company having several state employer identification numbers, even if the company does not have a physical presence in the state. For example, if a Floridian paper mill worker is stationed at the St. Marys, Georgia, location, the employer could be required to remit the employee's income taxes in Georgia.

Example:

Suppose that Jeremy receives a salary of $850 per week at his job in Joliet, Illinois. He has pre-tax deductions of $50 for insurance and $50 for 401(k). Using the Illinois state tax rate of 5%:

Taxable income	$750.00
State income tax	37.50

Local Income Taxes

Another mandatory tax is *local income tax* levied by certain municipalities and counties. Payroll accountants need to be aware of any local taxes that apply to their business. Information about applicable local taxes may be found through city and county governments, often through their Internet sites.

Denver, Colorado, has a local tax called the Occupational Privilege Tax (OPT), also known as the "Head Tax." The OPT is $5.75 per month for employees and $4.00 for employers of any business that has any activity in Denver, even if the employee or business does not exist or reside in Denver itself, on wages exceeding $500. The local income tax is applied after any pre-tax deductions. (Source: City and County of Denver, Colorado, Tax Guide)

State and Local Income Taxes

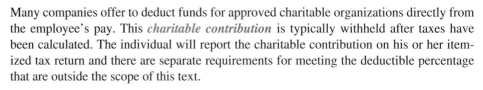

STOP & CHECK

1. April works as a research scientist in Coeur d'Alene, Idaho. She is married with two withholding allowances and earns $62,500 annually, paid biweekly. She has a pre-tax deduction of $150 for her 401(k) and $80 for qualified health insurance. Using the state tax listed in Appendix D, what is her state income tax?

2. Rick works as an accountant in Denver, Colorado. Colorado has a state income tax of a flat 4.63% per employee. Colorado's OPT is $5.75 per month. If Rick is paid monthly and earns $2,850 after pre-tax deductions, what are his state and local taxes?

LO 4-5   Explain Post-Tax Deductions

After the employer withholds the pre-tax and mandatory amounts from an employee's pay, other withholdings may apply. These other withholdings, known as post-tax deductions, comprise both voluntary and *mandated deductions.* An example of a voluntary post-tax deduction is a charitable contribution elected by the employee. Mandated post-tax deductions include *garnishments* and *union dues.* Post-tax deductions are amounts that the IRS has declared cannot reduce the employee's tax liability.

Charitable Contributions

Many companies offer to deduct funds for approved charitable organizations directly from the employee's pay. This *charitable contribution* is typically withheld after taxes have been calculated. The individual will report the charitable contribution on his or her itemized tax return and there are separate requirements for meeting the deductible percentage that are outside the scope of this text.

Court-Ordered Garnishments

There are several reasons that a court may order an employer to withhold amounts from an employee's pay and redirect those funds to a regulatory agency. The most common garnishments are for child support, alimony, and student loans. Garnishments apply to *disposable income,* which is the amount of employee pay after legally required deductions such as income taxes have been withheld. If an employee has one garnishment order for 10% and receives a second for 15%, any further garnishment requests will be deferred until the disposable income is at a level that is available for garnishments.

© Jamie Grill/Tetra Images/Getty Images, RF

Consumer credit:
   According to Title III of the **Consumer Credit Protection Act**, garnishments may be not more than: (a) 25% of the employee's disposable earnings OR (b) the amount by which an employee's disposable earnings are greater than 30 times the federal minimum wage, or $217.50.

Child support:
   Garnishments for child support or alimony may be up to 50% of disposable income, with an additional 5% for any child support that is more than 12 weeks in arrears.

Nontax debts owed to federal agencies:
   Garnishments for nontax amounts to federal agencies may not total more than 15% of disposable income.

Union Dues

When employees are part of a union for which they must remit regular dues, the employer must withhold those dues from the employee as a post-tax payroll deduction. The union uses dues to fund its activities, which include representation in employee–employer negotiations and political activism. Some employers may pay the union dues for their employee as part of their non-cash compensation.

Additional Withholding

If an employee has more than one job or a spouse that works, an option to avoid having to owe taxes at the end of the year is to withhold additional federal income taxes out of each check. Additional withholdings are requested within the employee's Form W-4. This can be either a straight dollar value or an additional percentage. These amounts are withheld from the employee and submitted with the normal federal payroll tax deposits by the employer. Additional withholdings reduce the employee's tax liability, the same as standard federal income taxes.

Once the payroll clerk determines each employee's gross pay, pre-tax deductions, and taxes withheld, the post-tax deductions are applied to the remaining amount. All deductions, both voluntary and mandatory, should be listed on an attachment to the paycheck, often in both period and yearly amounts. An example of a pay advice with deductions is in Figure 4-5.

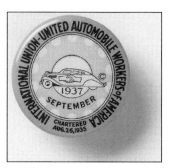

© Kevin Cavanagh/The McGraw-Hill Education, RF

FIGURE 4-5

Sample Employee Pay Advice

Payroll End Date	2/21/20XX		Payroll Pay Date		2/25/20XX		Check:	2156
Employee Name	I. M. Smith		Employee number		22692		Rate	$12.00/hour

Description	Earnings	YTD Gross	Description	Deductions	YTD Deductions
Regular	$480.00	$3,275.00	Federal W/H	$21.00	$247.00
Overtime	$36.00	$36.00	Social Security	$28.89	$183.58
			Medicare	$6.76	$42.94
			Section 125	$50.00	$350.00
Net Pay	$313.75	$1,818.28	401(k)	$25.00	$175.00
			Union Dues	$31.00	$217.00
			State W/H	$9.60	$67.20
			Garnishment	$30.00	$210.00
			Total Deductions	$202.25	$1,492.72

Post-Tax Deductions

1. Don has disposable pay of $1,790.00. He receives a court-ordered garnishment for credit card debt of $15,000. What is the maximum amount that may be withheld from Don's pay?

2. Don questions the amount of the garnishment, claiming that he has health insurance of $125 and union dues of $45 that must also be withheld from his pay. How much should be withheld for the garnishment? Explain.

LO 4-6   Analyze Employee Net Pay

Now that we have discussed the computation of gross income, the various taxes withheld, and miscellaneous voluntary or court-ordered deductions withheld, it is time to determine the employee's *net pay*.

Pay Computation Steps

This is the process to compute each employee's pay:

1. Start with the employee's gross pay.
2. Subtract the pre-tax deductions to get the total taxable earnings.
3. Compute the taxes to be withheld from the total taxable earnings.
4. Deduct the taxes.
5. Deduct any other voluntary or mandated deductions.
6. The result is the employee's net pay.

Example:

Marco receives a salary of $2,000 paid biweekly and has earned $46,000 year-to-date. He is married with two withholding allowances and works for KOR, Inc., in Charleston, West Virginia, where his state income tax is 6%. His pre-tax deductions are medical insurance of $50, a cafeteria plan of $75, and a 401(k) of 3% of his gross salary per pay period. He has charitable contributions of $10, union dues of $62, and a court-ordered garnishment for $120. Taxable income computation is the same for both Federal and state income tax purposes. Let us compute his net pay step by step:

Gross pay	$2,000.00
less: pre-tax medical insurance deduction	−50.00
less: cafeteria plan	−75.00
less: 401(k) contribution	−60.00
Total taxable earnings	$ 1,815.00
less: federal income tax (using wage-bracket method)	−140.00
less: Social Security tax*	−116.25
less: Medicare tax**	−27.19
less: West Virginia state income tax	−108.90
less: charitable contribution	−10.00
less: union dues	−62.00
less: garnishment	−120.00
Net pay	$ 1,230.66

*2000 − 50 − 75 = 1,875 × .062 = 116.25
**2000 − 50 − 75 = 1875 × .0145 = 27.19

An employer will occasionally want to pay an employee a specific net amount. However, all Federal, state, and local taxes must be applied. The amount of the employee's pay must be "grossed up" in order to satisfy tax liabilities and achieve the net pay desired.

Example:

Caitlyn Lanneker is an employee of Pacifica Enterprises, located in Washington state. The firm's president wants to award Caitlyn a bonus at the end of the year to reward her. Use the following steps to compute the gross-up amount:

1. Compute the tax rate for Federal income tax and FICA: The tax rate on bonuses is 28%. The Social Security (6.2%) and Medicare taxes (1.45%) must be added to this rate. For bonuses, the total tax rate equals 28% + 6.2% + 1.45%, or 35.65%.

(continued)

(concluded)

(For non-bonus gross-up, compute the tax rate using amounts from Appendix C.) Add any state or local income tax rates to this computation as necessary.

2. Subtract 100% − Tax rate% to get the Net tax rate. For this bonus, it is 100% − 35.65%, or 64.35% since no state or local income tax rates apply.

3. Gross-up amount equals the Net pay divided by the Net tax rate. For example, for Caitlyn to receive a $150 bonus, the equation is $150/64.35% = $233.10

STOP & CHECK

Computing Net Pay

1. Miguel has biweekly pay of $2,085 and works for a company in Biloxi, Mississippi, and is subject to a 5% tax rate. He is single with five allowances. He elects to have 3% of his biweekly pay withheld for his 401(k), and his qualified health insurance deduction is $80 per pay period, both of which are taken pre-tax. He has a garnishment of $200 per pay period. What is his taxable income for Federal income tax purposes?

2. What is Miguel's net pay?

LO 4-7   Discuss Employee Pay Methods

Once the net pay is computed, the next step is to give the employees access to their money. Four common types of payment methods are available: cash, check, direct deposit, and paycard. Each method has its benefits and drawbacks. We will explore each method separately.

Cash

Cash is one of the oldest forms of paying employees but is not widely used as a contemporary payroll practice. The most common use of cash as a payment method involves paying for day laborers, temporary helpers, and odd jobs. Cash is one of the most difficult forms of payroll to manage because it is difficult to track and control. Payments for wages in cash should involve a written receipt signed by the employee. Companies paying by cash must physically have the cash on hand for payroll, which increases the risk of theft from both internal and external sources. Payroll taxes could be withheld, which requires prior preparation so that the appropriate amount of cash is available to pay precisely what is due for each employee. For employees, cash is a very convenient pay method because of its inherent liquidity.

Cash is a convenient way to pay employees but can pose challenges in security of the funds for both the employer and the employee. Cash is difficult to trace and can be transmitted from bearer to bearer very rapidly. For the employer, ensuring that the employee receives and acknowledges the appropriate pay amount is the key. When using cash as a payment method for employees, a receipt that contains information about the gross pay, deductions, and net pay (called the *pay advice*) is important. The critical piece is to have the employee sign and date a copy of the pay advice, acknowledging receipt of the correct amount of cash on the specific date. Obtaining the employee's signature and date received can prevent future problems with perceived problems involving timely payments of employee compensation.

© Tetra Images/Corbis, RF

Check

Paper checks are a common method of remitting employee compensation. For the employer, a paper check offers traceability and simplicity of accounting records. The use

© Comstock Images/Getty Images, RF

of checks instead of cash means that the employer does not have to maintain large amounts of cash, reducing the vulnerability of keeping currency on hand. Programs such as Quick-Books and Sage50 allow employers to print paychecks directly from the program on specifically designed, pre-printed forms. Checks offer a level of security that cash does not because they are issued to a specific employee, the only person who can legally convert the check into cash.

The disadvantage to using paper checks for payroll purposes involves bank account reconciliation. Once issued, the employee may choose not to deposit it into his or her bank account, which can complicate the firm's reconciliation process. Paper checks could be lost or destroyed, requiring voiding of the old check and issuance of a new one. Paper checks may soon be phased out of current practice as other methods of employee pay grow in popularity because of the convenience for both the employer and the employee.

> According to the Pew Internet and American Life Project (2014), more than 53 million consumers in the United States use online banking. The practice of payroll disbursement using paper checks is declining as people shift from traditional banking methods to a culture of electronic money management. (Source: Smart Biz)

© Steve Cole/Photodisc/Getty Images, RF

For employers who use paper checks as a compensation method, two significant best practices exist: the use of a payroll-only checking account and a procedure for the handling of the payroll checks themselves. A separate payroll-dedicated checking account prevents problems that could occur if the company has difficulties (such as insufficient funds) in the business's main account. For the checks themselves, the payroll accountant needs to maintain a record that notes the use of each and every check, especially for checks that are voided, lost, or never cashed. If a company issues checks, it needs to maintain an unclaimed property account for payroll checks that are never cashed by the employee. The process of leaving a check uncashed, especially a payroll check, is called *escheatment* and is subject to state laws about the handling and distribution of such unclaimed money. Compliance with state escheatment laws is mandatory but not largely enforced–but that does not relieve the employer of the obligation to pay its employee. Use of a record in which the payroll accountant annotates each check's use (i.e., cashed, voided, lost) is imperative.

When a company pays employees by check, the numerical amount of the check must also be represented in specific words for the bank to accept the check for payment to the payee. The highlighted area in the image below shows how the information should appear on the face of the check.

Wings of the North			
121 Nicholas Street			
North Pole, AK 99705			Check No. 23445
Petra Smith		Date	1/3/2015
One Thousand One Hundred Twenty-four and 13/100		dollars	1.124.13
Payee: Petra Smith Address: 426 Candy Cane Lane City/State Zip: North Pole, AK 99705		Signed: *Rudolph Donner*	

Direct Deposit

Direct deposit of employee compensation into the individual's bank account offers employers some of the same advantages as checks. Like checks, employee compensation is traceable through both the employer's bank and the optional paper pay advice issued to the employee. Employees often prefer direct deposit because their pay is immediately

© Comstock/PunchStock, RF

available in their bank account, eliminating the need to travel to the bank to deposit the paper check. However, for employees to receive their pay through direct deposit, they must have a bank account.

An advantage of direct deposit is that it prevents paper waste, promoting "green" business. In 2009, the National Automated Clearing House Association (NACHA) estimated an average of approximately $175 per employee, amounting to $6.7 billion, was saved per year by using direct deposit. These savings came from lower waste collection, paper usage, and recycling costs. Not only does direct deposit save a company money, it reduces the time needed for payroll processing, which frees payroll accountants to complete other tasks.

When using direct deposit as an employee compensation method, a suggested best practice is to grant the employees access to a website or online portal by which they can securely view their pay advice and pay history, as this may substitute for paper payroll advices. Because direct deposit involves the use of electronic data transmittal, the posting of the pay advice on a secure site could be linked with the human resources data, allowing the employee an element of self-maintenance in payroll records. The potential pitfall in the use of a website for these highly sensitive records is the vulnerability of the information to computer hacking. If an employer chooses to use a website in this manner, they must take steps to prevent hacking through data encryption, identity verification, and site security.

> The Federal Communications Commission (FCC) has published guidelines for employer data security procedures, especially as pertains to employee information on websites and the use of paycards. The FCC guidelines include advice about the selection of data to be included on employee-accessible websites, password strength guidelines, update intervals, and data archiving. (Source: FCC)

Paycards

Paycards have been growing in popularity since the beginning of the 21st century. These cards are debit cards onto which an employer electronically transmits the employee's pay. The use of payroll cards started in the 1990s as a convenient way to compensate over-the-road truck drivers who could not be in a predictable place on each payday. Comerica started issuing the paycards that could be used anywhere a conventional MasterCard was accepted, which is nearly everywhere. Unlike the use of paper checks or direct deposit, the paycard does not require an employee to maintain a bank account to access his or her pay. The convenience and ease of use for employees makes the pay card an option that nearly 2 million workers in the United States have opted to use.

What is the disadvantage to paycard use? Unlike the limits to access that a bank has for its account holders, a paycard can be lost or stolen. Some employees may encounter challenges such as withdrawal limits or cash back at point-of-sale (POS) purchases. An issue that haunted the early use of paycards was *Regulation E* of the Federal Deposit Insurance Corporation (FDIC), which protects consumers from loss of the availability of their funds on deposit in the event of bank losses. Until 2006, Regulation E applied to funds on deposit in an FDIC-insured institution. Regulation E was extended to cover payroll funds transferred to paycards, according to 12 CFR Part 205. As a pay method that is growing in popularity among employers and employees, paycards offer more compensation options for employers.

Pay Methods

1. What are the different employee pay methods?
2. What regulation governs paycard loss or theft?
3. For which pay method(s) must an employee have a bank account?

TAXES AND PAYMENT METHODS

Mandatory and voluntary deductions from employee pay change each year because of changes in the laws governing these withholdings. Some developments in employee withholdings during the early 2010s include the following:

- Changes in the availability of day care centers and related pay deductions for employees.
- Additional Medicare tax deductions that were enacted as part of the Affordable Care Act.
- Changes in the amounts that employees may contribute on a tax-deferred basis to pension plans.
- Increases in the use of paycards as a form of employee compensation.

Some trends to watch in employee net pay include the following:

- Federally mandated wellness programs to reduce absenteeism and worker stress.
- Changes to rules governing overtime pay that will affect the net pay for salaried employees.
- Changes to employee net pay because of the Affordable Care Act health insurance requirements for employers.
- Increased public awareness of the effect of pay raises, especially for cost of living, on net pay.
- State-level legislation about the percent of disposable earnings that may be subject to garnishments.

Paycards require different types of security than the other types of employee compensation, but most elements remain the same. In addition to tracking hours and accurately compensating employees based on their marital status and withholdings, the employer must also keep the employee's paycard number in a secure file. Software such as QuickBooks offer password encryption abilities for the files of employees who have paycards. Like any other debit card, the funds are electronically coded to the account number. Although the card issuer (not the employer) must remain compliant with Regulation E as far as card loss or theft is concerned, the employer is responsible to ensure this extra step of payroll security.

In late 2013, Visa, Inc., introduced an improvement to its Visa Advanced Authorization technology, making compensation via paycards more secure and reliable. This new technology improved real-time fraud detection and was projected to prevent nearly $200 million in fraud within a five-year period. (Source: PR Newswire)

Summary of Employee Net Pay and Pay Methods

Employee pay is subject to a variety of deductions that can be both mandatory and voluntary. Deductions such as federal income tax and Medicare tax are virtually inescapable. Other taxes such as Social Security, state taxes, and local taxes are not applicable in every employee's situation and depend on a variety of factors such as year-to-date pay and state of residence. Of the other deductions, some can be withheld from an employee's pay before taxes are deducted, which benefits an employee by reducing their payroll tax liability. Other deductions must be taken after taxes are withheld. Understanding the difference between gross pay and net pay is vital for payroll accountants because the net pay, not the gross, is the pay that the employee actually receives.

The question of employee pay methods is complex. Which pay method is the best? It is not an easy answer. An employer should consider the needs of the employees, as well as the business, to decide if one method will suit everyone. Sometimes a combination of payment methods is the best solution, although it adds complexity for the payroll accountant. The most appropriate method for the organization will depend on many different factors. Most often, there is not a single method that an organization will use, but a combination of methods to serve the needs of its employees.

Key Points

- Pre-tax deductions are used for qualified deductions and to reduce the taxable wage base.
- Federal income tax applies to all workers, and the amount varies based on wages, pay frequency, marital status, and number of withholdings.
- Social Security tax has a maximum wage base that can change each year.
- Medicare tax has no maximum wage base, and an additional Medicare tax is levied on employees who earn more than $200,000.
- Certain pre-tax deductions are subject to FICA taxes.
- Post-tax deductions include garnishments, union dues, and charitable contributions.
- Garnishments are subject to maximum percentages of disposable income, depending on the type of garnishment.
- Net pay is gross pay less all deductions.
- Employees' pay may be disbursed in cash, by check, by paycard, or via direct deposit.

Vocabulary

401(k)	Flexible Spending	Pay advice
403(b)	Account	Paycard
Additional Medicare tax	Fringe Benefit	Percentage method
Cafeteria plans	Garnishments	Regulation E
Charitable contributions	Gross pay	SEP
Consumer Credit Protec-	Health Savings account	SIMPLE
tion Act	(HSA)	SIMPLE 401(k)
Defined benefit	IRA	Social Security tax
Defined contribution	Local income tax	State income tax
Direct deposit	Mandated deductions	Union dues
Disposable income	Mandatory deductions	Voluntary deductions
Escheatment	Medicare tax	Wage base
ESOP	Net pay	Wage-bracket method

Review Questions

1. What are the four factors that affect how much federal income tax is withheld from an employee's pay?

2. How is Social Security tax computed? What is the maximum wage base?

3. How is Medicare tax computed? What is the maximum wage base?

4. Name four states that do not have an income tax for employees.

5. What are two examples of voluntary deductions?

6. What are two examples of pre-tax deductions?

7. How is an employee's net income computed?

8. Why is the difference between gross pay and taxable income important?

9. What are garnishments and how must they be handled?

10. What are the four different pay methods?

11. What are an advantage and disadvantage of paycards?

12. What are an advantage and disadvantage of direct deposit?

13. How does the percentage method work? When should it be used instead of the wage-bracket method?

Exercises Set A

4-1A.
LO 4-1, 4-2

Karen and Katie are looking at the company's health care options and trying to determine how much their net pay will decrease if they sign up for the qualified cafeteria plan offered by the company. Explain the calculations of taxable income when qualified health care deductions are involved. Karen, a married woman with four exemptions, earns $2,000 per biweekly payroll. Katie, a single woman with one exemption, also earns $2,000 per biweekly payroll. The biweekly employee contribution to health care that would be subject to the cafeteria plan is $100.

Karen's taxable income if she declines to participate in the cafeteria plan: _____

Karen's taxable income if she participates in the cafeteria plan:

_____

Katie's taxable income if she declines to participate in the cafeteria plan: _____

Katie's taxable income if she participates in the cafeteria plan:

_____

4-2A.
LO 4-1, 4-2, 4-3, 4-6

Using the data in Exercise 4-1A, compute the net pay for Karen and Katie. Assume that they are subject to Federal income tax (using the wage-bracket method) and FICA taxes and have no other deductions from their pay.

Karen's net pay if she declines to participate in the cafeteria plan:

_____

Karen's net pay if she participates in the cafeteria plan: _____

Katie's net pay if she declines to participate in the cafeteria plan:

_____

Katie's net pay if she participates in the cafeteria plan: _____

4-3A.
LO 4-1, 4-2, 4-3, 4-5, 4-6

Tooka's Trees in Auburn, Tennessee, has six employees who are paid biweekly. Calculate the net pay from the information provided below for the November 15 pay date. Assume that all wages are subject to Social Security and Medicare taxes. Use the wage-bracket method of determining Federal income tax. All 401(k) and Section 125 amounts are pre-tax deductions. The wages are not subject to state taxes.

a. T. Taylor
Single, four withholdings
Gross pay: $1,500 per period
401(k) deduction: $125 per pay period
Net pay: _____

b. B. Walburn
Married, six withholdings
Gross pay: $2,225 per period
401(k) deduction: $250 per period
Net pay: _____

   c. H. Carpenter
      Single, no withholdings
      Gross pay: $2,100 per period
      Section 125 deduction: $75 per period
      401(k) deduction: $50 per period
      Net pay: _____

   d. J. Knight
      Married, three withholdings
      Gross pay: $1,875 per period
      United Way deduction: $50 per period
      Garnishment: $50 per period
      Net pay: _____

   e. C. Lunn
      Single, one withholding
      Gross pay: $1,200 per period
      Section 125 withholding: $50 per period
      401(k) deduction: 6% of gross pay
      Net pay: _____

   f. E. Smooter
      Married, eight withholdings
      Gross pay: $2,425 per period
      401(k) deduction: $75 per period
      Net pay: _____

4-4A.
LO 4-1, 4-2, 4-3, 4-4, 4-5, 4-6

The following employees of CIBA Ironworks in Bristol, Illinois, are paid in different frequencies. Some employees have union dues and/or garnishments deducted from their pay. Calculate their net pay, using the wage-bracket method to determine Federal income tax, and including Illinois income tax of 3.75% of taxable pay. No employee has exceeded the maximum FICA limits.

Employee	Frequency	Marital Status/ Withholdings	Pay	Union Dues per Period	Garnishment per Period	Net Pay
C. Whaley	Weekly	M, 2	$ 850		$ 50	
F. Paguaga	Semimonthly	M, 6	$2,800	$ 120		
K. Harvey	Monthly	S, 3	$8,000	$ 240	$ 75	
L. Bolling	Biweekly	M, 0	$2,500		$100	

4-5A.
LO 4-1, 4-2, 4-3, 4-4, 4-5, 4-6

Frances Newberry is the payroll accountant for Pack-it Services of Jackson, Arizona. The employees of Pack-it Services are paid semimonthly. An employee, Glen Riley, comes to her on November 10 and requests a pay advance of $750, which he will pay back in equal parts on the November 15 and December 15 paychecks. Glen is married with eight withholding allowances and is paid $50,000 per year. He contributes 3% of his pay to a 401(k) and has $25 per paycheck deducted for a Section 125 plan. Compute his net pay on his November 15th paycheck. The state income tax rate is 4%.

4-6A.
LO 4-1, 4-2

Milligan's Millworks pays its employees on a weekly basis. Using the wage-bracket tables from Appendix C, compute the federal income tax withholdings for the following employees of Milligan's Millworks:

Employee	Marital Status	No. of Exemptions	Weekly Pay	Federal Tax
D. Balestreri	S	4	$ 840	
Y. Milligan	S	2	$1,233	
H. Curran	M	7	$ 680	
D. Liberti	M	0	$ 755	

4-7A.

LO 4-2

Wynne and Associates has employees with pay schedules that vary based on job classification. Compute the Federal income tax withholding for each employee using the percentage method.

Employee	Marital Status	No. of Exemptions	Pay Frequency	Pay Amount	Federal Income Tax
S. Turner	S	1	Weekly	$ 3,000	
D. McGorray	S	4	Monthly	$ 15,000	
A. Kennedy	M	3	Daily	$ 500	
R. Thomas	M	5	Annually	$120,000	

4-8A.

LO 4-3

The employees of Agonnacultis, Inc., are paid on a semimonthly basis. Compute the FICA taxes for the employees for the November 15 payroll. All employees have been employed for the entire calendar year.

Employee	Semimonthly Pay	YTD Pay for Oct 31 Pay Date	Social Security Tax for Nov. 15 Pay Date	Medicare Tax for Nov. 15 Pay Date
T. Newberry	$7,500			
S. Smith	$3,500			
D. Plott	$4,225			
I. Ost	$6,895			
D. Bogard	$9,500			
M. Mallamace	$ 4,100			

4-9A.

LO 4-4

Fannon's Chocolate Factory operates in North Carolina. Using the state income tax rate of 5.75%, calculate the income tax for each employee.

Employee	Amount per Pay Period	North Carolina Income Tax
K. Jamieson	$ 550	
D. Macranie	$4,895	
G. Lockhart	$3,225	
K. McIntyre	$ 1,795	

4-10A.

LO 4-2

Using the percentage method, calculate the federal withholding amounts for the following employees.

Employee	Marital Status	Withholdings	Pay Frequency	Amount per Pay Period	Federal Income Tax
S. Calder	M	6	Quarterly	$20,000	
P. Singh	S	2	Annually	$90,000	
B. Nelson	M	0	Daily	$ 500	

4-11A.

LO 4-7

Margaret Wilson is the new accountant for a startup company. The company has cross-country drivers, warehouse personnel, and office staff at the main location. The company is looking at options that allow their employees flexibility with receiving their pay. Margaret has been asked to present the advantages and disadvantages of the various pay methods to senior management. Which would be the best option for each class of workers?

Exercises Set B

4-1B.

LO 4-1, 4-2

Will and Eric are looking at the company's health care options and trying to determine what their taxable income will be if they sign up for the qualified cafeteria plan offered by the company, which will allow them to deduct the health care contributions pre-tax. Explain the calculations of taxable income when qualified health care deductions are involved. Will, a single man with one deduction, earns $1,600 per semimonthly payroll. Eric, a married man with six deductions, earns $1,875 per semimonthly pay period. The semimonthly employee contribution to health care that would be subject to the cafeteria plan is $75 for Will, $250 for Eric.

Will's taxable income if he declines to participate in the cafeteria plan: _____

Will's taxable income if he participates in the cafeteria plan: _____

Eric's taxable income if he declines to participate in the cafeteria plan: _____

Eric's taxable income if he participates in the cafeteria plan: _____

4-2B.
LO 4-1, 4-2, 4-3, 4-6

Using the data in Exercise 4-1B, compute the net pay for Will and Eric. Assume that they are subject to Federal income tax (using the wage-bracket method in Appendix C) and FICA taxes and have no other deductions from their pay.

Will's net pay if he declines to participate in the cafeteria plan: _____

Will's net pay if he participates in the cafeteria plan: _____

Eric's net pay if he declines to participate in the cafeteria plan: _____

Eric's net pay if he participates in the cafeteria plan: _____

4-3B.
LO 4-1, 4-2, 4-3, 4-5, 4-6

Hark Enterprises in Taft, Wyoming, has six employees who are paid on a semimonthly basis. Calculate the net pay from the information provided below for the August 15 pay date. Assume that all wages are subject to Social Security and Medicare taxes. Use the wage-bracket tables in Appendix C to determine the Federal income tax withholding.

a. L. Fletcher:
   Married, five withholdings
   Gross pay: $1,320 per period
   401(k) deduction: 2% of gross pay per pay period
   Net pay: _____

b. S. Lince
   Single, no withholdings
   Gross pay: $1,745 per period
   401(k) deduction: $225 per pay period
   Net pay: _____

c. A. Brown
   Single, five withholdings
   Gross pay: $2,120 per period
   Section 125 deduction: $25 per pay period
   401(k) deduction: $150 per pay period
   Net pay: _____

d. R. Kimble
   Married, six withholdings
   Gross pay: $1,570 per period
   United Way deduction: $25 per pay period
   Garnishment: $75 per period
   Net pay: _____

e. F. Monteiro
   Married, no withholdings
   Gross pay: $2,200 per period
   Section 125 deduction: $100 per period

401(k) deduction: 4% of gross pay

Net pay: _____

f. K. Giannini

Single, two withholdings

Gross pay: $1,485 per period

401(k) deduction: $120 per period

Net pay: _____

4-4B.

LO 4-1, 4-2, 4-3, 4-5, 4-6

The following employees of Memory Bytes of Titusville, Washington, are paid in different frequencies. Some employees have union dues and/or garnishments deducted from their pay. Calculate their net pay (use the wage-bracket tables in Appendix C to determine Federal income tax unless otherwise noted). No employee has exceeded the maximum FICA limits.

Employee	Frequency	Marital Status/ Withholdings	Pay	Union Dues per Period	Garnishment per Period	Net Pay
N. Lawrence	Biweekly	M, 5	$ 1,680	$102		
D. Gaitan	Weekly	S, 0	$ 1,300		$70	
N. Ruggieri	Semimonthly	M, 2	$2,520	$110	$90	
P. Oceguera	Monthly	S, 2	$6,600		$45	

4-5B.

LO 4-1, 4-2, 4-3, 4-4, 4-5, 4-6

Jane Heinlein is the payroll accountant for Sia Lights of Carter, Nebraska. The employees of Sia Lights are paid biweekly. An employee, Melinda Gunnarson, comes to her on September 14 and requests a pay advance of $825, which she will pay back in equal parts on the September 28 and October 12 paychecks. Melinda is single with one withholding allowance and is paid $32,500 per year. She contributes 1% of her pay to a 401(k) plan and has $25 per paycheck deducted for a court-ordered garnishment. Compute her net pay for her September 28th paycheck. The state income tax rate is 5.01%. Use the wage-bracket tables in Appendix C to determine the Federal income tax withholding amount.

4-6B.

LO 4-2

Wolfe Industries pays its employees on a semimonthly basis. Using the wage-bracket tables from Appendix C, compute the federal income tax deductions for the following employees of Wolfe Industries:

Employee	Marital Status	No. of Exemptions	Semimonthly Pay	Federal Income Tax
T. Canter	M	1	$1,050	
M. McCollum	M	5	$1,390	
C. Hammond	S	2	$1,295	
T. Elliott	S	4	$ 1,165	

4-7B.

LO 4-2

GL Kennels has employees with pay schedules that vary based on job classification. Compute the federal income tax liability for each employee using the percentage method.

Employee	Marital Status	No. of Exemptions	Pay Frequency	Pay Amount	Percentage Method
C. Wells	M	2	Biweekly	$ 1,825	
L. Decker	M	0	Weekly	$ 750	
J. Swaby	S	5	Weekly	$ 875	
M. Ohlson	M	3	Semi-monthly	$2,025	

4-8B.

LO 4-3

The employees of Black Cat Designs are paid on a semimonthly basis. Compute the FICA taxes for the employees for the November 30, 2015, payroll. All employees have been employed for the entire calendar year.

Employee	Semimonthly Pay	YTD Pay for 11-15-2015	Social Security Tax for 11-30-2015 Pay	Medicare Tax for 11-30-2015 Pay
P. Gareis	$4,250			
E. Siliwon	$6,275			
G. De La Torre	$5,875			
L. Rosenthal	$2,850			
C. Bertozzi	$ 5,105			
T. Gennaro	$2,940			

4-9B.

LO 4-4

Christensen Ranch operates in Pennsylvania. Using the state income tax rate of 3.07%, calculate the state income tax for each employee.

Employee	Amount per Pay Period	Pennsylvania Income Tax
G. Zonis	$ 1,325	
V. Sizemore	$ 1,710	
R. Dawson	$ 925	
C. Couture	$2,550	

4-10B.

LO 4-2

Using the percentage method, calculate the federal withholding amounts for the following employees.

Employee	Marital Status	Withholdings	Pay Frequency	Amount per Pay Period	Federal Income Tax
L. Abbey	S	3	Annually	$63,500	
G. Narleski	M	0	Quarterly	$ 14,000	
T. Leider	S	1	Monthly	$ 1,200	

4-11B.

LO 4-7

David Adams has been retained as a consultant for Marionet Industries. The company has had difficulty with its cross-country drivers receiving their pay in a timely fashion because they are often away from their home banks. The company is looking at options that allow its employees flexibility with receiving their pay. Prepare a presentation depicting the advantages and disadvantages of the various pay methods for senior management.

Critical Thinking

4-1. Vicky Le, an employee of Sweet Shoppe Industries, receives a bonus of $5,000 for her stellar work. Her boss wants Vicky to receive $5,000 on the check. She contributes 3% of her pay in a pre-tax deduction to her 401(k). Calculate the gross pay amount that would result in $5,000 paid to Vicky.

4-2. Your boss approaches you in mid-December and requests that you pay certain employees their gross pay amount as if there were no deductions as their Christmas bonuses. None of the employees have reached the Social Security wage base for the year. What is the gross-up amount for each of the following employees? (Use the tax rate for bonuses and no state taxes.)

Employee	Regular Gross Pay per Period	Grossed-Up Amount
Yves St. John	$2,500	
Kim Johnson	$3,380	
Michael Hale	$ 3,178	

In the Real World: Scenario for Discussion

The State of Kansas passed legislation in 2007 that allowed employers to select their employee pay method. The legislation was known as the "paperless payroll law," and many employers opted to give their employees paycards instead of cash, check, or direct deposit. What are some issues with this practice? What are some benefits?

Internet Activities

4-1. Did you know that you can use an online calculator to see how your voluntary deductions will affect your paycheck? Many different payroll calculators exist. Go to one or more of the following sites and use the payroll calculator:

www.paycheckcity.com/

www.surepayroll.com/calculator/payroll-calculators.asp

www.adp.com/tools-and-resources.aspx

4-2. Health insurance is a rapidly changing and evolving field. Employers have many options and concerns to consider. Check out www.npr.org/sections/health-care/ to listen to podcasts about health insurance and employer issues. What issues do employers currently face?

4-3. Want to know more about the concepts in this chapter? Check out these sites:

www.healthcare.gov/law/index.html

www.aflac.com

www.investopedia.com

www.irs.gov/pub/irs-pdf/p15.pdf

www.americanpayroll.org/Visa-Paycard-Portal/

Continuing Payroll Project: Prevosti Farms and Sugarhouse

For the February 16 pay date, use the gross pay totals from the end of Chapter 3 and compute the net pay for each employee. Once you have computed the net pay (using the wage-bracket tables in Appendix C), complete the paycheck for each employee (assume that all employees are paid by check). State withholding tax for Vermont is computed at 3% of taxable wages (i.e., gross pay less pre-tax deductions). Date the checks February 16, 2015. The first check number is 5356. Note that the first paycheck comprises only one week of work during the pay period and that the Federal income tax should be determined using the biweekly tables in Appendix C.

Voluntary deductions for each employee are as follows:

Name	Deduction
Millen	Insurance: $155/paycheck 401(k): 3% of gross pay
Towle	Insurance: $100/paycheck 401(k): 5% of gross pay
Long	Insurance: $155/paycheck 401(k): 2% of gross pay
Shangraw	Insurance: $100/paycheck 401(k): 3% of gross pay
Lewis	Insurance: $155/paycheck 401(k): 4% of gross pay
Schwartz	Insurance: $100/paycheck 401(k): 5% of gross pay
Prevosti	Insurance: $155/paycheck 401(k): 6% of gross pay
You	Insurance: $100/paycheck 401(k): 2% of gross pay

Complete the net pay for the February 16 pay date and write the checks dated February 16, 2015. All insurance and 401(k) deductions are pre-tax. Update the Employee Earnings Records for February 16, 2015.

Prevosti Farms and Sugarhouse
820 Westminster Road
Bridgewater, VT 05520

	Date
	dollars

Payee:
Address:
City/State Zip   Signed:

Payroll End Date		Payroll Pay Date		Check:	
Employee Name		Employee number		Rate	

Description	Earnings	YTD Gross	Description	Deductions	YTD Deductions
Regular			Federal W/H		
Overtime			Social Security		
			Medicare		
			Pretax Insurance		
			401(k)		
			State W/H		
			Total Deductions		

Prevosti Farms and Sugarhouse
820 Westminster Road
Bridgewater, VT 05520

	Date
	dollars

Payee:
Address:
City/State Zip   Signed:

Payroll End Date		Payroll Pay Date		Check:	
Employee Name		Employee number		Rate	

Description	Earnings	YTD Gross	Description	Deductions	YTD Deductions
Regular			Federal W/H		
Overtime			Social Security		
			Medicare		
			Pretax Insurance		
			401(k)		
			State W/H		
			Total Deductions		

Prevosti Farms and Sugarhouse
820 Westminster Road
Bridgewater, VT 05520

	Date
	dollars

Payee:
Address:
City/State Zip   Signed:

Payroll End Date		Payroll Pay Date		Check:	
Employee Name		Employee number		Rate	

Description	Earnings	YTD Gross	Description	Deductions	YTD Deductions
Regular			Federal W/H		
Overtime			Social Security		
			Medicare		
			Pretax Insurance		
			401(k)		
			State W/H		
			Total Deductions		

Prevosti Farms and Sugarhouse
820 Westminster Road
Bridgewater, VT 05520

	Date
	dollars

Payee:
Address:
City/State Zip   Signed:

Payroll End Date		Payroll Pay Date		Check:	
Employee Name		Employee number		Rate	

Description	Earnings	YTD Gross	Description	Deductions	YTD Deductions
Regular			Federal W/H		
Overtime			Social Security		
			Medicare		
			Pretax Insurance		
			401(k)		
			State W/H		
			Total Deductions		

Prevosti Farms and Sugarhouse					
820 Westminster Road					
Bridgewater, VT 05520					

		Date	
	dollars		

Payee:
Address:
City/State Zip   Signed:

Payroll End Date		Payroll Pay Date		Check:	
Employee Name		Employee number		Rate	

Description	Earnings	YTD Gross	Description	Deductions	YTD Deductions
Regular			Federal W/H		
Overtime			Social Security		
			Medicare		
			Pretax Insurance		
			401(k)		
			State W/H		
			Total Deductions		

Prevosti Farms and Sugarhouse					
820 Westminster Road					
Bridgewater, VT 05520					

		Date	
	dollars		

Payee:
Address:
City/State Zip   Signed:

Payroll End Date		Payroll Pay Date		Check:	
Employee Name		Employee number		Rate	

Description	Earnings	YTD Gross	Description	Deductions	YTD Deductions
Regular			Federal W/H		
Overtime			Social Security		
			Medicare		
			Pretax Insurance		
			401(k)		
			State W/H		
			Total Deductions		

Prevosti Farms and Sugarhouse		
820 Westminster Road		
Bridgewater, VT 05520		

Date ▭

dollars ▭

Payee:
Address:
City/State Zip　　　　　　Signed:

Payroll End Date ▭　　Payroll Pay Date ▭　　Check: ▭

Employee Name ▭　　Employee number ▭　　Rate ▭

Description	Earnings	YTD Gross	Description	Deductions	YTD Deductions
Regular			Federal W/H		
Overtime			Social Security		
			Medicare		
			Pretax Insurance		
			401(k)		
			State W/H		
			Total Deductions		

Prevosti Farms and Sugarhouse		
820 Westminster Road		
Bridgewater, VT 05520		

Date ▭

dollars ▭

Payee:
Address:
City/State Zip　　　　　　Signed:

Payroll End Date ▭　　Payroll Pay Date ▭　　Check: ▭

Employee Name ▭　　Employee number ▭　　Rate ▭

Description	Earnings	YTD Gross	Description	Deductions	YTD Deductions
Regular			Federal W/H		
Overtime			Social Security		
			Medicare		
			Pretax Insurance		
			401(k)		
			State W/H		
			Total Deductions		

Prevosti Farms and Sugarhouse
820 Westminster Road
Bridgewater, VT 05520

	Date	
		dollars

Payee:
Address:
City/State Zip   Signed:

Payroll End Date		Payroll Pay Date		Check:
Employee Name		Employee number		Rate

Description	Earnings	YTD Gross	Description	Deductions	YTD Deductions
Regular			Federal W/H		
Overtime			Social Security		
			Medicare		
			Pretax Insurance		
			401(k)		
			State W/H		
			Total Deductions		

Answers to Stop & Check Exercises

What Counts as Pre-Taxable?

1. Insurance, various retirement plans, cafeteria plans
2. Affordable Care Act of 2010
3. 401(k), IRA, SIMPLE, SEP, ESOP

How Much Tax to Withhold?

1. (a) $183; (b) (($2,166.67 − (2 × 166.70) − 1,127) × 0.15) + $76.90 = $182.84

2. $168 = $2,166.67 gross pay − $100 for 401(k) deduction per pay period = $2,066.67 taxable pay. This is the amount used in conjunction with the wage-bracket table to calculate the Federal income tax withheld. The difference in taxes with the 401(k) deduction is $183 − 168 = $15.

3. $162 = $2,166.67 gross pay − $75 health insurance − $55 AFLAC = $2,036.67 taxable pay

FICA Taxes

1. $327.36 for Social Security, $76.56 for Medicare
2. ($327.36 + $76.56) × 2 = $807.84
3. a. $0 Social Security tax; Medicare taxable would be reduced by the qualified insurance deduction. Year-to-date salary $197,916.73 less the qualified insurance $1,425 ($75 × 19) gives $196,491.67. Medicare base for this payroll, $3,508.33 to reach the $200,000 cap and $6,833.34 ($10,416.67 − 3,508.33 − 75.00) that will be charged the surcharge. ($3,508.33 × 1.45%) + ($6,833.34 × 2.35%) = $50.87 + $160.58 = $211.45 Medicare tax.

   b. ($10,416.67 − 75.00) × 2.35% = $243.03 Medicare tax

State and Local Income Taxes

1. $34.78 ($62,500 annual salary/26 biweekly = $2,403.85 gross pay − $150 for 401(k) pre-tax deduction − $80 health insurance pre-tax deduction = $2,173.85 taxable pay × 1.6%. From Appendix D, Married.

2. $131.96 ($2,850 × 4.63%) state, $5.75 local

Post-Tax Deductions

1. $447.50 = $1,790 × 25%

2. $447.50. The health insurance and union dues deductions are not legal obligations and do not affect disposable income.

Computing Net Pay

1. Gross pay $2,085, 401(k) deduction $62.55, health insurance $80. Taxable income = $1,942.45.

2. Net pay is calculated as $1,942.45 from question 1. Federal income tax = $146 (wage-bracket method), state income tax = $97.12 (1,942.45 * 5%), Social Security tax = $124.31 ($2,085 − 80 = $2,005 × .062), Medicare tax = $29.07 ($2,085 − 80 = $2,005 × .0145), garnishment = $200. Net pay = $2,085 − 62.55 − 80 − 146 − 97.12 − 124.31 − 29.07 − 200 = $1,345.95.

Pay Methods

1. Cash, check, direct deposit, and paycard

2. Regulation E

3. Direct deposit

5

Employer Payroll Taxes and Labor Planning

All facets of payroll accounting are important because they affect the success of the company and its employees. A particularly important piece of the payroll puzzle is the employer's payroll tax responsibility. The reporting and remittance of payroll taxes is a significant aspect that requires scrupulous attention to detail. Many different tax forms exist that must be filed at regular intervals and with varying governmental bodies. Tax filing requires organizational skills, time management, and continued accuracy. Tax reporting is a huge responsibility of the business and its payroll accountant because of governmental oversight.

Other aspects of an employer's payroll tax responsibility include maintaining workers' compensation insurance, forwarding amounts withheld through employees' voluntary and mandated deductions, and determining both labor expenses and employee benefits. The Internal Revenue Service and state employment departments have websites that contain important information about filing requirements, due dates, guidelines, and penalties. (See Appendix E for state employment department contact information.) Insurance responsibilities are a vital consideration when determining labor expenses and employee benefits because they are a significant element in the cost of doing business.

LEARNING OBJECTIVES

After studying Chapter 5, you should be able to:

LO 5-1   List Employer-Paid and Employee-Paid Obligations

LO 5-2   Discuss Reporting Periods and Requirements for Employer Tax Deposits

LO 5-3   Prepare Mid-Year and Year-End Employer Tax Reporting and Deposits

© Beathan/Corbis RfF/Corbis, RF

LO 5-4   Describe Payroll Within the Context of Business Expenses

LO 5-5   Relate Labor Expenses to Company Profitability

LO 5-6   Complete Benefit Analysis as a Function of Payroll

Benefits Analysis and Employee Economic Security

Employers must weigh different options when considering what benefits they will provide their employees. Employee benefits are now viewed as a way to attract and retain valuable workers. However, offering benefits represents an additional labor expense. Depending on the industry, wages and salaries comprise between 18 and 55% of a firm's operating expenses. In a survey conducted by the SHRM, 28% of employers reported that they increased the amount of sponsored benefits during 2014. To achieve the best return for the investment in their employees, employers surveyed their employees to determine which benefits were the most valuable. The largest increases in benefits spending were reported in employee retirement funds and wellness coverage. (Source: SHRM)

> **Labor costs often make up a significant portion of a company's expense. Employee benefits such as company contributions to retirement plans, temporary disability insurance, and educational reimbursements represent additional business expenses. In Chapter 5, we will examine employer payroll tax responsibilities and how payroll is a tool in labor planning.**

The cost to have employees involves much more than the wage or salary that the employee earns. Employers must match amounts deducted from employee pay for FICA taxes and must contribute the entire amount of FUTA tax. The employer is responsible for the collection, reporting, deposit, and reconciliation of taxes withheld from the employee. When the cost of additional employee benefits, including paid time off, is added to the expense of having employees, it becomes apparent that an employee represents a significant investment by the company.

LO 5-1   List Employer-Paid and Employee-Paid Obligations

Employers must pay some of the same taxes that the employees do. However, a firm has additional liabilities that employees do not, such as certain unemployment taxes and workers' compensation insurance. A comparison of employee-paid and employer-paid taxes is given in Table 5-1.

The taxes that an employer must pay are often known as *statutory deductions*, meaning that governmental statutes have made the tax a mandatory deduction. An important element of employer tax responsibility is that it continues after writing the paychecks to the employees, often extending well after an employee leaves the firm. Employers must file mandatory reconciliation reports about amounts they have withheld from employee pay, track the employees throughout the company's accounting system, and maintain the personnel files for both current and terminated employees in accordance with the firm's payroll practices and governmental regulations.

TABLE 5-1
Employee-Paid and Employer-Paid Taxes

Tax	Employee Pays	Employer Pays
Social Security	XX	XX
Medicare	XX	XX
Federal Income Tax	XX	
Federal Unemployment Tax (FUTA)		XX
State Income Tax (where applicable)	XX	
State Unemployment Tax (SUTA)	Sometimes both are responsible at different percentages; see your local taxation authority for specific details.	XX
Local Income Taxes	XX	
Local Occupational Taxes (where applicable)	XX	XX
Workers' Compensation Premiums		XX
401(k)/Pension (if matching policy exists)	XX	XX
Other Voluntary Deductions	XX	

Social Security and Medicare Taxes

The *FICA* taxes, which includes both the Social Security and Medicare taxes, are among the statutory withholdings that employees and employers pay. Employees and employers must each contribute 6.2% (for a total of 12.4%) of the employee's pay up to the maximum withholding amount for Social Security. Additionally, employers must match the employees' payroll deductions for the Medicare tax in the amount of 1.45% (for a total of 2.9%) of the employees' gross pay less applicable deductions. In addition, the Affordable Care Act has mandated an additional 0.9% of Medicare tax for employees whose wages exceed $200,000 annually. The employer does not match this additional Medicare tax.

Let us look at an example of how the employer's share of the FICA tax works.

Courtney works as an hourly worker who earns an annual salary of $36,000 and is paid biweekly. Her gross pay is $1,384.62 per pay period ($36,000 per year/26 pay periods).

Courtney's share of the Social Security tax:	$1,384.62 × 6.2% = $85.85
Her employer's share of the Social Security tax:	$1,384.62 × 6.2% = $85.85
Total Social Security tax liability for Courtney's pay this period:	$171.70

As shown in the example, the employer and employee contribute the same amounts for the Social Security tax. Remember that the Social Security tax has a maximum withholding per year based on the employee's salary, which is $118,500 for 2015. After reaching that maximum, neither the employee nor the employer contribute any more Social Security tax.

William is the vice president of Sunny Glassworks. His annual salary is $225,000, which is paid semi-monthly. His gross pay per period is $9,375.00 ($225,000/24 pay periods). For the 12th pay period of the year, the Social Security tax withholding is as follows:

William's share of the Social Security tax:	$9,375 × 6.2% = $581.25
Sunny Glasswork's share of William's Social Security tax:	$9,375 × 6.2% = $581.25
Total Social Security tax liability for William's pay this period:	$1,162.50

After the 12th pay period, William's year-to-date pay is $9,375.00 × 12 = $112,500. After the 13th pay period, William's year-to-date pay will be $9,375 × 13 = $121,875, which exceeds the Social Security wage base. The amount subject to Social Security tax for the 13th pay period equals the wage base minus the 12th pay period YTD pay:

$118,500 − $112,500 = $6,000 of William's pay during the 13th pay period is subject to Social Security tax.

William's share of the Social Security tax:	$6,000 × 6.2% = $372.00
Sunny Glasswork's share of William's Social Security tax:	$6,000 × 6.2% = $372.00
Total Social Security tax liability for William's pay this period that must be remitted by Sunny Glassworks:	$744.00

Medicare tax, the other piece of the FICA taxes, has no maximum but does have an additional tax for high-wage employees. Let us look at Courtney's and William's pay again to see how the Medicare tax works. First Courtney, then William:

Courtney's share of the Medicare tax:	$1,384.62 × 1.45% = $20.08
Her employer's share of the Medicare tax:	$1,384.62 × 1.45% = $20.08
Total Medicare tax liability for Courtney's pay this period that must be remitted by Sunny Glassworks:	$40.16
Total FICA responsibility from Courtney's pay this period ($171.70 + $40.16):	$211.86

As of the 22nd pay period of the year, William's YTD pay is $206,250. Amount subject to the additional Medicare tax: $6,250.

Medicare tax amounts:	
William's standard Medicare tax liability:	$9,375 × 1.45% = $135.94
Sunny Glasswork's Medicare tax liability:	$9,375 × 1.45% = $135.94
William's additional Medicare tax liability:	$6,250 × 0.9% = 56.25
Total Medicare tax liability:	$328.13
Total FICA responsibility for William's pay this period	$328.13

Remember, no Social Security tax applies because William has exceeded the wage base.

Social Security and Medicare amounts may be listed separately when the company makes their tax deposit. The employer's tax deposit will also include the amount deducted from the employee for federal income tax.

Maintaining accurate records of taxes withheld through payroll registers and employee earnings records is a critical part of calculating proper FICA tax deductions. Whether a company uses a manual system, has an automated system, or outsources the payroll duties, it remains responsible for the accuracy of the deductions and maintenance of associated records.

Federal and State Unemployment Taxes

Another set of employer-paid payroll taxes includes those mandated by the Federal Unemployment Tax Act (*FUTA*) and State Unemployment Tax Act (*SUTA*). FUTA and SUTA are unemployment compensation funds established to provide for workers who have lost their jobs. Generally, the rate for FUTA tax is lower than that for SUTA tax because the states govern the disbursement of unemployment funds and because unemployment rates vary by region. FUTA taxes pay for the administrative expenses of the unemployment insurance fund. SUTA tax rates provide a localized and individual focus for employer taxes. The unemployment insurance fund pays for half of extended unemployment benefits as well as providing a fund of additional benefits against which states may borrow as necessary to cover unemployment claims. An interesting note is that FUTA and SUTA are employer-only taxes in all *but* three states: Alaska, New Jersey, and Pennsylvania.

FUTA pertains only to U.S. citizens and workers employed by American companies. According to the IRS, an American employer must meet the following criteria:

* An individual who is a resident of the United States,
* A partnership, if two-thirds or more of the partners are residents of the United States,

© Janis Christie/Photodisc/Getty Images, RF

- A trust, if all of the trustees are residents of the United States, or
- A corporation organized under the laws of the United States or of any State or the District of Columbia.

American citizens who work for companies outside of the United States who are not classified as American employers are not subject to FUTA provisions. Certain resident aliens and professions are exempt to FUTA provisions, as stipulated by Income Tax Regulation §31.3301-1. The professions from which employee compensation is exempt from FUTA provisions are:

- Compensation paid to agricultural workers.
- Compensation paid to household employees unless the compensation exceeds $1,000 during any calendar quarter of the current year or prior year.
- Compensation paid to employees of religious, charitable, educational, or certain other tax-exempt organizations.
- Compensation paid to employees of the U.S. government or any of its agencies.
- Compensation paid to employees of the government of any state of the United States, or any of its political subdivisions.
- Compensation paid to employees of the government of the District of Columbia, or any of its political subdivisions.

The 2015 rate for FUTA tax is 6.0% of the first $7,000 of an employee's wages paid during a calendar year. FUTA is paid by the employer. Employees that move to a different company will have the new employer paying additional FUTA taxes. Therefore, if an employer has a high turnover rate among its employees (i.e., a large number of employees remain employed for only a short period before terminating employment), the firm will pay FUTA tax for all employees for the first $7,000 of earnings. FUTA is subject to a 5.4% reduction, for which employers may qualify on two conditions:

- Employers make SUTA deposits on time and in full.
- As long as the state is not a credit reduction state.

Even with the credit, the employer's FUTA rate will be 0.6% on the first $7,000 of every employee's wage. The minimum FUTA tax rate is 0.6%, which means that a minimum of $42 ($7,000 × 0.006) may be paid per employee.

Establishment of the SUTA in each state provided states with local authority to offer unemployment or jobless benefits. Designed as an unemployment insurance program after the Great Depression of the 1930s, the remittance of SUTA payments follows many of the same procedures as other payroll taxes. As a state-run fund, each state can establish its own qualification requirements for both individual claims and business payments. The SUTA wage base and rate fluctuates among states, and can be an incentive for businesses to change operations from one state to another. A chart containing the SUTA wage base and rates is shown in Table 5-2.

As we noted, the nominal FUTA tax is 6.0%, of which the employer remits 0.6% to the federal government. The remaining 5.4% is a guideline, and many states have rates that vary based on employee retention and other factors. States examine employee turnover during an established period and determine if employers qualify for a credit against the nominal FUTA rate. SUTA is limited on wages collected. Depending upon the state the company is operating in, this limit may be equal to, higher, or lower than the FUTA rate. For example, Alaska's SUTA wage base was $38,700 in 2015.

An employer's SUTA rate is determined by a mix of state unemployment rates and company experience ratings. The SUTA rate for company A may be different from the rate for company B. For example, a construction company may experience higher unemployment claims because of the seasonal nature and higher risk associated with the industry, and therefore their rate may be 4.54%, whereas a similar-sized company in a professional services industry may have an unemployment rate of 3.28%. States issue letters on an annual basis to companies with the individually determined SUTA rate for the following year.

TABLE 5-2
SUTA Wage Base and Rates 2015

State	Wage Base	Min/Max Rate	State	Wage Base	Min/Max Rate
Alabama	$ 8,000	0.65%–6.8%	Montana	$29,500	0.02%–6.12%
Alaska	$38,700	1.0%–5.4%	Nebraska	$ 9,000	0.00%–5.4%
Arizona	$ 7,000	0.03%–7.79%	Nevada	$27,800	0.3%–5.4%
Arkansas	$12,000	0.9%–12.8%	New Hampshire	$14,000	0.1%–8.0%
California	$ 7,000	1.5%–6.2%	New Jersey	$32,000	1.2%–7.0%
Colorado	$11,800	0.78%–10.2%	New Mexico	$23,400	0.33%–5.4%
Connecticut	$15,000	1.9%–6.8%	New York	$10,500	2.1%–9.9%
Delaware	$18,500	0.3%–8.2%	North Carolina	$21,700	0.072%–6.912%
D.C.	$ 9,000	1.6%–7.0%	North Dakota	$35,600	0.1%–9.7%
Florida	$ 7,000	0.24%–5.4%	Ohio	$ 9,000	0.3%–10.8%
Georgia	$ 9,500	0.04%–8.10%	Oklahoma	$17,000	0.1%–5.5%
Hawaii	$40,900	0.2%–5.8%	Oregon	$35,700	1.5%–5.4%
Idaho	$36,000	0.453%–5.4%	Pennsylvania	$ 9,000	2.801%–14.0467%
Illinois	$12,960	0.55%–8.15%	Puerto Rico	$ 7,000	2.4%–5.4%
Indiana	$ 9,500	0.51%–9.568%	Rhode Island	$21,200	1.69%–9.79%
Iowa	$27,300	0.00%–7.5%	South Carolina	$14,000	0.06%–6.03%
Kansas	$12,000	0.09%–9.4%	South Dakota	$15,000	0.0%–10.03%
Kentucky	$ 9,900	1.0%–10.0%	Tennessee	$ 9,000	0.15%–10.0%
Louisiana	$ 7,700	0.10%–6.2%	Texas	$ 9,000	0.47%–7.49%
Maine	$12,000	0.8%–6.92%	Utah	$31,300	0.3%–7.3%
Maryland	$ 8,500	0.6%–9.0%	Vermont	$16,400	1.3%–8.4%
Massachusetts	$15,000	0.73%–11.13%	Virginia	$ 8,000	0.44%–6.54%
Michigan	$ 9,500	0.06%–13.3%	Washington	$42,100	0.17%–7.85%
Minnesota	$30,000	1.0%–9.0%	West Virginia	$12,000	1.5%–8.5%
Mississippi	$14,000	0.36%–5.56%	Wisconsin	$14,000	0.27%–12.0%
Missouri	$13,000	0.00%–13.65%	Wyoming	$24,700	0.27%–10.0%

*Employers in the highest tax group will have a wage base of $22,100.

Examples:
JayMac Communications, a California company, has 15 employees, all of whom have met the $7,000 threshold for the FUTA tax. The state portion for which JayMac is liable is 5.4%. The unemployment tax obligations are:

FUTA:	15 employees × $7,000 × 0.006 =	$ 630
SUTA:	15 employees × $7,000 × 0.054 =	$ 5,670
Total unemployment tax liability:		$ 6,300

Charmer Industries of Georgia has 20 employees: 18 employees have met the FUTA and SUTA thresholds, 2 employees have not, earning $5,400 and $2,500, respectively. The state obligation for Charmer is 2.3% owing to a favorable employer rating. Charmer's unemployment taxes would be computed as follows:

FUTA:	18 × $7,000 × 0.006 =	$ 756.00
	($5,400 + $2,500) × 0.006 =	$ 47.40
	Total FUTA liability:	$ 803.40
SUTA:	18 × $9,500 × 0.023 =	$3,933.00
	($5,400 + $2,500) × 0.023 =	$ 181.70
	Total SUTA liability:	$ 4,114.70
Total unemployment tax liability:		$ 4,918.10

Other State and Local Employer-Only Payroll Taxes

Some states have employer-only taxes unique to the area. Delaware, Colorado, Hawaii, and several other states have additional taxes that are remitted under different names.

- Georgia employers pay an administrative assessment of 0.08% on employee gross wages.
- Maine has an employer-paid Competitive Skills Scholarship tax of 0.06%.
- In California, employers pay an Employment Training Tax (ETT) of 0.1% on all wages up to the first $7,000 of wages.

As a payroll accountant, it is very important to be familiar with the tax withholding and employer responsibilities for each state in which the company does business.

Individual counties and cities can also impose occupational taxes on the businesses within their jurisdiction. For example, there is the Denver Occupational Privilege "Head" Tax. Individuals are responsible for $5.75 per month, and employers are responsible for $4.00 per employee per month. The reporting periods for the local and city taxes are separate from the filing requirements for federal or state. The payroll accountant must review all tiers of taxes to ensure compliance in collection, submission, and reporting.

FUTA and SUTA

1. AMS Enterprises in New Mexico has 30 employees. Of these, 25 have exceeded the FUTA and SUTA wage bases. This is the first quarter of the year, and AMS Enterprises has not yet paid any FUTA or SUTA taxes for the year. The other five employees' YTD wages are as follows: Employee A, $15,800; Employee B, $7,800; Employee C, $11,115; Employee D, $22,800; Employee E, $2,575. AMS Enterprises receives the full FUTA tax credit and pays a SUTA rate of 4.2%. How much are AMS Enterprises' FUTA and SUTA liabilities?

2. Noodle Noggins of Maine has 12 employees and is eligible for the full FUTA tax credit; the SUTA rate is 3.26%. Ten of the 12 employees have exceeded the FUTA wage base. Eight employees have exceeded the SUTA wage base. The remaining employees have the following YTD wages: $5,500, $6,800, $11,100, and $9,850. The Competitive Skills Scholarship tax applies to all employees. Noodle's YTD total wages are $279,580. What are the FUTA, SUTA, and Competitive Skills Scholarship tax liabilities for Noodle Noggins?

LO 5-2   Discuss Reporting Periods and Requirements for Employer Tax Deposits

The frequency of depositing federal income tax and FICA taxes depends on the size of the company's payroll. The IRS stipulates five different schedules for an employer's deposit of payroll taxes: annually, quarterly, monthly, semiweekly, and next business day. Of these, the most common deposit schedules are monthly and semiweekly. Electronic tax deposits are usually processed through the Electronic Federal Tax Payment System *(EFTPS)* website, although the IRS allows employers to transmit payments through certain financial institutions via *Automated Clearing House (ACH)* or wire transfer. When using the EFTPS, the employer must register with the IRS to access the site. The EFTPS is used for both Form 941 (Federal income tax, Social Security tax, and Medicare tax) and the quarterly/annual Form 940 FUTA tax deposit. The website for EFTPS is www.eftps.gov.

Lookback Period

The frequency of each company's deposits is determined through a *lookback period*, which is the amount of payroll taxes an employer has reported in the 12-month period prior to June 30 of the previous year. For example, the lookback period that the IRS would use for 2014 tax deposit frequency would be the July 1, 2012, through June 30, 2013, period. Employers receive notification about their deposit requirements in writing from the IRS in October of each year. Table 5-3 shows the lookback period.

TABLE 5-3
Lookback Period

Lookback Period for 2015 Taxes			
July 1, 2013, through September 30, 2013	October 1, 2013, through December 31, 2013	January 1, 2014, through March 31, 2014	April 1, 2014, through June 30, 2014

Source: IRS.

Deposit Frequencies

By using the lookback period, the IRS informs businesses if they need to deposit their payroll taxes annually, monthly, or semiweekly. Table 5-4 outlines the criteria for differences among deposit frequencies.

TABLE 5-4
Criteria for Deposit Frequencies

Frequency	Criteria	Due Date
Annually	$2,500 or less in employment taxes to be remitted annually with Form 944.	January 31 of the following year.
Quarterly	For any amounts not deposited during the quarter that may be due to rounding errors or other undeposited amounts.	15th of the month following the end of the quarter.
Monthly	Less than $50,000 in payroll tax liability during the lookback period. The amount of total tax liability is also found on Form 941, line 10. All new businesses are monthly schedule depositors unless they accrue in excess of $100,000 in payroll taxes for any pay period (see the Next Business Day rule frequency).	15th of the month following the month during which the company accrued payroll tax deposits. For example, taxes on March payroll would be due on **April 15,** or the next business day if April 15 falls on a weekend or a holiday.
Semiweekly	$50,000 or more in payroll tax liability during the lookback period. The amount of total tax liability is also found on Form 941, line 10. The exception to the semiweekly deposit schedule is the Next Business Day rule.	For payroll paid on a Wednesday, Thursday, or Friday, the payroll tax deposit is due by the following **Wednesday.** For payroll paid on a Saturday, Sunday, Monday, or Tuesday, the payroll tax is due by the following **Friday.**
Next Business Day	$100,000 or more in payroll tax liability for any payroll period.	The payroll tax deposit is due on the next business day.

Reporting Periods

1. Perry Plastics had $46,986 in payroll taxes during the lookback period. How often must the company deposit its payroll taxes?

2. For Perry Plastics, when is the deposit for June payroll taxes due?

3. Charlie's Kitchens has a payroll tax liability of $126,463 on its Friday payroll. When is the payroll tax deposit due?

LO 5-3 Prepare Mid-Year and Year-End Employer Tax Reporting and Deposits

Companies and payroll accountants are responsible for timely filing of the various tax documents required by governmental authorities. Note that the dates for depositing and reporting taxes are not always the same. For example, an employer may be required to file payroll tax deposits through the EFTPS on a semiweekly or monthly basis, depending upon their payroll tax liability during the lookback period. However, that same employer would not be required to file tax forms until after the end of the quarter. Like personal tax reporting, business reporting of statutory tax obligations has specific forms that employers must use. The most common forms used to deposit federal income tax and FICA taxes are Forms 941 (quarterly) and 944 (annual). An additional form used by agricultural businesses is Form 943, and it serves the same purpose as Form 941.

Form 941

Monthly payroll tax depositors file *Form 941* (see Figure 5-1), which is the employer's quarterly report of taxes deposited and taxes due. The form is used to reconcile the firm's deposits with the tax liability derived through mathematical computations on the form. It is common to encounter minor adjustments during the process of completing the form owing to rounding differences incurred during monthly tax deposits. Form 941 has specific instructions for its completion, as shown in Table 5-5.

TABLE 5-5

Instructions for Completing Form 941

Part 1:
Line 1: The number of employees during the quarter reported, as indicated in the box in the upper right-hand corner.
Line 2: Total wages subject to Federal income tax (less pre-tax deductions) for the quarter.
Line 3: Federal income tax withheld from wages paid during the quarter.
Line 4: Check box only if no wages paid during the quarter were subject to taxes (this is uncommon).
Lines 5a–5d: Column 1 is for the wages and tips subject to Social Security and Medicare taxes; column 2 is the amount of wages multiplied by the tax percent specified on the form.
Line 5e: Total of column 2, lines 5a–5d.
Line 5f: Tax on unreported tips.
Line 6: Total taxes due before adjustments.
Lines 7–9: Quarterly tax adjustments.
Line 10: Total tax less adjustments: line 6 minus lines 7, 8, and 9.
Line 11: Total taxes deposited during the quarter.
Line 12: Balance due.
Line 13: Overpayment.

Part 2:
Check the first box if the tax liability for the quarter is less than $2,500.
OR
Check the second box if the tax liability is greater than $2,500 and enter the taxes deposited each month during the quarter.
The total deposits must equal the total liability in Part 1.
If the business is a semiweekly depositor, then Schedule B must be completed.

FIGURE 5-1
Form 941

Form **941 for 2015:** Employer's QUARTERLY Federal Tax Return   950114
(Rev. January 2015)   Department of the Treasury — Internal Revenue Service   OMB No. 1545-0029

Employer identification number (EIN)   9 8 – 7 6 5 4 3 2 1

Name *(not your trade name)*   Patrick Rosenberg

Trade name *(if any)*   Rosenberg Enterprises

Address   1234 Any Street
          Number   Street   Suite or room number

          Mapletown   AR   55394
          City   State   ZIP code

          Foreign country name   Foreign province/county   Foreign postal code

Report for this Quarter of 2015
(Check one.)

☐ **1:** January, February, March

☒ **2:** April, May, June

☐ **3:** July, August, September

☐ **4:** October, November, December

Instructions and prior year forms are available at *www.irs.gov/form941.*

Read the separate instructions before you complete Form 941. Type or print within the boxes.

Part 1:   Answer these questions for this quarter.

1   Number of employees who received wages, tips, or other compensation for the pay period including: *Mar. 12* (Quarter 1), *June 12* (Quarter 2), *Sept. 12* (Quarter 3), or *Dec. 12* (Quarter 4)   **1**   12

2   Wages, tips, and other compensation . . . .   **2**   128356 ▪ 74

3   Federal income tax withheld from wages, tips, and other compensation . . . . . .   **3**   18432 ▪ 00

4   If no wages, tips, and other compensation are subject to social security or Medicare tax   ☐ Check and go to line 6.

		Column 1		Column 2
5a	Taxable social security wages . .	128356 ▪ 74	× .124 =	15916 ▪ 24
5b	Taxable social security tips . . .	▪	× .124 =	▪
5c	Taxable Medicare wages & tips. .	128356 ▪ 74	× .029 =	3722 ▪ 35
5d	Taxable wages & tips subject to Additional Medicare Tax withholding	▪	× .009 =	▪

5e   Add Column 2 from lines 5a, 5b, 5c, and 5d . . . .   **5e**   19638 ▪ 59

5f   Section 3121(q) Notice and Demand—Tax due on unreported tips (see instructions) . .   **5f**   ▪

6   Total taxes before adjustments. Add lines 3, 5e, and 5f . . . .   **6**   38070 ▪ 59

7   Current quarter's adjustment for fractions of cents . . . .   **7**   ▪ 01

8   Current quarter's adjustment for sick pay . . . .   **8**   ▪

9   Current quarter's adjustments for tips and group-term life insurance . . . . . .   **9**   ▪

10   Total taxes after adjustments. Combine lines 6 through 9 . . . .   **10**   38070 ▪ 60

11   Total deposits for this quarter, including overpayment applied from a prior quarter and overpayments applied from Form 941-X, 941-X (PR), 944-X, 944-X (PR), or 944-X (SP) filed in the current quarter . . . .   **11**   38070 ▪ 60

12   Balance due. If line 10 is more than line 11, enter the difference and see instructions . . .   **12**   ▪

13   Overpayment. If line 11 is more than line 10, enter the difference   ▪   Check one: ☐ Apply to next return. ☐ Send a refund.

▶ **You MUST complete both pages of Form 941 and SIGN it.**   Next ▶

For Privacy Act and Paperwork Reduction Act Notice, see the back of the Payment Voucher.   Cat. No. 17001Z   Form **941** (Rev. 1-2015)

Source: Internal Revenue Service.

950214

Name (not your trade name)	Employer identification number (EIN)
Patrick Rosenberg	98-7654321

Part 2: **Tell us about your deposit schedule and tax liability for this quarter.**

If you are unsure about whether you are a monthly schedule depositor or a semiweekly schedule depositor, see Pub. 15 (Circular E), section 11.

14 Check one: ☐ Line 10 on this return is less than $2,500 or line 10 on the return for the prior quarter was less than $2,500, and you did not incur a $100,000 next-day deposit obligation during the current quarter. If line 10 for the prior quarter was less than $2,500 but line 10 on this return is $100,000 or more, you must provide a record of your federal tax liability. If you are a monthly schedule depositor, complete the deposit schedule below; if you are a semiweekly schedule depositor, attach Schedule B (Form 941). Go to Part 3.

☒ **You were a monthly schedule depositor for the entire quarter.** Enter your tax liability for each month and total liability for the quarter, then go to Part 3.

Tax liability: **Month 1**   12690 . 20

Month 2   12690 . 20

Month 3   12690 . 20

Total liability for quarter   38070 . 60   Total must equal line 10.

☐ **You were a semiweekly schedule depositor for any part of this quarter.** Complete Schedule B (Form 941), Report of Tax Liability for Semiweekly Schedule Depositors, and attach it to Form 941.

Part 3: **Tell us about your business. If a question does NOT apply to your business, leave it blank.**

15 If your business has closed or you stopped paying wages . . . . ☐ Check here, and

enter the final date you paid wages   /   /   .

16 If you are a seasonal employer and you do not have to file a return for every quarter of the year . . . ☐ Check here.

Part 4: **May we speak with your third-party designee?**

Do you want to allow an employee, a paid tax preparer, or another person to discuss this return with the IRS? See the instructions for details.

☐ Yes. Designee's name and phone number

Select a 5-digit Personal Identification Number (PIN) to use when talking to the IRS. ☐ ☐ ☐ ☐ ☐

☒ No.

Part 5: **Sign here. You MUST complete both pages of Form 941 and SIGN it.**

Under penalties of perjury, I declare that I have examined this return, including accompanying schedules and statements, and to the best of my knowledge and belief, it is true, correct, and complete. Declaration of preparer (other than taxpayer) is based on all information of which preparer has any knowledge.

X Sign your name here   *Patrick J. Rosenberg*

Print your name here   Patrick Rosenberg

Print your title here   Owner

Date   1/31/2015

Best daytime phone   532-555-2340

Paid Preparer Use Only   Check if you are self-employed . . . ☐

Preparer's name		PTIN	
Preparer's signature		Date	/ /
Firm's name (or yours if self-employed)		EIN	
Address		Phone	
City		State		ZIP code	

Source: Internal Revenue Service.

Schedule B

Semiweekly depositors must file Schedule B (Figure 5-2) in addition to Form 941. This form allows firms to enter the details of payroll tax liabilities that occur multiple times during a month. On *Schedule B*, the payroll tax liability is entered on the days of the month on which the payroll occurred. The total tax liability for each month is entered in the right-hand column. The total tax liability for the quarter must equal line 10 of Form 941.

Example:

Nicholas Lindeman is the owner of a company that is a semiweekly payroll tax depositor. The company pays its employees on the 15th and the last day of the month. Pay dates that fall on the weekend are paid on the preceding Friday. Because he is a semiweekly schedule depositor, he must file Schedule B in addition to Form 941. For the first quarter of 2015, Lindeman's company had the following pay dates and payroll tax liabilities:

Pay Date	Payroll Tax Liability
January 15	$ 41,486.47
January 31	$ 41,486.47
February 14	$ 41,486.47
February 28	$ 41,486.47
March 15	$ 41,486.47
March 31	$ 41,486.47
Total Tax Liability for the Quarter	**$ 248,918.82**

Note that the payroll tax liability is (a) listed on the payroll date, and (b) includes the FICA taxes (employee and employer share) and the federal income tax withheld.

State Tax Remittance

Each state that charges income tax has its own form that it uses for employee income *tax remittance* purposes. State tax forms are similar to federal forms as far as the information included is concerned and generally have similar due dates. An important note is that each state has its own unique taxes. For example, California has an employee-only State Disability Insurance (SDI) tax of 0.9% on earnings up to $104,378 per employee, as well as an employer-only Employment Training Tax (ETT) of 0.1% on the first $7,000 of each employee's earnings. These additional taxes are included on the state's payroll tax return.

Additionally, employers are responsible for reporting any other local or regional taxes. Employers must abide by the filing requirements for each of the taxes or face fines or penalties depending upon state/local tax code. The purpose of these taxes can include the provision of social services and the funding of infrastructure costs. The Denver Head tax was designed to fulfill both of these purposes, with the increase of infrastructure and the availability of municipal programs for residents.

Form 944

Firms with a total annual tax liability of less than $2,500 use *Form 944* (see Figure 5-3). Like Form 941, the firm enters the details of wages paid and computes the taxes due. The firm reports the monthly deposits and liabilities in Part 2. However, instead of entering a quarterly liability, the firm enters the annual liability, which is the sum of all the monthly liabilities. The IRS must notify a company in writing of the requirement to file a Form 944.

FIGURE 5-2
Schedule B for Form 941

Schedule B (Form 941):

Report of Tax Liability for Semiweekly Schedule Depositors

960311

(Rev. January 2014)   Department of the Treasury — Internal Revenue Service

OMB No. 1545-0029

Employer identification number (EIN)   1 3 – 2 5 6 9 7 0 4

Name *(not your trade name)*   Nicholas Lindeman

Calendar year   2 0 1 4   (Also check quarter)

Report for this Quarter...
(Check one.)

- [X] **1:** January, February, March
- [ ] **2:** April, May, June
- [ ] **3:** July, August, September
- [ ] **4:** October, November, December

Use this schedule to show your **TAX LIABILITY** for the quarter; DO NOT use it to show your deposits. When you file this form with Form 941 or Form 941-SS, DO NOT change your tax liability by adjustments reported on any Forms 941-X or 944-X. You must fill out this form and attach it to Form 941 or Form 941-SS if you are a semiweekly schedule depositor or became one because your accumulated tax liability on any day was $100,000 or more. Write your daily tax liability on the numbered space that corresponds to the date wages were paid. See Section 11 in Pub. 15 (Circular E), Employer's Tax Guide, for details.

Month 1

#		#		#		#		Tax liability for Month 1
1	.	9	.	17	.	25	.	
2	.	10	.	18	.	26	.	82972 . 94
3	.	11	.	19	.	27	.	
4	.	12	.	20	.	28	.	
5	.	13	.	21	.	29	.	
6	.	14	.	22	.	30	.	
7	.	15	41486 . 47	23	.	31	41486 . 47	
8	.	16	.	24				

Month 2

#		#		#		#		Tax liability for Month 2
1	.	9	.	17	.	25	.	
2	.	10	.	18	.	26	.	82972 . 94
3	.	11	.	19	.	27	.	
4	.	12	.	20	.	28	41486 . 47	
5	.	13	.	21	.	29	.	
6	.	14	41486 . 47	22	.	30	.	
7	.	15	.	23	.	31	.	
8	.	16	.	24	.			

Month 3

#		#		#		#		Tax liability for Month 3
1	.	9	.	17	.	25	.	
2	.	10	.	18	.	26	.	82972 . 94
3	.	11	.	19	.	27	.	
4	.	12	.	20	.	28	.	
5	.	13	.	21	.	29	.	
6	.	14	.	22	.	30	.	
7	.	15	41486 . 47	23	.	31	41486 . 47	
8	.	16	.	24	.			

Fill in your total liability for the quarter (Month 1 + Month 2 + Month 3) ▶
Total must equal line 10 on Form 941 or Form 941-SS.

Total liability for the quarter

248918 . 82

For Paperwork Reduction Act Notice, see separate instructions.   IRS.gov/form941   Cat. No. 11967Q   **Schedule B (Form 941)** (Rev. 1-2014)

Source: Internal Revenue Service.

FIGURE 5-3
Form 944

Form **944 for 2014:** **Employer's ANNUAL Federal Tax Return**

Department of the Treasury — Internal Revenue Service

OMB No. 1545-2007

Employer identification number (EIN)   2 4 – 8 9 7 6 5 0 4

Name *(not your trade name)*   Madison K. Poole

Trade name *(if any)*   MP Pool Service

Address   18196 Arabella Street

Number	Street		Suite or room number

Fountain Grove	CA	93020
City	State	ZIP code

Foreign country name	Foreign province/county	Foreign postal code

Who Must File Form 944

You must file annual Form 944 instead of filing quarterly Forms 941 **only if the IRS notified you in writing.**
Instructions and prior-year forms are available at *www.irs.gov/form944.*

Read the separate instructions before you complete Form 944. Type or print within the boxes.

Part 1:   Answer these questions for this year. Employers in American Samoa, Guam, the Commonwealth of the Northern Mariana Islands, the U.S. Virgin Islands, and Puerto Rico can skip lines 1 and 2.

1	Wages, tips, and other compensation	1	8952 . 20
2	Federal income tax withheld from wages, tips, and other compensation	2	800 . 00
3	If no wages, tips, and other compensation are subject to social security or Medicare tax	3 ☐	Check and go to line 5.
4	Taxable social security and Medicare wages and tips:		

		Column 1		Column 2
4a	Taxable social security wages	8952 . 20	× .124 =	1110 . 07
4b	Taxable social security tips	.	× .124 =	.
4c	Taxable Medicare wages & tips	8952 . 20	× .029 =	259 . 61
4d	Taxable wages & tips subject to Additional Medicare Tax withholding	.	× .009 =	.

	4e Add Column 2 from lines 4a, 4b, 4c, and 4d	4e	1369 . 68
5	Total taxes before adjustments. Add lines 2 and 4e	5	2169 . 68
6	Current year's adjustments (see instructions)	6	.
7	Total taxes after adjustments. Combine lines 5 and 6	7	.
8	Total deposits for this year, including overpayment applied from a prior year and overpayments applied from Form 944-X, 944-X (PR), 944-X (SP), 941-X, or 941-X (PR) .	8	2169 . 68
9a	Reserved		
9b	Reserved		
10	Reserved		
11	Balance due. If line 7 is more than line 8, enter the difference and see instructions	11	2169 . 68
12	Overpayment. If line 8 is more than line 7, enter the difference	.	Check one: ☐ Apply to next return. ☐ Send a refund.

▶ **You MUST complete both pages of Form 944 and SIGN it.**

Next ▶

For Privacy Act and Paperwork Reduction Act Notice, see the back of the Payment Voucher.   Cat. No. 39316N   Form **944** (2014)

Name *(not your trade name)*	Employer identification number (EIN)
Madison K. Poole	24-8976504

Part 2: **Tell us about your deposit schedule and tax liability for this year.**

13 Check one: ☒ Line 7 is less than $2,500. Go to Part 3.

☐ Line 7 is $2,500 or more. Enter your tax liability for each month. If you are a semiweekly depositor or you accumulate $100,000 or more of liability on any day during a deposit period, you must complete Form 945-A instead of the boxes below.

	Jan.		Apr.		Jul.		Oct.
13a	.	13d	.	13g	.	13j	.
	Feb.		May		Aug.		Nov.
13b	.	13e	.	13h	.	13k	.
	Mar.		Jun.		Sep.		Dec.
13c	.	13f	.	13i	.	13l	.

Total liability for year. Add lines 13a through 13l. Total must equal line 7. **13m** .

Part 3: **Tell us about your business. If question 14 does NOT apply to your business, leave it blank.**

14 If your business has closed or you stopped paying wages...

☐ Check here and enter the final date you paid wages.

Part 4: **May we speak with your third-party designee?**

Do you want to allow an employee, a paid tax preparer, or another person to discuss this return with the IRS? See the instructions for details.

☐ Yes. Designee's name and phone number

Select a 5-digit Personal Identification Number (PIN) to use when talking to IRS. ☐ ☐ ☐ ☐ ☐

☒ No.

Part 5: **Sign Here. You MUST complete both pages of Form 944 and SIGN it.**

Under penalties of perjury, I declare that I have examined this return, including accompanying schedules and statements, and to the best of my knowledge and belief, it is true, correct, and complete. Declaration of preparer (other than taxpayer) is based on all information of which preparer has any knowledge.

X **Sign your name here** *Madison K. Poole*

Print your name here Madison K. Poole

Print your title here President

Date 1/31/2015

Best daytime phone 909-555-8760

Paid Preparer Use Only

Check if you are self-employed ☐

Preparer's name		PTIN	
Preparer's signature		Date	
Firm's name (or yours if self-employed)		EIN	
Address		Phone	
City		State	ZIP code

Page **2**

Form **944** (2014)

Source: Internal Revenue Service.

Example:
Madison Poole owns MP Pool Service. MP Pool Service is a sole proprietorship with one part-time employee who works only five months of the year. The IRS has notified Mr. Poole that MP Pool Service is required to report federal payroll tax liabilities using Form 944. The total wages paid to the employee during 2015 were $8,952.20. The federal income tax liability was $800, and total payroll tax liability for the year was $2,169.98. Because the total annual payroll tax liability is less than $2,500, MP Pool Service must file an annual return. The due date for Form 944 is January 31 of the following year.

Unemployment Tax Reporting

Form 940 is the employer's annual report of federal unemployment taxes due, based on employee wages paid during the year. This report is for a calendar year and is due by January 31 of the following year.

According to 26 IRC section 3306, certain fringe benefits are not subject to federal unemployment taxes because they represent noncash compensation that is not intended to be used as disposable income. Specific examples of these fringe benefits are employee retirement plans, such as the 401(k) and 403(b), and qualified section 125 "cafeteria" plans. For tax reporting purposes, amounts contributed by employees to these exempt items must be treated in one of two ways on Form 940:

- Deducted from Line 3 "Total payments to all employees."
- Reported on Line 4 "Payments exempt from FUTA taxes."

An example of Form 940 for CJS Creations is found in Figure 5-4.

Example:
Cheryl Sullivan owns CJS Creations. She filed the Annual FUTA Tax Return (Form 940) to report unemployment tax contributions during 2014. CJS Creations has 12 employees. Lines 9 through 11 are adjustments to the FUTA deposited, which are rare and do not apply in this scenario (see pages 8–10 of Publication 15 for more details).

Line 1a: If the company pays unemployment tax in only one state, then the state abbreviation is entered here; otherwise, the company must check the box on line 1b and complete schedule A. CJS Creations has only one location, in Hawaii.

Line 3: All wages paid during the calendar year are entered here.

Line 4: Wages exempt from FUTA Tax. None of CJS Creations' wages are exempt from FUTA tax.

Line 5: Wages for the year that are in excess of $7,000 per employee are entered here. The FUTA wage base is $7,000 per employee. In this example, all employees worked for the entire calendar year, so CJS Creations is responsible for FUTA tax on $7,000 per employee. To compute Line 5:

Total wages	$364,039.32
less FUTA wage base ($7,000 × 12 employees)	(84,000.00)
Wages in excess of $7,000	$280,039.32

Line 6: This is the sum of lines 4 and 5.

Line 7: FUTA Taxable wages, which are $84,000 for CJS Creations.

Line 8: FUTA Tax ($84,000 × 0.06) or $504.00.

Line 12: Total FUTA Tax of $504.00.

Line 13: Total FUTA Tax deposited during the year. This total must match Line 17 (side 2). Because all of CJS Creations' employees exceeded their wage base during the first quarter, all FUTA tax had been deposited.

FIGURE 5-4
Form 940

Form **940 for 2014:** **Employer's Annual Federal Unemployment (FUTA) Tax Return**   850113

Department of the Treasury — Internal Revenue Service

OMB No. 1545-0028

Employer identification number (EIN)   1 2 – 5 0 7 9 8 6 4

Name *(not your trade name)*   Cheryl J. Sullivan

Trade name *(if any)*   CJS Creations

Address   23953 Island Way

Number   Street   Suite or room number

Millilani   HI   99403

City   State   ZIP code

Foreign country name   Foreign province/county   Foreign postal code

Type of Return
(Check all that apply.)

☐ **a.** Amended

☐ **b.** Successor employer

☐ **c.** No payments to employees in 2014

☐ **d.** Final: Business closed or stopped paying wages

Instructions and prior-year forms are available at *www.irs.gov/form940.*

Read the separate instructions before you complete this form. Please type or print within the boxes.

Part 1: **Tell us about your return. If any line does NOT apply, leave it blank.**

1a	If you had to pay state unemployment tax in one state only, enter the state abbreviation .	**1a** H I
1b	If you had to pay state unemployment tax in more than one state, you are a multi-state employer	**1b** ☐ Check here. Complete Schedule A (Form 940).
2	If you paid wages in a state that is subject to CREDIT REDUCTION	**2** ☐ Check here. Complete Schedule A (Form 940).

Part 2: **Determine your FUTA tax before adjustments for 2014. If any line does NOT apply, leave it blank.**

3	Total payments to all employees	**3**	364039 ▪ 32
4	Payments exempt from FUTA tax	**4**	▪

Check all that apply: **4a** ☐ Fringe benefits   **4c** ☐ Retirement/Pension   **4e** ☐ Other
4b ☐ Group-term life insurance   **4d** ☐ Dependent care

5	Total of payments made to each employee in excess of $7,000	**5** 280039 ▪ 32	
6	Subtotal (line 4 + line 5 = line 6)	**6**	280039 ▪ 32
7	Total taxable FUTA wages (line 3 – line 6 = line 7) (see instructions)	**7**	84000 ▪ 00
8	FUTA tax before adjustments (line 7 x .006 = line 8)	**8**	504 ▪ 00

Part 3: **Determine your adjustments. If any line does NOT apply, leave it blank.**

9	If ALL of the taxable FUTA wages you paid were excluded from state unemployment tax, multiply line 7 by .054 (line 7 × .054 = line 9). Go to line 12	**9**	▪
10	If SOME of the taxable FUTA wages you paid were excluded from state unemployment tax, OR you paid ANY state unemployment tax late (after the due date for filing Form 940), complete the worksheet in the instructions. Enter the amount from line 7 of the worksheet . .	**10**	▪
11	If credit reduction applies, enter the total from Schedule A (Form 940)	**11**	▪

Part 4: **Determine your FUTA tax and balance due or overpayment for 2014. If any line does NOT apply, leave it blank.**

12	Total FUTA tax after adjustments (lines 8 + 9 + 10 + 11 = line 12)	**12**	504 ▪ 00
13	FUTA tax deposited for the year, including any overpayment applied from a prior year .	**13**	504 ▪ 00
14	Balance due (If line 12 is more than line 13, enter the excess on line 14.) • If line 14 is more than $500, you must deposit your tax. • If line 14 is $500 or less, you may pay with this return. (see instructions)	**14**	▪
15	Overpayment (If line 13 is more than line 12, enter the excess on line 15 and check a box below.)	**15**	▪

▶ You **MUST** complete both pages of this form and **SIGN** it.   Check one: ☐ Apply to next return. ☐ Send a refund.

Next ▶

For Privacy Act and Paperwork Reduction Act Notice, see the back of Form 940-V, Payment Voucher.   Cat. No. 11234O   Form **940** (2014)

Source: Internal Revenue Service.

FIGURE 5-4 *(concluded)*   850212

Name *(not your trade name)*	Employer identification number (EIN)
Cheryl J. Sullivan	12-5079864

Part 5:   Report your FUTA tax liability by quarter only if line 12 is more than $500. If not, go to Part 6.

16   Report the amount of your FUTA tax liability for each quarter; do NOT enter the amount you deposited. If you had no liability for a quarter, leave the line blank.

16a   **1st quarter** (January 1 – March 31) . . . . **16a** [.   ]

16b   **2nd quarter** (April 1 – June 30) . . . . **16b** [.   ]

16c   **3rd quarter** (July 1 – September 30) . . . . **16c** [.   ]

16d   **4th quarter** (October 1 – December 31) . . . . . . **16d** [.   ]

17   Total tax liability for the year (lines 16a + 16b + 16c + 16d = line 17) **17** [.   ]   **Total must equal line 12.**

Part 6:   May we speak with your third-party designee?

Do you want to allow an employee, a paid tax preparer, or another person to discuss this return with the IRS? See the instructions for details.

☐ **Yes.**   Designee's name and phone number [   ]   [   ]

Select a 5-digit Personal Identification Number (PIN) to use when talking to IRS [ ] [ ] [ ] [ ] [ ]

☒ **No.**

Part 7:   Sign here. You MUST complete both pages of this form and SIGN it.

Under penalties of perjury, I declare that I have examined this return, including accompanying schedules and statements, and to the best of my knowledge and belief, it is true, correct, and complete, and that no part of any payment made to a state unemployment fund claimed as a credit was, or is to be, deducted from the payments made to employees. Declaration of preparer (other than taxpayer) is based on all information of which preparer has any knowledge.

✗ **Sign your name here**	*Cheryl J. Sullivan*	Print your name here	Cheryl J. Sullivan
		Print your title here	President
Date	1/31/2015	Best daytime phone	808-555-9876

Paid Preparer Use Only   Check if you are self-employed . ☐

Preparer's name		PTIN	
Preparer's signature		Date	/ /
Firm's name (or yours if self-employed)		EIN	
Address		Phone	
City		State		ZIP code	

Source: Internal Revenue Service.

Matching Final Annual Pay to Form W-2

One of the more common questions payroll accountants receive following the release of W-2s from the employees at the end of the year is "why doesn't this match my final paycheck?" In short, it should—if you know how to calculate the income that belongs in each block of the W-2. The W-2 reflects all gross wages received by the employee, less any pre-tax deductions: health insurance, qualified retirement contributions, and other deductions. The total federal income taxes that the employer withheld from the employee and remitted as part of their 941 tax deposits also appears on the W-2 and acts as supporting documentation for the total wages reported on Forms 941 and 940.

Similarly, Form W-2 contains the employee's Social Security and Medicare wages. These wages are not reduced by contributions by the employee to qualified pension accounts (401(k), 403(b), etc.), and therefore may be higher than box 1. The only difference between boxes 3 and 5 will come when employees earn more than the maximum Social Security wage in the given year, $118,500 for 2015. When this occurs, the Medicare wages reported in box 5 will be greater than Social Security wages displayed in box 3. Boxes 4 and 6 contain the Social Security and Medicare taxes withheld from the employee and remitted through 941 deposits. Employees who receive tuition reimbursement benefits from their employer may receive up to $5,250 annually, per IRS publication 970. Any tuition reimbursed to the employee in excess of $5,250 during a calendar year must be treated as taxable income for the year and included in Box 1 wages.

Tipped employees will have amounts represented in boxes 7 and 8 for their reported tips. Box 10 is used to report Dependent Care Benefits. Contributions to nonqualifying retirement plans will be represented in box 11. Employee contributions to qualifying plans are represented in box 12. An alphabetical code is assigned to the specific type of qualified retirement plan the contributions are made to (A through EE). Box 13 denotes specific contributions to deferred compensation plans. Box 14 is used to report other information to employees, such as union dues, health insurance premiums (not pre-tax), educational assistance payments, and other similar items. State and local taxes and wages are represented in boxes 15 through 20.

When completing a *Form W-2*, you will have several copies of the same form. A sample Form W-2 is found in Figure 5-5. According to the order in which they print, the copies of Form W-2 are as follows:

Which Copy?	What Is It For?
Copy A	Social Security Administration
Copy 1	State, City, or Local Tax Department
Copy B	Filing with the Employee's Federal Tax Return
Copy C	Employee's Records
Copy 2	State, City, or Local Tax Department
Copy D	Employer

The following is an example of a Form W-2 for Jill M. Martin.

Example:

Jill Meri Martin worked for LC Enterprises during 2015. The following is on her W-2 for 2015.

> **Box 1** contains the wages, tips, and other compensation. Jill earned $36,523.34 during 2015.
>
> **Box 2** contains the federal income tax withheld: Jill had $3,671.04 withheld based on her W-4 information.
>
> **Boxes 3 and 5** contain the Social Security and Medicare wages. Note that these two boxes contain a higher amount than box 1. Jill has a retirement plan into which she contributed $2,000 during 2015.
>
> **Boxes 4 and 6** contain the Social Security tax withheld ($2,388.45) and the Medicare tax withheld ($558.59).
>
> **Box 12** contains amounts for nontaxable items. Codes for Box 12 are contained in *Figure 5-6.*
>
> **Boxes 15–17** contain the state tax information. Jill had $1,826.17 withheld for state taxes based on the state withholding certificate that she filed in January 2015.

FIGURE 5-5

Form W-2

22222 | Void ☐ | a Employee's social security number 555-55-5555 | For Official Use Only ▶ OMB No. 1545-0008

b Employer identification number (EIN) 34-1029386	1 Wages, tips, other compensation 36,523.34	2 Federal income tax withheld 3,671.04
c Employer's name, address, and ZIP code LC Enterprises 1234 A Street Anytown, IL 66734	3 Social security wages 38,523.34	4 Social security tax withheld 2,388.45
	5 Medicare wages and tips 38,523.34	6 Medicare tax withheld 558.59
	7 Social security tips	8 Allocated tips
d Control number	9	10 Dependent care benefits
e Employee's first name and initial / Last name / Suff.	11 Nonqualified plans	12a See instructions for box 12 Code D 2,000.00
Jill M Martin 573 First Street Anytown, IL 66734	13 Statutory employee ☐ Retirement plan ☒ Third-party sick pay ☐	12b Code
	14 Other	12c Code
f Employee's address and ZIP code		12d Code

15 State	Employer's state ID number	16 State wages, tips, etc.	17 State income tax	18 Local wages, tips, etc.	19 Local income tax	20 Locality name
IL	00071053723	36,523.34	1,826.17			

Form **W-2** **Wage and Tax Statement** **2015**

Department of the Treasury—Internal Revenue Service

For Privacy Act and Paperwork Reduction Act Notice, see the separate instructions.

Copy A For Social Security Administration — Send this entire page with Form W-3 to the Social Security Administration; photocopies are **not** acceptable.

Cat. No. 10134D

Do Not Cut, Fold, or Staple Forms on This Page

Source: Internal Revenue Service.

FIGURE 5-6

Box 12 Codes for Form W-2

A	Uncollected social security or RRTA tax on lips	K	20% excise tax on excess golden parachute payments	V	Income from exercise of nonstatutory stock option(s)
B	Uncollected Medicare tax on tips (but not Additional Medicare Tax)	L	Substantiated employee business expense reimbursements	W	Employer contributions (including employee contributions through a cafeteria plan) to an employee's health savings account (HSA)
C	Taxable cost of group-term life insurance over $50,000	M	Uncollected social security or RRTA tax on taxable cost of group-term life insurance over $50,000 (former employees only)	Y	Deferrals under a section 409A nonqualified deferred compensation plan
D	Elective deferrals to a section 401(k) cash or deferred arrangement plan (including a SIMPLE 401(k) arrangement)	N	Uncollected Medicare tax on taxable cost of group-term life insurance over $50,000 (but not Additional Medicare Tax)(former employees only)	Z	Income under a nonqualified deferred compensation plan that fails to satisfy section 409A
E	Elective deferrals under a section 403(b) salary reduction agreement	P	Excludable moving expense reimbursements paid directly to employee	AA	Designated Roth contributions under a section 401(k) plan
F	Elective deferrals under a section 408(k)(6) salary reduction SEP	Q	Nontaxable combat pay	BB	Designated Roth contributions under a section 403(b) plan
G	Elective deferrals and employer contributions (including nonelective deferrals) to a section 457(b) deferred compensation plan	R	Employer contributions to an Archer MSA	DD	Cost of employer-sponsored health coverage
H	Elective deferrals to a section 501(c)(18)(D) tax-exempt organization plan	S	Employee salary reduction contributions under a section 408(p) SIMPLE plan	EE	Designated Roth contributions under a governmental section 457(b) plan
J	Nontaxable sick pay	T	Adoption benefits		

Form W-3 is the transmittal form that accompanies the submission of Copy A to the Social Security Administration. It contains the aggregate data for all W-2s issued by an employer. Form W-3 and all accompanying W-2s must be filed by February 28 (if filing a paper W-3 form) or March 31 (if filing an electronic W-3). The total annual wages reported on the W-3 must match the annual wages reported on Forms 941 and 940.

The following example from Feola's Cafe depicts the completion of Form W-3 for a company. (See Figure 5-7.)

Example:
Kevin Feola is the owner of Feola's Cafe, 125 Flat Avenue, Brooklyn, New York, 12002, EIN 49-0030594, phone number 929-555-0904.

Box b: Feola's Cafe will file Form 941 to report quarterly tax liability, so box 941-SS is checked.

Box c: Feola's Cafe had 25 employees who received W-2s.

Box 1: Gross wages and tips for 2015 were $654,087.35.

Box 2: The amount of federal income tax withheld for the 2015 wages was $117,735.

Box 3: Social Security wages were $546,333.35.

Box 4: Social Security tax withheld was $33,872.67.

Box 5: Medicare wages and tips were $570,838.35.

Box 6: Medicare tax withheld was $8,277.16.

Box 7: Social Security tips were $24,505.

Box 12a: Deferred compensation was $83,249.

FIGURE 5-7
Form W-3

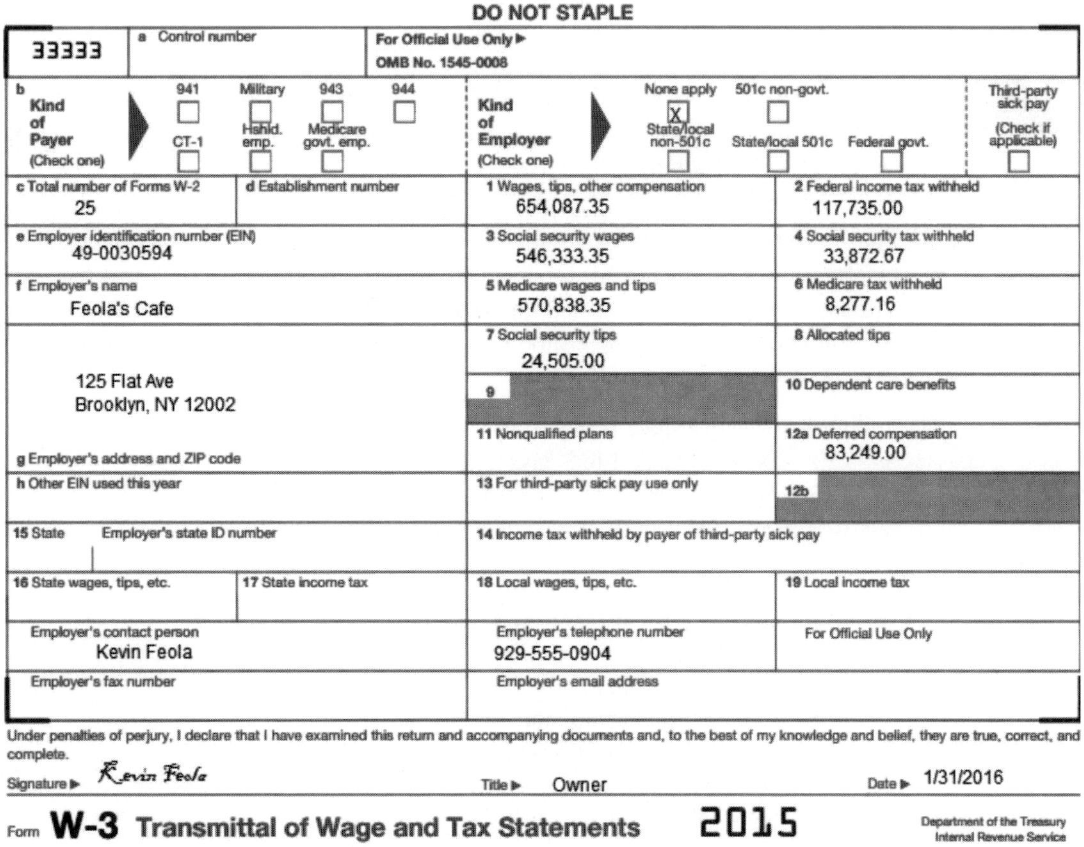

DO NOT STAPLE

33333 | a Control number | For Official Use Only ▶ OMB No. 1545-0008

b Kind of Payer (Check one) ▶ 941 | Military | 943 | 944 | CT-1 | Hshld. emp. | Medicare govt. emp.

Kind of Employer (Check one) ▶ None apply [X] | 501c non-govt. | State/local non-501c | State/local 501c | Federal govt.

Third-party sick pay (Check if applicable)

c Total number of Forms W-2: 25	d Establishment number
1 Wages, tips, other compensation: 654,087.35	2 Federal income tax withheld: 117,735.00
e Employer identification number (EIN): 49-0030594	
3 Social security wages: 546,333.35	4 Social security tax withheld: 33,872.67
f Employer's name: Feola's Cafe	
5 Medicare wages and tips: 570,838.35	6 Medicare tax withheld: 8,277.16
7 Social security tips: 24,505.00	8 Allocated tips
9	10 Dependent care benefits
11 Nonqualified plans	12a Deferred compensation: 83,249.00
g Employer's address and ZIP code: 125 Flat Ave, Brooklyn, NY 12002	
h Other EIN used this year	
13 For third-party sick pay use only	12b
15 State / Employer's state ID number	14 Income tax withheld by payer of third-party sick pay
16 State wages, tips, etc. / 17 State income tax	18 Local wages, tips, etc. / 19 Local income tax
Employer's contact person: Kevin Feola	Employer's telephone number: 929-555-0904 / For Official Use Only
Employer's fax number	Employer's email address

Under penalties of perjury, I declare that I have examined this return and accompanying documents and, to the best of my knowledge and belief, they are true, correct, and complete.

Signature ▶ Kevin Feola   Title ▶ Owner   Date ▶ 1/31/2016

Form **W-3 Transmittal of Wage and Tax Statements** 2015   Department of the Treasury Internal Revenue Service

	Tax Forms

STOP & CHECK

1. Jacobucci Enterprises is a monthly schedule depositor. According to the information it reported on Form 941, its quarterly tax liability is $8,462.96. During the quarter, it made deposits of $2,980.24 and $3,068.24. How much must it remit with its tax return?

2. Corrado's Corrals paid annual wages totaling $278,452.76 to 15 employees. Assuming that all employees were employed for the entire year, what is the amount of FUTA wages?

3. For Corrado's Corrals in the previous question, what is the FUTA tax liability?

4. Skyrockets, Inc., had the following wage information reported in box 1 of its W-2s:

   Employee A: $25,650
   Employee B: $30,025
   Employee C: $28,550
   Employee D: $31,970
   What amount must they report as total wages on its Form W-3?

LO 5-4 Describe Payroll Within the Context of Business Expenses

© John Flournoy/McGraw-Hill
Education, RF

Understanding employer payroll expenses is important because of the wide range of mandatory activities and lesser-known expenses associated with maintaining employees. Compensation expenses and employer payroll-related liabilities must be accurately maintained in an accounting system. The scope of payroll-related employer responsibilities contribute to the need for knowledgeable payroll accountants.

The amounts withheld from employee pay and the employer liabilities must be deposited in a timely manner with the appropriate authorities. The omission of any of the required filings, activities, or any inaccuracy in the accounting system can lead to problems that could include governmental sanctions and penalties. The IRS will waive penalties under two conditions:

1. The amount of the shortfall does not exceed the greater of $100 or 2% of the required tax deposit.
2. The amount of the shortfall is deposited either (A) by the due date of the period return (monthly and semiweekly depositors), or (B) the first Wednesday or Friday that falls after the 15th of the month (semiweekly depositors only).

The following penalties apply to late filings and underpayments:

2% - Deposits made 1 to 5 days late.

5% - Deposits made 6 to 15 days late.

10% - Deposits made 16 or more days late. Also applies to amounts paid within 10 days of the date of the first notice the IRS sent asking for the tax due.

10% - Amounts (that should have been deposited) paid directly to the IRS, or paid with your tax return. But see Payment with return, earlier in this section, for an exception.

15% - Amounts still unpaid more than 10 days after the date of the first notice the IRS sent asking for the tax due or the day on which you received notice and demand for immediate payment, whichever is earlier.

Source: Internal Revenue Service.

A quick summary of general employer payroll expenses and responsibilities follows:

Employee compensation	Tax withholding	Tax matching
Tax remittance	Voluntary deductions from employee pay	Remittance of voluntary deductions
Tax reporting	Tax deposits	Accountability

Employees and Company Framework

© Steve Allen/Brand X Pictures, RF

Beyond the expenses and responsibilities of the payroll accounting system is the understanding of how the employees fit within the larger framework of the company. Payroll is one part of the cost of employing people. Before the employee ever becomes productive for a company, employers will incur recruiting, hiring, and training costs that vary based on the company's location and minimum job requirements. Other costs include any tools, uniforms, and specific equipment that employees need to perform their jobs. Expenses associated with hiring and retaining well-qualified employees may comprise a significant amount of a company's overhead.

> According to *Entrepreneur* magazine, hiring new employees costs an average of $4,000 each. This figure includes recruiting, hiring, and training costs. Other hidden costs associated with employing people involve workplace integration and worker productivity, which may not peak for several weeks after the initial hire. (Source: *Entrepreneur*)

We mentioned the interrelation of accounting and human resources as it pertains to the employee earnings record. The employee earnings record serves more than a single purpose. Besides the tracking of employee wages as they pertain to tax maximums and periodic reporting, the employee earnings record links directly with the company's budgeting and cost analysis functions. Companies need the information generated by payroll records to ensure profitability and competitiveness.

Payroll-Related Business Expenses

STOP & CHECK

1. What are examples of employer-related business expenses?
2. How do payroll expenses relate to other business functions?

LO 5-5 Relate Labor Expenses to Company Profitability

Compensating employees is far more complex than simply paying the hourly wage. The employer's expenses related to taxes, insurance, and benefits are an addition to the employee's annual salary. (See Figure 5-8.) Having employees affects the profitability of a company but is a vital part of doing business. Managers need to associate the proper amount of payroll costs with their department so they can make informed decisions about employee productivity and future budgets.

The Labor Distribution Report

The number of employees in a department is known as the *labor distribution*. Payroll accounting is a powerful tool in understanding the labor distribution of a company.

FIGURE 5-8
Employer Costs for Employee Compensation

Source: *Bureau of Labor Statistics, 2015.*

Compensation component	Civilian workers	Private industry	State and local government
Wages and salaries	68.4%	69.4%	64.1%
Benefits	31.6	30.6	35.9
Paid leave	7.0	6.9	7.3
Supplemental pay	3.0	3.5	0.8
Insurance	8.8	8.1	11.9
Health benefits	8.4	7.6	11.6
Retirement and savings	5.3	4.2	10.1
Defined benefit	3.3	2.0	9.2
Defined contribution	1.9	2.2	0.9
Legally required	7.6	8.0	5.9

Accounting records facilitate departmental identification of the number and type of employees, time worked, overtime used, and benefits paid. Integrating the department information into the employee earnings records facilitates labor distribution analysis.

For example, ABD Industries has three departments: administration, sales, and manufacturing. The employees are distributed as follows:

Administration: 15	Sales: 10	Manufacturing: 60

Without *departmental classifications*, the payroll costs associated with the 85 employees at ABD would be allocated evenly among the departments. This allocation would result in the administration and sales departments absorbing an amount of the payroll costs that is disproportionate to the number of employees. The departmental classification yields an accurate picture of how the labor is distributed across a company.

Example: No departmental classification

Total payroll amount of $500,000 for ABD industries.
Each department would have $166,666.67 of payroll costs assigned.

Example: With departmental classification

Total payroll for ABD: $500,000 or $5,882.35 per employee (if allocated evenly per employee).
Administration payroll costs = $5,882.35 × 15 = $88,235
Sales payroll costs = $5,882.35 × 10 = $58,823
Manufacturing payroll costs = $5,882.35 ×60 = $352,942

Allocating costs according to the number of employees in each department yields a more accurate amount than equal distribution of the labor costs across the three departments at ABD. However, allocating by number of departmental employees assumes that each employee has equal compensation, which is improbable. A payroll accounting system allows accurate allocation based on the precise amounts paid to each employee per payroll period. Labor distribution reports are among the tools that managers use to determine the productivity and costs specifically associated with their department.

Labor distribution reports may be used to reveal whatever information is important to a business. Funding sources, payroll accuracy, and budget projections are three common uses of labor distribution reports. Vanderbilt University uses a labor distribution report to ensure that payroll costs are linked to appropriate departments and to specific grant funding. (Source: *Small Business Chronicle*)

Labor Distribution Report

STOP & CHECK

1. Pine Banks Tree Farms has 10 employees on staff: three office staff, five agricultural workers, and two drivers. Their annual payroll expense is $300,000.

   a. What would be the labor distribution if Pine Banks Tree Farms uses departmental classification?

   b. What would be the labor distribution if Pine Banks Tree Farms does not use departmental classification?

2. Which method, departmental classification or nondepartmental classification, is most appropriate? Why?

LO 5-6   Complete Benefit Analysis as a Function of Payroll

Accuracy, as we have emphasized repeatedly, is the cornerstone of a payroll system. Accuracy is critical in employee compensation and satisfies governmental reporting requirements; additionally, it assists in the large-scale decision-making process of a company. Payroll-related employee costs need to be compared to the advantages of maintaining the employee—namely, the profitability of the department. To achieve the analysis required, a *benefit analysis* report needs to be compiled. The payroll records of the company facilitate the compilation of the benefit analysis report.

Wages and salaries are a company's largest employee expense. The second largest expense to employers is employee benefits. Benefits can include paid time off, holiday pay, bonuses, and insurance. Many companies pay a percentage of the employee's insurance benefits, ranging from 70 to 100% in some cases. With the rising costs and mandatory nature of health insurance for certain employers, employee costs have become a major budget concern for many managers. Accurate reporting of the benefits costs to employers provides the management with guidance for budget analysis and employee compensation. A sample benefit analysis report is contained in Figure 5-9.

Note the differences between total employee benefit costs and total employer benefit costs. Mandatory and voluntary employee payroll deduction represent a significant monetary investment. When added to the employee's wages and the costs involved with recruitment and hiring, the amount of money dedicated to labor costs becomes a significant portion of a company's expenses.

Taking the information prepared above, the payroll accountant can determine the cost of each individual employee to the company. This information can also be used to determine the total cost of offering a particular benefit to the employees. The latter is used when the company is looking at annual renewals of health insurance benefits for comparison.

The analysis of employee benefits considers all of the variables that comprise their compensation. Many managers are unaware of the full cost of having an employee added to or removed from their department, so the benefit analysis report serves the following purposes:

- Benefit analysis helps employers benchmark their employees' compensation to other companies with similar profiles or in certain geographic locations.

- The report also helps employers with labor distribution and budgeting tasks by providing data for decision making.

- The benefit analysis facilitates managerial understanding of departmental impacts prior to hiring or dismissing employees.

FIGURE 5-9
Sample Benefit Analysis Report

Statement for: Elizabeth M. Charette

Annual Gross Salary:	**$44,137.60**
Total Hours Worked Annually:	**2,080 Hours**

Health & Welfare Benefits:	Annual Employee Cost	Annual Employer Cost
Medical/Dental:	$600	$6,000
Life Insurance:	$0	$1,200
AD&D Coverage:	$0	$980
Dependent Life Insurance:	$300	$600
Disability Insurance:	$600	$3,000
Total Health & Welfare:	$1,500	$11,780
Retirement Plan Benefits:	Employee Cost	Employer Cost
401k Employee Contribution:	$1,324.13	$662.07
Profit Sharing:	$0	$3,000
Total Retirement Plan:	$1,324.13	$3,662.07
PTO & Holiday Pay	Employee Cost	Employer Cost
Paid Time Off:	$0	$1,697.60
Holiday Pay:	$0	$1,867.36
Total PTO and Holiday Pay:	$0	$3,564.96
Additional Compensation:	Employee Cost	Employer Cost
Annual Bonus:	$0	$2,500
Bereavement Pay:	$0	$509.28
Production Bonus:	$0	$500
Tuition Reimbursement:	$0	$5,250
Total Additional Comp:	$0	$8,759.28
Government Mandated:	Employee Cost	Employer Cost
Social Security:	$2,736.53	$2,736.53
Medicare:	$640.00	$640.00
Federal Unemployment:	$0	$253.28
State Unemployment:	$0	$2,279.53
Workers' Compensation:	$0	$353.10
Total Government Mandated:	$3,376.53	$6,262.44
Total Cost of Benefit Provided by WLA Industries	$6,200.66	$34,028.75
Total Cost of Employing E. M. Charette		$78,166.35

Annual Total Compensation Report

Some companies provide their employees with an ***annual total compensation report***. The annual total compensation report is similar to the benefit analysis report because it contains detailed analysis of employee costs. The difference between the two reports is the intended audience. The benefit analysis report is an internal report for the company's management, and the annual total compensation report is meant to be distributed to the employee. The work going into the total compensation report can come from either the human resources department or the accounting department, depending on the structure of the company. Either way, the payroll accountant contributes vital information to the report.

To prepare the information for the benefit analysis and total compensation reports, the payroll accountant will gather information from many sources: payroll registers, accounts payable invoices, *payroll tax reports*, and contributions to retirement programs (when employer matching is involved). The payroll accountant will start by printing the annual earnings report for the employee in question. A computerized earnings register can be configured to include taxes and other deductions from the employee's pay. When the total compensation report covers periods greater than one year, it may be necessary for the payroll accountant to obtain Social Security and Medicare tax rates for the years in question. Employer portions of unemployment insurance, workers' compensation, and taxes are added to the benefits provided to the employees in the determination of the total cost.

The payroll accountant will request copies of invoices for health insurance, life insurance, and any other benefits the employer provides, such as on-site meals and gym facilities/memberships, from the accounts payable accountant. Other items that may be added to the cost per employee for benefit analysis could be company-provided awards, meals, clothing, or special facilities (break room, locker room, etc.). Once complete, the annual compensation report is distributed to employees to help them understand the total value of their annual compensation. A sample total compensation report is in Figure 5-10.

Benefit Analysis Report

1. What are the purposes of compiling a benefit analysis report?
2. What is the difference between a benefit analysis report and an annual total compensation report?

Trends to Watch

EMPLOYER TAXES AND BENEFIT ANALYSIS

Tax rates and remittance methods for employers tend to change annually based on directives issued by federal, state, and local governments. Some developments in employer taxes that have changed during the early 2010s include the following:

- The use of the EFTPS as a mandatory tax remittance method for new employers and the preferred method for existing employers.
- Temporary tax deductions for portions of COBRA policies for displaced workers.
- The Work Opportunity Tax Credit that reduces tax liabilities for employers who hired certain groups of workers.
- A reduction in the FUTA tax rate due to the expiration of a 0.2% surtax.

Some trends to watch in employer taxes and benefit analysis include the following:

- Employer-sponsored wellness programs in response to Affordable Care Act and ADA legislation.
- Very small health insurance networks that allow small employers to deliver cost-effective, tailored health insurance.
- Transference of health insurance provider choice from the employer to the employee, allowing employees to choose the health plan that suits their needs.
- Some states are challenging the constitutionality of the personal income tax, claiming that it violates prohibitions of taxing individual persons.

FIGURE 5-10
Total Compensation Report

CASH COMPENSATION AND BENEFITS SUMMARY

The amount of your total compensation from ABC Company is much more than what is indicated in your yearly earnings statement. In addition to direct pay, it includes the value of your health care insurance, disability and life insurance, retirement benefits, and government mandated benefits. Below, we break out your total compensation.

CASH COMPENSATION	Amount
Base Salary	$52,000.00
Total:	**$52,000.00**

Base Salary as of 12/31/2013.

BENEFITS	Plan	Coverage	Your Contribution	Company Contribution
Medical Insurance	ABC One		$600.00	$5,400.00
Vision Insurance	ABC Vision		$0.00	$600.00
Dental Insurance	NL Dental		$120.00	$1,080.00
Total:			**$720.00**	**$7,080.00**

The above benefit elections are based on 12/31/2013.

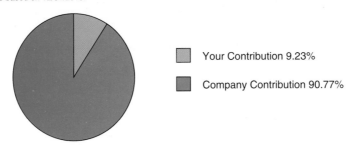

- Your Contribution 9.23%
- Company Contribution 90.77%

TOTAL COMPENSATION VALUE

The true value of your ABC Company total compensation includes your direct pay, the company's contribution to your benefits, and the consequent tax savings to you.

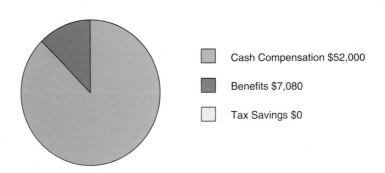

- Cash Compensation $52,000
- Benefits $7,080
- Tax Savings $0

THE TOTAL VALUE OF YOUR COMPENSATION:	$59,080.00

OTHER VALUABLE BEBEFITS

ABC Company provides other valuable benefits that are not listed above. Below is a summary of those plans.

Paid Time Off (PTO)	10 Days	$4,520.00
Total:		**$4,520.00**

Summary of Employer Payroll Taxes and Labor Planning

Taxes are a part of conducting business. Whether taxes are income- or employee-related, a business must abide by the regulations for the timely submission and reporting of taxes. Employers have responsibilities for collecting federal income tax, Social Security, and Medicare taxes from their employees. In addition, the company is responsible for setting aside federal unemployment taxes per employee based upon taxable wages. Apart from the federal taxes, employers may be liable for the collecting, reporting, and submission of state and local income and unemployment taxes. Privilege taxes may also be collected in specific districts, such as the Denver Head Tax. Employers who fail to meet the reporting, deposit, or submission requirements may be subject to fines and penalties.

Understanding the connection between the W-2 form and the final paycheck of the year can save payroll accountants hours of work in searching to find the answers to each individual employee's query. When the payroll accountant can explain the elements of the W-2 with confidence, fewer employees will come to ask why the difference, especially if the payroll accountant provides a written explanation with the final annual paycheck or W-2.

Although the human resources department could prepare the benefit analysis report, in smaller companies this duty can fall to the payroll accountant. Even in larger organizations, the human resources department will need specific information from the payroll accountant to feed into the benefit analysis report. Managers can examine the benefit analysis to understand how much their employees cost the department. Once receiving a total annual compensation report, the employee has a more complete understanding of their compensation package, thereby feeding wage discussions, and building a data-driven understanding of cost changes.

Key Points

- Employers share some of the same tax obligations as their employees. Some examples are the Social Security, Medicare, and (in some states) SUTA taxes.
- FUTA taxes are paid only on the first $7,000 of each employee's annual taxable wage; SUTA tax wage base limits vary by state.
- Payroll tax deposit frequency is determined by the amount of payroll taxes paid during a "lookback" period.
- All new employers are monthly schedule depositors until the next lookback period.
- Most employers file quarterly payroll tax returns on Form 941.
- Employers who deposit payroll taxes on a semiweekly basis must also file a Schedule B with their Form 941.
- Employers with less than $2,500 of annual tax liability file a Form 944 at the end of the calendar year.
- Employers report FUTA tax liability on an annual basis by using Form 940.
- Employers file an annual Form W-2 for each employee with the Social Security Administration.
- Form W-3 is the transmittal form used to report a company's aggregate annual wages and withholdings.
- Labor distribution has an effect on company profitability, and benefit costs are a significant factor in managerial decisions.
- A total annual compensation report is used to communicate to employees the complete compensation package that they receive.

Vocabulary

Annual total compensation report	FICA	Lookback period
Automated clearing house (ACH)	Form 940	Payroll tax reports
	Form 941	Schedule B
Benefit analysis	Form 944	Semiweekly depositors
Departmental classification	Form W-2	Statutory deductions
	Form W-3	SUTA
EFTPS	FUTA	Tax remittance
	Labor distribution	

Review Questions

1. What taxes are paid by the employer only?

2. What taxes are the shared responsibility of the employer and employee?

3. What taxes are paid by the employee only?

4. What determines the deposit requirements for employer taxes?

5. How often must a company report Form 941 earnings/withholdings?

6. How often must a company report Form 940 earnings/withholdings?

7. Which of the mandatory withholdings have a maximum wage base?

8. How did the Affordable Care Act change Medicare tax withholding percentages?

9. What is Form 941?

10. Which employers must use Schedule B?

11. How do employers know that they must use Form 944?

12. What is Form 940?

13. What is the difference between Form W-2 and Form W-3?

14. What are the employer's payroll responsibilities?

15. How does payroll relate to a company's costs of doing business?

16. What is meant by the term *labor distribution?*

17. How do payroll records inform managers about labor distribution?

18. What is a benefit analysis report?

19. How can a manager use the benefit analysis report in the decision-making process?

20. How do the payroll reports inform managers about department and company profitability?

Exercises Set A

5-1A.
LO 5-1

Bob works for Seymour Engines, which pays employees on a semi-monthly basis. Bob's annual salary is $120,000. Calculate the following:

Pay Date	Prior YTD Earnings	Social Security Taxable Wages	Medicare Taxable Wages	Employer Share Social Security Tax	Employer Share Medicare Tax
November 15					
December 31					

5-2A.
LO 5-1, 5-3

Eyeseeyou Cameras has the following employees:

Employee Name	Annual Taxable Wages
Mia Haskell	$26,000
Viktor Papadopoulos	$35,000
Puja Anderson	$32,000
Cady Billingmeier	$29,000
Carl Johnson	$46,000

Eyeseeyou Cameras' SUTA tax rate is 5.4% and applies to the first $8,000 of employee wages. What is the annual amount due for each employee?

Employee	FUTA Due	SUTA Due
Mia Haskell		
Viktor Papadopoulos		
Puja Anderson		
Cady Billingmeier		
Carl Johnson		

5-3A.

LO 5-1, 5-2, 5-3

Freedom, Inc., has 16 employees within Denver City and County. All of the employees worked a predominate number of hours within the city. The employees earned $7.25 per hour and worked 160 hours each during the month. The employer must remit $4.00 per month per employee that earns more than $500 per month. Additionally, employees who earn more than $500 per month must have $5.75 withheld from their pay. What is the employee and company Occupational Privilege Tax for these employees?

Employee: _____

Employer: _____

5-4A.

LO 5-1, 5-3

Joseph earned $68,000 in 2015 for a company in Kentucky. He is single with 1 dependent and is paid annually. Compute the following employee share of the taxes, using the wage-bracket tables in Appendix C.

Federal income tax withholding _____

Social Security tax _____

Medicare tax _____

5-5A.

LO 5-3

Using the information from Exercise 5-4A, compute the employer's share of the taxes. The FUTA rate in Kentucky for 2015 is 0.6% on the first $7,000 of employee wages, and the SUTA rate is 5.4% with a wage base of $9,900. $3,200 of Joseph's wages are exempt from FUTA taxes

Federal income tax withholding _____

Social Security tax _____

Medicare tax _____

FUTA tax _____

SUTA tax _____

5-6A.

LO 5-2

Veryclear Glassware is a new business owned by Samantha Peoples, who is the company president. Her first year of operations commenced on April 1, 2015. What schedule depositor would she be for the first year of operations?

5-7A.

LO 5-3

Using the information from Exercise 5-6A, complete the following Form 941 for second quarter 2015.

EIN: 78-7654398

Address: 23051 Old Redwood Highway, Sebastopol, California 95482, phone 707-555-5555

Number of employees: 7

Wages, tips, and other compensation paid during second quarter 2015: $244,798

Income tax withheld: $48,000

Social Security tax withheld: $15,177.48

Medicare tax withheld: $3,549.57

Monthly tax liability:

April	$28,484.79
May	28,484.79
June	28,484.80

Form **941 for 2015:** Employer's QUARTERLY Federal Tax Return

(Rev. January 2015)

Department of the Treasury — Internal Revenue Service

950114

OMB No. 1545-0029

Employer identification number (EIN) ☐☐ – ☐☐☐☐☐☐☐

Name *(not your trade name)*

Trade name *(if any)*

Address

Number   Street   Suite or room number

City   State   ZIP code

Foreign country name   Foreign province/county   Foreign postal code

Report for this Quarter of 2015
(Check one.)

☐ 1: January, February, March

☐ 2: April, May, June

☐ 3: July, August, September

☐ 4: October, November, December

Instructions and prior year forms are available at *www.irs.gov/form941*.

Read the separate instructions before you complete Form 941. Type or print within the boxes.

Part 1:   Answer these questions for this quarter.

1   Number of employees who received wages, tips, or other compensation for the pay period including: *Mar. 12* (Quarter 1), *June 12* (Quarter 2), *Sept. 12* (Quarter 3), or *Dec. 12* (Quarter 4)   1 ▢

2   Wages, tips, and other compensation . . . .   2 ▢

3   Federal income tax withheld from wages, tips, and other compensation . . . . . .   3 ▢

4   If no wages, tips, and other compensation are subject to social security or Medicare tax   ☐ Check and go to line 6.

	Column 1		Column 2
5a Taxable social security wages . .	▢	× .124 =	▢
5b Taxable social security tips . . .	▢	× .124 =	▢
5c Taxable Medicare wages & tips. .	▢	× .029 =	▢
5d Taxable wages & tips subject to Additional Medicare Tax withholding	▢	× .009 =	▢

5e   Add Column 2 from lines 5a, 5b, 5c, and 5d . . . .   5e ▢

5f   Section 3121(q) Notice and Demand—Tax due on unreported tips (see instructions) . .   5f ▢

6   Total taxes before adjustments. Add lines 3, 5e, and 5f . . . .   6 ▢

7   Current quarter's adjustment for fractions of cents . . . .   7 ▢

8   Current quarter's adjustment for sick pay . . . .   8 ▢

9   Current quarter's adjustments for tips and group-term life insurance . . . . . .   9 ▢

10   Total taxes after adjustments. Combine lines 6 through 9 . . . .   10 ▢

11   Total deposits for this quarter, including overpayment applied from a prior quarter and overpayments applied from Form 941-X, 941-X (PR), 944-X, 944-X (PR), or 944-X (SP) filed in the current quarter . . . .   11 ▢

12   Balance due. If line 10 is more than line 11, enter the difference and see instructions . . .   12 ▢

13   Overpayment. If line 11 is more than line 10, enter the difference ▢   Check one: ☐ Apply to next return.   ☐ Send a refund.

▶ You MUST complete both pages of Form 941 and SIGN it.

Next ▶

For Privacy Act and Paperwork Reduction Act Notice, see the back of the Payment Voucher.   Cat. No. 17001Z   Form **941** (Rev. 1-2015)

950214

Name *(not your trade name)*	Employer identification number (EIN)

Part 2: Tell us about your deposit schedule and tax liability for this quarter.

If you are unsure about whether you are a monthly schedule depositor or a semiweekly schedule depositor, see Pub. 15 (Circular E), section 11.

14 Check one: ☐ Line 10 on this return is less than $2,500 or line 10 on the return for the prior quarter was less than $2,500, and you did not incur a $100,000 next-day deposit obligation during the current quarter. If line 10 for the prior quarter was less than $2,500 but line 10 on this return is $100,000 or more, you must provide a record of your federal tax liability. If you are a monthly schedule depositor, complete the deposit schedule below; if you are a semiweekly schedule depositor, attach Schedule B (Form 941). Go to Part 3.

☐ **You were a monthly schedule depositor for the entire quarter.** Enter your tax liability for each month and total liability for the quarter, then go to Part 3.

Tax liability: Month 1   [.   ]

Month 2   [.   ]

Month 3   [.   ]

Total liability for quarter   [.   ]   Total must equal line 10.

☐ **You were a semiweekly schedule depositor for any part of this quarter.** Complete Schedule B (Form 941), Report of Tax Liability for Semiweekly Schedule Depositors, and attach it to Form 941.

Part 3: Tell us about your business. If a question does NOT apply to your business, leave it blank.

15 **If your business has closed or you stopped paying wages** . . . . ☐ Check here, and

enter the final date you paid wages   [/   /   ] .

16 **If you are a seasonal employer and you do not have to file a return for every quarter of the year** . . ☐ Check here.

Part 4: May we speak with your third-party designee?

Do you want to allow an employee, a paid tax preparer, or another person to discuss this return with the IRS? See the instructions for details.

☐ Yes. Designee's name and phone number   [   ]   [   ]

Select a 5-digit Personal Identification Number (PIN) to use when talking to the IRS.   ☐ ☐ ☐ ☐ ☐

☐ No.

Part 5: Sign here. You MUST complete both pages of Form 941 and SIGN it.

Under penalties of perjury, I declare that I have examined this return, including accompanying schedules and statements, and to the best of my knowledge and belief, it is true, correct, and complete. Declaration of preparer (other than taxpayer) is based on all information of which preparer has any knowledge.

X **Sign your name here**   [   ]   Print your name here   [   ]

Print your title here   [   ]

Date   [/   /   ]   Best daytime phone   [   ]

Paid Preparer Use Only   Check if you are self-employed . . . ☐

Preparer's name		PTIN	
Preparer's signature		Date	/ /
Firm's name (or yours if self-employed)		EIN	
Address		Phone	
City	State	ZIP code	

Form **941** (Rev. 1-2015)

Source: Internal Revenue Service.

5-8A.
LO 5-3

Using the information from 5-6A and 5-7A for Veryclear Glassware (California Employer Account Number 999-9999-9), complete the following State of California Form DE-9, Quarterly Contribution and Report of Wages Report. Use 5.4% as the UI rate, 0.1% as the ETT rate, and 0.9% as the SDI rate. All employees have worked a full calendar year with the company, and all wages are subject to UI, ETT, and SDI. The California PIT taxes withheld for the quarter are $22,406. The company has deposited $38,073.07 for the quarter.

EDD Employment Development Department
State of California

QUARTERLY CONTRIBUTION RETURN AND REPORT OF WAGES
REMINDER: File your DE 9 and DE 9C together.
PLEASE TYPE THIS FORM—DO NOT ALTER PREPRINTED INFORMATION

00090112

QUARTER ENDED   DUE   DELINQUENT IF NOT POSTMARKED OR RECEIVED BY   YR   QTR

EMPLOYER ACCOUNT NO.

DO NOT ALTER THIS AREA

DEPT. USE ONLY

P1   P2   C   P   U   S   A

T

EFFECTIVE DATE   Mo.   Day   Yr.

FEIN

A. NO WAGES PAID THIS QUARTER ☐   **B.** OUT OF BUSINESS/NO EMPLOYEES ☐

ADDITIONAL FEINS

B1.   OUT OF BUSINESS DATE
M M D D Y Y Y Y

C. TOTAL SUBJECT WAGES PAID THIS QUARTER ....

D. UNEMPLOYMENT INSURANCE (UI) (Total Employee Wages up to $ per employee per calendar year)

(D1) UI Rate %   (D2) UI TAXABLE WAGES FOR THE QUARTER   (D3) UI CONTRIBUTIONS
                         TIMES   =

E. EMPLOYMENT TRAINING TAX (ETT)

(E1) ETT Rate %   TIMES   UI Taxable Wages for the Quarter (D2) ...... =   (E2) ETT CONTRIBUTIONS

F. STATE DISABILITY INSURANCE (SDI) (Total Employee Wages up to $ per employee per calendar year)

(F1) SDI Rate %   (F2) SDI TAXABLE WAGES FOR THE QUARTER   (F3) SDI EMPLOYEE CONTRIBUTIONS WITHHELD
                         TIMES   =

G. CALIFORNIA PERSONAL INCOME TAX (PIT) WITHHELD ....

H. SUBTOTAL (Add Items D3, E2, F3, and G) ....

I. LESS: CONTRIBUTIONS AND WITHHOLDINGS PAID FOR THE QUARTER ....
    (**DO NOT** INCLUDE PENALTY AND INTEREST PAYMENTS)

J. TOTAL TAXES DUE OR OVERPAID   (Item H minus Item I) ....

If amount due, prepare a *Payroll Tax Deposit* (DE 88), include the correct payment quarter, and mail to: Employment Development Department, P.O. Box 826276, Sacramento, CA 94230-6276. **NOTE:** Do not mail payments along with the DE 9 and *Quarterly Contribution Return and Report of Wages (Continuation)* (DE 9C), as this may delay processing and result in erroneous penalty and interest charges. **Mandatory Electronic Funds Transfer (EFT)** filers must remit all SDI/PIT deposits by EFT to avoid a noncompliance penalty.

K. I declare that the above, to the best of my knowledge and belief, is true and correct. If a refund was claimed, a reasonable effort was made to refund any erroneous deductions to the affected employee(s).

Signature *Required* _____   Title _____   Phone (____) _____   Date_____
                                          (Owner, Accountant, Preparer, etc.)

⊙   SIGN AND MAIL TO: State of California / Employment Development Department / P.O. Box 989071 / West Sacramento CA 95798-9071

DE 9 Rev. 1 (1-12) **(INTERNET)**   Page 1 of 2   Fast, Easy, and Convenient! Visit EDD's Web site at **www.edd.ca.gov**

Source: Employment Development Department.

5-9A.
LO 5-3

ZRT, Inc., paid its 25 employees a total of $863,428.49 during 2014. Of these wages, $5,400 is exempt fringe benefits (Section 125 cafeteria plans) and $9,850 is exempt retirement benefits (employer contributions to 401(k) plans). All employees have worked there for the full calendar year and reached the FUTA wage base during the first quarter, taxes were deposited then. ZRT, Inc., is located at 3874 Palm Avenue, Sebring, Florida, 20394. The owner is Hope Daniels, EIN is 99-2039485, phone number 461-555-9485. Complete Form 940 for ZRT, Inc.

Form **940 for 2015:** Employer's Annual Federal Unemployment (FUTA) Tax Return
Department of the Treasury — Internal Revenue Service

850113

OMB No. 1545-0028

Employer identification number (EIN)

Name (not your trade name)

Trade name (if any)

Address

Number   Street   Suite or room number

City   State   ZIP code

Foreign country name   Foreign province/county   Foreign postal code

Type of Return
(Check all that apply.)

a. Amended
b. Successor employer
c. No payments to employees in 2014
d. Final: Business closed or stopped paying wages

Instructions and prior-year forms are available at *www.irs.gov/form940.*

Read the separate instructions before you complete this form. Please type or print within the boxes.

Part 1: Tell us about your return. If any line does NOT apply, leave it blank.

1a   If you had to pay state unemployment tax in one state only, enter the state abbreviation .   1a
1b   If you had to pay state unemployment tax in more than one state, you are a multi-state employer . . . .   1b   Check here. Complete Schedule A (Form 940).
2   If you paid wages in a state that is subject to CREDIT REDUCTION   2   Check here. Complete Schedule A (Form 940).

Part 2: Determine your FUTA tax before adjustments for 2014. If any line does NOT apply, leave it blank.

3   Total payments to all employees   3
4   Payments exempt from FUTA tax   4

Check all that apply: 4a Fringe benefits   4c Retirement/Pension   4e Other
4b Group-term life insurance   4d Dependent care

5   Total of payments made to each employee in excess of $7,000   5
6   Subtotal (line 4 + line 5 = line 6)   6
7   Total taxable FUTA wages (line 3 – line 6 = line 7) (see instructions)   7
8   FUTA tax before adjustments (line 7 x .006 = line 8)   8

Part 3: Determine your adjustments. If any line does NOT apply, leave it blank.

9   If ALL of the taxable FUTA wages you paid were excluded from state unemployment tax, multiply line 7 by .054 (line 7 x .054 = line 9). Go to line 12   9
10   If SOME of the taxable FUTA wages you paid were excluded from state unemployment tax, OR you paid ANY state unemployment tax late (after the due date for filing Form 940), complete the worksheet in the instructions. Enter the amount from line 7 of the worksheet . .   10
11   If credit reduction applies, enter the total from Schedule A (Form 940)   11

Part 4: Determine your FUTA tax and balance due or overpayment for 2014. If any line does NOT apply, leave it blank.

12   Total FUTA tax after adjustments (lines 8 + 9 + 10 + 11 = line 12)   12
13   FUTA tax deposited for the year, including any overpayment applied from a prior year   13
14   Balance due (If line 12 is more than line 13, enter the excess on line 14.)
   • If line 14 is more than $500, you must deposit your tax.
   • If line 14 is $500 or less, you may pay with this return. (see instructions)   14
15   Overpayment (If line 13 is more than line 12, enter the excess on line 15 and check a box below.)   15
   ▶ You **MUST** complete both pages of this form and **SIGN** it.   Check one: Apply to next return. Send a refund.

Next ▶

For Privacy Act and Paperwork Reduction Act Notice, see the back of Form 940-V, Payment Voucher.   Cat. No. 11234O   Form **940** (2015)

850212

Name *(not your trade name)*	Employer identification number (EIN)

Part 5: Report your FUTA tax liability by quarter only if line 12 is more than $500. If not, go to Part 6.

16 Report the amount of your FUTA tax liability for each quarter; do NOT enter the amount you deposited. If you had no liability for a quarter, leave the line blank.

16a 1st quarter (January 1 – March 31) . . . . 16a ▪

16b 2nd quarter (April 1 – June 30) . . . . 16b ▪

16c 3rd quarter (July 1 – September 30) . . . . 16c ▪

16d 4th quarter (October 1 – December 31) . . . . 16d ▪

17 Total tax liability for the year (lines 16a + 16b + 16c + 16d = line 17) 17 ▪ **Total must equal line 12.**

Part 6: May we speak with your third-party designee?

Do you want to allow an employee, a paid tax preparer, or another person to discuss this return with the IRS? See the instructions for details.

☐ Yes. Designee's name and phone number

Select a 5-digit Personal Identification Number (PIN) to use when talking to IRS

☐ No.

Part 7: Sign here. You MUST complete both pages of this form and SIGN it.

Under penalties of perjury, I declare that I have examined this return, including accompanying schedules and statements, and to the best of my knowledge and belief, it is true, correct, and complete, and that no part of any payment made to a state unemployment fund claimed as a credit was, or is to be, deducted from the payments made to employees. Declaration of preparer (other than taxpayer) is based on all information of which preparer has any knowledge.

✗ **Sign your name here**

Print your name here

Print your title here

Date / /

Best daytime phone

Paid Preparer Use Only

Check if you are self-employed . ☐

Preparer's name		PTIN	
Preparer's signature		Date	/ /
Firm's name (or yours if self-employed)		EIN	
Address		Phone	
City	State	ZIP code	

Form **940** (2015)

Source: Internal Revenue Service.

5-10A.
LO 5-3
Leda, Inc. is located at 433 Augusta Road, Caribou, Maine, 04736, phone number 201-555-1212. The Federal EIN is 54-3910394, and it has a Maine Revenue Services number of 3884019. Owner, Amanda Leda, has asked you to prepare Form W-2 for each of the following employees of Leda, Inc. as of December 31, 2015.

Sarah C. Niehaus
122 Main Street, #3
Caribou, ME 04736
SSN: 477-30-2234
Dependent Care Benefit:
$1,800.00

Total 2015 wages: $34,768.53
401(k) contribution: $1,043.06
Section 125 contribution: $1,500.00
Federal income tax withheld: $4,833.82
Social Security tax withheld: $2,062.65
Medicare tax withheld: $482.39
State income tax withheld $2,561.92

Maxwell S. Law
1503 22nd Street
New Sweden, ME 04762
SSN: 493-55-2049

Total 2015 wages: $36,729.37
401(k) contribution: $1,469.18
Section 125 contribution: $1,675.00
Federal income tax withheld: $4,407.52
Social Security tax withheld: $2,173.37
Medicare tax withheld: $508.29
State income tax withheld $2,670.02

Siobhan E. Manning
1394 West Highway 59
Woodland, ME 04694
SSN: 390-39-1002
Tuition in excess of $5,250:
$1,575.00

Total 2015 wages: $30,034.87
401(k) contribution: $712.75
Section 125 contribution: $1,000.00
Federal income tax withheld: $4,833.82
Social Security tax withheld: $1,800.16
Medicare tax withheld: $421.01
State income tax withheld $2,130.38

Donald A. Hendrix
1387 Rimbaud Avenue
Caribou, ME 04736
SSN: 288-30-5940

Total 2015 wages: $22,578.89
401(k) contribution: $1,354.73
Section 125 contribution: $2,250.00
Federal income tax withheld: $2,709.47
Social Security tax withheld: $1,260.39
Medicare tax withheld: $294.77
State income tax withheld $1,508.45

Alison K. Sutter
3664 Fairfield Street
Washburn, ME 04786
SSN: 490-55-0293

Total 2015 wages: $45,908.34
401(k) contribution: $2,754.50
Section 125 contribution: $1,750.00
Federal income tax withheld: $5,509.00
Social Security tax withheld: $2,737.82
Medicare tax withheld: $640.30
State income tax withheld $3,291.61

22222	a Employee's social security number	OMB No. 1545-0008		
b Employer identification number (EIN)			1 Wages, tips, other compensation	2 Federal income tax withheld
c Employer's name, address, and ZIP code			3 Social security wages	4 Social security tax withheld
			5 Medicare wages and tips	6 Medicare tax withheld
			7 Social security tips	8 Allocated tips
d Control number			9	10 Dependent care benefits
e Employee's first name and initial Last name Suff.			11 Nonqualified plans	12a
		13 Statutory employee Retirement plan Third-party sick pay	12b
		14 Other	12c
			12d
f Employee's address and ZIP code				

15 State Employer's state ID number	16 State wages, tips, etc.	17 State income tax	18 Local wages, tips, etc.	19 Local income tax	20 Locality name

Form **W-2** Wage and Tax Statement
Copy 1—For State, City, or Local Tax Department

2015

Department of the Treasury—Internal Revenue Service

22222	**a** Employee's social security number	OMB No. 1545-0008		
b Employer identification number (EIN)			**1** Wages, tips, other compensation	**2** Federal income tax withheld
c Employer's name, address, and ZIP code			**3** Social security wages	**4** Social security tax withheld
			5 Medicare wages and tips	**6** Medicare tax withheld
			7 Social security tips	**8** Allocated tips
d Control number		**9**		**10** Dependent care benefits
e Employee's first name and initial Last name Suff.			**11** Nonqualified plans	**12a**
		13 Statutory employee ☐ Retirement plan ☐ Third-party sick pay ☐		**12b**
		14 Other		**12c**
				12d
f Employee's address and ZIP code				

15 State Employer's state ID number	**16** State wages, tips, etc.	**17** State income tax	**18** Local wages, tips, etc.	**19** Local income tax	**20** Locality name

Form **W-2** Wage and Tax Statement   **2015**   Department of the Treasury—Internal Revenue Service
Copy 1—For State, City, or Local Tax Department

22222	**a** Employee's social security number	OMB No. 1545-0008		
b Employer identification number (EIN)			**1** Wages, tips, other compensation	**2** Federal income tax withheld
c Employer's name, address, and ZIP code			**3** Social security wages	**4** Social security tax withheld
			5 Medicare wages and tips	**6** Medicare tax withheld
			7 Social security tips	**8** Allocated tips
d Control number		**9**		**10** Dependent care benefits
e Employee's first name and initial Last name Suff.			**11** Nonqualified plans	**12a**
		13 Statutory employee ☐ Retirement plan ☐ Third-party sick pay ☐		**12b**
		14 Other		**12c**
				12d
f Employee's address and ZIP code				

15 State Employer's state ID number	**16** State wages, tips, etc.	**17** State income tax	**18** Local wages, tips, etc.	**19** Local income tax	**20** Locality name

Form **W-2** Wage and Tax Statement   **2015**   Department of the Treasury—Internal Revenue Service
Copy 1—For State, City, or Local Tax Department

22222	**a** Employee's social security number	OMB No. 1545-0008		
b Employer identification number (EIN)			**1** Wages, tips, other compensation	**2** Federal income tax withheld
c Employer's name, address, and ZIP code			**3** Social security wages	**4** Social security tax withheld
			5 Medicare wages and tips	**6** Medicare tax withheld
			7 Social security tips	**8** Allocated tips
d Control number		**9**		**10** Dependent care benefits
e Employee's first name and initial Last name Suff.			**11** Nonqualified plans	**12a**
		13 Statutory employee ☐ Retirement plan ☐ Third-party sick pay ☐		**12b**
		14 Other		**12c**
				12d
f Employee's address and ZIP code				

15 State Employer's state ID number	**16** State wages, tips, etc.	**17** State income tax	**18** Local wages, tips, etc.	**19** Local income tax	**20** Locality name

Form **W-2** Wage and Tax Statement   **2015**   Department of the Treasury—Internal Revenue Service
Copy 1—For State, City, or Local Tax Department

a Employee's social security number		
22222	OMB No. 1545-0008	

b Employer identification number (EIN)	1 Wages, tips, other compensation	2 Federal income tax withheld
c Employer's name, address, and ZIP code	3 Social security wages	4 Social security tax withheld
	5 Medicare wages and tips	6 Medicare tax withheld
	7 Social security tips	8 Allocated tips
d Control number	9	10 Dependent care benefits
e Employee's first name and initial Last name Suff.	11 Nonqualified plans	12a
	13 Statutory employee Retirement plan Third-party sick pay	12b
	14 Other	12c
		12d
f Employee's address and ZIP code		

15 State Employer's state ID number	16 State wages, tips, etc.	17 State income tax	18 Local wages, tips, etc.	19 Local income tax	20 Locality name

Form **W-2** Wage and Tax Statement   **2015**   Department of the Treasury—Internal Revenue Service

Copy 1—For State, City, or Local Tax Department

5-11A.
LO 5-3

Using the information from Exercise 5-10A for Leda Inc., complete Form W-3 that must accompany the company's W-2 Forms. Leda Inc. is a 941-SS payer and is a private, for-profit company. Amanda Leda is the owner; phone number of 207-555-8978; no email address to disclose; fax number 207-555-9898. No third-party sick pay applied for 2015.

DO NOT STAPLE OR FOLD

a Control number	For Official Use Only ▶
33333	OMB No. 1545-0008

b Kind of Payer (Check one)	941-SS Military 943 944 Hshld. emp. Medicare govt. emp.	Kind of Employer (Check one)	None apply 501c non-govt. State/local non-501c State/local 501c Federal govt.	Third-party sick pay (Check if applicable)
c Total number of Forms W-2	d Establishment number	1 Wages, tips, other compensation	2 Income tax withheld	
e Employer identification number (EIN)		3 Social security wages	4 Social security tax withheld	
f Employer's name		5 Medicare wages and tips	6 Medicare tax withheld	
		7 Social security tips	8	
		9	10	
		11 Nonqualified plans	12a Deferred compensation	
g Employer's address and ZIP code				
h Other EIN used this year		13 For third-party sick pay use only	12b	
15 Employer's territorial ID number		14 Income tax withheld by payer of third-party sick pay		
Employer's contact person		Employer's telephone number	For Official Use Only	
Employer's fax number		Employer's email address		

Copy 1—For Local Tax Department

Under penalties of perjury, I declare that I have examined this return and accompanying documents, and, to the best of my knowledge and belief, they are true, correct, and complete.

Signature ▶   Title ▶   Date ▶

Form W-3SS Transmittal of Wage and Tax Statements   **2015**   Department of the Treasury Internal Revenue Service

5-12A.
LO 5-4, 5-6

Pete's Shelby Shop is a company that restores vintage Ford Mustangs. He has 7 employees. Pete wants to perform a benefits analysis report for one of his employees, Kristina Mallhoff for the year. Kristina's benefits package is as follows:

Salary: $40,000

401(k) contribution: 3% of salary, company match is 50% of employee contribution

Medical insurance deduction: $150 per month

Dental insurance: $25 per month

Complete the following Benefits Analysis Report for Kristina Mallhoff for the year. Do not include FUTA and SUTA taxes.

Yearly Benefit Costs	Company Cost	Kristina's Cost
Medical insurance	$ 7,200	$
Dental insurance	$ 1,000	$
Life insurance	$ 200	-0-
AD&D	$ 50	-0-
Short-term disability	$ 500	-0-
Long-term disability	$ 250	-0-
401(k)	$	$
Social Security	$	$
Medicare	$	$
Tuition reimbursement	$ 2,000	-0-
Total yearly benefit costs	$	
Kristina's annual salary	$	
Total yearly benefit costs	$	
Total value of Kristina's compensation	$	

5-13A.
LO 5-4, 5-5

Hoxter Printing has 35 employees distributed among the following departments:

Sales: 10	Factory: 15	Administration: 10

The total annual payroll for Hoxter Printing is $700,000.

Compute the labor distribution based on equal distribution among the departments.

Sales: _____

Factory: _____

Administration: _____

5-14A.
LO 5-4, 5-5

For Hoxter Printing in Exercise 5-13A, compute the labor distribution based on the number of employees per department:

Sales: _____

Factory: _____

Administration: _____

Exercises Set B

5-1B.
LO 5-1

Jill works for Mjelde & Fletcher, which pays employees on a semi-monthly basis. Jill's annual salary is $210,000. Calculate the following:

Pay Date	Prior YTD Earnings	Social Security Taxable Wages	Medicare Taxable Wages	Employer Share Social Security Tax	Employer Share Medicare Tax
November 30					
December 31					

5-2B.
LO 5-1, 5-3

Barry's Grill of Andrews, Texas, has the following employees as of December 31:

Employee Name	Annual Taxable Wages
Mark English	$45,750
Shelly Morris	$21,250
TL Radford	$29,850
James Morrow	$36,280
Trella Lyons	$34,900

The company's SUTA tax rate is 6.25% and has a wage base of $9,000. What is the amount of FUTA and SUTA taxes due for each employee?

Employee	FUTA Due	SUTA Due
Mark English		
Shelly Morris		
TL Radford		
James Morrow		
Trella Lyons		

5-3B.
LO 5-1, 5-2, 5-3

Semolians has 22 employees within Denver City and County. The employees earned $8.50 per hour and worked 160 hours each during the month. The employer must remit $4.00 per month per employee that earns more than $500 per month. Additionally, employees who earn more than $500 per month must have $5.75 withheld from their pay. What is the employee and company Occupational Privilege Tax for these employees?

Employee: _____

Employer: _____

5-4B.
LO 5-1, 5-2, 5-3

Leslie earned $155,000 in 2015 for a company in Pennsylvania. She is single with four dependents and is paid annually. Leslie contributed $3,550 to her 401(k) plan and $2,000 to her Section 125 plan. Employees in Pennsylvania contribute 0.07% of their gross pay toward SUTA tax, which has a wage base for 2015 of $9,000. Compute Leslie's share of the taxes, using the wage bracket tables in Appendix C to determine Federal income tax.

Federal income tax _____

Social Security tax _____

Medicare tax _____

SUTA tax _____

5-5B.
LO 5-2, 5-3

Using the information from Exercise 5-4B, compute the employer's share of the taxes. The FUTA rate within Pennsylvania for 2015 is 0.6% on the first $7,000 of employee wages, and the SUTA rate is 3.456% with a wage base of $9,000.

Federal income tax _____

Social Security tax _____

Medicare tax _____

FUTA tax _____

SUTA tax _____

5-6B.
LO 5-1

Fideaux is a new business owned by Lewis Brooks. His first year of operations commenced on June 1, 2015. What schedule depositor would his company be for the first year of operations?

5-7B.
LO 5-3

Using the information from Exercise 5-6B, complete the following Form 941 for third quarter 2015.

EIN: 98-0050036

Address: 1021 Old Plainfield Road, Salina, California 95670

Phone: 707-555-0303

Number of employees: 8

Wages, tips, and other compensation paid during third quarter 2014: $302,374

Income tax withheld: $51,000

Monthly tax liability:

July	$32,421.08
August	32,421.08
September	32,421.07

Form **941 for 2015:** **Employer's QUARTERLY Federal Tax Return**

950114

(Rev. January 2015)   Department of the Treasury — Internal Revenue Service

OMB No. 1545-0029

Employer identification number (EIN) [ ] [ ] — [ ] [ ] [ ] [ ] [ ] [ ]

Name *(not your trade name)* [   ]

Trade name *(if any)* [   ]

Address [   ]
Number   Street   Suite or room number

[   ]
City   State   ZIP code

[   ]
Foreign country name   Foreign province/county   Foreign postal code

Report for this Quarter of 2015
(Check one.)

[ ] **1:** January, February, March

[ ] **2:** April, May, June

[ ] **3:** July, August, September

[ ] **4:** October, November, December

Instructions and prior year forms are available at *www.irs.gov/form941.*

Read the separate instructions before you complete Form 941. Type or print within the boxes.

Part 1:   Answer these questions for this quarter.

1   Number of employees who received wages, tips, or other compensation for the pay period including: *Mar. 12* (Quarter 1), *June 12* (Quarter 2), *Sept. 12* (Quarter 3), or *Dec. 12* (Quarter 4)   **1** [   ]

2   Wages, tips, and other compensation . . . .   **2** [   ]

3   Federal income tax withheld from wages, tips, and other compensation . . . . . .   **3** [   ]

4   If no wages, tips, and other compensation are subject to social security or Medicare tax   [ ] Check and go to line 6.

		Column 1		Column 2
5a	Taxable social security wages . .	[ ]	× .124 =	[ ]
5b	Taxable social security tips . . .	[ ]	× .124 =	[ ]
5c	Taxable Medicare wages & tips. .	[ ]	× .029 =	[ ]
5d	Taxable wages & tips subject to Additional Medicare Tax withholding	[ ]	× .009 =	[ ]

5e   Add Column 2 from lines 5a, 5b, 5c, and 5d . . . .   **5e** [   ]

5f   Section 3121(q) Notice and Demand—Tax due on unreported tips (see instructions) . .   **5f** [   ]

6   Total taxes before adjustments. Add lines 3, 5e, and 5f . . . .   **6** [   ]

7   Current quarter's adjustment for fractions of cents . . . .   **7** [   ]

8   Current quarter's adjustment for sick pay . . . .   **8** [   ]

9   Current quarter's adjustments for tips and group-term life insurance . . . . .   **9** [   ]

10   Total taxes after adjustments. Combine lines 6 through 9 . . . .   **10** [   ]

11   Total deposits for this quarter, including overpayment applied from a prior quarter and overpayments applied from Form 941-X, 941-X (PR), 944-X, 944-X (PR), or 944-X (SP) filed in the current quarter . . . .   **11** [   ]

12   Balance due. If line 10 is more than line 11, enter the difference and see instructions . .   **12** [   ]

13   Overpayment. If line 11 is more than line 10, enter the difference [   ] Check one: [ ] Apply to next return. [ ] Send a refund.

▶ **You MUST complete both pages of Form 941 and SIGN it.**

Next ▶

For Privacy Act and Paperwork Reduction Act Notice, see the back of the Payment Voucher.   Cat. No. 17001Z   Form **941** (Rev. 1-2015)

950214

Name *(not your trade name)*

Employer identification number (EIN)

Part 2:   Tell us about your deposit schedule and tax liability for this quarter.

If you are unsure about whether you are a monthly schedule depositor or a semiweekly schedule depositor, see Pub. 15 (Circular E), section 11.

14 Check one: ☐ Line 10 on this return is less than $2,500 or line 10 on the return for the prior quarter was less than $2,500, and you did not incur a $100,000 next-day deposit obligation during the current quarter. If line 10 for the prior quarter was less than $2,500 but line 10 on this return is $100,000 or more, you must provide a record of your federal tax liability. If you are a monthly schedule depositor, complete the deposit schedule below; if you are a semiweekly schedule depositor, attach Schedule B (Form 941). Go to Part 3.

☐ **You were a monthly schedule depositor for the entire quarter.** Enter your tax liability for each month and total liability for the quarter, then go to Part 3.

Tax liability: Month 1   [.   ]

Month 2   [.   ]

Month 3   [.   ]

Total liability for quarter   [.   ]   Total must equal line 10.

☐ **You were a semiweekly schedule depositor for any part of this quarter.** Complete Schedule B (Form 941), Report of Tax Liability for Semiweekly Schedule Depositors, and attach it to Form 941.

Part 3:   Tell us about your business. If a question does NOT apply to your business, leave it blank.

15 If your business has closed or you stopped paying wages . . . .   ☐ Check here, and

enter the final date you paid wages   [/   /   ] .

16 If you are a seasonal employer and you do not have to file a return for every quarter of the year . .   ☐ Check here.

Part 4:   May we speak with your third-party designee?

Do you want to allow an employee, a paid tax preparer, or another person to discuss this return with the IRS? See the instructions for details.

☐ Yes. Designee's name and phone number   [   ]   [   ]

Select a 5-digit Personal Identification Number (PIN) to use when talking to the IRS.   ☐ ☐ ☐ ☐ ☐

☐ No.

Part 5:   Sign here. You MUST complete both pages of Form 941 and SIGN it.

Under penalties of perjury, I declare that I have examined this return, including accompanying schedules and statements, and to the best of my knowledge and belief, it is true, correct, and complete. Declaration of preparer (other than taxpayer) is based on all information of which preparer has any knowledge.

X   Sign your name here   [   ]

Print your name here   [   ]

Print your title here   [   ]

Date   [/   /   ]

Best daytime phone   [   ]

Paid Preparer Use Only   Check if you are self-employed . . . ☐

Preparer's name   [   ]   PTIN   [   ]

Preparer's signature   [   ]   Date   [/   /   ]

Firm's name (or yours if self-employed)   [   ]   EIN   [   ]

Address   [   ]   Phone   [   ]

City   [   ]   State [   ]   ZIP code   [   ]

Source: Internal Revenue Service.

5-8B.
LO 5-3

Using the information from 5-6B and 5-7B for Fideaux, complete the following State of California Form DE-9, Quarterly Contribution Return and Report of Wages. The California employer account number is 989-8877-1. Use 5.4% as the UI rate, 0.1% as the ETT rate, and 0.9% as the SDI rate. All employees have worked since July 1 with the company. The California PIT taxes withheld for the quarter are $40,000. The company has deposited no taxes for the quarter.

EDD Employment Development Department
State of California

QUARTERLY CONTRIBUTION RETURN AND REPORT OF WAGES
REMINDER: File your DE 9 and DE 9C together.

00090112

PLEASE TYPE THIS FORM—DO NOT ALTER PREPRINTED INFORMATION

			YR	QTR
QUARTER ENDED	DUE	DELINQUENT IF NOT POSTMARKED OR RECEIVED BY		

EMPLOYER ACCOUNT NO.

DO NOT ALTER THIS AREA

DEPT. USE ONLY

P1   P2   C   P   U   S   A

T

EFFECTIVE DATE   Mo.   Day   Yr.

FEIN

A. NO WAGES PAID THIS QUARTER ☐   **B.** OUT OF BUSINESS/NO EMPLOYEES ☐

ADDITIONAL FEINS

B1.   OUT OF BUSINESS DATE
M M D D Y Y Y Y

C. TOTAL SUBJECT WAGES PAID THIS QUARTER ....

D. UNEMPLOYMENT INSURANCE (UI) (Total Employee Wages up to $ per employee per calendar year)

(D1) UI Rate %   TIMES   (D2) UI TAXABLE WAGES FOR THE QUARTER   =   (D3) UI CONTRIBUTIONS

E. EMPLOYMENT TRAINING TAX (ETT)

(E1) ETT Rate %   TIMES   UI Taxable Wages for the Quarter (D2) ......   =   (E2) ETT CONTRIBUTIONS

F. STATE DISABILITY INSURANCE (SDI) (Total Employee Wages up to $ per employee per calendar year)

(F1) SDI Rate %   TIMES   (F2) SDI TAXABLE WAGES FOR THE QUARTER   =   (F3) SDI EMPLOYEE CONTRIBUTIONS WITHHELD

G. CALIFORNIA PERSONAL INCOME TAX (PIT) WITHHELD ....

H. SUBTOTAL (Add Items D3, E2, F3, and G) ....

I. LESS: CONTRIBUTIONS AND WITHHOLDINGS PAID FOR THE QUARTER ....
(**DO NOT** INCLUDE PENALTY AND INTEREST PAYMENTS)

J. TOTAL TAXES DUE OR OVERPAID   (Item H minus Item I) ....

If amount due, prepare a *Payroll Tax Deposit* (DE 88), include the correct payment quarter, and mail to: Employment Development Department, P.O. Box 826276, Sacramento, CA 94230-6276. **NOTE:** Do not mail payments along with the DE 9 and *Quarterly Contribution Return and Report of Wages (Continuation)* (DE 9C), as this may delay processing and result in erroneous penalty and interest charges. **Mandatory Electronic Funds Transfer (EFT)** filers must remit all SDI/PIT deposits by EFT to avoid a noncompliance penalty.

K. I declare that the above, to the best of my knowledge and belief, is true and correct. If a refund was claimed, a reasonable effort was made to refund any erroneous deductions to the affected employee(s).

Signature *Required* _____ Title _____ Phone (___) _____ Date_____
(Owner, Accountant, Preparer, etc.)

SIGN AND MAIL TO: State of California / Employment Development Department / P.O. Box 989071 / West Sacramento CA 95798-9071

DE 9 Rev. 1 (1-12) **(INTERNET)**   Page 1 of 2   Fast, Easy, and Convenient! Visit EDD's Web site at **www.edd.ca.gov**

Source: Employment Development Department.

5-9B.
LO 5-3

Blier's Bears paid its nine employees a total of $432,586.40 during 2014. All employees have worked there for the full calendar year and reached the FUTA wage base during the first quarter. Taxes were deposited. The employer contributed $12,470 to Section 125 plans during the year (payments exempt from FUTA). Blier's Bears is located at 783 Morehead Street, Fargo, ND 68383, phone number 701-555-3432. The owner is Noah Jackson, and the EIN is 73-4029848. Complete Form 940 for Blier's Bears.

Form **940 for 2015:** **Employer's Annual Federal Unemployment (FUTA) Tax Return**   850113

Department of the Treasury — Internal Revenue Service

OMB No. 1545-0028

Employer identification number (EIN) ☐☐ – ☐☐☐☐☐☐☐

Name *(not your trade name)*

Trade name *(if any)*

Address
Number   Street   Suite or room number
City   State   ZIP code
Foreign country name   Foreign province/county   Foreign postal code

Type of Return
(Check all that apply.)
☐ a. Amended
☐ b. Successor employer
☐ c. No payments to employees in 2014
☐ d. Final: Business closed or stopped paying wages

Instructions and prior-year forms are available at *www.irs.gov/form940.*

Read the separate instructions before you complete this form. Please type or print within the boxes.

Part 1:   Tell us about your return. If any line does NOT apply, leave it blank.

1a   If you had to pay state unemployment tax in one state only, enter the state abbreviation . **1a** ☐ ☐

1b   If you had to pay state unemployment tax in more than one state, you are a multi-state employer . . . . **1b** ☐ Check here. Complete Schedule A (Form 940).

2   If you paid wages in a state that is subject to CREDIT REDUCTION . . . . . **2** ☐ Check here. Complete Schedule A (Form 940).

Part 2:   Determine your FUTA tax before adjustments for 2014. If any line does NOT apply, leave it blank.

3   Total payments to all employees . . . . **3** ☐ .

4   Payments exempt from FUTA tax . . . . . **4** ☐ .

Check all that apply: **4a** ☐ Fringe benefits   **4c** ☐ Retirement/Pension   **4e** ☐ Other
4b ☐ Group-term life insurance   **4d** ☐ Dependent care

5   Total of payments made to each employee in excess of $7,000 . . . . **5** ☐ .

6   Subtotal (line 4 + line 5 = line 6) . . . . **6** ☐ .

7   Total taxable FUTA wages (line 3 – line 6 = line 7) (see instructions) . . . . . **7** ☐ .

8   FUTA tax before adjustments (line 7 x .006 = line 8) . . . . . . **8** ☐ .

Part 3:   Determine your adjustments. If any line does NOT apply, leave it blank.

9   If ALL of the taxable FUTA wages you paid were excluded from state unemployment tax, multiply line 7 by .054 (line 7 x .054 = line 9). Go to line 12 . . . . . **9** ☐ .

10   If SOME of the taxable FUTA wages you paid were excluded from state unemployment tax, OR you paid ANY state unemployment tax late (after the due date for filing Form 940), complete the worksheet in the instructions. Enter the amount from line 7 of the worksheet . . **10** ☐ .

11   If credit reduction applies, enter the total from Schedule A (Form 940) . . . . . **11** ☐ .

Part 4:   Determine your FUTA tax and balance due or overpayment for 2014. If any line does NOT apply, leave it blank.

12   Total FUTA tax after adjustments (lines 8 + 9 + 10 + 11 = line 12) . . . . . **12** ☐ .

13   FUTA tax deposited for the year, including any overpayment applied from a prior year . **13** ☐ .

14   Balance due (If line 12 is more than line 13, enter the excess on line 14.)
• If line 14 is more than $500, you must deposit your tax.
• If line 14 is $500 or less, you may pay with this return. (see instructions) . . . . . **14** ☐ .

15   Overpayment (If line 13 is more than line 12, enter the excess on line 15 and check a box below.) . . . . . **15** ☐ .

▶ You **MUST** complete both pages of this form and **SIGN** it.   Check one: ☐ Apply to next return. ☐ Send a refund.

Next ▶

For Privacy Act and Paperwork Reduction Act Notice, see the back of Form 940-V, Payment Voucher.   Cat. No. 112340   Form **940** (2015)

850212

Name *(not your trade name)*	Employer identification number (EIN)

Part 5:   **Report your FUTA tax liability by quarter only if line 12 is more than $500. If not, go to Part 6.**

16   Report the amount of your FUTA tax liability for each quarter; do NOT enter the amount you deposited. If you had no liability for a quarter, leave the line blank.

   16a   1st quarter (January 1 – March 31) . . . .   **16a**   [.   ]

   16b   2nd quarter (April 1 – June 30) . . . .   **16b**   [.   ]

   16c   3rd quarter (July 1 – September 30) . . . .   **16c**   [.   ]

   16d   4th quarter (October 1 – December 31) . . . .   **16d**   [.   ]

17   Total tax liability for the year (lines 16a + 16b + 16c + 16d = line 17) **17**   [.   ]   **Total must equal line 12.**

Part 6:   **May we speak with your third-party designee?**

Do you want to allow an employee, a paid tax preparer, or another person to discuss this return with the IRS? See the instructions for details.

☐ **Yes.**   Designee's name and phone number   [   ]   [   ]

            Select a 5-digit Personal Identification Number (PIN) to use when talking to IRS   [ ][ ][ ][ ][ ]

☐ **No.**

Part 7:   **Sign here. You MUST complete both pages of this form and SIGN it.**

Under penalties of perjury, I declare that I have examined this return, including accompanying schedules and statements, and to the best of my knowledge and belief, it is true, correct, and complete, and that no part of any payment made to a state unemployment fund claimed as a credit was, or is to be, deducted from the payments made to employees. Declaration of preparer (other than taxpayer) is based on all information of which preparer has any knowledge.

✗ **Sign your name here**   [   ]   Print your name here [   ]

                            Print your title here [   ]

         Date   [/ /]   Best daytime phone [   ]

Paid Preparer Use Only   Check if you are self-employed . ☐

Preparer's name	[ ]	PTIN [ ]
Preparer's signature	[ ]	Date [/ /]
Firm's name (or yours if self-employed)	[ ]	EIN [ ]
Address	[ ]	Phone [ ]
City	[ ] State [ ]	ZIP code [ ]

Source: Internal Revenue Service.

5-10B.

LO 5-3

Philip Castor, owner of Castor Corporation is located at 1310 Garrick Way, Sun Valley, Arizona, 86029, phone number 928-555-8842. The Federal EIN is 20-1948348, and the state employer identification number is 9040-2038-1. Prepare Form W-2 for each of the following employees of Castor Corporation as of December 31, 2015. The same deductions are allowed for state income tax as for federal.

Paul M. Parsons
5834 Moon Drive
Sun Valley, AZ 86029
SSN: 578-33-3049

Total 2015 wages: $47,203.78
401(k) contribution: $2,832.23
Section 125 contribution: $1,400.00
Federal income tax withheld: $5,664.45
Social Security tax withheld: $2,839.83
Medicare tax withheld: $664.15
State income tax withheld: $1,443.84

Rachel Y. Maddox
32 Second Street
Holbrook, AZ 86025
SSN: 734-00-1938
Tuition in excess of $5,250: $750

Total 2015 wages: $37,499.02
401(k) contribution: $1,124.97
Section 125 contribution: $500.00
Federal income tax withheld: $4,409.88
Social Security tax withheld: $2,293.94
Medicare tax withheld: $536.49
State income tax withheld: $1,180.92

Ari J. Featherstone
7784 Painted Desert Road
Sun Valley, AZ 86029
SSN: 290-03-4992

Total 2015 wages: $41,904.29
401(k) contribution: $1,885.69
Federal income tax withheld: $5,028.52
Social Security tax withheld: $2,600.30
Medicare tax withheld: $608.13
State income tax withheld: $1,344.63

Connor L. Clearwater
7384 Ridge Road
Woodruff, AZ 85942
SSN: 994-20-4837

Total 2015 wages: $29,874.37
401(k) contribution: $597.49
Section 125 contribution: $250.00
Federal income tax withheld: $3,584.92
Social Security tax withheld: $1,836.71
Medicare tax withheld: $429.55
State income tax withheld: $975.30

Tieya L. Millen
229 Second Street #4A
Holbrook, AZ 86025
SSN: 477-30-2234

Total 2015 wages: $15,889.04
Federal income tax withheld: $1,906.69
Social Security tax withheld: $985.12
Medicare tax withheld: $230.39
State income tax withheld: $533.87

22222	a Employee's social security number	OMB No. 1545-0008	
b Employer identification number (EIN)		1 Wages, tips, other compensation	2 Federal income tax withheld
c Employer's name, address, and ZIP code		3 Social security wages	4 Social security tax withheld
		5 Medicare wages and tips	6 Medicare tax withheld
		7 Social security tips	8 Allocated tips
d Control number		9	10 Dependent care benefits
e Employee's first name and initial Last name Suff.		11 Nonqualified plans	12a
		13 Statutory employee Retirement plan Third-party sick pay	12b
		14 Other	12c
			12d
f Employee's address and ZIP code			

15 State	Employer's state ID number	16 State wages, tips, etc.	17 State income tax	18 Local wages, tips, etc.	19 Local income tax	20 Locality name

Form **W-2**   Wage and Tax Statement   **2015**   Department of the Treasury—Internal Revenue Service
Copy 1—For State, City, or Local Tax Department

22222	**a** Employee's social security number	OMB No. 1545-0008		
b Employer identification number (EIN)			**1** Wages, tips, other compensation	**2** Federal income tax withheld
c Employer's name, address, and ZIP code			**3** Social security wages	**4** Social security tax withheld
			5 Medicare wages and tips	**6** Medicare tax withheld
			7 Social security tips	**8** Allocated tips
d Control number		**9**	**10** Dependent care benefits	
e Employee's first name and initial Last name Suff.		**11** Nonqualified plans	**12a**	
		13 Statutory employee Retirement plan Third-party sick pay	**12b**	
		14 Other	**12c**	
			12d	
f Employee's address and ZIP code				
15 State Employer's state ID number	**16** State wages, tips, etc.	**17** State income tax	**18** Local wages, tips, etc.	**19** Local income tax **20** Locality name

Form **W-2** Wage and Tax Statement   **2015**   Department of the Treasury—Internal Revenue Service
Copy 1—For State, City, or Local Tax Department

22222	**a** Employee's social security number	OMB No. 1545-0008		
b Employer identification number (EIN)			**1** Wages, tips, other compensation	**2** Federal income tax withheld
c Employer's name, address, and ZIP code			**3** Social security wages	**4** Social security tax withheld
			5 Medicare wages and tips	**6** Medicare tax withheld
			7 Social security tips	**8** Allocated tips
d Control number		**9**	**10** Dependent care benefits	
e Employee's first name and initial Last name Suff.		**11** Nonqualified plans	**12a**	
		13 Statutory employee Retirement plan Third-party sick pay	**12b**	
		14 Other	**12c**	
			12d	
f Employee's address and ZIP code				
15 State Employer's state ID number	**16** State wages, tips, etc.	**17** State income tax	**18** Local wages, tips, etc.	**19** Local income tax **20** Locality name

Form **W-2** Wage and Tax Statement   **2015**   Department of the Treasury—Internal Revenue Service
Copy 1—For State, City, or Local Tax Department

22222	**a** Employee's social security number	OMB No. 1545-0008		
b Employer identification number (EIN)			**1** Wages, tips, other compensation	**2** Federal income tax withheld
c Employer's name, address, and ZIP code			**3** Social security wages	**4** Social security tax withheld
			5 Medicare wages and tips	**6** Medicare tax withheld
			7 Social security tips	**8** Allocated tips
d Control number		**9**	**10** Dependent care benefits	
e Employee's first name and initial Last name Suff.		**11** Nonqualified plans	**12a**	
		13 Statutory employee Retirement plan Third-party sick pay	**12b**	
		14 Other	**12c**	
			12d	
f Employee's address and ZIP code				
15 State Employer's state ID number	**16** State wages, tips, etc.	**17** State income tax	**18** Local wages, tips, etc.	**19** Local income tax **20** Locality name

Form **W-2** Wage and Tax Statement   **2015**   Department of the Treasury—Internal Revenue Service
Copy 1—For State, City, or Local Tax Department

Chapter 5 Employer Payroll Taxes and Labor Planning 197

	a Employee's social security number			
22222		OMB No. 1545-0008		
b Employer identification number (EIN)			**1** Wages, tips, other compensation	**2** Federal income tax withheld
c Employer's name, address, and ZIP code			**3** Social security wages	**4** Social security tax withheld
			5 Medicare wages and tips	**6** Medicare tax withheld
			7 Social security tips	**8** Allocated tips
d Control number			**9**	**10** Dependent care benefits
e Employee's first name and initial Last name Suff.			**11** Nonqualified plans	**12a**
			13 Statutory employee / Retirement plan / Third-party sick pay	**12b**
			14 Other	**12c**
				12d
f Employee's address and ZIP code				
15 State Employer's state ID number	**16** State wages, tips, etc.	**17** State income tax	**18** Local wages, tips, etc.	**19** Local income tax **20** Locality name

Form **W-2** Wage and Tax Statement   2015   Department of the Treasury—Internal Revenue Service
Copy 1—For State, City, or Local Tax Department

5-11B.
LO 5-3

Using the information from Exercise 5-10B for Castor Corporation, complete Form W-3 that must accompany the company's Forms W-2. Castor Corporation is a 941-SS payer and is a private, for-profit company. No third-party sick pay was applied for 2015.

DO NOT STAPLE OR FOLD

	a Control number		For Official Use Only ▶ OMB No. 1545-0008		
33333					
b Kind of Payer (Check one)	941-SS ☐ Military ☐ 943 ☐ 944 ☐ Hshld. emp. ☐ Medicare govt. emp. ☐		**Kind of Employer** (Check one)	None apply ☐ 501c non-govt. ☐ State/local non-501c ☐ State/local 501c ☐ Federal govt. ☐	Third-party sick pay (Check if applicable) ☐
c Total number of Forms W-2	**d** Establishment number		**1** Wages, tips, other compensation	**2** Income tax withheld	
e Employer identification number (EIN)			**3** Social security wages	**4** Social security tax withheld	
f Employer's name			**5** Medicare wages and tips	**6** Medicare tax withheld	
			7 Social security tips	**8**	
			9	**10**	
			11 Nonqualified plans	**12a** Deferred compensation	
g Employer's address and ZIP code			**13** For third-party sick pay use only	**12b**	
h Other EIN used this year					
15 Employer's territorial ID number			**14** Income tax withheld by payer of third-party sick pay		
Employer's contact person			Employer's telephone number	For Official Use Only	
Employer's fax number			Employer's email address		

Copy 1—For Local Tax Department

Under penalties of perjury, I declare that I have examined this return and accompanying documents, and, to the best of my knowledge and belief, they are true, correct, and complete.

Signature ▶   Title ▶   Date ▶

Form **W-3SS** Transmittal of Wage and Tax Statements   2015   Department of the Treasury Internal Revenue Service

5-12B.
LO 5-5, 5-6

Nanco is a company that makes custom signs and has 12 employees. The owner wants to perform a benefits analysis report for the year for one of its employees, Ben Loomes. Ben's benefits package is as follows:

Salary: $38,950

401(k) contribution: 5% of salary, company match is half of employee's contribution up to 6%

Medical insurance deduction: $140 per month

Dental insurance: $36 per month

Complete the following Benefits Analysis Report for Ben Loomes for the year.

Yearly Benefit Costs	Company Cost	Ben's Cost
Medical insurance	$ 9,600	$
Dental insurance	$ 800	$
Life insurance	$ 1200	-0-
AD&D	$ 125	-0-
Short-term disability	$ 500	-0-
Long-term disability	$ 250	-0-
401(k)	$	$
Social Security	$	$
Medicare	$	$
Tuition reimbursement	$ 5,000	-0-
Total yearly benefit costs	$	
Ben's annual salary	$	
Total yearly benefit costs	$	
Total value of Ben's compensation	$	

5-13B.
LO 5-4, 5-5

Hammond Enterprises has 52 employees distributed among the following departments:

Sales: 14	Factory: 26	Administration: 12

The total annual payroll for Hammond Enterprises is $1,280,550.

Compute the labor distribution based on equal distribution among the departments.

Sales: _____

Factory: _____

Administration: _____

5-14B.
LO 5-4, 5-5

For Hammond Enterprises in Exercise 5-13B, compute the labor distribution based on the number of employees per department:

Sales: _____

Factory: _____

Administration: _____

Critical Thinking

5-1. Maggie's Memories is a semiweekly depositor. Following the success of a special project, Maggie, the owner, pays each of the 250 employees a $20,000 bonus on August 17, 2015. Assuming a 25% income tax rate, when will Maggie need to deposit the payroll taxes?

5-2. Chris is the president of a military regalia antique business, War Arts. His employee, Barry Williams, is due a raise. Barry's current benefit analysis is as follows:

Yearly Benefit Costs	Company Cost (Current)	Employee Cost (Current)
Medical insurance	$ 8,000	$ 1,200
Dental insurance	$ 120	$ 120
Life insurance	$ 300	-0-
AD&D	$ 150	-0-
Short-term disability	$ 60	-0-
Long-term disability	$ 30	-0-
401(k)	$ 750	$ 1,500
Social Security	$ 3,018.16	$ 3,018.16
Medicare	$ 705.86	$ 705.86
Tuition reimbursement	$ 2,000	-0-
Total yearly benefit costs (employer)	$15,134.02	
Employee's annual salary	$50,000	
Total value of employee's compensation	$65,134.02	

Compute the benefit analysis assuming:

7% increase in pay

3% contribution to 401(k) will remain the same with a company match of 50%

10% increase in medical and dental insurance premiums

Yearly Benefit Costs	Company Cost (New)	Employee Cost (New)
Medical insurance	$	$
Dental insurance	$	$
Life insurance	$	-0-
AD&D	$	-0-
Short-term disability	$	-0-
Long-term disability	$	-0-
401(k)	$	$
Social Security	$	$
Medicare	$	$
Tuition reimbursement	$	-0-
Total yearly benefit costs (employer)	$	
Barry's annual salary	$	
Total value of employee's compensation	$	

In the Real World: Scenario for Discussion

In Little Rock, Arkansas, a church pastor was found guilty of payroll tax fraud by withholding employee payroll taxes and failing to remit them from 2006 through 2010. The pastor is serving a sentence of 33 months in prison with 5 years of supervised release and $450,000 in restitution to the IRS. Do you think this was a fair sentence? Why or why not?

Internet Activities

5-1. Try the withholding calculator from the IRS. Go to www.irs.gov/individuals and use the withholding calculator.

5-2. Go to www.bizfilings.com/toolkit/sbg/tax-info/payroll-taxes/unemployment.aspx and check out the unemployment tax laws for your state.

5-3. Want to know more about the concepts in this chapter? Go to one or more of the following sites. What are two or three things you notice about the information on the site?

www.smallbusiness.chron.com/example-employee-compensation-plan-10068.html

http://yourbusiness.azcentral.com/labor-cost-distribution-report-26061.html

www.lectlaw.com/files/tax22.htm

www.irs.gov/publications/p80/ar02.html

Continuing Payroll Project: Prevosti Farms and Sugarhouse

The first quarter tax return needs to be filed for Prevosti Farms and Sugarhouse by April 15. For the purpose of the taxes, assume the February 27 payroll amounts were duplicated for both of March's payroll periods.

EIN	89-6589801
Number of employees	8
Quarterly wages	$32,010.17
Federal income tax withheld	$988.00
401(k) contributions	$1,257.65
Insurance withheld	$4,080.00
Month 1	-0-
Month 2	$2,133.22
Month 3	$3,128.12

Complete Form 941 for Prevosti Farms and Sugarhouse.

Form **941 for 2015:** Employer's QUARTERLY Federal Tax Return

(Rev. January 2015)   Department of the Treasury — Internal Revenue Service

950114

OMB No. 1545-0029

Employer identification number (EIN) ☐☐ – ☐☐☐☐☐☐☐

Name *(not your trade name)* ☐

Trade name *(if any)* ☐

Address ☐
Number   Street   Suite or room number
☐ ☐ ☐
City   State   ZIP code
☐ ☐ ☐
Foreign country name   Foreign province/county   Foreign postal code

Report for this Quarter of 2015
(Check one.)

☐ **1:** January, February, March

☐ **2:** April, May, June

☐ **3:** July, August, September

☐ **4:** October, November, December

Instructions and prior year forms are available at *www.irs.gov/form941*.

Read the separate instructions before you complete Form 941. Type or print within the boxes.

Part 1:	Answer these questions for this quarter.

1   Number of employees who received wages, tips, or other compensation for the pay period including: *Mar. 12* (Quarter 1), *June 12* (Quarter 2), *Sept. 12* (Quarter 3), or *Dec. 12* (Quarter 4)   **1** ☐

2   Wages, tips, and other compensation . . . .   **2** ☐

3   Federal income tax withheld from wages, tips, and other compensation . . . . .   **3** ☐

4   If no wages, tips, and other compensation are subject to social security or Medicare tax   ☐ Check and go to line 6.

		Column 1		Column 2	
5a	Taxable social security wages . .	☐	× .124 =	☐	
5b	Taxable social security tips . . .	☐	× .124 =	☐	
5c	Taxable Medicare wages & tips. .	☐	× .029 =	☐	
5d	Taxable wages & tips subject to Additional Medicare Tax withholding	☐	× .009 =	☐	

5e   Add Column 2 from lines 5a, 5b, 5c, and 5d . . . .   **5e** ☐

5f   Section 3121(q) Notice and Demand—Tax due on unreported tips (see instructions) . .   **5f** ☐

6   Total taxes before adjustments. Add lines 3, 5e, and 5f . . . .   **6** ☐

7   Current quarter's adjustment for fractions of cents . . . .   **7** ☐

8   Current quarter's adjustment for sick pay . . . .   **8** ☐

9   Current quarter's adjustments for tips and group-term life insurance . . . . . .   **9** ☐

10   Total taxes after adjustments. Combine lines 6 through 9 . . . .   **10** ☐

11   Total deposits for this quarter, including overpayment applied from a prior quarter and overpayments applied from Form 941-X, 941-X (PR), 944-X, 944-X (PR), or 944-X (SP) filed in the current quarter . . . .   **11** ☐

12   Balance due. If line 10 is more than line 11, enter the difference and see instructions . . .   **12** ☐

13   Overpayment. If line 11 is more than line 10, enter the difference ☐   Check one: ☐ Apply to next return. ☐ Send a refund.

▶ **You MUST complete both pages of Form 941 and SIGN it.**

Next ▶

For Privacy Act and Paperwork Reduction Act Notice, see the back of the Payment Voucher.   Cat. No. 17001Z   Form **941** (Rev. 1-2015)

950214

Name *(not your trade name)*	Employer identification number (EIN)

Part 2: **Tell us about your deposit schedule and tax liability for this quarter.**

If you are unsure about whether you are a monthly schedule depositor or a semiweekly schedule depositor, see Pub. 15 (Circular E), section 11.

14 Check one: ☐ **Line 10 on this return is less than $2,500 or line 10 on the return for the prior quarter was less than $2,500, and you did not incur a $100,000 next-day deposit obligation during the current quarter.** If line 10 for the prior quarter was less than $2,500 but line 10 on this return is $100,000 or more, you must provide a record of your federal tax liability. If you are a monthly schedule depositor, complete the deposit schedule below; if you are a semiweekly schedule depositor, attach Schedule B (Form 941). Go to Part 3.

☐ **You were a monthly schedule depositor for the entire quarter.** Enter your tax liability for each month and total liability for the quarter, then go to Part 3.

Tax liability: Month 1 [_____ . __]

Month 2 [_____ . __]

Month 3 [_____ . __]

Total liability for quarter [_____ . __] **Total must equal line 10.**

☐ **You were a semiweekly schedule depositor for any part of this quarter.** Complete Schedule B (Form 941), Report of Tax Liability for Semiweekly Schedule Depositors, and attach it to Form 941.

Part 3: **Tell us about your business. If a question does NOT apply to your business, leave it blank.**

15 **If your business has closed or you stopped paying wages** . . . . ☐ Check here, and

enter the final date you paid wages [__ / __ / __] .

16 **If you are a seasonal employer and you do not have to file a return for every quarter of the year** . . ☐ Check here.

Part 4: **May we speak with your third-party designee?**

Do you want to allow an employee, a paid tax preparer, or another person to discuss this return with the IRS? See the instructions for details.

☐ Yes. Designee's name and phone number [_____] [_____]

Select a 5-digit Personal Identification Number (PIN) to use when talking to the IRS. ☐ ☐ ☐ ☐ ☐

☐ No.

Part 5: **Sign here. You MUST complete both pages of Form 941 and SIGN it.**

Under penalties of perjury, I declare that I have examined this return, including accompanying schedules and statements, and to the best of my knowledge and belief, it is true, correct, and complete. Declaration of preparer (other than taxpayer) is based on all information of which preparer has any knowledge.

X **Sign your name here** [_____]   Print your name here [_____]

Print your title here [_____]

Date [__ / __ / __]   Best daytime phone [_____]

Paid Preparer Use Only   Check if you are self-employed . . . . ☐

Preparer's name	[_____]	PTIN	[_____]
Preparer's signature	[_____]	Date	[__ / __ / __]
Firm's name (or yours if self-employed)	[_____]	EIN	[_____]
Address	[_____]	Phone	[_____]
City	[_____]	State [____]	ZIP code	[_____]

Answers to Stop & Check Exercises

FUTA and SUTA

1.

FUTA: $7,000 × 29 × 0.006 =	$	1,218.00
$2,575 × 0.006 =	$	15.45
FUTA Liability	$	1,233.45
SUTA: $23,400 × 25 × 0.042 =	$	24,570.00
$60,090 × 0.042 =	$	2,523.78
SUTA Liability	$	27,093.78
Total combined FUTA/SUTA liability	$	28,327.23

2.

FUTA: $7,000 × 10 × 0.006 =	$	420.00
($5,500 + 6,800) × 0.006 =		73.80
Total FUTA liability	$	493.80
SUTA: $12,000 × 8 × 0.0326 =	$	3,129.60
$33,250 × 0.0326 =	$	1,083.95
Total SUTA liability	$	4,213.55

Competitive Skills Scholarship tax liability: $279,580 × 0.0006 = $167.75

Reporting Periods

1. Monthly
2. July 15
3. Monday, the next business day

Tax Forms

1. $2,414.48
2. $105,000 (15 employees × $7,000)
3. $630.00 ($105,000 (from problem 2) × 0.006 FUTA rate)
4. $116,195

Payroll-Related Business Expenses

1. Workers' Compensation Insurance, FUTA and SUTA taxes, Social Security and Medicare employer-share taxes, retirement matching, training, any tools or uniforms, office furniture, and so on.
2. Payroll expenses relate to the company's profitability, worker productivity analyses, employee retention, and business competitiveness.

Labor Distribution Report

1. a. office, $90,000; agricultural, $150,000; drivers, $60,000
   b. Each department would be allocated $100,000 of the payroll.
2. Department classification is the most appropriate because it matches the costs more closely to each department.

Benefit Analysis Report

1. One of the purposes of compiling a benefit analysis report is to represent graphically all of the variables that make up an employee's compensation package. The benefit analysis report provides managers and supervisors a budgetary tool to understand the full cost of hiring or dismissing employees. Additionally, the benefit analysis allows companies to compare benefits and employee costs to geographic or industry standards.
2. The benefit analysis report is an internal report for the company's management, and the annual total compensation report is meant to be distributed to the employee.

The Payroll Register, Employees' Earning Records, and Accounting System Entries

In this chapter, we will examine the need for and use of a payroll register and employees' earnings records. In previous chapters, we have examined the effects of payroll on employees, employers, and governmental agencies. This chapter links Generally Accepted Accounting Principles with payroll elements. We will discuss the debits and credits associated with payroll accrual and payment. For this chapter, we will use the accrual basis of accounting, which means that transactions are recognized at the time they are incurred.

Accounting entries are the transactions that place the payroll amounts into the correct ledger accounts. In automated systems, the software is designed to code each payroll item automatically to the correct general ledger account. However, for the payroll accountant to record accurate expenses and period end accruals in the correct month, manual entries are necessary. This is the final step of the payroll cycle for each pay period and is the most important piece of the process from an accounting perspective.

LEARNING OBJECTIVES

After studying Chapter 6, you should be able to:

LO 6-1   Create a Payroll Register

LO 6-2   Transfer Payroll Data to the Employees' Earnings Records

© Tom Grill/Photographer's Choice RF/Getty Images, RF

LO 6-3 Describe Financial Accounting Concepts

LO 6-4 Complete Payroll-Related General Journal Entries

LO 6-5 Generate Payroll-Related General Ledger Entries

LO 6-6 Describe Payroll Effects on the Accounting System

LO 6-7 Explain Payroll Entries in Accounting Reports

Employee Retention Becomes a C-Level Concern

Companies in the United States have reported growth during recent years. Pay-Scale surveyed 4,700 employers and found that more than half expected to see improved financial performance. These employers reported an intent to hire additional employees to meet growth needs. However, 80% of chief financial officers in the United States expressed concern with employee retention, citing a need to offer existing employees pay raises and promotions to retain their top performers. Payroll data is a critical element that informs decisions regarding employee compensation. The payroll piece of financial reports fosters both analysis of employee pay and benchmarking within appropriate business contexts. (Source: *CGMA Magazine,* PayScale)

> Workforce expansion leads to competition for skilled employees. Accurate reporting of payroll costs in the financial statement is a key part of decision making. In Chapter 6, we will examine the accounting system entries for payroll costs, then the effect on the company's financial reports, and finally how those reports influence managerial decisions.

LO 6-1   Create a Payroll Register

A payroll register is the payroll accountant's internal tool that helps ensure accuracy of employee compensation. A payroll register can be completed manually, in a spreadsheet program such as Microsoft Excel, in accounting software programs such as QuickBooks, or by payroll outsourcing companies such as ADP or Zen Payroll. Like other worksheets that accountants use, the payroll register is a company confidential document that is not made public.

The payroll register is annotated at the top with the beginning and ending dates of the payroll period. Each employee has a separate row in the register. The register contains columns to reflect each employee's specific pay information, such as:

1. Employee name

2. Marital status

3. Number of withholdings

4. Salary or hourly rate

5. Number of regular hours worked

6. Number of overtime hours worked

7. Regular pay

8. Overtime pay

9. Gross pay

10. Federal income tax withheld

11. Social Security tax withheld

12. Medicare tax withheld

13. State income tax withheld (where applicable)

14. Other state taxes

15. Local taxes (if applicable)

16. 401(k) or other retirement plan deductions

17. Insurance deductions

18. Garnishments or levies

19. Union dues

20. Any other deductions

21. Net pay

22. Check or payment ID number

It may seem tedious to complete a register each payroll period, but the register offers more information than just the employee compensation. The register also contains information about employer liabilities for taxes and the employees' voluntary deductions that the employer must remit to the appropriate places at a future date. A sample payroll register is shown in Figure 6-1.

FIGURE 6-1
Sample Payroll Register

Date	Employee ID	Name	Hourly Wage	Hours	Gross Pay	Federal Allow.	State Tax	Federal Income Tax	Social Security 6.2%	Medicare 1.45%	Total Tax Withheld	Insurance Deduction	Net Pay

A separate payroll register is maintained for each pay period. To ensure accuracy, the accountant totals, proves, and rules the register.

What does total, prove, and rule mean?

Total: Each column and row are totaled.

Prove: The column totals are added horizontally *and* row totals are totaled vertically. The aggregate column and row totals must be equal.

Rule: Column totals are double underlined to show that the totals have been proven.

Payroll Register Retention

Although no regulations exist for the retention and archiving of the payroll register, a general guideline is that the payroll register should be stored with the other payroll accounting records and destroyed in accordance with accounting record guidelines, which is three years under FLSA. One cautionary note on record destruction: Recall that the IRS requires all submitted records be retained for four years. Like other confidential records, the payroll register must be destroyed by shredding or incineration at the appropriate time.

The payroll register has a related set of documents called the employee earnings records. The employees' earnings records form the link between the accounting and the human resource departments. The information contained within each row of the payroll register is transferred to the employees' earnings records.

The Payroll Register

1. What is the purpose of the payroll register?
2. What are five of the columns that usually appear in a payroll register?
3. What do total, prove, and rule mean?

LO 6-2   Transfer Payroll Data to the Employees' Earnings Records

Employee earnings records form the link between the accounting and the human resource departments and connect closely with the payroll register. The information contained within each row of the payroll register is transferred to the employee's earnings record, an example of which is shown in Figure 6-2.

EMPLOYEE EARNINGS RECORD   Page A-16

Year _____

Employee's Name: _____
Address: _____   Number of Exemptions: (FED) _____   (STATE) _____
City: _____ State: _____ Zip: _____
Social Security Number: _____   Additional Withholding: (FED) _____   (STATE) _____

Payroll Period Ending	Total Hours	Gross Wages	Withholdings				Net Pay
			FICA	Federal Tax	State Tax	Other:	
J A N							
Monthly Total							
F E B							
Monthly Total							
M A R							
Monthly Total							
Quarterly Total							
A P R							
Monthly Total							
M A Y							
Monthly Total							
J U N							
Monthly Total							
Quarter Total							
Year to Date Total							

Payroll Period Ending	Total Hours	Gross Wages	Withholdings				Net Pay
			FICA	Federal Tax	State Tax	Other:	
J U L							
Monthly Total							
A U G							
Monthly Total							
S E P							
Monthly Total							
Quarterly Total							
O C T							
Monthly Total							
N O V							
Monthly Total							
D E C							
Monthly Total							
Quarter Total							
Year to Date Total							

FIGURE 6-2
Employee Earnings Record

The employee earnings record is the master document accountants use to track employees' marital status, deductions (mandatory, voluntary, and mandated), and year-to-date earnings. Remember that Social Security, FUTA, and SUTA taxes have annual earnings limits for each employee. Accountants update the employees' earnings records during each pay period to track all pay and tax deductions. Any employee changes including pay rate, marital status, and number of withholding allowances should be annotated in the earnings records as soon as possible to ensure the accuracy of the payroll.

The Employees' Earnings Records and Periodic Tax Reports

Period totals are also included on the earnings record. These totals facilitate the preparation of the quarterly and annual reports. Like any payroll record, the earnings records should be retained and destroyed at the same interval as other accounting records. Earning records are typically included as supporting documents for internal copies of quarterly filings of Form 941 as well as state, and local tax returns (where applicable). During a payroll audit, the documentation attached to the tax returns provides verification of the information contained in the reports. A secondary use is that, in the event of computer data failure, documents attached to payroll records can be used to re-create files.

Employee Earnings Register

1. How do the employees' earnings records relate to the payroll register?
2. Which of the following fields exist on both the payroll register and the employees' earnings records:
    a. Name
    b. Pay rate

c. Social Security tax

d. Net pay

e. Marital status

3. What reports and forms use information from the employees' earnings records?

LO 6-3 Describe Financial Accounting Concepts

In an accounting system, the fundamental accounting equation is **Assets = Liabilities + Owners' Equity.**

> *Assets*: Cash or other items that are used in the operation of the business and amounts owed to the business by customers.
>
> *Liabilities*: Amounts owed by the business to other people or companies.
>
> *Owners' Equity*: The net investment that the owner has in the business, including earnings kept in the business.

Financial business transactions, such as the movement of cash, are tracked in the accounting system. A fundamental concept in accounting involves the accounting equation, which must remain in balance at all times. As such, transactions will either increase an account (or multiple accounts), decrease an account (or multiple accounts), or a combination thereof. To understand the concept of equation balance, T-accounts are the first step in understanding the classification process that is part of transaction analysis.

> **Example:**
> Barry Larson, the owner of Riptide Sails, invested $4,000 into his business on August 1, 2015. Accountants classify the transaction into two accounts: assets and owner's equity. The cash account would increase because the money was invested in the business. Barry's owner's capital account would increase because he increased his net investment in the business. Using the T-account approach, the transaction would look like this:
>
> | Cash | |
> |---|---|
> | Dr. | Cr. |
> | 4,000 | |
>
> | Larson, Capital | |
> |---|---|
> | Dr. | Cr. |
> | | 4,000 |

Debits and Credits

If accountants were to maintain T-accounts for all of a business's transactions, their work would be tedious and vulnerable to a large number of errors. To simplify the addition and subtraction involved, accountants use the terms "debit" (abbreviated Dr.)

and "credit" (abbreviated Cr.) to explain the transaction. In accounting parlance, *debit* simply means "the left side of the T-account," and *credit* simply means "the right side of the T-account." No connotation exists about good or bad with the use of these terms in accounting.

Debits Increase:	Credits Increase:
Expenses	Liabilities
Assets	Equity (Capital)
Drawing	Revenue

The General Journal

To simplify the use of T-accounts, accountants use a journal (called the *General Journal*) to record the daily financial transactions. The General Journal is maintained in chronological order. The General Journal is one big T-account and has columns to record the debits and credits involved in each transaction. Complementing the General Journal is the *General Ledger*, in which all journal transactions are recorded in their specific accounts.

In the transaction above, the General Journal version would appear as follows:

Trans.	Date	Account Name & Description	Post Ref	Debit	Credit
1	8/1/2015	Cash	101	4,000.00	
		B. Larson, Capital	301		4,000.00
		Started business			

Note certain accounting conventions present in the journal entry:

- The date of the transaction is noted.
- The debit part of the transaction is on the first line and is flush-left in the column.
- The credit part of the transaction is on the second line and is indented slightly.
- A brief description of the transaction is on line three.
- Account numbers are annotated in the Post Reference (Post Ref.) column.
- The post reference in the General Journal is the General Ledger account number.

The General Ledger

Once the transaction has been recorded in the General Journal, the accountant posts the entry to corresponding General Ledger accounts. In the following table, note that (1) the transaction itself is listed, and (2) the balance of each account is adjusted accordingly. The General Ledger account balances are used to generate the payroll reports that we have been discussing so far. The elements of the General Ledger and specific posting practices will appear later in this chapter.

			Account: 101 – Cash		
Date	Description	Post Ref.	Debit	Credit	Balance
8/1/2015	Initial Contribution	J1	4,000.00		4,000.00
			Account: 301 – B. Larson, Capital		
Date	Description	Post Ref.	Debit	Credit	Balance
8/1/2015	Initial Contribution	J1		4,000.00	4,000.00

Financial Accounting Concepts

1. What is the fundamental accounting equation?
2. What increases the Wages and Salaries Payable account, a debit or a credit?
3. What increases the Wages and Salaries Expense account, a debit or a credit?

LO 6-4   Complete Payroll-Related General Journal Entries

Recording the specific General Journal entries that correspond to payroll activities is the next step in the process. General Journal entries are the original entry point for events to be recorded within the accounting system. A sample period payroll for NC Bikes follows.

NC Bikes pays its employees biweekly and operates on a calendar fiscal year (i.e., the year-end is December 31). The payroll accountant for NC Bikes has completed the payroll register for the January 28, 2015, payroll. Pay checks will be issued on January 31. Payroll totals are as follows:

Gross pay: $18,050.00

Federal income tax withheld: $1,500.00

Social Security tax withheld: $1,084.38

Medicare tax withheld: $253.61

State income tax withheld: $577.60

401(k) contributions withheld: $750.00

Health insurance premiums withheld: $560.00

United Way contributions withheld: $180.00

Net pay: $13,144.41

Employee Pay-Related Journal Entries

The General Journal entry to record the employee's portion of the payroll and the issuance of the checks to employees is in two parts:

Date	Description	Account	Debit	Credit
Jan. 28	Salaries and Wages Expense	511	$18,050.00	
	FIT Payable	221		$1,500.00
	Social Security Tax Payable	222		1,084.38
	Medicare Tax Payable	223		253.61
	State Income Tax Payable	224		577.60
	401(k) Contributions Payable	225		750.00
	Health Insurance Premiums Payable	226		560.00
	United Way Contributions Payable	227		180.00
	Salaries and Wages Payable	231		13,144.41
Jan. 31	Salaries and Wages Payable	231	13,144.41	
	Cash	101		13,144.41

Employer Payroll-Related Journal Entries

The employer's share of the payroll is similarly recorded. NC Bikes' share of the payroll expenses is:

> Social Security tax: $1,084.38
>
> Medicare tax: $253.61
>
> FUTA tax: $104.94
>
> SUTA tax: $974.70

The General Journal entry for the employer's share of the payroll taxes is:

Date	Description	Account	Debit	Credit
Jan. 28	Payroll Taxes Expense	512	$2,417.63	
	Social Security Tax Payable	222		$1,084.38
	Medicare Tax Payable	223		253.61
	FUTA Tax Payable	228		104.94
	SUTA Tax Payable	229		974.70

Other Payroll-Related Journal Entries

What about the other deductions that NC Bikes withheld from its employees' pay? These other deductions, including federal and state income tax, 401(k) contributions, health insurance premiums and United Way contributions, are liabilities of the company. These amounts will remain in the liability accounts until NC Bikes *remits* them. Upon remittance, the General Journal entries will appear as a debit to the Liability account and a credit to Cash. An example for the January 28 payroll's voluntary deductions, paid to the appropriate companies on January 31, follows:

Date	Description	Account	Debit	Credit
Jan. 31	401(k) Contributions Payable	225	$750.00	
	Health Insurance Payable	226	560.00	
	United Way Contribution Payable	227	180.00	
	Cash	101		$1,490.00

Remember that the remittance for the governmental taxes has a specific schedule. The General Journal entry for the tax remittances would follow the same pattern as the voluntary deductions: debit the Liability account(s) and credit Cash.

Payroll Accruals and Reversals

A common occurrence is that a payroll may be split between two months, as will be the case for NC Bikes. For example, the majority of the pay for the end of March (i.e., the end of the first quarter) will be paid on the April 1, 2015, payday. For accounting purposes, the accountant needs to record the *accrual* of the payroll for March to represent accurately the *expenses* and liabilities incurred during the period. Some companies choose to record the period's expenses through *adjusting entries*, and then reverse the entries after the start of the next period to prevent confusion in the payroll accounting process.

In the case of NC Bikes, the adjusting entry would appear as follows for the end of March:

Gross pay: $16,245.00

Federal income tax withheld: $1,350.00

Social Security tax withheld: $1,007.19

Medicare tax withheld: $235.55

State income tax withheld: $519.84

Net pay: $13,132.42

The adjusting entry for March 31, 2015, would be:

Date	Description	Account	Debit	Credit
Mar. 31	Salaries and Wages Expense	511	$16,245.00	
	FIT Payable	221		$1,350.00
	Social Security Tax Payable	222		1,007.19
	Medicare Tax Payable	223		235.55
	State Income Tax Payable	224		519.84
	Salaries and Wages Payable	231		13,132.42

The amount for the employer's share would be:

Date	Description	Account	Debit	Credit
Mar. 31	Payroll Taxes Expense	512	$2,217.17	
	Social Security Tax Payable	222		$1,007.19
	Medicare Tax Payable	223		235.55
	FUTA Tax Payable	228		97.47
	SUTA Tax Payable	229		876.96

On April 1, 2015, the accountant could record a reversing entry as follows:

Date	Description	Account	Debit	Credit
Apr. 1	FIT Payable	221	$1,350.00	
	Social Security Tax Payable	222	1,007.19	
	Medicare Tax Payable	223	235.55	
	State Income Tax Payable	224	519.84	
	Salaries and Wages Payable	231	13,132.42	
	Salaries and Wages Expense	511		$16,245.00

The *reversal* of the employer's share of payroll expenses would be:

Date	Description	Account	Debit	Credit
Apr. 1	Social Security Tax Payable	222	$1,007.19	
	Medicare Tax Payable	223	235.55	
	FUTA Tax Payable	224	129.96	
	SUTA Tax Payable	229	876.96	
	Payroll Taxes Expense	512		$2,217.17

Note that not all companies and accountants use reversing entries. An advantage of using the reversing entry is that it simplifies the payroll process by avoiding calculating partial payroll periods that occur due to the period end. A disadvantage is that the reversing entry becomes an additional entry that the accountant has to journalize and post. The use of the reversing entry is at the company's discretion.

Payroll and the General Journal

STOP & CHECK

1. In the following General Journal entry, which account represents the employees' gross pay?

Description	Debit	Credit
Wages and Salaries Expense	$124,785.00	
Federal Income Tax Payable		$15,280.00
Social Security Tax Payable		$ 7,736.67
Medicare Tax Payable		$ 1,809.38
State Income Tax Payable		$ 4,741.83
Wages and Salaries Payable		$ 95,217.12

2. Based on the above General Journal entry, what would be the entry for the employer's share of the payroll taxes? Omit FUTA/SUTA taxes.

3. In the above General Journal entry, assume that $42,795 of the gross pay was accrued for the following period. The accrual amounts are:

Wages and Salaries Expense	$42,795.00	
Federal Income Tax Payable		$15,280.00
Social Security Tax Payable		$ 2,653.29
Medicare Tax Payable		$ 620.53
State Income Tax Payable		$ 1,626.21
Wages and Salaries Payable		$ 22,614.97

What would be the reversing entry?

LO 6-5   Generate Payroll-Related General Ledger Entries

As mentioned before, the process of updating the General Ledger accounts with the transactions that the accountant records in the General Journal is called *posting*. Each account used in the General Journal has a corresponding General Ledger account used to track individual balances of a firm.

For the January 28 payroll and January 31 remittances that we discussed in the previous section, the postings to the General Ledger would appear as depicted in Figure 6-3. Note that the entries shown reflect only the payroll entries for the end of January and for the end of the first quarter in March.

FIGURE 6-3
General Ledger

					Balance		
							Account: 101 – Cash
Date		**Description**	**Post Ref**	**Debit**	**Credit**	**Debit**	**Credit**
		Beginning Balance				122,367.43	
Jan	31		J1		13,144.91	109,222.52	
Jan	31		J4		750.00	108,472.52	
Jan	31		J4		560.00	107,912.52	
Jan	31		J4		180.00	107,732.52	

					Balance		
							Account: 221 – FIT Payable
Date		**Description**	**Post Ref**	**Debit**	**Credit**	**Debit**	**Credit**
Jan	28		J1		1,500.00		1,500.00
Mar	31	Accrue Payroll	J5		1,350.00		2,850.00
Apr	1	Reverse Payroll	J7	1,350.00			1,500.00

					Balance		
							Account: 222 – Social Security Tax Payable
Date		**Description**	**Post Ref**	**Debit**	**Credit**	**Debit**	**Credit**
Jan	28		J1		1,084.38		1,084.38
Jan	28		J1		1,084.38		2,168.76
Mar	31	Accrue Payroll	J5		974.70		3,143.46
Mar	31	Accrue Payroll – Employer	J6		974.70		4,118.16
Apr	1	Reverse Payroll	J7	974.70			3,143.46
Apr	1	Reverse Payroll – Employer	J7	974.70			2,168.76

					Balance		
							Account: 223 – Medicare Tax Payable
Date		**Description**	**Post Ref**	**Debit**	**Credit**	**Debit**	**Credit**
Jan	28		J1		253.61		253.61
Jan	28		J1		253.61		507.22
Mar	31	Accrue Payroll	J5		235.55		742.77
Mar	31	Accrue Payroll – Employer	J6		235.55		978.32
Apr	1	Reverse Payroll	J7	235.55			742.77
Apr	1	Reverse Payroll – Employer	J8	235.55			507.22

					Balance		
							Account: 224 – State Income Tax Payable
Date		**Description**	**Post Ref**	**Debit**	**Credit**	**Debit**	**Credit**
Jan	28		J1		577.60		577.60
Mar	31	Accrue Payroll	J5		519.84		1,097.44
Apr	1	Reverse Payroll	J7	519.84			577.60

(continued)

Account: 225 – 401(k) Contributions Payable

Date		Description	Post Ref	Debit	Credit	Balance Debit	Balance Credit
Jan	28		J1		750.00		750.00
Jan	31		J4	750.00			–

Account: 226 – Health Insurance Payable

Date		Description	Post Ref	Debit	Credit	Balance Debit	Balance Credit
Jan	28		J1		560.00		560.00
Jan	31		J4	560.00			–

Account: 227 – United Way Contributions Payable

Date		Description	Post Ref	Debit	Credit	Balance Debit	Balance Credit
Jan	28		J1		180.00		180.00
Jan	31		J4	180.00			–

Account: 228 – FUTA Tax Payable

Date		Description	Post Ref	Debit	Credit	Balance Debit	Balance Credit
Jan	28		J1		144.40		144.40
Mar	31	Accrue Payroll – Employer	J6		129.96		274.36
Apr	1	Reverse Payroll – Employer	J8	129.96			144.40

Account: 229 – SUTA Tax Payable

Date		Description	Post Ref	Debit	Credit	Balance Debit	Balance Credit
Jan	28		J1		974.40		974.40
Mar	31	Accrue Payroll – Employer	J6		876.96		1,851.36
Apr	1	Reverse Payroll – Employer	J8	876.96			974.40

Account: 231 – Salaries and Wages Payable

Date		Description	Post Ref	Debit	Credit	Balance Debit	Balance Credit
Jan	28		J1		13,144.41		13,144.41
Jan	31		J1	13,144.41			–
Mar	31	Accrue Payroll	J5		13,164.91		13,164.91
Apr	1	Reverse Payroll	J7	13,164.91			–

Account: 512 – Payroll Taxes Expense

Date		Description	Post Ref	Debit	Credit	Balance Debit	Balance Credit
Jan	28		J1	2,457.09		2,457.09	
Mar	31	Accrue Payroll	J6	2,217.17		4,674.26	
Apr	1	Reverse Payroll	J7		2,217.17	2,217.17	

(concluded)

					Account: 511 – Salaries and Wages Expense		
Date		**Description**	**Post Ref**	**Debit**	**Credit**	**Balance**	
						Debit	**Credit**
Jan	28		J1	18,050.00		18,050.00	
Mar	31	Accrue Payroll	J6	16,245.00		34,295.00	
Apr	1	Reverse Payroll	J7		16,245.00	18,050.00	

General Ledger Posting Practices

Note that the columns in the General Ledger are similar to those in the General Journal. Some specific practices in the General Ledger are worth noting:

- Each line has a date (in the General Journal, only the first line of each transaction is dated).
- The description is usually left blank, except for adjusting, closing, and reversing entries.

The post reference number is a combination of letters and numbers. The letters denote which journal the entry correlates. In this case, "J" means that the original entry may be found in the General Journal. The number in the post reference column reflects the page of the journal on which the entry is recorded.

The first pair of debit and credit columns is used to record the General Journal entry. If the account had a debit in the General Journal transaction, then the amount would appear in the debit column in the first pair of columns in the General Ledger. The same practice is used for credits.

The second pair of debit and credit columns is used to maintain a running balance of the total in the account. These account balances are the foundation for the financial reports generated by the accountant and reviewed by managers, officers, customers, vendors, and governmental agencies.

General Ledger Entries

1. The Medicare Tax Payable account had a credit balance on June 23 of $2,540. As of the June 30 payroll, credits totaling $220 were posted to the Medicare Tax Payable account. What is the balance in the account as of June 30?

2. The post reference for the June 30 journal entry is J34. What does this post reference mean?

LO 6-6   Describe Payroll Effects on the Accounting System

Entries in the payroll system are posted into the General Ledger. When a company has an automated payroll system, the journal entries discussed previously are automatically updated to the General Ledger. A payroll accountant needs to understand how the accounts should look after a payroll is completed to ensure the automated system has performed correctly. Glitches within computer programs may cause the payroll entry to be one-sided, in which only the debit or credit entry will flow through to the General Ledger. When this occurs, the payroll accountant must discover what has not posted to ensure the entire transaction posts correctly.

Payroll-Related Business Expenses

Payroll represents an expense to the business. As such, it reduces the company's profitability proportional to the wages earned and taxes paid. When the payroll accountant accrues the

© PhotoDisc/Getty Images, RF

expenses related to the payroll, the company's expenses will also increase. Companies that operate using a cash basis (i.e., recording activities only when cash is received or spent) will witness the payroll expenses reducing the income when wages and salaries are paid to the employees and when taxes are remitted to governmental agencies.

Besides administering specific payroll tasks, a responsibility of the payroll accountant is to allocate the employee expenses to specific accounts, departments, or business activities. Regardless of the employee's job description, some amount of time can be allocable to jobs or customers. For example, a fabric manufacturing company will have sewing, accounting, and managerial staff. The bulk of the sewing staff's time will be allocable to specific jobs; however, some time will be considered overhead—cleaning or meetings, for example. The bulk of the accounting department's time will be considered overhead. However, if the accountant is working on the analysis of a specific client's project, that time may be billed to the client. Managerial positions may also have specific times allocated to jobs depending upon the needs of the client and the position.

The Business Effects of Payroll

STOP & CHECK

1. Does the payment of employee wages increase or decrease the profitability of a business?
2. Why is it important to allocate payroll-related expenses properly?

LO 6-7   Explain Payroll Entries in Accounting Reports

When examining the *income statement*, *balance sheet*, and *trial balance* (Figures 6-4, 6-5, and 6-6), the payroll accountant must know what effect his or her work has on each statement. Within the expense section of the income statement, you will see several accounts that relate to payroll. Starting with the wages categories, there are salary and hourly divisions. Each of the taxes we have discussed is listed. Note that the expenses related to the taxes are paid by the employer and forwarded to the taxing authority; thus, there is no Federal income tax expense. Expenses related to the employer portion of retirement fund matching, health benefits, or other benefits are also located within the income statement.

Moving on to the balance sheet, any unpaid liabilities will be reported in the current liability section. If there are employees who have taken payroll advances, which are amounts to be repaid by the employee, these will show in the current assets section. In accrual accounting, there may also be end-of-period entries to accrue for payroll earned

FIGURE 6-4
Income Statement Presentation (Partial)

NC Bikes Income Statement For the Quarter Ended March 31, 2OXX		
Expenses:		
Salaries and Wages Expense	$ 34,295.00	
Payroll Taxes Expense	4,674.26	
Utilities Expense	1,725.00	
Telephone Expense	884.00	
Rent Expense	5,175.00	
Total Expenses		46,753.26
Net Income for Quarter		$ 31,55014

FIGURE 6-5
Balance Sheet Presentation

NC Bikes Balance Sheet March 31, 2OXX		
Assets:		
Cash		$ 107,732.52
Accounts Receivable		23,948.30
Equipment		15,289.00
Inventory		225,960.00
Total Assets		$ 372,929.82
Liabilities		
Accounts Payable		4,085.27
FIT Payable		2,850.00
Social Security Tax Payable		4,118.16
Medicare Tax Payable		978.32
State Income Tax Payable		1,097.44
Health Insurance Payable		560.00
FUTA Tax Payable		274.36
SUTA Tax Payable		1,851.36
Salaries and Wages Payable		13,164.91
Total Liabilities		28,979.82
Owners' Equity		
J. Nelson, Capital		178,530.00
A. Nelson, Capital		120,420.00
Total Owners' Equity		298,950.00
Total Liabilities and Owners' Equity		$ 327,929.82

FIGURE 6-6
Trial Balance Presentation

Account	Debit	Credit
Cash	$ 107,732.52	
Accounts Receivable	23,948.30	
Equipment	15,289.00	
Inventory	225,960.00	
Accounts Payable		$ 4,085.27
FIT Payable		2,850.00
Social Security Tax Payable		4,118.16
Medicare Tax Payable		978.32
State Income Tax Payable		1,097.44
Health Insurance Payable		560.00
FUTA Tax Payable		274.36
SUTA Tax Payable		1,851.36
Salaries and Wages Payable		13,164.91
J. Nelson, Capital		162,755.00
A. Nelson, Capital		104,645.74
Sales		123,302.52
Salaries and Wages Expense	34,295.00	
Payroll Taxes Expense	4,674.26	
Utilities Expense	1,725.00	
Telephone Expense	884.00	
Rent Expense	5,175.00	
	$ 419,683.08	$ 419,683.08

by the employees. Additional liability accounts for accrued salaries, accrued hourly wages, accrued holiday pay, and accrued paid time off could also appear, depending on the timing of the end of the period and the types of employees and benefits with which the company operates.

The trial balance contains all accounts the company uses, spanning all of the financial statements. The accounts listed on the trial balance appear in the order of the chart of accounts. Typically, assets are listed first: short term, then long term. Following are liabilities: short term, then long term. Equity accounts are listed next, followed by revenues and expenses. The important thing to remember when examining the trial balance is that it should balance: Debits must equal credits. Should one side not balance with the other, the accountant must determine why and correct the error.

Labor Reports

The payroll accountant may provide specific *labor reports* to management or department heads, and these reports may have a variety of names and content depending on the needs of the business.

- The labor usage report designates where the labor is used within the company. When a company has several employees that work in different departments, the labor usage report can be useful in determining overhead *allocations* by department and the need for additional or lower staff within a specific department.

- The billable vs. nonbillable report tracks the time employees have spent specifically on projects for which customers are paying. This report allows managers to determine if the time allocated to the job in job costing is accurate, the efficiency of the operation, or if the employee is taking too long on a specific job.

- Overtime reports allow managers to determine how much overtime has been paid to employees during a specified time period. This report allows managers to monitor labor distribution and scheduling to ensure adherence with budget guidelines.

- Employers can also make use of trend reports for payroll staffing needs. Trend reports of income over the period of the year can reveal seasonal increases or decreases in business. An informed business manager will know if the company needs to have seasonal or temporary workers for short-term increases. If the trend reflects a steady increase in business, the manager may determine that hiring a new employee would be beneficial.

Analyzing the staffing needs of the company compared to income projections may also lead managers to know if they need to lay off personnel or reduce hours of existing employees.

Labor Reports

1. Which of the following reports are affected by the payroll of an organization?
   a. Trial balance
   b. Statement of owners' equity
   c. Interest statement
   d. Income summary
   e. Balance sheet
2. What is a specific type of report that the payroll accountant provides to managerial staff?
3. What are trend reports?

ECONOMIC EFFECTS OF PAYROLL

Although payroll accounting principles remain relatively stable, the role that payroll plays in the broader context of a business is subject to change. Some developments in payroll accounting in the business context that have changed during the early 2010s include the following:

- Issues with employment vulnerability stemming from the economic downturn during which employers restructured their operations to remain viable.
- Grassroots movements ("Occupy") that brought the issue of wage disparity into the public eye.
- Changes in workforce composition, worker skills, and the jobs that businesses need performed to meet 21st century needs.
- An increase in the proportion and number of service businesses and a shift away from manufacturing jobs.

Some trends to watch in payroll's economic effects include the following:

- Company revenues have increased, prompting a need for additional skilled workers.
- Employer-sponsored wellness programs have become a part of strategic human resource management because of the correlation with employee sick time and retention.
- Technology use such as cloud-based payroll services foster employee mobility and create challenges to work–life balance.

Summary of Payroll Register, Employees' Earnings Records, and Accounting System Entries

The payroll register and employees' earnings records are two tools that payroll accountants need to maintain their work accurately. Both records track employee compensation and contain information about company liabilities to governmental agencies and other organizations. These records also provide information for company decision makers by yielding data about labor distribution and cost allocation. Payroll records provide information about benefits given to employees and how those benefits affect a business's profitability. Information contained in these sources and tools used by payroll accountants provides integral insights for managerial functions.

The final piece of the payroll cycle is the creation of accounting system entries. Similar to other business transactions, recording, paying the payroll, remitting money to governmental agencies and other firms requires General Journal and General Ledger entries. Business owners and departmental managers use this accounting information to measure the effectiveness of business plans and to plan both short- and long-term strategies. As an integral part of business operations, payroll-related expenses and liabilities affect the financial reports and company viability as a whole.

With this chapter's explanation of accounting system entries, we have now completed our journey through the payroll process. We have investigated the history of payroll, its many aspects and functions, and the importance of employee compensation within a business context.

We hope that on finishing this book you will have taken away that payroll accounting is complex, involves many different decisions along the way, and deserves your close attention. Figure 6-7 is a depiction of the basic elements of the payroll process that we have discussed.

FIGURE 6-7
Payroll Process Flowchart

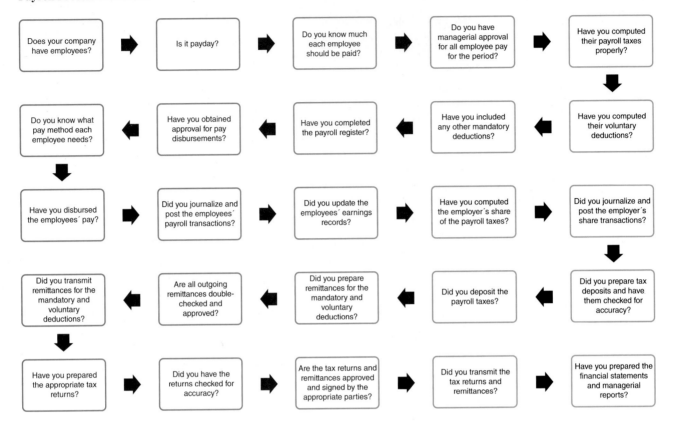

Key Points

- The payroll register is a tool used by payroll accountants to ensure the accuracy of employee compensation.
- The payroll register yields information about totals for mandatory and voluntary deductions, assisting the accountant with remittances.
- The employees' earnings records are the link between accounting and human resources and contain information from the payroll register.
- Accounting principles assist in the classification of payroll costs and organizational performance.
- Payroll transactions are recorded in the General Journal and posted to General Ledger accounts.
- The balances in the General Ledger accounts form the foundation of financial reports.
- Payroll costs represent an expense of the business.
- Employees are assigned to departments to foster accurate measurements of business segment profitability.
- Trend reports offer business leaders insight about changes in labor costs over a period.

Vocabulary

Accrual	General Journal	Remit
Adjusting entries	General Ledger	Reversal
Allocation	Income statement	Rule
Assets	Labor reports	Total
Balance sheet	Liabilities	Trial balance
Credit	Owner's equity	
Debit	Posting	
Expense	Prove	

REVIEW QUESTIONS

1. What types of accounts does a debit increase?

2. What types of accounts does a credit increase?

3. Where are daily accounting entries recorded?

4. Once recorded, to what are the entries posted?

5. What is the purpose of the payroll register?

6. What information is contained in employees' earnings records?

7. How are the payroll register and the employees' earnings records related?

8. For the employee share of the payroll, what type of account is debited for the gross pay?

9. What are three of the accounts that may be credited for the employee payroll?

10. What two accounts are affected upon issuance of paychecks?

11. What accounts are debited and credited for the employer share of the payroll expenses?

12. How do payroll expenses affect the income statement and balance sheet?

13. How can companies use payroll information that is reported in the financial statements to determine labor distribution?

14. How can a company's payroll information contained in financial reports assist in corporate planning?

15. How do the payroll register and employees' earnings records help employers meet their responsibilities to different groups, such as the employees and governmental agencies?

Exercises Set A

6-1A.
LO 6-1

As the accountant for Tooka's Trees, you need to prepare the payroll register for the payroll dated October 15, 2015. Employees are paid biweekly and are subject to a flat 3% state income tax. Use the wage bracket method in the federal tax table in Appendix C. No employee has exceeded the Social Security wage base. The employees are:

a. T. Taylor

Single, 4 withholdings

Gross pay: $1,500 per period

401(k) deduction: $125 per pay period

b. B. Walburn

Married, 6 withholdings

Gross pay: $2,225 per period

401(k) deduction: $250 per period

c. H. Carpenter

Single, 0 withholdings

Gross pay: $1,500 per period

Section 125 deduction: $75 per period

401(k) deduction: $50 per period

d. J. Knight

Married, 3 withholdings

Gross pay: $1,875 per period

United Way deduction: $50 per period

Garnishment: $50 per period

e. C. Lunn

Single, 1 withholding

Gross pay: $2,200 per period

Section 125 withholding: $50 per period

401(k) deduction: 6% of gross pay

f. E. Smooter

Married, 8 withholdings

Gross pay: $2,425 per period

Complete the payroll register for Tooka's Trees for the payroll dated October 15.

401(k) deduction: $75 per period

Run Date [_____]   Company Name _____

P/R Date [_____]

Name	Marital Status	No. of Withholdings	Hourly Rate	No. of Regular Hours	No. of Overtime Hours	Gross Earning	Federal Inc. Tax	Social Security Tax	Medicare W/H	State Tax	401(k)	Garnishment	United Way	Sec. 125	Net Pay

6-2A.
LO 6-1

Charles Merrill owns a housekeeping service, Charles' Cleaners, in Florida. For the weekly payroll dated July 12, 2015, complete the payroll register. Use the wage bracket method in the federal tax table in Appendix C. No employee has exceeded the Social Security tax wage base. Total, prove, and rule the entries.

Name	Marital Status	No. of With-holdings	Hourly Rate	No. of Regular Hours	No. of Overtime Hours	Gross Earning	Taxable Income	Federal Income Tax	Social Security Tax	Medicare Tax	401(k)	Garnishment	United Way	Sec. 125	Net Pay
M. Clark	M	3	8.50	40	3						50				
B. Toonen	S	1	9.20	35							75		10		
P. Dahl	S	0	10.10	37.5								100			
S. Steverman	S	1	8.04	40									25		
L. Bromley	M	4	8.90	38							60			20	
R. Matte	S	2	10.50	40	5						75		10		
F. Maddox	S	1	9.95	40								75		15	

6-3A.
LO 6-2

Below is the employee earnings record for Sean Steverman of Charles' Cleaners. Record his earnings on the July 12 pay from Exercise 6-2A.

EMPLOYEE EARNING RECORD

NAME: Sean Steverman   Hire Date May 22, 2011

ADDRESS 2326 Vinings Drive   Date of Birth Nov. 15, 1991

CITY/STATE/ZIP
Lodi, FL 32039   Position House Cleaner   PT/(FT)

TELEPHONE 305-555-5698   No. of exemptions 1   M/(S)

SOCIAL SECURITY
NUMBER   188-56-7316   Pay Rate $8.04   (Hr)/Wk/Mo

Period Ended	Hrs. Worked	Reg Pay	OT Pay	Gross Pay	Social Sec. Tax	Medicare	Fed Inc. Tax	State Inc. Tax	Other Tax	401(k)	Other	Total Deduc	Net Pay	YTD
7/5/2014	40	321.60	0.00	321.60	19.94	4.66	22.00	0.00	0.00	0.00	0.00	25	250.00	4502.40

6-4A.
LO 6-3, 6-4

Using the payroll register from 6-2A for Charles' Cleaners, complete the General Journal entry for the employees' pay for the July 12 pay date. Paychecks will be issued in the future.

	Date	Description	Post Ref.	Debit	Credit	
1						1
2						2
3						3
4						4
5						5
6						6
7						7
8						8
9						9
10						10
11						11
12						12

6-5A. Using the payroll register from 6-2A for Charles' Cleaners, complete
LO 6-3, 6-4 the General Journal entry for the employer's share of the payroll taxes
for the July 12 pay date. Assume 5.4% SUTA and 0.6% FUTA tax rates
and that $1,352.40 is subject to FUTA/SUTA taxes.

	Date	Description	Post Ref.	Debit	Credit	
1						1
2						2
3						3
4						4
5						5
6						6
7						7
8						8
9						9

6-6A. Using the employee payroll entry from 6-4A, post the July 12 employee
LO 6-3, 6-4 pay for Charles' Cleaners to the selected General Ledger accounts below:

Account: Salaries and Wages Payable

	Date	Description	Post Ref.	Debit	Credit	Balance Debit	Balance Credit	
1								1
2								2
3								3
4								4
5								5
6								6

Account: Employee Federal Income Tax Payable

	Date	Description	Post Ref.	Debit	Credit	Balance Debit	Balance Credit	
1								1
2								2
3								3
4								4
5								5
6								6

Account: Social Security Tax Payable

	Date	Description	Post Ref.	Debit	Credit	Balance Debit	Balance Credit	
1								1
2								2
3								3
4								4
5								5
6								6

Account: Medicare Tax Payable

	Date	Description	Post Ref.	Debit	Credit	Balance Debit	Balance Credit	
1								1
2								2
3								3
4								4
5								5
6								6

Account: Salaries and Wages Expense

	Date	Description	Post Ref.	Debit	Credit	Balance Debit	Balance Credit	
1								1
2								2
3								3
4								4
5								5
6								6
7								7

6-7A.

LO 6-3, 6-4

Using the employee payroll entry from 6-4A, complete the General Journal entry for the issuance of the pay for the July 12 pay date. The date of the checks is July 15.

	Date	Description	Post Ref.	Debit	Credit	
1						1
2						2
3						3
4						4
5						5

6-8A.

LO 6-3, 6-4, 6-5

Using the employer payroll entry from 6-5A, post the employer's share of payroll taxes for the July 12 pay at Charles' Cleaners to the appropriate General Ledger accounts. Assume that $1,352.40 is subject to FUTA/SUTA taxes.

Account: Social Security Tax Payable

	Date	Description	Post Ref.	Debit	Credit	Balance Debit	Balance Credit	
1								1
2								2
3								3
4								4
5								5
6								6
7								7

Account: Medicare Tax Payable

	Date	Description	Post Ref.	Debit	Credit	Balance Debit	Balance Credit	
1								1
2								2
3								3
4								4
5								5
6								6
7								7

Account: Federal Unemployment Tax Payable

	Date	Description	Post Ref.	Debit	Credit	Balance Debit	Balance Credit	
1								1
2								2
3								3
4								4
5								5
6								6
7								7

Account: State Unemployment Tax Payable

	Date	Description	Post Ref.	Debit	Credit	Balance Debit	Balance Credit	
1								1
2								2
3								3
4								4
5								5
6								6
7								7

Account: Payroll Taxes Expense

	Date	Description	Post Ref.	Debit	Credit	Balance Debit	Balance Credit	
1								1
2								2
3								3
4								4
5								5
6								6
7								7

6-9A.   KMH Industries is a monthly schedule depositor of payroll taxes. For
LO 6-3, 6-4   the month of August, the payroll taxes (employee and employer share)
were as follows:

    Social Security tax: $3,252.28

    Medicare tax: $760.61

    Employee Federal income tax: $2,520

Create the General Journal entry for the remittance of the taxes. Use
check 2052 in the description.

	Date	Description	Post Ref.	Debit	Credit	
1						1
2						2
3						3
4						4
5						5
6						6
7						7
8						8

6-10A.   Sophie Sue Breeders has the following voluntary withholdings to remit:
LO 6-3, 6-4   AFLAC payable: $560.00

    401(k) payable: $1,280.00

    Garnishments payable: $375.00

    United Way contributions payable: $200.00

Create the General Journal entry for the remittance of these withheld
amounts.

	Date	Description	Post Ref.	Debit	Credit	
1						1
2						2
3						3
4						4
5						5
6						6
7						7

6-11A.   Sheronda Rowe is the payroll accountant for Great Lake Lamps. The
LO 6-6, 6-7   company's management has requested an analysis of the payroll
effects on the expenses of the company. Explain which accounting report(s) you would use to construct your analysis. How would
you explain the purpose of labor expenses as they affect company
productivity?

Exercises Set B

6-1B.   As the accountant for TJ's Tire Company in Illinois, you need to pre-
LO 6-1   pare the payroll register for the payroll dated November 21, 2015.
Employees are paid semimonthly and are subject to a flat 5% state
income tax.

Use the wage bracket method in the federal tax table in Appendix C. No employee has met the Social Security wage base. The employees are:

a. P. Hamel
Married, 1 withholding
Gross pay: $2,357 per period
401(k) deduction: $175 per pay period

b. J. Roberts
Single, 1 withholding
Gross pay: $1,725 per period
401(k) deduction: $100 per period

c. M. Meyer
Married, 4 withholdings
Gross pay: $2,625 per period
Garnishment: $125 per period
401(k) deduction: $175 per period

d. C. Moriarty
Married, 7 withholdings
Gross pay: $2,430 per period
Section 125 deduction: $80 per period
401(k) deduction: $150 per period

e. T. Brock
Single, 3 withholdings
Gross pay: $1,590 per period
United Way deduction: $25 per period
401(k) deduction: 3% of gross pay

f. R. Leigh
Married, 2 withholdings
Gross pay: $2,210 per period
Garnishment: $45 per period
United Way: $10 per period
401(k) deduction: 2% of gross pay

Complete the payroll register for TJ's Tire Company for the payroll dated November 21. Use the wage bracket table in Appendix C.

Run Date [＿＿＿]   Company Name ＿＿＿＿＿＿＿＿＿＿
P/R Date [＿＿＿]

Name	Marital Status	No. of With-holdings	Hourly Rate	Reg. Earnings	Overtime Earnings	Gross Earning	Taxable Income for Federal and State Income Tax	Taxable Income for Social Security and Medicare	Federal Inc. Tax	Medicare Tax	State Income Tax	State Tax	401(k)	Garnishment	United Way	Net Pay	Sec. 125

6-2B. Tony Stanford owns Cosmic Comics in Greensboro, North Carolina. For the
LO 6-1 weekly payroll dated September 19, 2015, complete the payroll register.
Use the wage bracket method in the federal tax table in Appendix C.
Assume 5.8% state income tax. No employee has exceeded the Social
Security wage base. Total, prove, and rule the entries.

Run Date [ ]   Company Name _____

P/R Date [ ]

Name	Marital Status	No. of With-holdings	Hourly Rate	No. of Regular Hours	No. of Overtime Hours	Gross Earnings	401(k)	Garnish-ment	Federal and State Taxable Income	Social Security and Medicare Taxable Income	Federal Income Tax	Social Security Tax	Medicare Tax	State Tax	United Way	Sec. 125	Net Pay
N. Camacho	M	2	12.20	40	2		50								10.00		
A. Rea	S	4	9.45	39												20.00	
P. Dahl	M	5	11.30	40	5		35								10.00		
R. Hayes	S	1	8.95	37			20										
Y. Fortanier	S	0	10.05	38.5				60									
S. Cronan	M	2	13.45	40	6			50									
A. Murner	S	2	10.65	37			45									15.00	
E. Zinsli	M	0	9.50	40	1		25										
Totals																	

6-3B. Below is the employee earnings record for Ally Murner of Cosmic Comics.
LO 6-2 Record her earnings on the September 12 pay from Exercise 6-2B.

EMPLOYEE EARNING RECORD

NAME: Ally Murner   Hire Date April 2, 2009

ADDRESS 522 Shady Lane   Date of Birth July 1, 1989

CITY/STATE/ZIP
Winslow, NC 22203   Position House Cleaner   PT/FT

TELEPHONE 704-553-5967   No. of exemptions 2   M/S

SOCIAL SECURITY

NUMBER 660-30-2938   Pay Rate $10.65   Hr/Wk/Mo

Period Ended	Hrs. Worked	Reg Pay	OT Pay	Gross Pay	Social Sec. Tax	Medicare	Fed Inc. Tax	State Inc. Tax	Other Tax	401(k)	Other	Total Deduc	Net Pay	YTD
9/5/2014	40	426.00	0.00	426.00	26.41	6.18	20.00	24.70	0	45.00	0.00	122.90	303.71	8256.80

6-4B. Using the payroll register from 6-2B for Cosmic Comics, complete the
LO 6-1, 6-3, General Journal entry for the employees' pay for the September 12
6-4   pay date. Employees' paychecks will be issued on September 15.

	Date	Description	Post Ref.	Debit	Credit
1					
2					
3					
4					
5					
6					
7					
8					
9					

6-5B.
LO 6-1, 6-3, 6-4

Using the payroll register from 6-2B for Cosmic Comics, complete the General Journal entry for the employer's share of the payroll taxes for the September 12 pay date. Assume a 5.4% SUTA rate and 0.6% FUTA rate and that $954.05 of the gross pay is subject to SUTA/FUTA taxes.

	Date	Description	Post Ref.	Debit	Credit
1					
2					
3					
4					
5					
6					
7					
8					
9					

6-6B.
LO 6-4, 6-5

Using the employee payroll entry from 6-4B, post the September 12 employee pay for Cosmic Comics to the selected General Ledger accounts that follow.

Account: Salaries and Wages Payable

	Date	Description	Post Ref.	Debit	Credit	Balance Debit	Balance Credit
1							
2							
3							
4							
5							
6							

Account: Employee Federal Income Tax Payable

	Date	Description	Post Ref.	Debit	Credit	Balance Debit	Balance Credit
1							
2							
3							
4							
5							
6							

Account: Social Security Tax Payable

	Date	Description	Post Ref.	Debit	Credit	Balance Debit	Balance Credit
1							
2							
3							
4							
5							
6							

Account: Medicare Tax Payable

	Date	Description	Post Ref.	Debit	Credit	Balance Debit	Balance Credit
1							
2							
3							
4							
5							
6							

Account: Employee State Income Tax Payable

	Date	Description	Post Ref.	Debit	Credit	Balance Debit	Balance Credit
1							
2							
3							
4							
5							
6							

Account: Salaries and Wages Expense

	Date	Description	Post Ref.	Debit	Credit	Balance Debit	Balance Credit
1							
2							
3							
4							
5							
6							
7							

6-7B.   Using the employee payroll entry from 6-4B, complete the General
LO 6-3, 6-4   Journal entry for the issuance of Cosmic Comics pay on September 15.

	Date	Description	Post Ref.	Debit	Credit	
1						1
2						2
3						3
4						4
5						5

6-8B.   Using the employer payroll entry from 6-5B, post the employer's share
LO 6-4, 6-5   of payroll taxes for the September 12 pay period at Cosmic Comics to
the appropriate General Ledger accounts:

Account: Payroll Taxes Expense

	Date	Description	Post Ref.	Debit	Credit	Balance Debit	Balance Credit	
1								1
2								2
3								3
4								4
5								5
6								6
7								7

Account: Social Security Tax Payable

	Date	Description	Post Ref.	Debit	Credit	Balance Debit	Balance Credit	
1								1
2								2
3								3
4								4
5								5
6								6
7								7

Account: Medicare Tax Payable

	Date	Description	Post Ref.	Debit	Credit	Balance Debit	Balance Credit	
1								1
2								2
3								3
4								4
5								5
6								6
7								7

Account: Federal Unemployment Tax Payable

	Date	Description	Post Ref.	Debit	Credit	Balance Debit	Balance Credit	
1								1
2								2
3								3
4								4
5								5
6								6
7								7

Account: State Unemployment Tax Payable

	Date	Description	Post Ref.	Debit	Credit	Balance Debit	Balance Credit	
1								1
2								2
3								3
4								4
5								5
6								6
7								7

6-9B.

LO 6-3, 6-4

Legends Leadworks is a monthly schedule depositor of payroll taxes. For the month of April, the payroll taxes (employee and employer share) were as follows:

Social Security tax: $5,386.56

Medicare tax: $1,259.76

Employee federal income tax: $4,978

Create the General Journal entry for the remittance of the taxes. Use check 1320 in the description.

	Date	Description	Post Ref.	Debit	Credit	
1						1
2						2
3						3
4						4
5						5
6						6
7						7
8						8

6-10B.

LO 6-3, 6-4

Candy Farms, Inc., has the following voluntary withholdings to remit:

AFLAC payable: $687.00

Worker's compensation insurance payable: $1,042.00

401(k) payable: $2,104.00

Garnishments payable: $450.00

U.S. savings bonds payable: $200.00

Create the General Journal entry for the remittance of these withheld amounts.

	Date	Description	Post Ref.	Debit						Credit						
1																1
2																2
3																3
4																4
5																5
6																6
7																7
8																8

6-11B.
LO 6-6, 6-7   Pujah Srinivasan is the controller for HHT Industries. She has been asked to explain the payroll accounts on the financial statements for the preceding month. What information will she find about payroll on the income statement? What information will be located on the balance sheet? How could she use the information in the accounting reports to explain the payroll effects on the company?

Critical Thinking

6-1. Your boss asks you for a five-year labor cost trend chart. The labor costs per year are as follows:

2011	$178,967
2012	$185,923
2013	$172,245
2014	$179,905
2015	$182,478

Construct a line chart to depict the data. What conclusions can you derive from the data about labor costs and trends over the last five years? Why?

6-2. Giblin's Goodies pays employees weekly on Fridays. As they approach the end of December, they notice that December 31 is a Thursday. The payroll data for December 28–31 is as follows:

Gross pay: $4,500

Federal income tax: $520

Social Security tax: $279

Medicare tax: $65.25

State income tax: $90

Give the adjusting entry in the General Journal to recognize the employee and employer share of the payroll for the week of December 28. Date the entry December 31. Then, give the journal entry to reverse the adjustment on January 1, 2016.

	Date	Description	Post Ref.	Debit				Credit				
1												1
2												2
3												3
4												4
5												5
6												6
7												7
8												8
9												9
10												10
11												11
12												12
13												13
14												14
15												15

In the Real World: Scenario for Discussion

An ongoing discussion among business managers is the return on employee investment (ROEI). Employers want to maximize business profitability, and employees are a significant part of organizational success. An example of this issue faces Uber. The company has a cadre of drivers across the United States who are demanding to be classified as employees. What are some issues Uber faces if it classifies its drivers as employees? How could these issues affect ROEI and company profitability? (Source: *Forbes*)

Internet Activities

6-1. Would you like to know about personal experiences as a payroll accountant? How about videos that detail the completion of payroll-related forms? Go to www.youtube.com and search the term "payroll accounting" to read personal perspectives about payroll practice, outsourcing, and tax form completion. What were three insights you found that were new to you?

6-2. Would you like to build your own favorites list of payroll accounting tools? Go to one or more of the following sites. What are three important items you noticed?

www.accountingtools.com

http://payroll.softwareinsider.com/

www.accountantsworld.com

www.americanpayroll.org

6-3. Join a conversation about payroll accounting with industry professionals. Go to www.linkedin.com and establish a profile (if you do not have one). Search groups for payroll accounting and follow the conversations. Which topics did you choose? Why?

6-4. Want to know more about the concepts in this chapter? Check out:

www.na.sage.com/Sage-HRMS/lp/roei

www.americanpayroll.org/payrollmetrics/challenges/

www.moneyinstructor.com/lesson/accountingconcepts.asp

www.cs.thomsonreuters.com/resources/white-papers/15962_Payroll_Opportunity_WP_.pdf

Continuing Payroll Project: Prevosti Farms and Sugarhouse

Complete the Payroll Register for the 2/13 and 2/27 pay periods. Complete the General Journal entries as follows:

February 13	Journalize employee pay.
February 13	Journalize employer payroll tax for the February 13 pay period. Use 5.4% SUTA and 0.6% FUTA. No employees will exceed the FUTA or SUTA wage base.
February 16	Issue employee pay.
February 27	Journalize employee pay.
February 27	Journalize the employer payroll tax for the February 27 pay period. Use 5.4% SUTA and 0.6% FUTA. No employees will exceed FUTA or SUTA wage base.
March 2	Issue employee pay.

Post all journal entries to the appropriate General Ledger accounts.

Run Date [   ]   Company Name _____

P/R Date [   ]

Name	Marital Status	No. of Withholdings	Hourly Rate	No. of Regular Hours	No. of Overtime Hours	Gross Earning	Federal W/H	Social Security Tax	Medicare W/H	State Tax	401(k)	Insurance	Net Pay

Run Date [   ]   Company Name _____

P/R Date [   ]

Name	Marital Status	No. of Withholdings	Hourly Rate	No. of Regular Hours	No. of Overtime Hours	Gross Earning	Federal W/H	Social Security Tax	Medicare W/H	State Tax	401(k)	Insurance	Net Pay

	Date	Description	Post Ref.	Debit	Credit	
1						1
2						2
3						3
4						4
5						5
6						6
7						7
8						8
9						9
10						10
11						11
12						12
13						13
14						14
15						15
16						16
17						17
18						18
19						19
20						20
21						21
22						22
23						23
24						24
25						25
26						26
27						27
28						28
29						29
30						30
31						31
32						32
33						33
34						34
35						35

Account: Cash   **101**

	Date	Description	Post Ref.	Debit	Credit	Balance Debit	Balance Credit	
1							15 0 0 0 00	1
2								2
3								3
4								4
5								5
6								6

Account: Employee Federal Income Tax Payable   **203**

	Date	Description	Debit	Credit	Balance Debit	Balance Credit	
1							1
2							2
3							3
4							4
5							5
6							6

Account: Social Security Tax Payable   **204**

	Date	Description	Debit	Credit	Balance Debit	Balance Credit	
1							1
2							2
3							3
4							4
5							5
6							6

Account: Medicare Tax Payable   **205**

	Date	Description	Debit	Credit	Balance Debit	Balance Credit	
1							1
2							2
3							3
4							4
5							5
6							6

Account: Employee State Income Tax Payable   **206**

	Date	Description	Debit	Credit	Balance Debit	Balance Credit	
1							1
2							2
3							3
4							4
5							5
6							6

Account: 401(k) Contributions Payable   **208**

	Date	Description	Debit	Credit	Balance Debit	Balance Credit	
1							1
2							2
3							3
4							4
5							5
6							6

Account: Health Insurance Payable   **209**

	Date	Description	Debit	Credit	Balance Debit	Balance Credit	
1							1
2							2
3							3
4							4
5							5
6							6

Account: Salaries and Wages Payable   **210**

	Date	Description	Debit	Credit	Balance Debit	Balance Credit	
1							1
2							2
3							3
4							4
5							5
6							6

Account: FUTA Tax Payable   **211**

	Date	Description	Debit	Credit	Balance Debit	Balance Credit	
1							1
2							2
3							3
4							4
5							5
6							6

Account: SUTA Tax Payable   **212**

	Date	Description	Debit	Credit	Balance Debit	Balance Credit	
1							1
2							2
3							3
4							4
5							5
6							6

Account: Payroll Taxes Expense   **514**

	Date	Description	Debit	Credit	Balance Debit	Balance Credit	
1							1
2							2
3							3
4							4
5							5
6							6

Account: Salaries and Wages Expense   **515**

	Date	Description	Debit	Credit	Balance Debit	Balance Credit	
1							1
2							2
3							3
4							4
5							5
6							6

Answers to Stop & Check Exercises

The Payroll Register

1. The purpose of the payroll register is to ensure the accuracy of employee compensation.

2. Some fields included are employee name, marital status, number of exemptions, pay rate, regular hours, overtime hours, gross pay, deductions, total deductions, and net pay.

3. Total means to compute the total of each row and each column. Prove means to demonstrate that the sum of all rows equals the sum of all columns. Rule means to double-underline each column total.

Employees' Earnings Records

1. The payroll register contains the period payroll information for all employees. The employee earnings record lists all payroll data for a single employee.

2. All fields exist on both the employees' earnings records and the payroll register.

3. Quarterly and annual tax reports use the totals from the employees' earnings records.

Financial Accounting Concepts

1. Assets = Liabilities + Owners' Equity
2. Credit
3. Debit

Payroll and the General Journal

1. Dr. Wages and Salaries Expense $124,785.00

2.

Account	Debit	Credit
Payroll Taxes Expense	$9,546.05	
Social Security Tax Payable		$7,736.67
Medicare Tax Payable		$1,809.38

	Debit	Credit
Federal Income Tax Payable	$15,280.00	
Social Security Tax Payable	$2,653.29	
Medicare Tax Payable	$620.53	
State Income Tax Payable	$1,626.21	
Wages and Salaries Payable	$22,614.97	
Wages and Salaries Expense		$42,795.00

General Ledger Entries

1. $2,760 Cr.

2. The transaction may be found in the General Journal on page 34.

The Business Effects of Payroll

1. The payment of employee wages decreases profitability because it increases the expenses of a business.

2. Allocation of payroll expenses to specific jobs, clients, and so on allows the company to understand the costs associated with the activity.

Labor Reports

1. Trial balance, balance sheet, and statement of owners' equity

2. Labor reports

3. Trend reports are used by managers to identify business patterns, needs, and opportunities.

Appendix

Comprehensive Payroll Project: Wayland Custom Woodworking

Wayland Custom Woodworking is a firm that manufactures custom cabinets and woodwork for business and residential customers. Students will have the opportunity to establish payroll records and to complete at least a month of payroll information for Wayland.

Wayland Custom Woodworking is located at 1716 Nichol Street, Logan, UT 84321, phone number 435-555-9877. The owner is Mark Wayland. Wayland's EIN is 91-7444533, and the Utah Employer Account Number is 999-9290-1. Wayland has determined it will pay its employees on a semimonthly basis.

Students will complete the payroll for the final quarter of 2015 and will file fourth quarter and annual tax reports on the appropriate dates. When writing out the dollar amount for each check, spell out all words and present cents as fractions of 100. For example, $1,250.50 would be One Thousand Two Hundred Fifty and 50/100.

At the instructor's discretion, students may complete a short version, which contains the payroll transactions beginning December 1. Directions for completion of the short version follow the November 30 transactions.

The SUTA (UI) rate for Wayland Custom Woodworking is 2.6% on the first $31,300. The state income tax rate is 5.0%.

Rounding can create a challenge. For these exercises, the rate for the individuals is not rounded. So take their salary and divide by 2,080 (52 weeks times 40 hours per week) for full time, nonexempt employees. For example, Varden's salary is $42,000, and he is a nonexempt employee, so the calculation will be $42,000/2,080, which would give you $20.19231 per hour. After this hourly rate is determined, then it can be applied to the number of hours worked.

Exempt employees salaries are divided by 24 (the number of payroll periods with a semimonthly pay frequency). For example, Chinson's salary is $24,000, and he is a full-time exempt employee, so the calculation will be $24,000/24, which would give you $1,000 per pay period. After the gross pay has been calculated, round the result to only two decimal points prior to calculating taxes or other withholdings.

Federal Withholding Allowance	$166.70 per allowance claimed
FUTA Rate (less Section 125 health insurance)	0.6% on the first $7,000 of wages
Semimonthly Federal Percentage Method Tax (less 401(k), less Section 125 health insurance)	Appendix C, Page 270, Table 3
Utah SUTA (UI) Rate (Employer) (less Section 125 health insurance)	2.6% on the first $31,300 of wages
Utah State Income Tax Withholding (Employee) (less 401(k), less Section 125 health insurance)	5.0% (see Table 1)

UTAH SCHEDULE 3				SEMIMONTHLY Payroll Period (24 pay periods per year)		

SINGLE

1. Utah taxable wages		
2. Multiply line 1 by .05 (5%)		
3. Number of withholding allowances		
4. Multiply line 3 by $ 5		
5. Base allowance	10	
6. Add lines 4 and 5		
7. Line 1 less $500 (not less than 0)		
8. Multiply line 7 by .013 (1.3%)		
9. Line 6 less line 8 (not less than 0)		
10. Withholding tax - line 2 less line 9 (not less than 0)		

MARRIED

1. Utah taxable wages		
2. Multiply line 1 by .05 (5%)		
3. Number of withholding allowances		
4. Multiply line 3 by $ 5		
5. Base allowance	16	
6. Add lines 4 and 5		
7. Line 1 less $750 (not less than 0)		
8. Multiply line 7 by .013 (1.3%)		
9. Line 6 less line 8 (not less than 0)		
10. Withholding tax - line 2 less line 9 (not less than 0)		

TABLE 1

October 1

Wayland Custom Woodworking (WCW) pays its employees according to their job classification. The following employees comprise Wayland's staff:

Employee Number	Name and Address	Payroll Information
00-Chins	Anthony Chinson 530 Sylvann Ave Logan, UT 84321 435-555-1212 Job Title: Account Executive	Married, 1 withholding allowance Exempt $24,000/year + commission Start Date: 10/1/201X SSN: 511-22-3333
00-Wayla	Mark Wayland 1570 Lovett Street Logan, UT 84321 435-555-1110 Job Title: President/Owner	Married, 5 withholding allowances Exempt $75,000/year Start Date: 10/1/201X SSN: 505-33-1775
01-Peppi	Sylvia Peppinico 291 Antioch Road Logan, UT 84321 435-555-2244 Job Title: Craftsman	Married, 7 withholding allowances Exempt $43,500/year Start Date: 10/1/201X SSN: 047-55-9951
01-Varde	Stevon Varden 333 Justin Drive Logan, UT 84321 435-555-9981 Job Title: Craftsman	Married, 2 withholding allowances Nonexempt $42,000/year Start Date: 10/1/201X SSN: 022-66-1131
02-Hisso	Leonard Hissop 531 5th Street Logan, UT 84321 435-555-5858 Job Title: Purchasing/ Shipping	Single, 4 withholding allowances Nonexempt $49,500/year Start Date: 10/1/201X SSN: 311-22-6698

The departments are as follows:

- Department 00: Sales and Administration
- Department 01: Factory Workers
- Department 02: Delivery and Customer Service

You have been hired as of October 1 as the new accounting clerk. Your employee number is 00-XXXXX, where "XXXXX" is the first five letters of your last name. If your last name is fewer than five letters, use the first few letters of your first name to complete the employee number. Your Utah drivers' license number is 887743 expiring in 7/2018 and Social Security number is 555-55-5555. You are nonexempt and paid at a rate of $36,000 per year. Complete the W-4 and, using the given information, complete the I-9 form to start your employee file. Complete it as if you are single with 1 withholding, you decide to contribute 3% to a 401(k), and health insurance is $50 per pay period.

Complete the headers of the Employee' Earnings Record for all company employees. The Balance Sheet for Wayland Custom Woodworking as of September 30, 2015, is as follows:

Wayland Custom Woodworking
Balance Sheet
9/30/2015

Assets		Liabilities & Equity	
Cash	$1,125,000	Accounts Payable	$ 112,490
Supplies	27,240	Salaries and Wages Payable	
Office Equipment	87,250	Federal Unemployment Tax Payable	
Inventory	123,000	Social Security Tax Payable	
Vehicle	25,000	Medicare Tax Payable	
Accumulated Depreciation, Vehicle		State Unemployment Tax Payable	
Building	164,000	Employee Federal Income Tax Payable	
Accumulated Depreciation, Building		Employee State Income Tax Payable	
Land	35,750	Employee State Income Tax Payable	
Total Assets	$1,587,240	401(k) Contributions Payable	
		Employee Medical Premiums Payable	
		Notes Payable	224,750
		Utilities Payable	
		Total Liabilities	337,240
		Owners' Equity	1,250,000
		Retained Earnings	-
		Total Equity	1,250,000
		Total Liabilities and Equity	$ 1,587,240

October 15

October 15 is the end of the first pay period for the month of October. Employee pay will be disbursed on October 18, 201X. Any time worked in excess of 88 hours is considered overtime. Remember that the employees are paid on a semimonthly basis. The hours for the employees are as follows:

Name	Hourly Rate	Hours Worked 10/1–10/15	Gross Pay	Overtime	Commission
Chinson		88 hours (exempt)			$1,500.00
Wayland		88 hours (exempt)			
Peppinico		88 hours (exempt)			
Varden		98 hours			
Hissop		95.25 hours			
You		88 hours			

Update the Employee' Earning Records for the period's pay and update the YTD amount.

Compute the Net Pay for each employee using the payroll register on page 250. Once you have computed the net pay, complete the paycheck for each employee (assume that all employees are paid by check). Date the checks 10/18/1X. The first check number is 174556.

Name	Deduction
Chinson	Section 125 Health Insurance: $50/paycheck 401(k): 3% of gross pay
Wayland	Section 125 Health Insurance: $75/paycheck 401(k): 6% of gross pay
Peppinico	Section 125 Health Insurance: $75/paycheck 401(k): $50 per paycheck
Varden	Section 125 Health Insurance: $50/paycheck 401(k): 4% of gross pay
Hissop	Section 125 Health Insurance: $75/paycheck 401(k): 3% of gross pay
You	Section 125 Health Insurance: $50/paycheck 401(k): 3% of gross pay

---

Wayland Custom Woodworking
8530 San Pablo Road
Santa Clarita, CA 90210

174556

Anthony Chinson   Date   10/18/1X

dollars   -

Payee: Anthony Chinson
Address: 530 Sylvann Ave
City/State Zip: Newhall, CA 91234   Signed: *Mark Wayland*

| Payroll End Date | 10/15/1X | | Payroll Pay Date | 10/18/1X | | Check: | 174556 |

| Employee Name | Anthony Chinson | | Employee number | 00-CHINS | Rate | 11.54 |

Description	Earnings	YTD Gross	Description	Deductions	YTD Deductions
Regular		-	Federal W/H		-
Holiday			FICA		-
Commissions		-	Medicare		-
			State SDI		-
			Pretax Insurance		-
Total Earnings	-	-	State PIT		-
			401(k)		-
			Total Deductions	-	

Wayland Custom Woodworking
8530 San Pablo Road
Santa Clarita, CA 90210

174557

Mark Wayland   Date   10/18/1X

dollars   -

Payee: Mark Wayland
Address: 1570 Lovett St
City/State Zip: Val Verde, CA 91496   Signed: *Mark Wayland*

| Payroll End Date | 10/15/1X | | Payroll Pay Date | 10/18/1X | | Check: | 174557 |

| Employee Name | Mark Wayland | | Employee number | 00-Wayla | Rate | 36.06 |

Description	Earnings	YTD Gross	Description	Deductions	YTD Deductions
Regular		-	Federal W/H		-
Holiday		-	FICA		-
			Medicare		-
			State SDI		-
Total Earnings	-	-	Pretax Insurance		-
			State PIT		-
			401(k)		-
			Total Deductions	-	

Wayland Custom Woodworking
8530 San Pablo Road
Santa Clarita, CA 90210

174558

Sylvia Peppinico   Date   10/18/1X

dollars   -

Payee: Sylvia Peppinico
Address: 291 Antioch Rd
City/State Zip: Newhall, CA 91234   Signed: *Mark Wayland*

Payroll End Date	10/15/1X	Payroll Pay Date	10/18/1X	Check:	174558
Employee Name	Sylvia Peppinico	Employee number	01-PEPPI	Rate	20.91

Description	Earnings	YTD Gross	Description	Deductions	YTD Deductions
Regular		-	Federal W/H		-
Holiday		-	FICA		-
			Medicare		-
			State SDI		-
Total Earnings	-	-	Pretax Insurance		-
			State PIT		-
			401(k)		-
			Total Deductions	-	-

Wayland Custom Woodworking
8530 San Pablo Road
Santa Clarita, CA 90210

174559

Stevon Varden   Date   10/18/1X

dollars   -

Payee: Stevon Varden
Address: 333 Justin Dr
City/State Zip: Pico, CA 91452   Signed: *Mark Wayland*

Payroll End Date	10/15/1X	Payroll Pay Date	10/18/1X	Check:	174559
Employee Name	Stevon Varden	Employee number	01-VARDE	Rate	29.81

Description	Earnings	YTD Gross	Description	Deductions	YTD Deductions
Regular		-	Federal W/H		-
Overtime		-	FICA		-
Holiday		-	Medicare		-
			State SDI		-
Total Earnings	-	-	Pretax Insurance		-
			State PIT		-
			401(k)		-
			Total Deductions	-	-

Wayland Custom Woodworking
8530 San Pablo Road
Santa Clarita, CA 90210

174560

Leonard Hissop   Date   10/18/1X

dollars   -

Payee: Leonard Hissop
Address: 531 5th St
City/State Zip: Santa Clarita, CA 91552   Signed: *Mark Wayland*

Payroll End Date	10/15/1X	Payroll Pay Date	10/18/1X	Check:	174560
Employee Name	Leonard Hissop	Employee number	02-HISSO	Rate	23.8

Description	Earnings	YTD Gross	Description	Deductions	YTD Deductions
Regular		-	Federal W/H		-
Overtime		-	FICA		-
Holiday		-	Medicare		-
			State SDI		-
Total Earnings	-	-	Pretax Insurance		-
			State PIT		-
			401(k)		-
			Total Deductions	-	-

Wayland Custom Woodworking		
8530 San Pablo Road		
Santa Clarita, CA 90210		174561

Student Name Here	Date	10/18/1X
	dollars	-

Payee: Student name here
Address: address from student
City/State Zip: City/State/Zip

Signed: *Mark Wayland*

Payroll End Date	10/15/1X	Payroll Pay Date	10/18/1X	Check:	174561
Employee Name	Student Name Here	Employee number	00-STUDE	Rate	17.31

Description	Earnings	YTD Gross	Description	Deductions	YTD Deductions
Regular		-	Federal W/H		-
Overtime		-	FICA		-
Holiday		-	Medicare		-
			State SDI		-
Total Earnings	-	-	Pretax Insurance		-
			State PIT		-
			401(k)		
			Total Deductions	-	-

Complete the Payroll Register for October 15

Run Date _____   Wayland Custom Woodworking
P/R Date _____

Name	Marital Status	No. With-holdings	Hourly Rate	No. of Regular Hours	No. of Overtime Hours	Gross Earning	Federal W/H	Social Security Tax	Medicare W/H	State W/H Tax	401(k)	Insurance	Net Pay	Check No.	Check Date
Anthony Chinson															
Mark Wayland															
Sylvia Peppinico															
Stevon Varden															
Leonard Hissop															
Student															

General Journal Entries

Complete the General Journal entries as follows:

Oct 15	Journalize employee pay for the period.
Oct 15	Journalize employer payroll tax for the October 15 pay date.
Oct 18	Journalize payment of payroll to employees (use one entry for all checks).

Date		Description	Post Ref.	Debit	Credit

Date		Description	Post Ref.	Debit	Credit

Post all journal entries to the appropriate General Ledger accounts.

October 31

October 31 is the end of the final pay period for the month. Employee pay will be disbursed on November 5, 201X. Any hours exceeding 96 are considered overtime. Compute the employee gross pay below.

The hours for the employees are as follows:

Name	Hourly Rate	Hours Worked 10/16–10/31	Gross Pay	Overtime	Commission
Chinson		96 hours (exempt)			$1,750.00
Wayland		96 hours (exempt)			
Peppinico		96 hours (exempt)			
Varden		98 hours			
Hissop		97.5 hours			
You		99 hours			

Update the Employee' Earning Records' for the period's pay and update the YTD amount.

Compute the net pay for each employee. Once you have computed the gross pay, complete the paycheck for each employee (assume that all employees are paid by check). Date the checks 11/5/201X.

Wayland Custom Woodworking
8530 San Pablo Road
Santa Clarita, CA 90210

174562

Anthony Chinson

Date   11/05/1X

dollars   -

Payee: Anthony Chinson
Address: 530 Sylvann Ave
City/State Zip: Newhall, CA 91234

Signed: *Mark Wayland*

Payroll End Date	10/31/1X		Payroll Pay Date	11/05/1X		Check:	174562

Employee Name	Anthony Chinson		Employee number	00-CHINS	Rate	11.54

Description	Earnings	YTD Gross	Description	Deductions	YTD Deductions
Regular		-	Federal W/H		
Holiday			FICA		-
Commissions		-	Medicare		-
			State SDI		-
			Pretax Insurance		-
Total Earnings	-	-	State PIT		-
			401(k)		
			Total Deductions	-	-

Wayland Custom Woodworking
8530 San Pablo Road
Santa Clarita, CA 90210

174563

Mark Wayland   Date   11/05/1X

dollars   -

Payee: Mark Wayland
Address: 1570 Lovett St
City/State Zip: Val Verde, CA 91496   Signed: *Mark Wayland*

Payroll End Date	10/31/1X	Payroll Pay Date	11/05/1X	Check:	174563
Employee Name	Mark Wayland	Employee number	00-Wayla	Rate	36.06

Description	Earnings	YTD Gross	Description	Deductions	YTD Deductions
Regular		-	Federal W/H		-
Holiday		-	FICA		-
			Medicare		-
			State SDI		-
Total Earnings	-	-	Pretax Insurance		-
			State PIT		-
			401(k)		-
			Total Deductions	-	-

Wayland Custom Woodworking
8530 San Pablo Road
Santa Clarita, CA 90210

174564

Sylvia Peppinico   Date   11/05/1X

dollars   -

Payee: Sylvia Peppinico
Address: 291 Antioch Rd
City/State Zip: Newhall, CA 91234   Signed: *Mark Wayland*

Payroll End Date	10/31/1X	Payroll Pay Date	11/05/1X	Check:	174564
Employee Name	Sylvia Peppinico	Employee number	01-PEPPI	Rate	20.91

Description	Earnings	YTD Gross	Description	Deductions	YTD Deductions
Regular		-	Federal W/H		-
Holiday		-	FICA		-
			Medicare		-
			State SDI		-
Total Earnings	-	-	Pretax Insurance		-
			State PIT		-
			401(k)		-
			Total Deductions	-	-

Wayland Custom Woodworking
8530 San Pablo Road
Santa Clarita, CA 90210

174565

Stevon Varden   Date   11/05/1X

dollars   -

Payee: Stevon Varden
Address: 333 Justin Dr
City/State Zip: Pico, CA 91452   Signed: *Mark Wayland*

Payroll End Date	10/31/1X	Payroll Pay Date	11/05/1X	Check:	174565
Employee Name	Stevon Varden	Employee number	01-VARDE	Rate	29.81

Description	Earnings	YTD Gross	Description	Deductions	YTD Deductions
Regular		-	Federal W/H		-
Overtime		-	FICA		-
Holiday		-	Medicare		-
			State SDI		-
Total Earnings	-	-	Pretax Insurance		-
			State PIT		-
			401(k)		-
			Total Deductions	-	-

Wayland Custom Woodworking
8530 San Pablo Road
Santa Clarita, CA 90210

174566

Leonard Hissop   Date   11/05/1X

dollars   -

Payee: Leonard Hissop
Address: 531 5th St
City/State Zip: Santa Clarita, CA 91552   Signed: *Mark Wayland*

Payroll End Date   10/31/1X   Payroll Pay Date   11/05/1X   Check: 174566

Employee Name Leonard Hissop   Employee number   02-HISSO   Rate $ 23.80

Description	Earnings	YTD Gross	Description	Deductions	YTD Deductions
Regular		-	Federal W/H		-
Overtime		-	FICA		-
Holiday		-	Medicare		-
			State SDI		
Total Earnings	-	-	Pretax Insurance		-
			State PIT		-
			401(k)		-
			Total Deductions	-	-

Wayland Custom Woodworking
8530 San Pablo Road
Santa Clarita, CA 90210

174567

Student Name Here   Date   11/05/1X

dollars   -

Payee: Student name here
Address: address from student
City/State Zip: City/State/Zip   Signed: *Mark Wayland*

Payroll End Date   10/31/1X   Payroll Pay Date   11/05/1X   Check: 174567

Employee Name Student Name Here   Employee number   00-STUDE   Rate   17.31

Description	Earnings	YTD Gross	Description	Deductions	YTD Deductions
Regular		-	Federal W/H		-
Overtime		-	FICA		-
Holiday		-	Medicare		-
			State SDI		-
Total Earnings	-	-	Pretax Insurance		-
			State PIT		-
			401(k)		-
			Total Deductions	-	-

Complete the Payroll Register for October 31

Run Date [   ]   Wayland Custom Woodworking
P/R Date [   ]

Name	Marital Status	No. With-holdings	Hourly Rate	No. of Regular Hours	No. of Overtime Hours	Gross Earning	Federal W/H	Social Security Tax	Medicare W/H	State W/H Tax	401(k)	Insurance	Net Pay	Check No.	Check Date
Anthony Chinson															
Mark Wayland															
Sylvia Peppinico															
Stevon Varden															
Leonard Hissop															
Student															

General Journal Entries

Complete the General Journal entries as follows:

Oct 31	Journalize employee pay for the period.
Oct 31	Journalize employer payroll tax for the October 31 pay date.
Nov 5	Journalize payment of payroll to employees (use one entry for all checks).
Nov 5	Journalize remittance of 401(k) and Section 125 health insurance premiums deducted.
Nov 5	Journalize remittance of monthly payroll taxes.

Date		Description	Post Ref.	Debit	Credit

Post all journal entries to the appropriate General Ledger accounts.

November 15

Complete the chart below. Any hours exceeding 88 are considered overtime. Remember that the employees are paid semimonthly. The hours for the employees during the pay period are as follows:

Name	Hourly Rate	Hours Worked 11/01–11/15	Gross Pay	Overtime	Commission
Chinson		88 hours (exempt)			$1,050.00
Wayland		88 hours (exempt)			
Peppinico		88 hours (exempt)			
Varden		96 hours			
Hissop		91 hours			
You		93 hours			

Update the Employees' Earning Records for the period's pay and update the YTD amount.

Compute the net pay for each employee. Once you have computed the gross pay, complete the paycheck for each employee (assume that all employees are paid by check). Date the checks 11/18/1X.

Wayland Custom Woodworking
8530 San Pablo Road
Santa Clarita, CA 90210

174568

Anthony Chinson   Date   11/18/1X

dollars   -

Payee: Anthony Chinson
Address: 530 Sylvann Ave
City/State Zip: Newhall, CA 91234   Signed: *Mark Wayland*

Payroll End Date	11/15/1X	Payroll Pay Date	11/18/1X	Check:	174568
Employee Name	Anthony Chinson	Employee number	00-CHINS	Rate	11.54

Description	Earnings	YTD Gross	Description	Deductions	YTD Deductions
Regular		-	Federal W/H		-
Holiday			FICA		-
Commissions		-	Medicare		-
			State SDI		-
			Pretax Insurance		-
Total Earnings	-	-	State PIT		-
			401(k)		-
			Total Deductions	-	-

Wayland Custom Woodworking
8530 San Pablo Road
Santa Clarita, CA 90210

174569

Mark Wayland   Date   11/18/1X

dollars   -

Payee: Mark Wayland
Address: 1570 Lovett St
City/State Zip: Val Verde, CA 91496   Signed: *Mark Wayland*

Payroll End Date	11/15/1X	Payroll Pay Date	11/18/1X	Check:	174569
Employee Name	Mark Wayland	Employee number	00-Wayla	Rate	36.06

Description	Earnings	YTD Gross	Description	Deductions	YTD Deductions
Regular		-	Federal W/H		-
Holiday		-	FICA		-
			Medicare		-
			State SDI		-
Total Earnings	-	-	Pretax Insurance		-
			State PIT		-
			401(k)		-
			Total Deductions	-	-

Wayland Custom Woodworking
8530 San Pablo Road
Santa Clarita, CA 90210

174570

Sylvia Peppinico   Date   11/18/1X

dollars   -

Payee: Sylvia Peppinico
Address: 291 Antioch Rd
City/State Zip: Newhall, CA 91234   Signed: *Mark Wayland*

Payroll End Date	11/15/1X	Payroll Pay Date	11/18/1X	Check:	174570
Employee Name	Sylvia Peppinico	Employee number	01-PEPPI	Rate	20.91

Description	Earnings	YTD Gross	Description	Deductions	YTD Deductions
Regular		-	Federal W/H		-
Holiday		-	FICA		-
			Medicare		-
			State SDI		-
Total Earnings	-	-	Pretax Insurance		-
			State PIT		-
			401(k)		-
			Total Deductions	-	-

Wayland Custom Woodworking
8530 San Pablo Road
Santa Clarita, CA 90210

174571

Stevon Varden   Date   11/18/1X

dollars   -

Payee: Stevon Varden
Address: 333 Justin Dr
City/State Zip: Pico, CA 91452   Signed: *Mark Wayland*

Payroll End Date	11/15/1X	Payroll Pay Date	11/18/1X	Check:	174571
Employee Name	Stevon Varden	Employee number	01-VARDE	Rate	29.81

Description	Earnings	YTD Gross	Description	Deductions	YTD Deductions
Regular		-	Federal W/H		-
Overtime		-	FICA		-
Holiday		-	Medicare		-
			State SDI		-
Total Earnings	-	-	Pretax Insurance		-
			State PIT		-
			401(k)		-
			Total Deductions	-	-

Wayland Custom Woodworking
8530 San Pablo Road
Santa Clarita, CA 90210

174572

Leonard Hissop   Date   11/18/1X

dollars   -

Payee: Leonard Hissop
Address: 531 5th St
City/State Zip: Santa Clarita, CA 91552   Signed: *Mark Wayland*

Payroll End Date	11/15/1X	Payroll Pay Date	11/18/1X	Check:	174572
Employee Name	Leonard Hissop	Employee number	02-HISSO	Rate	$ 23.80

Description	Earnings	YTD Gross	Description	Deductions	YTD Deductions
Regular		-	Federal W/H		-
Overtime		-	FICA		-
Holiday		-	Medicare		-
			State SDI		-
Total Earnings	-	-	Pretax Insurance		-
			State PIT		-
			401(k)		-
			Total Deductions	-	-

Wayland Custom Woodworking
8530 San Pablo Road
Santa Clarita, CA 90210

174573

Student Name Here   Date   11/18/1X

dollars   -

Payee: Student name here
Address: address from student
City/State Zip: City/State/Zip   Signed: *Mark Wayland*

Payroll End Date	11/15/1X	Payroll Pay Date	11/18/1X	Check:	174573
Employee Name	Student Name Here	Employee number	00-STUDE	Rate	17.31

Description	Earnings	YTD Gross	Description	Deductions	YTD Deductions
Regular		-	Federal W/H		-
Overtime		-	FICA		-
Holiday		-	Medicare		-
			State SDI		-
Total Earnings	-	-	Pretax Insurance		-
			State PIT		-
			401(k)		-
			Total Deductions	-	-

Complete the Payroll Register for November 15.

Run Date [　　　　　]   Wayland Custom Woodworking
P/R Date [　　　　　]

Name	Marital Status	No. With-holdings	Hourly Rate	No. of Regular Hours	No. of Overtime Hours	Gross Earning	Federal W/H	Social Security Tax	Medicare W/H	State W/H Tax	401(k)	Insurance	Net Pay	Check No.	Check Date
Anthony Chinson															
Mark Wayland															
Sylvia Peppinico															
Stevon Varden															
Leonard Hissop															
Student															

General Journal Entries

Complete the General Journal entries as follows:

Nov 15	Journalize employee pay for the period.
Nov 15	Journalize employer payroll tax for the November 15 pay date.
Nov 18	Journalize payment of payroll to employees (use one entry for all checks).

Date		Description	Post Ref.	Debit	Credit

Post all journal entries to the appropriate General Ledger accounts.

November 30

Compute the employee gross pay and update the Employees' Earnings Record with the November 30 pay and the new YTD amount.

The company is closed and pays for the Friday following Thanksgiving. The employees will receive holiday pay for Thanksgiving and the Friday following. Any hours worked in excess of 88 hours is considered overtime.

The hours for the employees are as follows:

Name	Hourly Rate	Hours Worked 11/16–11/30	Gross Pay	Holiday	Overtime	Commission
Chinson		88 hours (exempt) (16 Holiday)				$2,325.00
Wayland		88 hours (exempt) (16 Holiday)				
Peppinico		88 hours (exempt) (16 Holiday)				
Varden		90 hours(16 Holiday)				
Hissop		91 hours(16 Holiday)				
You		89 hours(16 Holiday)				

Update the Employees' Earnings Records for the period's pay and update the YTD amount. Compute the net pay for each employee. Once you have computed the gross pay, complete the paycheck for each employee (assume that all employees are paid by check). Date the checks 12/03/1X.

Wayland Custom Woodworking
8530 San Pablo Road
Santa Clarita, CA 90210

174574

Anthony Chinson   Date   12/03/1x

dollars   -

Payee: Anthony Chinson
Address: 530 Sylvann Ave
City/State Zip: Newhall, CA 91234   Signed: *Mark Wayland*

Payroll End Date	11/30/1x	Payroll Pay Date	12/03/1x	Check:	174574

Employee Name: Anthony Chinson   Employee number: 00-CHINS   Rate: 11.54

Description	Earnings	YTD Gross	Description	Deductions	YTD Deductions
Regular		-	Federal W/H		-
Holiday		-	FICA		-
Commissions		-	Medicare		-
			State SDI		-
			Pretax Insurance		
Total Earnings	-	-	State PIT		-
			401(k)		-
			Total Deductions	-	-

Wayland Custom Woodworking
8530 San Pablo Road
Santa Clarita, CA 90210

174575

Mark Wayland   Date   12/03/1x

dollars   -

Payee: Mark Wayland
Address: 1570 Lovett St
City/State Zip: Val Verde, CA 91496   Signed: *Mark Wayland*

Payroll End Date	11/30/1x	Payroll Pay Date	12/03/1x	Check:	174575

Employee Name: Mark Wayland   Employee number: 00-Wayla   Rate: 36.06

Description	Earnings	YTD Gross	Description	Deductions	YTD Deductions
		-	Federal W/H		-
Holiday		-	FICA		-
			Medicare		-
			State SDI		-
Total Earnings	-	-	Pretax Insurance		-
			State PIT		-
			401(k)		-
			Total Deductions	-	-

Wayland Custom Woodworking
8530 San Pablo Road
Santa Clarita, CA 90210

174576

Sylvia Peppinico   Date   12/03/1x

dollars   -

Payee: Sylvia Peppinico
Address: 291 Antioch Rd
City/State Zip: Newhall, CA 91234   Signed: *Mark Wayland*

Payroll End Date	11/30/1x	Payroll Pay Date	12/03/1x		Check:	174576
Employee Name	Sylvia Peppinico		Employee number	01-PEPP1	Rate	20.91

Description	Earnings	YTD Gross	Description	Deductions	YTD Deductions
Regular		-	Federal W/H		-
Holiday		-	FICA		-
			Medicare		-
			State SDI		-
Total Earnings	-	-	Pretax Insurance		-
			State PIT		-
			401(k)		-
			Total Deductions	-	-

Wayland Custom Woodworking
8530 San Pablo Road
Santa Clarita, CA 90210

174577

Stevon Varden   Date   12/03/1x

dollars   -

Payee: Stevon Varden
Address: 333 Justin Dr
City/State Zip: Pico, CA 91452   Signed: *Mark Wayland*

Payroll End Date	11/30/1x	Payroll Pay Date	12/03/1x		Check:	174577
Employee Name	Stevon Varden		Employee number	01-VARDE	Rate	29.81

Description	Earnings	YTD Gross	Description	Deductions	YTD Deductions
Regular		-	Federal W/H		-
Overtime		-	FICA		-
Holiday		-	Medicare		-
			State SDI		-
Total Earnings	-	-	Pretax Insurance		-
			State PIT		-
			401(k)		-
			Total Deductions	-	-

Wayland Custom Woodworking
8530 San Pablo Road
Santa Clarita, CA 90210

174578

Leonard Hissop   Date   12/03/1x

dollars   -

Payee: Leonard Hissop
Address: 531 5th St
City/State Zip: Santa Clarita, CA 91552   Signed: *Mark Wayland*

Payroll End Date	11/30/1x	Payroll Pay Date	12/03/1x		Check:	174578
Employee Name	Leonard Hissop		Employee number	02-HISSO	Rate	23.80

Description	Earnings	YTD Gross	Description	Deductions	YTD Deductions
Regular		-	Federal W/H		-
Overtime		-	FICA		-
Holiday		-	Medicare		-
			State SDI		-
Total Earnings	-	-	Pretax Insurance		-
			State PIT		-
			401(k)		-
			Total Deductions	-	-

Wayland Custom Woodworking		
8530 San Pablo Road		
Santa Clarita, CA 90210		174579

Student Name Here	Date	12/03/1x
	dollars	-

Payee: Student name here
Address: address from student
City/State Zip: City/State/Zip

Signed: *Mark Wayland*

Payroll End Date	11/30/1x	Payroll Pay Date	12/03/1x	Check:	174579
Employee Name	Student Name Here	Employee number	00-STUDE	Rate	17.31

Description	Earnings	YTD Gross	Description	Deductions	YTD Deductions
Regular		-	Federal W/H		-
Overtime		-	FICA		-
Holiday		-	Medicare		-
			State SDI		-
Total Earnings	-	-	Pretax Insurance		-
			State PIT		-
			401(k)		-
			Total Deductions	-	-

Complete the Payroll Register for November 30.

Run Date [   ]   Wayland Custom Woodworking
P/R Date [   ]

Name	Marital Status	No. With-holdings	Hourly Rate	No. of Regular Hours	No. of Overtime Hours	Gross Earning	Federal W/H	Social Security Tax	Medicare W/H	State W/H Tax	401(k)	Insurance	Net Pay	Check No.	Check Date
Anthony Chinson															
Mark Wayland															
Sylvia Peppinico															
Stevon Varden															
Leonard Hissop															
Student															

General Journal Entries

Complete the General Journal entries as follows:

Nov 30	Journalize employee pay for the period.
Nov 30	Journalize employer payroll tax for the November 30 pay date.
Dec 3	Journalize payment of payroll to employees (use one entry for all checks).
Dec 3	Journalize remittance of 401(k) and Section 125 health insurance premiums deducted.
Dec 3	Journalize remittance of payroll taxes.

Date		Description	Post Ref.	Debit	Credit

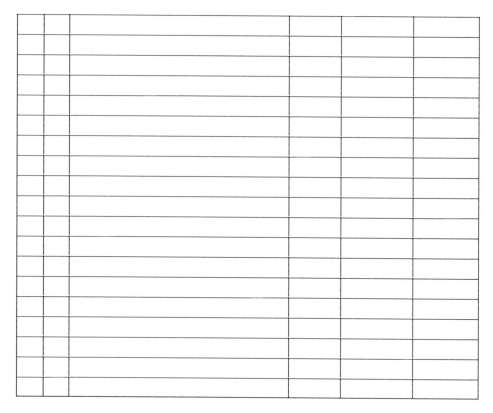

Post all journal entries to the appropriate General Ledger accounts.

Short Version

If desired, students may complete the payroll for one month only. When using the short version, students should start with the November 30, 2015, Balance Sheet:

Wayland Custom Woodworking **Balance Sheet** **November 30, 2015**			
Assets		**Liabilities & Equity**	
Cash	$ 1,085,334.77	Accounts Payable	$ 149,272.68
Supplies	10,283.15	Salaries and Wages Payable	10,314.54
Office Equipment	130,202.16	Employee Federal Income Tax Payable	1,930.23
Inventory	221,163.81	Social Security Tax Payable	3,219.22
Vehicle	25,000.00	Medicare Tax Payable	752.88
Accumulated Depreciation, Vehicle	(1,420.00)	Federal Unemployment Tax Payable	88.85
Building	164,000.00	State Unemployment Tax Payable	694.49
Accumulated Depreciation, Building	(3,221.00)	Employee State Income Tax Payable	1,088.86
Land	35,750.00	401(k) Contributions Payable	1,018.66
Total Assets	$ 1,667,092.89	Employee Medical Premiums Payable	750.00
		Notes Payable	211,000.00
		Utilities Payable	2,825.43
		Total Liabilities	382,955.84
		Owners' Equity	1,250,000.00
		Retained Earnings	34,137.05
		Total Equity	1,284,137.05
		Total Liabilities and Equity	$ 1,667,092.89

When using the short version, students will need to enter the payroll-related balances in the November 30 Balance Sheet as the beginning balances in the General Ledger accounts.

Students should enter the following Year-To-Date earnings balances in the Employees' Earnings Records:

Employee	YTD Net Pay	YTD Gross Pay
Chinson	$ 7,761.64	$10,625.00
Wayland	$ 9,149.52	$12,500.00
Peppinico	$ 5,971.04	$ 7,250.00
Varden	$ 5,957.97	$ 7,935.58
Hissop	$ 6,713.80	$ 9,903.84
Student	$ 4,618.66	$ 6,464.42

(Short version only: December 3:

Journalize the following, using the balances given in the November 30 Balance Sheet:

- Payment of Salaries and Wages Payable
- Remittance of 401(k) Contributions and Employee Medical Premiums
- Remittance of November Taxes

Students should then continue with the December payroll transactions on December 15.)

December 15

Compute the employee gross pay and update the Employees' Earnings Record with the December 15 pay and the new YTD amount.

Complete the chart below:

Name	Hourly Rate	Hours Worked 12/01–12/15	Gross Pay	Overtime	Commission
Chinson		80 hours (exempt)			$1,680.00
Wayland		80 hours (exempt)			
Peppinico		80 hours (exempt)			
Varden		84 hours			
Hissop		80 hours			
You		83 hours			

Update the Employees' Earning Records for the period pay and update the YTD amount. Compute the net pay for each employee. Once you have computed the gross pay, complete the paycheck for each employee (assume that all employees are paid by check). Date the checks 12/18/201X.

Wayland Custom Woodworking					
8530 San Pablo Road					
Santa Clarita, CA 90210				174580	
Anthony Chinson			Date	12/18/1X	
				dollars	-
Payee: Anthony Chinson					
Address: 530 Sylvann Ave					
City/State Zip: Newhall, CA 91234		Signed: *Mark Wayland*			

Payroll End Date	12/15/1X		Payroll Pay Date	12/18/1X		Check:	174580
Employee Name	Anthony Chinson			Employee number	00-CHINS	Rate	11.54

Description	Earnings	YTD Gross	Description	Deductions	YTD Deductions
Regular		-	Federal W/H		-
Holiday		-	FICA		-
Commissions		-	Medicare		-
			State SDI		-
			Pretax Insurance		-
Total Earnings	-	-	State PIT		-
			401(k)		-
			Total Deductions	-	-

Wayland Custom Woodworking
8530 San Pablo Road
Santa Clarita, CA 90210

174581

Mark Wayland

Date 12/18/1X

dollars -

Payee: Mark Wayland
Address: 1570 Lovett St
City/State Zip: Val Verde, CA 91496

Signed: *Mark Wayland*

Payroll End Date	12/15/1X		Payroll Pay Date	12/18/1X	Check:	174581
Employee Name	Mark Wayland		Employee number	00-Wayla	Rate	36.06

Description	Earnings	YTD Gross	Description	Deductions	YTD Deductions
Regular		-	Federal W/H		-
Holiday		-	FICA		-
			Medicare		-
			State SDI		-
Total Earnings	-	-	Pretax Insurance		-
			State PIT		-
			401(k)		-
			Total Deductions	-	-

Wayland Custom Woodworking
8530 San Pablo Road
Santa Clarita, CA 90210

174582

Sylvia Peppinico

Date 12/18/1X

dollars -

Payee: Sylvia Peppinico
Address: 291 Antioch Rd
City/State Zip: Newhall, CA 91234

Signed: *Mark Wayland*

Payroll End Date	12/15/1X		Payroll Pay Date	12/18/1X	Check:	174582
Employee Name	Sylvia Peppinico		Employee number	01-PEPPI	Rate	20.91

Description	Earnings	YTD Gross	Description	Deductions	YTD Deductions
Regular		-	Federal W/H		-
Holiday		-	FICA		-
			Medicare		-
			State SDI		-
Total Earnings	-	-	Pretax Insurance		-
			State PIT		-
			401(k)		-
			Total Deductions	-	-

Wayland Custom Woodworking
8530 San Pablo Road
Santa Clarita, CA 90210

174583

Stevon Varden

Date 12/18/1X

dollars -

Payee: Stevon Varden
Address: 333 Justin Dr
City/State Zip: Pico, CA 91452

Signed: *Mark Wayland*

Payroll End Date	12/15/1X		Payroll Pay Date	12/18/1X	Check:	174583
Employee Name	Stevon Varden		Employee number	01-VARDE	Rate	29.81

Description	Earnings	YTD Gross	Description	Deductions	YTD Deductions
Regular		-	Federal W/H		-
Overtime		-	FICA		-
Holiday		-	Medicare		-
			State SDI		-
Total Earnings	-	-	Pretax Insurance		-
			State PIT		-
			401(k)		-
			Total Deductions	-	-

Wayland Custom Woodworking
8530 San Pablo Road
Santa Clarita, CA 90210

174584

Leonard Hissop

Date   12/18/1X

dollars   -

Payee: Leonard Hissop
Address: 531 5th St
City/State Zip: Santa Clarita, CA 91552

Signed: *Mark Wayland*

| Payroll End Date | 12/15/1X | Payroll Pay Date | 12/18/1X | Check: | 174584 |

| Employee Name | Leonard Hissop | Employee number | 02-HISSO | Rate | 23.80 |

Description	Earnings	YTD Gross	Description	Deductions	YTD Deductions
Regular		-	Federal W/H		-
Overtime		-	FICA		-
Holiday		-	Medicare		-
			State SDI		-
Total Earnings	-	-	Pretax Insurance		-
			State PIT		-
			401(k)		-
			Total Deductions	-	-

Wayland Custom Woodworking
8530 San Pablo Road
Santa Clarita, CA 90210

174585

Student Name Here

Date   12/18/1X

dollars   -

Payee: Student name here
Address: address from student
City/State Zip: City/State/Zip

Signed: *Mark Wayland*

| Payroll End Date | 12/15/1X | Payroll Pay Date | 12/18/1X | Check: | 174585 |

| Employee Name | Student Name Here | Employee number | 00-STUDE | Rate | 17.31 |

Description	Earnings	YTD Gross	Description	Deductions	YTD Deductions
Regular		-	Federal W/H		-
Overtime		-	FICA		-
Holiday		-	Medicare		-
			State SDI		-
Total Earnings	-	-	Pretax Insurance		-
			State PIT		-
			401(k)		-
			Total Deductions	-	-

Complete the Payroll Register for December 15.

Run Date
P/R Date

Wayland Custom Woodworking

Name	Marital Status	No. With-holdings	Hourly Rate	No. of Regular Hours	No. of Overtime Hours	Gross Earning	Federal W/H	Social Security Tax	Medicare W/H	State W/H Tax	401(k)	Insurance	Net Pay	Check No.	Check Date
Anthony Chinson															
Mark Wayland															
Sylvia Peppinico															
Stevon Varden															
Leonard Hissop															
Student															

General Journal Entries

Complete the General Journal entries as follows:

Dec 15	Journalize employee pay for the period.
Dec 15	Journalize employer payroll tax for the December 15 pay date.
Dec 18	Journalize payment of payroll to employees (use one entry for all checks).

Date	Description	Post Ref.	Debit	Credit

Post all journal entries to the appropriate General Ledger accounts.

December 31

Compute the employee gross pay and update the Employee Earning Record with the December 31 pay and the new YTD amount.

The company pays for the day before and the day of Christmas, and if the holiday is on a weekend, the company pays for the Friday before. Christmas fell on a Tuesday, so employees will be paid for both the Monday and Tuesday as holiday pay.

Complete the chart below. The hours for the employees are as follows:

Name	Hourly Rate	Hours Worked 12/16–12/31	Gross Pay	Holiday	Overtime	Commission
Chinson		88 hours (exempt) (16 Holiday)				$1,015.00
Wayland		88 hours (exempt) (16 Holiday)				
Peppinico		88 hours (exempt) (16 Holiday)				
Varden		92 hours (16 Holiday)*				
Hissop		90 hours (16 Holiday)*				
You		91 hours (16 Holiday)*				

*Employees worked extra hours on Saturday during the week of 12/23–12/29. Remember, holidays and vacations do not incur overtime if the employee does not *work* more than 8 hours in a day.

Update the Employees' Earning Records for the period pay and update the YTD amount. Compute the net pay for each employee. Once you have computed the gross pay, complete the paycheck for each employee (assume that all employees are paid by check). Date the checks 1/3/201X.

Wayland Custom Woodworking
8530 San Pablo Road
Santa Clarita, CA 90210

174586

Anthony Chinson   Date   01/03/1X

                                                 dollars

Payee: Anthony Chinson
Address: 530 Sylvann Ave
City/State Zip: Newhall, CA 91234   Signed: *Mark Wayland*

Payroll End Date	12/30/1X		Payroll Pay Date	01/03/1X		Check:	174586
Employee Name	Anthony Chinson			Employee number	00-CHINS	Rate	11.54

Description	Earnings	YTD Gross	Description	Deductions	YTD Deductions
Regular		-	Federal W/H		-
Holiday			FICA		-
Commissions		-	Medicare		-
			State SDI		-
			Pretax Insurance		-
Total Earnings	-	-	State PIT		-
			401(k)		-
			Total Deductions	-	-

Wayland Custom Woodworking
8530 San Pablo Road
Santa Clarita, CA 90210

174587

Mark Wayland   Date   01/03/1X

                                                 dollars

Payee: Mark Wayland
Address: 1570 Lovett St
City/State Zip: Val Verde, CA 91496   Signed: *Mark Wayland*

Payroll End Date	12/30/1X		Payroll Pay Date	01/03/1X		Check:	174587
Employee Name	Mark Wayland			Employee number	00-Wayla	Rate	36.06

Description	Earnings	YTD Gross	Description	Deductions	YTD Deductions
Regular		-	Federal W/H		-
Holiday		-	FICA		-
			Medicare		-
			State SDI		-
Total Earnings	-	-	Pretax Insurance		-
			State PIT		-
			401(k)		-
			Total Deductions	-	-

Wayland Custom Woodworking
8530 San Pablo Road
Santa Clarita, CA 90210

174588

Sylvia Peppinico		Date	01/03/1X

dollars | - |

Payee: Sylvia Peppinico
Address: 291 Antioch Rd
City/State Zip: Newhall, CA 91234   Signed: *Mark Wayland*

Payroll End Date	12/30/1X		Payroll Pay Date	01/03/1X		Check:	174588

| Employee Name | Sylvia Peppinico | | Employee number | 01-PEPPI | Rate | 20.91 |

Description	Earnings	YTD Gross	Description	Deductions	YTD Deductions
Regular		-	Federal W/H		-
Holiday		-	FICA		-
			Medicare		-
			State SDI		-
Total Earnings	-	-	Pretax Insurance		-
			State PIT		-
			401(k)		-
			Total Deductions	-	-

Wayland Custom Woodworking
8530 San Pablo Road
Santa Clarita, CA 90210

174589

Stevon Varden		Date	01/03/1X

dollars | - |

Payee: Stevon Varden
Address: 333 Justin Dr
City/State Zip: Pico, CA 91452   Signed: *Mark Wayland*

Payroll End Date	12/30/1X		Payroll Pay Date	01/03/1X		Check:	174589

| Employee Name | Stevon Varden | | Employee number | 01-VARDE | Rate | 29.81 |

Description	Earnings	YTD Gross	Description	Deductions	YTD Deductions
Regular		-	Federal W/H		-
Overtime		-	FICA		-
Holiday		-	Medicare		-
			State SDI		-
Total Earnings	-	-	Pretax Insurance		-
			State PIT		-
			401(k)		-
			Total Deductions	-	-

Wayland Custom Woodworking
8530 San Pablo Road
Santa Clarita, CA 90210

174590

Leonard Hissop		Date	01/03/1X

dollars | - |

Payee: Leonard Hissop
Address: 531 5th St
City/State Zip: Santa Clarita, CA 91552   Signed: *Mark Wayland*

Payroll End Date	12/30/1X		Payroll Pay Date	01/03/1X		Check:	174590

| Employee Name | Leonard Hissop | | Employee number | 02-HISSO | Rate | 23.80 |

Description	Earnings	YTD Gross	Description	Deductions	YTD Deductions
Regular		-	Federal W/H		-
Overtime		-	FICA		-
Holiday		-	Medicare		-
			State SDI		-
Total Earnings	-	-	Pretax Insurance		-
			State PIT		-
			401(k)		-
			Total Deductions	-	-

```
┌─────────────────────────────────────────────────────────────────┐
│  Wayland Custom Woodworking                                       │
│     8530 San Pablo Road                                           │
│      Santa Clarita, CA 90210                                      │
│                                                      174591        │
│                                                                   │
│  Student Name Here                    Date      01/03/1X          │
│                                                                   │
│                                              dollars    [      -]  │
│                                                                   │
│  Payee: Student name here                                         │
│  Address: address from student                                    │
│  City/State Zip: City/State/Zip       Signed:  Mark Wayland       │
│                                                                   │
│  Payroll End Date  12/30/1X    Payroll Pay Date  01/03/1X   Check: 174591 │
│                                                                   │
│  Employee Name Student Name Here   Employee number 00-STUDE  Rate  17.31  │
│                                                                   │
│  Description   Earnings  YTD Gross   Description  Deductions  YTD Deductions │
│                                                                   │
│  Regular                     -   Federal W/H                  -   │
│  Overtime                    -   FICA                         -   │
│  Holiday                     -   Medicare                     -   │
│                                  State SDI                    -   │
│  Total Earnings       -      -   Pretax Insurance             -   │
│                                  State PIT                    -   │
│                                  401(k)                       -   │
│                                                                   │
│                                  Total Deductions     -      -    │
└─────────────────────────────────────────────────────────────────┘
```

Complete the Payroll Register for December 31.

Run Date [   ]   Wayland Custom Woodworking
P/R Date [   ]

Name	Marital Status	No. With-holdings	Hourly Rate	No. of Regular Hours	No. of Overtime Hours	Gross Earning	Federal W/H	Social Security Tax	Medicare W/H	State W/H Tax	401(k)	Insurance	Net Pay	Check No.	Check Date
Anthony Chinson															
Mark Wayland															
Sylvia Peppinico															
Stevon Varden															
Leonard Hissop															
Student															

Complete Form 941 for the remittance of quarterly federal taxes.
Complete forms for the remittance of quarterly state taxes.
Complete Form 940 for the remittance of FUTA taxes.

General Journal Entries

Complete the General Journal entries as follows:

Dec 31	Journalize employee pay for the period.
Dec 31	Journalize employer payroll tax for the December 31 pay date.
Jan 3	Journalize payment of payroll to employees (use one entry for all checks).
Jan 3	Journalize remittance of 401(k) and Section 125 health insurance premiums deducted.
Jan 3	Journalize remittance of monthly payroll taxes.

Date		Description	Post Ref.	Debit	Credit

Date		Description	Post Ref.	Debit	Credit

Post all journal entries to the appropriate General Ledger accounts.

<table>
<tr><td></td><td style="text-align:center">

Employment Eligibility Verification

Department of Homeland Security
U.S. Citizenship and Immigration Services
</td><td style="text-align:center">

USCIS
Form I-9
OMB No. 1615-0047
Expires 03/31/2016
</td></tr>
</table>

▶**START HERE.** **Read instructions carefully before completing this form. The instructions must be available during completion of this form.**
ANTI-DISCRIMINATION NOTICE: It is illegal to discriminate against work-authorized individuals. Employers **CANNOT** specify which document(s) they will accept from an employee. The refusal to hire an individual because the documentation presented has a future expiration date may also constitute illegal discrimination.

Section 1. Employee Information and Attestation *(Employees must complete and sign Section 1 of Form I-9 no later than the **first day of employment**, but not before accepting a job offer.)*

Last Name *(Family Name)*	First Name *(Given Name)*	Middle Initial	Other Names Used *(if any)*

Address *(Street Number and Name)*	Apt. Number	City or Town	State	Zip Code

Date of Birth *(mm/dd/yyyy)*	U.S. Social Security Number	E-mail Address	Telephone Number
	☐☐☐-☐☐-☐☐☐☐		

I am aware that federal law provides for imprisonment and/or fines for false statements or use of false documents in connection with the completion of this form.

I attest, under penalty of perjury, that I am (check one of the following):

☐ A citizen of the United States

☐ A noncitizen national of the United States *(See instructions)*

☐ A lawful permanent resident (Alien Registration Number/USCIS Number): _____

☐ An alien authorized to work until (expiration date, if applicable, mm/dd/yyyy) _____ . Some aliens may write "N/A" in this field.
(See instructions)

*For aliens authorized to work, provide your Alien Registration Number/USCIS Number **OR** Form I-94 Admission Number:*

1. Alien Registration Number/USCIS Number:_____

OR

2. Form I-94 Admission Number: _____

If you obtained your admission number from CBP in connection with your arrival in the United States, include the following:

Foreign Passport Number: _____

Country of Issuance: _____

Some aliens may write "N/A" on the Foreign Passport Number and Country of Issuance fields. *(See instructions)*

3-D Barcode **Do Not Write in This Space**	

Signature of Employee:	Date *(mm/dd/yyyy)*:

Preparer and/or Translator Certification *(To be completed and signed if Section 1 is prepared by a person other than the employee.)*

I attest, under penalty of perjury, that I have assisted in the completion of this form and that to the best of my knowledge the information is true and correct.

Signature of Preparer or Translator:	Date *(mm/dd/yyyy)*:

Last Name *(Family Name)*	First Name *(Given Name)*

Address *(Street Number and Name)*	City or Town	State	Zip Code

🛑 ***Employer Completes Next Page*** 🛑

Form W-4 (2015)

Purpose. Complete Form W-4 so that your employer can withhold the correct federal income tax from your pay. Consider completing a new Form W-4 each year and when your personal or financial situation changes.

Exemption from withholding. If you are exempt, complete **only** lines 1, 2, 3, 4, and 7 and sign the form to validate it. Your exemption for 2015 expires February 16, 2016. See Pub. 505, Tax Withholding and Estimated Tax.

Note. If another person can claim you as a dependent on his or her tax return, you cannot claim exemption from withholding if your income exceeds $1,050 and includes more than $350 of unearned income (for example, interest and dividends).

  Exceptions. An employee may be able to claim exemption from withholding even if the employee is a dependent, if the employee:

• Is age 65 or older,

• Is blind, or

• Will claim adjustments to income; tax credits; or itemized deductions, on his or her tax return.

The exceptions do not apply to supplemental wages greater than $1,000,000.

Basic instructions. If you are not exempt, complete the **Personal Allowances Worksheet** below. The worksheets on page 2 further adjust your withholding allowances based on itemized deductions, certain credits, adjustments to income, or two-earners/multiple jobs situations.

  Complete all worksheets that apply. However, you may claim fewer (or zero) allowances. For regular wages, withholding must be based on allowances you claimed and may not be a flat amount or percentage of wages.

Head of household. Generally, you can claim head of household filing status on your tax return only if you are unmarried and pay more than 50% of the costs of keeping up a home for yourself and your dependent(s) or other qualifying individuals. See Pub. 501, Exemptions, Standard Deduction, and Filing Information, for information.

Tax credits. You can take projected tax credits into account in figuring your allowable number of withholding allowances. Credits for child or dependent care expenses and the child tax credit may be claimed using the **Personal Allowances Worksheet** below. See Pub. 505 for information on converting your other credits into withholding allowances.

Nonwage income. If you have a large amount of nonwage income, such as interest or dividends, consider making estimated tax payments using Form 1040-ES, Estimated Tax for Individuals. Otherwise, you may owe additional tax. If you have pension or annuity income, see Pub. 505 to find out if you should adjust your withholding on Form W-4 or W-4P.

Two earners or multiple jobs. If you have a working spouse or more than one job, figure the total number of allowances you are entitled to claim on all jobs using worksheets from only one Form W-4. Your withholding usually will be most accurate when all allowances are claimed on the Form W-4 for the highest paying job and zero allowances are claimed on the others. See Pub. 505 for details.

Nonresident alien. If you are a nonresident alien, see Notice 1392, Supplemental Form W-4 Instructions for Nonresident Aliens, before completing this form.

Check your withholding. After your Form W-4 takes effect, use Pub. 505 to see how the amount you are having withheld compares to your projected total tax for 2015. See Pub. 505, especially if your earnings exceed $130,000 (Single) or $180,000 (Married).

Future developments. Information about any future developments affecting Form W-4 (such as legislation enacted after we release it) will be posted at *www.irs.gov/w4.*

Personal Allowances Worksheet (Keep for your records.)

A   Enter "1" for **yourself** if no one else can claim you as a dependent . . . . **A** _____

B   Enter "1" if: { • You are single and have only one job; or
                              • You are married, have only one job, and your spouse does not work; or   } . . . **B** _____
                              • Your wages from a second job or your spouse's wages (or the total of both) are $1,500 or less.

C   Enter "1" for your **spouse.** But, you may choose to enter "-0-" if you are married and have either a working spouse or more
          than one job. (Entering "-0-" may help you avoid having too little tax withheld.) . . . . **C** _____

D   Enter number of **dependents** (other than your spouse or yourself) you will claim on your tax return . . . . **D** _____

E   Enter "1" if you will file as **head of household** on your tax return (see conditions under **Head of household** above) . . **E** _____

F   Enter "1" if you have at least $2,000 of **child or dependent care expenses** for which you plan to claim a credit . . . **F** _____
          (**Note.** Do **not** include child support payments. See Pub. 503, Child and Dependent Care Expenses, for details.)

G   **Child Tax Credit** (including additional child tax credit). See Pub. 972, Child Tax Credit, for more information.
          • If your total income will be less than $65,000 ($100,000 if married), enter "2" for each eligible child; then **less** "1" if you
          have two to four eligible children or **less** "2" if you have five or more eligible children.
          • If your total income will be between $65,000 and $84,000 ($100,000 and $119,000 if married), enter "1" for each eligible child . . . **G** _____

H   Add lines A through G and enter total here. (**Note.** This may be different from the number of exemptions you claim on your tax return.) ▶ **H** _____

For accuracy, complete all worksheets that apply.	{	• If you plan to **itemize** or **claim adjustments to income** and want to reduce your withholding, see the **Deductions and Adjustments Worksheet** on page 2.
• If you are **single and have more than one job** or are **married and you and your spouse both work** and the combined earnings from all jobs exceed $50,000 ($20,000 if married), see the **Two-Earners/Multiple Jobs Worksheet** on page 2 to avoid having too little tax withheld.
• If **neither** of the above situations applies, **stop here** and enter the number from line H on line 5 of Form W-4 below.

-------------------- **Separate here and give Form W-4 to your employer. Keep the top part for your records.** --------------------

Form **W-4** Department of the Treasury Internal Revenue Service	**Employee's Withholding Allowance Certificate** ▶ **Whether you are entitled to claim a certain number of allowances or exemption from withholding is subject to review by the IRS. Your employer may be required to send a copy of this form to the IRS.**	OMB No. 1545-0074 2015

1 Your first name and middle initial	Last name	**2** Your social security number

Home address (number and street or rural route)	**3** ☐ Single ☐ Married ☐ Married, but withhold at higher Single rate.
	Note. If married, but legally separated, or spouse is a nonresident alien, check the "Single" box.
City or town, state, and ZIP code	**4** If your last name differs from that shown on your social security card, check here. You must call 1-800-772-1213 for a replacement card. ▶ ☐

5   Total number of allowances you are claiming (from line **H** above **or** from the applicable worksheet on page 2)   **5** _____

6   Additional amount, if any, you want withheld from each paycheck . . . . **6** $ _____

7   I claim exemption from withholding for 2015, and I certify that I meet **both** of the following conditions for exemption.
          • Last year I had a right to a refund of **all** federal income tax withheld because I had **no** tax liability, **and**
          • This year I expect a refund of **all** federal income tax withheld because I expect to have **no** tax liability.
          If you meet both conditions, write "Exempt" here . . . . ▶ **7** _____

Under penalties of perjury, I declare that I have examined this certificate and, to the best of my knowledge and belief, it is true, correct, and complete.

Employee's signature
(This form is not valid unless you sign it.) ▶ _____   Date ▶ _____

8 Employer's name and address (Employer: Complete lines 8 and 10 only if sending to the IRS.)	**9** Office code (optional)	**10** Employer identification number (EIN)

For Privacy Act and Paperwork Reduction Act Notice, see page 2.   Cat. No. 10220Q   Form **W-4** (2015)

EMPLOYEE EARNING RECORD

NAME: Hire Date

ADDRESS   Date of Birth

CITY/STATE/ZIP

Position   PT/FT

TELEPHONE   No. of exemptions   M/S

SOCIAL SECURITY

NUMBER   Pay Rate   Hr/Wk/Mo

Period Ended	Reg Pay	OT Pay	Holiday	Comm	Gross Pay	Fed Inc. Tax	Social Sec. Tax	Medicare	SDI	PIT	Ins	401(k)	Total Deduc	Net pay	YTD

EMPLOYEE EARNING RECORD

NAME: Hire Date

ADDRESS   Date of Birth

CITY/STATE/ZIP

Position   PT/FT

TELEPHONE   No. of exemptions   M/S

SOCIAL SECURITY

NUMBER   Pay Rate   Hr/Wk/Mo

Period Ended	Reg Pay	OT Pay	Holiday	Comm	Gross Pay	Fed Inc. Tax	Social Sec. Tax	Medicare	SDI	PIT	Ins	401(k)	Total Deduc	Net pay	YTD

EMPLOYEE EARNING RECORD

NAME: Hire Date

ADDRESS   Date of Birth

CITY/STATE/ZIP

Position   PT/FT

TELEPHONE   No. of exemptions   M/S

SOCIAL SECURITY

NUMBER   Pay Rate   Hr/Wk/Mo

Period Ended	Reg Pay	OT Pay	Holiday	Comm	Gross Pay	Fed Inc. Tax	Social Sec. Tax	Medicare	SDI	PIT	Ins	401(k)	Total Deduc	Net pay	YTD

EMPLOYEE EARNING RECORD

NAME: _____ Hire Date _____

ADDRESS _____ Date of Birth _____

CITY/STATE/ZIP _____

Position _____ PT/FT _____

TELEPHONE _____ No. of exemptions _____ M/S _____

SOCIAL SECURITY

NUMBER _____ Pay Rate _____ Hr/Wk/Mo _____

Period Ended	Reg Pay	OT Pay	Holiday	Comm	Gross Pay	Fed Inc. Tax	Social Sec. Tax	Medicare	SDI	PIT	Ins	401(k)	Total Deduc	Net pay	YTD

EMPLOYEE EARNING RECORD

NAME: _____ Hire Date _____

ADDRESS _____ Date of Birth _____

CITY/STATE/ZIP _____

Position _____ PT/FT _____

TELEPHONE _____ No. of exemptions _____ M/S _____

SOCIAL SECURITY

NUMBER _____ Pay Rate _____ Hr/Wk/Mo _____

Period Ended	Reg Pay	OT Pay	Holiday	Comm	Gross Pay	Fed Inc. Tax	Social Sec. Tax	Medicare	SDI	PIT	Ins	401(k)	Total Deduc	Net pay	YTD

EMPLOYEE EARNING RECORD

NAME: _____ Hire Date _____

ADDRESS _____ Date of Birth _____

CITY/STATE/ZIP _____

Position _____ PT/FT _____

TELEPHONE _____ No. of exemptions _____ M/S _____

SOCIAL SECURITY

NUMBER _____ Pay Rate _____ Hr/Wk/Mo _____

Period Ended	Reg Pay	OT Pay	Holiday	Comm	Gross Pay	Fed Inc. Tax	Social Sec. Tax	Medicare	SDI	PIT	Ins	401(k)	Total Deduc	Net pay	YTD

Account: Cash   **101**

	Date		Description	Post Ref.	Debit	Credit	Balance Debit	Balance Credit	
Beg Bal							1,125,000.00		
1									1
2									2
3									3
4									4
5									5
6									6
7									7
8									8
9									9
10									10
11									11
12									12

Account: Employee Federal Income Tax Payable   **203**

	Date		Description	Post Ref.	Debit	Credit	Balance Debit	Balance Credit	
1									1
2									2
3									3
4									4
5									5
6									6
7									7
8									8
9									9

Account: Social Security Tax Payable   **204**

	Date		Description	Post Ref.	Debit	Credit	Balance Debit	Balance Credit	
1									1
2									2
3									3
4									4
5									5
6									6
7									7
8									8
9									9
10									10
11									11
12									12
13									13
14									14
15									15

Account: Medicare Tax Payable   205

	Date		Description	Post Ref.	Debit	Credit	Balance Debit	Balance Credit	
1									1
2									2
3									3
4									4
5									5
6									6
7									7
8									8
9									9
10									10
11									11
12									12
13									13
14									14
15									15

Account: Employee State Income Tax Payable   206

	Date		Description	Post Ref.	Debit	Credit	Balance Debit	Balance Credit	
1									1
2									2
3									3
4									4
5									5
6									6
7									7
8									8
9									9

Account: 401(k) Contributions Payable   208

	Date		Description	Post Ref.	Debit	Credit	Balance Debit	Balance Credit	
1									1
2									2
3									3
4									4
5									5
6									6
7									7

Account: Employee Medical Premiums Payable   **209**

	Date		Description	Post Ref.	Debit	Credit	Balance Debit	Balance Credit	
1									1
2									2
3									3
4									4
5									5
6									6
7									7

Account: Salaries and Wages Payable   **210**

	Date		Description	Post Ref.	Debit	Credit	Balance Debit	Balance Credit	
1									1
2									2
3									3
4									4
5									5
6									6
7									7

Account: Federal Unemployment Tax Payable   **211**

	Date		Description	Post Ref.	Debit	Credit	Balance Debit	Balance Credit	
1									1
2									2
3									3
4									4
5									5
6									6
7									7

Account: State Unemployment Tax Payable   **212**

	Date		Description	Post Ref.	Debit	Credit	Balance Debit	Balance Credit	
1									1
2									2
3									3
4									4
5									5
6									6
7									7

Account: Payroll Taxes Expense 514

	Date		Description	Post Ref.	Debit	Credit	Balance		
							Debit	Credit	
1									1
2									2
3									3
4									4
5									5
6									6
7									7

Account: Salaries and Wages Expense 515

	Date		Description	Post Ref.	Debit	Credit	Balance		
							Debit	Credit	
1									1
2									2
3									3
4									4
5									5
6									6
7									7

Form **941 for 2015:** **Employer's QUARTERLY Federal Tax Return**
(Rev. January 2015)   Department of the Treasury — Internal Revenue Service

950114

OMB No. 1545-0029

Employer identification number (EIN) ☐☐ – ☐☐☐☐☐☐☐

Name *(not your trade name)* _____

Trade name *(if any)* _____

Address _____
Number   Street   Suite or room number

_____
City   State   ZIP code

_____
Foreign country name   Foreign province/county   Foreign postal code

Report for this Quarter of 2015
(Check one.)

☐ **1:** January, February, March

☐ **2:** April, May, June

☐ **3:** July, August, September

☐ **4:** October, November, December

Instructions and prior year forms are available at *www.irs.gov/form941*.

Read the separate instructions before you complete Form 941. Type or print within the boxes.

Part 1:   Answer these questions for this quarter.

1   Number of employees who received wages, tips, or other compensation for the pay period including: *Mar. 12* (Quarter 1), *June 12* (Quarter 2), *Sept. 12* (Quarter 3), or *Dec. 12* (Quarter 4)   **1** _____

2   Wages, tips, and other compensation   . . . .   **2** _____ ▪

3   Federal income tax withheld from wages, tips, and other compensation   **3** _____ ▪

4   If no wages, tips, and other compensation are subject to social security or Medicare tax   ☐ Check and go to line 6.

	Column 1		Column 2
5a Taxable social security wages . .	_____ ▪	× .124 =	_____ ▪
5b Taxable social security tips . . .	_____ ▪	× .124 =	_____ ▪
5c Taxable Medicare wages & tips. .	_____ ▪	× .029 =	_____ ▪
5d Taxable wages & tips subject to Additional Medicare Tax withholding	_____ ▪	× .009 =	_____ ▪

5e   Add Column 2 from lines 5a, 5b, 5c, and 5d   . . . . .   **5e** _____ ▪

5f   Section 3121(q) Notice and Demand—Tax due on unreported tips (see instructions)   . .   **5f** _____ ▪

6   Total taxes before adjustments. Add lines 3, 5e, and 5f   . . . .   **6** _____ ▪

7   Current quarter's adjustment for fractions of cents   . . . .   **7** _____ ▪

8   Current quarter's adjustment for sick pay   . . . .   **8** _____ ▪

9   Current quarter's adjustments for tips and group-term life insurance   . . . . . .   **9** _____ ▪

10   Total taxes after adjustments. Combine lines 6 through 9   . . . . .   **10** _____ ▪

11   Total deposits for this quarter, including overpayment applied from a prior quarter and overpayments applied from Form 941-X, 941-X (PR), 944-X, 944-X (PR), or 944-X (SP) filed in the current quarter   . . . .   **11** _____ ▪

12   Balance due. If line 10 is more than line 11, enter the difference and see instructions   . . .   **12** _____ ▪

13   Overpayment. If line 11 is more than line 10, enter the difference _____ ▪   Check one: ☐ Apply to next return. ☐ Send a refund.

▶ **You MUST complete both pages of Form 941 and SIGN it.**

For Privacy Act and Paperwork Reduction Act Notice, see the back of the Payment Voucher.   Cat. No. 17001Z   Form **941** (Rev. 1-2015)

Next ▶

950214

Name *(not your trade name)*	Employer identification number (EIN)

Part 2: Tell us about your deposit schedule and tax liability for this quarter.

If you are unsure about whether you are a monthly schedule depositor or a semiweekly schedule depositor, see Pub. 15 (Circular E), section 11.

14 Check one: ☐ Line 10 on this return is less than $2,500 or line 10 on the return for the prior quarter was less than $2,500, and you did not incur a **$100,000 next-day deposit obligation during the current quarter.** If line 10 for the prior quarter was less than $2,500 but line 10 on this return is $100,000 or more, you must provide a record of your federal tax liability. If you are a monthly schedule depositor, complete the deposit schedule below; if you are a semiweekly schedule depositor, attach Schedule B (Form 941). Go to Part 3.

☐ **You were a monthly schedule depositor for the entire quarter.** Enter your tax liability for each month and total liability for the quarter, then go to Part 3.

Tax liability:	Month 1		.	
	Month 2		.	
	Month 3		.	
Total liability for quarter			.	**Total must equal line 10.**

☐ **You were a semiweekly schedule depositor for any part of this quarter.** Complete Schedule B (Form 941), Report of Tax Liability for Semiweekly Schedule Depositors, and attach it to Form 941.

Part 3: Tell us about your business. If a question does NOT apply to your business, leave it blank.

15 If your business has closed or you stopped paying wages . . . . ☐ Check here, and

enter the final date you paid wages [/ /].

16 If you are a seasonal employer and you do not have to file a return for every quarter of the year . . ☐ Check here.

Part 4: May we speak with your third-party designee?

Do you want to allow an employee, a paid tax preparer, or another person to discuss this return with the IRS? See the instructions for details.

☐ Yes. Designee's name and phone number [   ] [   ]

Select a 5-digit Personal Identification Number (PIN) to use when talking to the IRS. ☐ ☐ ☐ ☐ ☐

☐ No.

Part 5: Sign here. You MUST complete both pages of Form 941 and SIGN it.

Under penalties of perjury, I declare that I have examined this return, including accompanying schedules and statements, and to the best of my knowledge and belief, it is true, correct, and complete. Declaration of preparer (other than taxpayer) is based on all information of which preparer has any knowledge.

X **Sign your name here** [   ]

Print your name here [   ]

Print your title here [   ]

Date [/ /]

Best daytime phone [   ]

Paid Preparer Use Only

Check if you are self-employed . . . ☐

Preparer's name		PTIN	
Preparer's signature		Date	/ /
Firm's name (or yours if self-employed)		EIN	
Address		Phone	
City	State	ZIP code	

Form **940 for 2014:**   **Employer's Annual Federal Unemployment (FUTA) Tax Return**   850113

Department of the Treasury — Internal Revenue Service

OMB No. 1545-0028

Employer identification number (EIN) ☐☐ – ☐☐☐☐☐☐☐

Name *(not your trade name)*

Trade name *(if any)*

Address

Number   Street   Suite or room number

City   State   ZIP code

Foreign country name   Foreign province/county   Foreign postal code

Type of Return
(Check all that apply.)

☐ **a.** Amended

☐ **b.** Successor employer

☐ **c.** No payments to employees in 2014

☐ **d.** Final: Business closed or stopped paying wages

Instructions and prior-year forms are available at *www.irs.gov/form940*.

Read the separate instructions before you complete this form. Please type or print within the boxes.

Part 1:   **Tell us about your return. If any line does NOT apply, leave it blank.**

1a	If you had to pay state unemployment tax in one state only, enter the state abbreviation .	1a ☐☐
1b	If you had to pay state unemployment tax in more than one state, you are a multi-state employer	1b ☐ Check here. Complete Schedule A (Form 940).
2	If you paid wages in a state that is subject to CREDIT REDUCTION	2 ☐ Check here. Complete Schedule A (Form 940).

Part 2:   **Determine your FUTA tax before adjustments for 2014. If any line does NOT apply, leave it blank.**

| 3 | Total payments to all employees . . . . | 3 | ⬚ . |
| 4 | Payments exempt from FUTA tax . . . . | 4 | ⬚ . |

Check all that apply: **4a** ☐ Fringe benefits   **4c** ☐ Retirement/Pension   **4e** ☐ Other
                    4b ☐ Group-term life insurance   **4d** ☐ Dependent care

5	Total of payments made to each employee in excess of $7,000	5	⬚ .
6	Subtotal (line 4 + line 5 = line 6)	6	⬚ .
7	Total taxable FUTA wages (line 3 – line 6 = line 7) (see instructions)	7	⬚ .
8	FUTA tax before adjustments (line 7 x .006 = line 8)	8	⬚ .

Part 3:   **Determine your adjustments. If any line does NOT apply, leave it blank.**

9	If ALL of the taxable FUTA wages you paid were excluded from state unemployment tax, multiply line 7 by .054 (line 7 × .054 = line 9). Go to line 12	9	⬚ .
10	If SOME of the taxable FUTA wages you paid were excluded from state unemployment tax, OR you paid ANY state unemployment tax late (after the due date for filing Form 940), complete the worksheet in the instructions. Enter the amount from line 7 of the worksheet . .	10	⬚ .
11	If credit reduction applies, enter the total from Schedule A (Form 940)	11	⬚ .

Part 4:   **Determine your FUTA tax and balance due or overpayment for 2014. If any line does NOT apply, leave it blank.**

12	Total FUTA tax after adjustments (lines 8 + 9 + 10 + 11 = line 12)	12	⬚ .
13	FUTA tax deposited for the year, including any overpayment applied from a prior year .	13	⬚ .
14	Balance due (If line 12 is more than line 13, enter the excess on line 14.) • If line 14 is more than $500, you must deposit your tax. • If line 14 is $500 or less, you may pay with this return. (see instructions)	14	⬚ .
15	Overpayment (If line 13 is more than line 12, enter the excess on line 15 and check a box below.)	15	⬚ .

▶ You **MUST** complete both pages of this form and **SIGN** it.

Check one: ☐ Apply to next return.   ☐ Send a refund.

Next ▶

For Privacy Act and Paperwork Reduction Act Notice, see the back of Form 940-V, Payment Voucher.   Cat. No. 11234O   Form **940** (2014)

850212

Name *(not your trade name)*	Employer identification number (EIN)

Part 5:   Report your FUTA tax liability by quarter only if line 12 is more than $500. If not, go to Part 6.

16   Report the amount of your FUTA tax liability for each quarter; do NOT enter the amount you deposited. If you had no liability for a quarter, leave the line blank.

    16a   1st quarter (January 1 – March 31) . . . .   **16a** [＿＿＿＿＿ . ＿]

    16b   2nd quarter (April 1 – June 30) . . . .   **16b** [＿＿＿＿＿ . ＿]

    16c   3rd quarter (July 1 – September 30) . . . .   **16c** [＿＿＿＿＿ . ＿]

    16d   4th quarter (October 1 – December 31) . . . .   **16d** [＿＿＿＿＿ . ＿]

17   **Total tax liability for the year** (lines 16a + 16b + 16c + 16d = line 17)   **17** [＿＿＿＿＿ . ＿]   **Total must equal line 12.**

Part 6:   May we speak with your third-party designee?

Do you want to allow an employee, a paid tax preparer, or another person to discuss this return with the IRS? See the instructions for details.

☐ **Yes.**   Designee's name and phone number [＿＿＿＿＿＿＿]   [＿＿＿＿＿＿＿]

            Select a 5-digit Personal Identification Number (PIN) to use when talking to IRS   ☐ ☐ ☐ ☐ ☐

☐ **No.**

Part 7:   Sign here. You MUST complete both pages of this form and SIGN it.

Under penalties of perjury, I declare that I have examined this return, including accompanying schedules and statements, and to the best of my knowledge and belief, it is true, correct, and complete, and that no part of any payment made to a state unemployment fund claimed as a credit was, or is to be, deducted from the payments made to employees. Declaration of preparer (other than taxpayer) is based on all information of which preparer has any knowledge.

✗ **Sign your name here** [＿＿＿＿＿＿＿]   Print your name here [＿＿＿＿＿＿＿]

                                 Print your title here [＿＿＿＿＿＿＿]

    Date [＿ / ＿ / ＿]   Best daytime phone [＿＿＿＿＿＿＿]

Paid Preparer Use Only   Check if you are self-employed . ☐

Preparer's name	[＿＿＿＿＿＿＿]	PTIN	[＿＿＿＿＿＿＿]
Preparer's signature	[＿＿＿＿＿＿＿]	Date	[＿ / ＿ / ＿]
Firm's name (or yours if self-employed)	[＿＿＿＿＿＿＿]	EIN	[＿＿＿＿＿＿＿]
Address	[＿＿＿＿＿＿＿]	Phone	[＿＿＿＿＿＿＿]
City	[＿＿＿＿＿] State [＿＿]	ZIP code	[＿＿＿＿＿＿＿]

Clear form

94182

9998

This form is ONLY for use by
MINERAL PRODUCERS.
Employers must file the annual
reconciliation electronically.

Name and address

Utah State Tax Commission
**Utah Annual Mineral Production
Withholding Reconciliation**

TC-941R

Rev. 7/15

☐ Check here to close
your account.

Utah Account ID

Federal EIN

Tax Period (yyyy)

Due Date (mmddyyyy)

☐ Check if AMENDED
(replacement, not net difference)

1. Total number of TC-675Rs issued   • 1 _____

2. Total Utah distributions reported on TC-675Rs   • 2 _____ . ___

3. Tax Commission use only   • 3 _____ . ___

4. Total Utah income tax withheld on TC-675Rs   • 4 _____ . ___

5. Utah tax withheld as reported on TC-941 return(s)

    Jan - Mar   • 5a _____ . ___   Jul - Sep   • 5c _____ . ___

    Apr - Jun   • 5b _____ . ___   Oct - Dec   • 5d _____ . ___

6. Add lines 5a through 5d and enter the total here   6 _____ . ___

7. Subtract line 6 from line 4 and enter amount here (see instructions)   7 _____ . ___

File online at taxexpress.utah.gov.

Under penalties provided by law, I declare to the best of my knowledge this return is true and correct.

Signature   Date   Phone
X _____   _____   _____

• _____
    USTC use only

• USTC use only (box no.)

Return ENTIRE form, coupon and payment to the Utah State Tax Commission

- -

Payment Coupon for Mineral Production Withholding Reconciliation, TC-941RPC

TC-941RPC Rev. 6/15

Tax Type **Withholding**	Utah Account ID	Payment Period Ending (mmddyyyy)	Payment Due Date (mmddyyyy)

**W
T
R**

Account name: _____

Amount Paid

Do not send cash. Do not staple check
to this coupon. Detach any check stub.

UTAH STATE TAX COMMISSION
210 N 1950 W
SLC UT 84134-0600
IIıIıIıIııIıIıIıIıIııIıIIıııIıIıIııIııIııII

DWS-UIC
Form 33H
REV 1213

Utah Employer Quarterly Wage List and Contribution Report
Utah Department of Workforce Services, Unemployment Insurance
140 E. 300 S., PO Box 45233, Salt Lake City UT 84145-0233
1-801-526-9235 option 5; 1-800-222-2857 option 5

The preferred method of filing this report is on-line at our website:

http://jobs.utah.gov

<u>Instructions on Back</u>

EMPLOYER NAME & ADDRESS:

Registration #: _____
FEIN: _____

■ FEIN change:_____

A report must be filed even if no wages are paid for the quarter. See Instructions

Yr/Quarter: _____
Qtr End Date: _____
Due Date: _____

Number of Employees this quarter:

1st Month	2nd Month	3rd Month

Type or machine print preferred.

Employee Social Security Number	Employee Name First	Middle Initial	Last	Total Wages Paid to Employee for this Qtr

The Taxable Wage Base for each employee is $ _____

Grand Total Wages (All Pages)	

■ ☐ Close account, last payroll date:_____

Please Select Reason   ☐ Out of Business
☐ New Owner

Wages in Excess (See Instruction 9)	
Subject Wages	

■ ☐ Change name, address, or phone: ☐ New Owner

Please Select Reason   ☐ Current Owner

Contribution Rate   X _____

Please enter phone number if missing or incorrect.

Name:_____
Address:_____

Contribution Due

Interest (1% per month)

Late Penalty ($25.00 min)

Total Payment Due

Current Phone
_____

Phone:_____

(Make check payable to Utah Unemployment Compensation Fund)

(___) ___ - ___

_____
Name   Title   Date   Contact Phone Number

I certify the information on this report is true and correct to the best of my knowledge.

_____
Signature

94181

9998

Name and address

Utah State Tax Commission	**TC-941**
Utah Withholding Return	Rev. 7/15

☐ Check here to stop receiving paper forms.

☐ Check here to close your account.

Utah Account ID

Federal EIN

Tax Period (mmddyyyy)

From   To

Due Date (mmddyyyy)

☐ Check if AMENDED
(replacement, not net difference)

1. Utah wages, compensation and distributions for this period   • 1 _____ . ____

2. Federal income tax withheld this period for Utah employees   • 2 _____ . ____

3. Utah tax withheld this period   • 3 _____ . ____

➜ Pay online at **taxexpress.utah.gov**, or use the payment coupon (form TC-941PC), available at **tax.utah.gov/forms**.

Under penalties provided by law, I declare to the best of my knowledge this return is true and correct.

Signature   Date   Phone
X _____   _____   _____

≡TaxExpress
taxexpress.utah.gov

You can save money!
See the instructions and learn about **taxexpress.utah.gov**.

• _____
USTC use only

Special Classes of Federal Tax Withholding

Special Classes of Employment and Special Types of Payments	Treatment Under Employment Taxes		
	Income Tax Withholding	Social Security and Medicare (including Additional Medicare Tax when wages are paid in excess of $200,000)	FUTA
Aliens, nonresident.	See Publication 515, Withholding of Tax on Nonresident Aliens and Foreign Entities, and Publication 519, U.S. Tax Guide for Aliens.		
Aliens, resident:			
1. Service performed in the United States.	Same as U.S. citizen.	Same as U.S. citizen. (Exempt if any part of service as crew member of foreign vessel or aircraft is performed outside United States.)	Same as U.S. citizen.
2. Service performed outside United States.	Withhold	Taxable if (1) working for an American employer or (2) an American employer by agreement covers U.S. citizens and residents employed by its foreign affiliates.	Exempt unless on or in connection with an American vessel or aircraft and either performed under contract made in United States, or alien is employed on such vessel or aircraft when it touches U.S. port.
Cafeteria plan benefits under section 125.	If employee chooses cash, subject to all employment taxes. If employee chooses another benefit, the treatment is the same as if the benefit was provided outside the plan. See Publication 15-B for more information.		
Deceased worker:			
1. Wages paid to beneficiary or estate in same calendar year as worker's death. See the Instructions for Forms W-2 and W-3 for details.	Exempt	Taxable	Taxable
2. Wages paid to beneficiary or estate after calendar year of worker's death.	Exempt	Exempt	Exempt

(continued)

(continued)

Special Classes of Employment and Special Types of Payments	Treatment Under Employment Taxes		
	Income Tax Withholding	Social Security and Medicare (including Additional Medicare Tax when wages are paid in excess of $200,000)	FUTA
Dependent care assistance programs.	Exempt to the extent it is reasonable to believe amounts are excludable from gross income under section 129.		
Disabled worker's wages paid after year in which worker became entitled to disability insurance benefits under the Social Security Act.	Withhold	Exempt, if worker did not perform any service for employer during period for which payment is made.	Taxable
Employee business expense reimbursement:			
1. Accountable plan. a. Amounts not exceeding specified government rate for per diem or standard mileage.	Exempt	Exempt	Exempt
b. Amounts in excess of specified government rate for per diem or standard mileage.	Withhold	Taxable	Taxable
2. Nonaccountable plan. See section 5 of IRS Publication 15 for details.	Withhold	Taxable	Taxable
Family employees:			
1. Child employed by parent (or partnership in which each partner is a parent of the child).	Withhold	Exempt until age 18; age 21 for domestic service.	Exempt until age 21.
2. Parent employed by child.	Withhold	Taxable if in course of the son's or daughter's business. For domestic services, see section 3 of IRS Publication 15.	Exempt
3. Spouse employed by spouse. See section 3 of IRS Publication 15 for more information.	Withhold	Taxable if in course of spouse's business.	Exempt
Fishing and related activities.	See Publication 334, Tax Guide for Small Business.		
Foreign governments and international organizations.	Exempt	Exempt	Exempt
Foreign service by U.S. citizens:			
1. As U.S. government employees.	Withhold	Same as within United States.	Exempt
2. For foreign affiliates of American employers and other private employers.	Exempt if at time of payment (1) it is reasonable to believe employee is entitled to exclusion from income under	Exempt unless (1) an American employer by agreement covers U.S. citizens employed by its foreign affiliates or (2) U.S. citizen works for American employer.	Exempt unless (1) on American vessel or aircraft and work is performed under contract made in United States or worker is employed on vessel when it touches U.S. port

Special Classes of Employment and Special Types of Payments	Treatment Under Employment Taxes		
	Income Tax Withholding	Social Security and Medicare (including Additional Medicare Tax when wages are paid in excess of $200,000)	FUTA
	section 911 or (2) the employer is required by law of the foreign country to withhold income tax on such payment.		or (2) U.S. citizen works for American employer (except in a contiguous country with which the United States has an agreement for unemployment compensation) or in the U.S. Virgin Islands.
Fringe benefits.	Taxable on excess of fair market value of the benefit over the sum of an amount paid for it by the employee and any amount excludable by law. However, special valuation rules may apply. Benefits provided under cafeteria plans may qualify for exclusion from wages for Social Security, Medicare, and FUTA taxes. See Publication 15-B for details.		
Government employment: State/local governments and political subdivisions, employees of:			
1. Salaries and wages (includes payments to most elected and appointed officials).	Withhold	Generally, taxable for (1) services performed by employees who are either (a) covered under a section 218 agreement or (b) not covered under a section 218 agreement and not a member of a public retirement system (mandatory Social Security and Medicare coverage), and (2) (for Medicare tax only) for services performed by employees hired or rehired after 3/31/86 who are not covered under a section 218 agreement or the mandatory Social Security provisions, unless specifically excluded by law. See Publication 963.	Exempt
2. Election workers. Election individuals are workers who are employed to perform services for state or local governments at election booths in connection with national, state, or local elections. **Note.** File Form W-2 for payments of $600 or more even if no Social Security or Medicare taxes were withheld.	Exempt	Taxable if paid $1,600 or more in 2015 (lesser amount if specified by a section 218 Social Security agreement). See Revenue Ruling 2000–6.	Exempt
3. Emergency workers. Emergency workers who were hired on a temporary basis in response to a specific unforeseen emergency and are not intended to become permanent employees.	Withhold	Exempt if serving on a temporary basis in case of fire, storm, snow, earthquake, flood, or similar emergency.	Exempt

(continued)

(continued)

Special Classes of Employment and Special Types of Payments	Treatment Under Employment Taxes		
	Income Tax Withholding	Social Security and Medicare (including Additional Medicare Tax when wages are paid in excess of $200,000)	FUTA
U.S. federal government employees.	Withhold	Taxable for Medicare. Taxable for Social Security unless hired before 1984. See Section 3121(b)(5).	Exempt
Homeworkers (industrial, cottage industry):			
1. Common law employees.	Withhold	Taxable	Taxable
2. Statutory employees. See section 2 of IRS Publication 15 for details.	Exempt	Taxable if paid $100 or more in cash in a year.	Exempt
Hospital employees:			
1. Interns.	Withhold	Taxable	Exempt
2. Patients.	Withhold	Taxable (exempt for state or local government hospitals).	Exempt
Household employees:			
1. Domestic service in private homes. Farmers, see Publication 51 (Circular A).	Exempt (withhold if both employer and employee agree).	Taxable if paid $1,900 or more in cash in 2015. Exempt if performed by an individual younger than age 18 during any portion of the calendar year and is not the principal occupation of the employee.	Taxable if employer paid total cash wages of $1,000 or more in any quarter in the current or preceding calendar year.
2. Domestic service in college clubs, fraternities, and sororities.	Exempt (withhold if both employer and employee agree).	Exempt if paid to regular student; also exempt if employee is paid less than $100 in a year by an income-tax-exempt employer.	Taxable if employer paid total cash wages of $1,000 or more in any quarter in the current or preceding calendar year.
Insurance for employees:			
1. Accident and health insurance premiums under a plan or system for employees and their dependents generally or for a class or classes of employees and their dependents.	Exempt (except 2% shareholder-employees of S corporations).	Exempt	Exempt
2. Group-term life insurance costs. See Publication 15-B for details.	Exempt	Exempt, except for the cost of group-term life insurance includible in the employee's gross income. Special rules apply for former employees.	Exempt
Insurance agents or solicitors:			
1. Full-time life insurance salesperson.	Withhold only if employee under common law. See section 2 of IRS Publication 15.	Taxable	Taxable if (1) employee under common law and (2) not paid solely by commissions.
2. Other salesperson of life, casualty, and so on, insurance.	Withhold only if employee under common law.	Taxable only if employee under common law.	Taxable if (1) employee under common law and (2) not paid solely by commissions.

Special Classes of Employment and Special Types of Payments	Treatment Under Employment Taxes		
	Income Tax Withholding	Social Security and Medicare (including Additional Medicare Tax when wages are paid in excess of $200,000)	FUTA
Interest on loans with below-market interest rates (foregone interest and deemed original issue discount).	See Publication 15-A.		
Leave-sharing plans: Amounts paid to an employee under a leave-sharing plan.	Withhold	Taxable	Taxable
Newspaper carriers and vendors: Newspaper carriers younger than age 18; newspaper and magazine vendors buying at fixed prices and retaining receipts from sales to customers. See Publication 15-A for information on statutory nonemployee status.	Exempt (withhold if both employer and employee voluntarily agree).	Exempt	Exempt
Noncash payments:			
1. For household work, agricultural labor, and service not in the course of the employer's trade or business.	Exempt (withhold if both employer and employee voluntarily agree).	Exempt	Exempt
2. To certain retail commission salespersons ordinarily paid solely on a cash commission basis.	Optional with employer, except to the extent employee's supplemental wages during the year exceed $1 million.	Taxable	Taxable
Nonprofit organizations.	See Publication 15-A.		
Officers or shareholders of an S Corporation. Distributions and other payments by an S corporation to a corporate officer or shareholder must be treated as wages to the extent the amounts are reasonable compensation for services to the corporation by an employee. See the Instructions for Form 1120S.	Withhold	Taxable	Taxable
Partners: Payments to general or limited partners of a partnership. See Publication 541, Partnerships, for partner reporting rules.	Exempt	Exempt	Exempt
Railroads: Payments subject to the Railroad Retirement Act. See Publication 915, Social Security, and Equivalent Railroad Retirement Benefits, for more details.	Withhold	Exempt	Exempt

(continued)

(continued)

Special Classes of Employment and Special Types of Payments	Treatment Under Employment Taxes		
	Income Tax Withholding	Social Security and Medicare (including Additional Medicare Tax when wages are paid in excess of $200,000)	FUTA
Religious exemptions.	See Publication 15-A and Publication 517, Social Security and Other Information for Members of the Clergy and Religious Workers.		
Retirement and pension plans:			
1. Employer contributions to a qualified plan.	Exempt	Exempt	Exempt
2. Elective employee contributions and deferrals to a plan containing a qualified cash or deferred compensation arrangement (for example, 401(k)).	Generally exempt, but see section 402(g) for limitation.	Taxable	Taxable
3. Employer contributions to individual retirement accounts under simplified employee pension plan (SEP).	Generally exempt, but see section 402(g) for salary reduction SEP limitation.	Exempt, except for amounts contributed under a salary reduction SEP agreement.	
4. Employer contributions to section 403(b) annuities.	Generally exempt, but see section 402(g) for limitation.	Taxable if paid through a salary reduction agreement (written or otherwise).	
5. Employee salary reduction contributions to a SIMPLE retirement account.	Exempt	Taxable	Taxable
6. Distributions from qualified retirement and pension plans and section 403(b) annuities. See Publication 15-A for information on pensions, annuities, and employer contributions to nonqualified deferred compensation arrangements.	Withhold, but recipient may elect exemption on Form W-4P in certain cases; mandatory 20% withholding applies to an eligible rollover distribution that is not a direct rollover; exempt for direct rollover. See Publication 15-A.	Exempt	Exempt
7. Employer contributions to a section 457(b) plan.	Generally exempt but see section 402(g) limitation.	Taxable	Taxable
8. Employee salary reduction contributions to a section 457(b) plan.	Generally exempt but see section 402(g) salary reduction limitation.	Taxable	Taxable
Salespersons:			
1. Common law employees.	Withhold	Taxable	Taxable
2. Statutory employees.	Exempt	Taxable	Taxable, except for full-time life insurance sales agents.
3. Statutory nonemployees (qualified real estate agents, direct sellers, and certain companion sitters). See Publication 15-A for details.	Exempt	Exempt	Exempt

Special Classes of Employment and Special Types of Payments	Treatment Under Employment Taxes		
	Income Tax Withholding	Social Security and Medicare (including Additional Medicare Tax when wages are paid in excess of $200,000)	FUTA
Scholarships and fellowship grants (includible in income under section 117(c)):	Withhold	Taxability depends on the nature of the employment and the status of the organization. See *Students, scholars, trainees, teachers,* and so on.	
Severance or dismissal pay.	Withhold	Taxable	Taxable
Service not in the course of the employer's trade or business (other than on a farm operated for profit or for household employment in private homes).	Withhold only if employee earns $50 or more in cash in a quarter and works on 24 or more different days in that quarter or in the preceding quarter.	Taxable if employee receives $100 or more in cash in a calendar year.	Taxable only if employee earns $50 or more in cash in a quarter and works on 24 or more different days in that quarter or in the preceding quarter.
Sick pay. See Publication 15-A for more information.	Withhold	Exempt after end of 6 calendar months after the calendar month employee last worked for employer.	
Students, scholars, trainees, teachers, etc.: 1. Student enrolled and regularly attending classes, performing services for:			
a. Private school, college, or university.	Withhold	Exempt	Exempt
b. Auxiliary nonprofit organization operated for and controlled by school, college, or university.	Withhold	Exempt unless services are covered by a section 218 (Social Security Act) agreement.	Exempt
c. Public school, college, or university.	Withhold	Exempt unless services are covered by a section 218 (Social Security Act) agreement.	Exempt
2. Full-time student performing service for academic credit, combining instruction with work experience as an integral part of the program.	Withhold	Taxable	Exempt unless program was established for or on behalf of an employer or group of employers.
3. Student nurse performing part-time services for nominal earnings at hospital as incidental part of training.	Withhold	Exempt	Exempt
4. Student employed by organized camps.	Withhold	Taxable	Exempt
5. Student, scholar, trainee, teacher, and so on, as nonimmigrant alien under section 101(a)(15)(F), (J), (M), or (Q) of Immigration and Nationality Act (that is, aliens holding F-1, J-1, M-1, or Q-1 visas).	Withhold unless excepted by regulations.	Exempt if service is performed for purpose specified in section 101(a)(15)(F), (J), (M), or (Q) of Immigration and Nationality Act. However, these taxes may apply if the employee becomes a resident alien.	

(continued)

(continued)

Special Classes of Employment and Special Types of Payments	Treatment Under Employment Taxes		
	Income Tax Withholding	Social Security and Medicare (including Additional Medicare Tax when wages are paid in excess of $200,000)	FUTA
Supplemental unemployment compensation plan benefits.	Withhold	Exempt under certain conditions. See Publication 15-A.	
Tips:			
1. If $20 or more in a month.	Withhold	Taxable	Taxable for all tips reported in writing to employer.
2. If less than $20 in a month. See section 6 of IRS Publication 15 for more information.	Exempt	Exempt	Exempt
Workers' compensation.	Exempt	Exempt	Exempt

Appendix C

Federal Income Tax Tables*

Payroll Period	One Withholding Allowance
Weekly..	$ 76.90
Biweekly	153.80
Semimonthly...	166.70
Monthly	333.30
Quarterly..	1,000.00
Semiannually	2,000.00
Annually..	4,000.00
Daily or miscellaneous (each day of the payroll period)	15.40

*Note: Appendix C is derived from IRS Publication 15. A comment to refer to pages 41 and 43 exists at the section end for wage-bracket tables when the taxable wages exceed the table. These page references are for Publication 15 itself and refers to pages 268 and 269 of this text.

Percentage Method Tables for Income Tax Withholding

(For Wages Paid in 2015)

TABLE 1—WEEKLY Payroll Period

(a) SINGLE person (including head of household)—

If the amount of wages (after subtracting withholding allowances) is:

Not over $44 . . . . $0

The amount of income tax to withhold is:

Over—	But not over—		of excess over—
$44	—$222 . .	$0.00 plus 10%	—$44
$222	—$764 . .	$17.80 plus 15%	—$222
$764	—$1,789 . .	$99.10 plus 25%	—$764
$1,789	—$3,685 . .	$355.35 plus 28%	—$1,789
$3,685	—$7,958 . .	$886.23 plus 33%	—$3,685
$7,958	—$7,990 . .	$2,296.32 plus 35%	—$7,958
$7,990	. . . .	$2,307.52 plus 39.6%	—$7,990

(b) MARRIED person—

If the amount of wages (after subtracting withholding allowances) is:

Not over $165 . . . . $0

The amount of income tax to withhold is:

Over—	But not over—		of excess over—
$165	—$520 . .	$0.00 plus 10%	—$165
$520	—$1,606 . .	$35.50 plus 15%	—$520
$1,606	—$3,073 . .	$198.40 plus 25%	—$1,606
$3,073	—$4,597 . .	$565.15 plus 28%	—$3,073
$4,597	—$8,079 . .	$991.87 plus 33%	—$4,597
$8,079	—$9,105 . .	$2,140.93 plus 35%	—$8,079
$9,105	. . . .	$2,500.03 plus 39.6%	—$9,105

TABLE 2—BIWEEKLY Payroll Period

(a) SINGLE person (including head of household)—

If the amount of wages (after subtracting withholding allowances) is:

Not over $88 . . . . $0

The amount of income tax to withhold is:

Over—	But not over—		of excess over—
$88	—$443 . .	$0.00 plus 10%	—$88
$443	—$1,529 . .	$35.50 plus 15%	—$443
$1,529	—$3,579 . .	$198.40 plus 25%	—$1,529
$3,579	—$7,369 . .	$710.90 plus 28%	—$3,579
$7,369	—$15,915 . .	$1,772.10 plus 33%	—$7,369
$15,915	—$15,981 . .	$4,592.28 plus 35%	—$15,915
$15,981	. . . .	$4,615.38 plus 39.6%	—$15,981

(b) MARRIED person—

If the amount of wages (after subtracting withholding allowances) is:

Not over $331 . . . . $0

The amount of income tax to withhold is:

Over—	But not over—		of excess over—
$331	—$1,040 . .	$0.00 plus 10%	—$331
$1,040	—$3,212 . .	$70.90 plus 15%	—$1,040
$3,212	—$6,146 . .	$396.70 plus 25%	—$3,212
$6,146	—$9,194 . .	$1,130.20 plus 28%	—$6,146
$9,194	—$16,158 . .	$1,983.64 plus 33%	—$9,194
$16,158	—$18,210 . .	$4,281.76 plus 35%	—$16,158
$18,210	. . . .	$4,999.96 plus 39.6%	—$18,210

TABLE 3—SEMIMONTHLY Payroll Period

(a) SINGLE person (including head of household)—

If the amount of wages (after subtracting withholding allowances) is:

Not over $96 . . . . $0

The amount of income tax to withhold is:

Over—	But not over—		of excess over—
$96	—$480 . .	$0.00 plus 10%	—$96
$480	—$1,656 . .	$38.40 plus 15%	—$480
$1,656	—$3,877 . .	$214.80 plus 25%	—$1,656
$3,877	—$7,983 . .	$770.05 plus 28%	—$3,877
$7,983	—$17,242 . .	$1,919.73 plus 33%	—$7,983
$17,242	—$17,313 . .	$4,975.20 plus 35%	—$17,242
$17,313	. . . .	$5,000.05 plus 39.6%	—$17,313

(b) MARRIED person—

If the amount of wages (after subtracting withholding allowances) is:

Not over $358 . . . . $0

The amount of income tax to withhold is:

Over—	But not over—		of excess over—
$358	—$1,127 . .	$0.00 plus 10%	—$358
$1,127	—$3,479 . .	$76.90 plus 15%	—$1,127
$3,479	—$6,658 . .	$429.70 plus 25%	—$3,479
$6,658	—$9,960 . .	$1,224.45 plus 28%	—$6,658
$9,960	—$17,504 . .	$2,149.01 plus 33%	—$9,960
$17,504	—$19,727 . .	$4,638.53 plus 35%	—$17,504
$19,727	. . . .	$5,416.58 plus 39.6%	—$19,727

TABLE 4—MONTHLY Payroll Period

(a) SINGLE person (including head of household)—

If the amount of wages (after subtracting withholding allowances) is:

Not over $192 . . . . $0

The amount of income tax to withhold is:

Over—	But not over—		of excess over—
$192	—$960 . .	$0.00 plus 10%	—$192
$960	—$3,313 . .	$76.80 plus 15%	—$960
$3,313	—$7,754 . .	$429.75 plus 25%	—$3,313
$7,754	—$15,967 . .	$1,540.00 plus 28%	—$7,754
$15,967	—$34,483 . .	$3,839.64 plus 33%	—$15,967
$34,483	—$34,625 . .	$9,949.92 plus 35%	—$34,483
$34,625	. . . .	$9,999.62 plus 39.6%	—$34,625

(b) MARRIED person—

If the amount of wages (after subtracting withholding allowances) is:

Not over $717 . . . . $0

The amount of income tax to withhold is:

Over—	But not over—		of excess over—
$717	—$2,254 . .	$0.00 plus 10%	—$717
$2,254	—$6,958 . .	$153.70 plus 15%	—$2,254
$6,958	—$13,317 . .	$859.30 plus 25%	—$6,958
$13,317	—$19,921 . .	$2,449.05 plus 28%	—$13,317
$19,921	—$35,008 . .	$4,298.17 plus 33%	—$19,921
$35,008	—$39,454 . .	$9,276.88 plus 35%	—$35,008
$39,454	. . . .	$10,832.98 plus 39.6%	—$39,454

Percentage Method Tables for Income Tax Withholding (continued)

(For Wages Paid in 2015)

TABLE 5—QUARTERLY Payroll Period

(a) SINGLE person (including head of household)—				(b) MARRIED person—			
If the amount of wages (after subtracting withholding allowances) is:		The amount of income tax to withhold is:		If the amount of wages (after subtracting withholding allowances) is:		The amount of income tax to withhold is:	
Not over $575		$0		Not over $2,150		$0	
Over—	But not over—		of excess over—	Over—	But not over—		of excess over—
$575	—$2,881 . .	$0.00 plus 10%	—$575	$2,150	—$6,763 . .	$0.00 plus 10%	—$2,150
$2,881	—$9,938 . .	$230.60 plus 15%	—$2,881	$6,763	—$20,875 . .	$461.30 plus 15%	—$6,763
$9,938	—$23,263 . .	$1,289.15 plus 25%	—$9,938	$20,875	—$39,950 . .	$2,578.10 plus 25%	—$20,875
$23,263	—$47,900 . .	$4,620.40 plus 28%	—$23,263	$39,950	—$59,763 . .	$7,346.85 plus 28%	—$39,950
$47,900	—$103,450 . .	$11,518.76 plus 33%	—$47,900	$59,763	—$105,025 . .	$12,894.49 plus 33%	—$59,763
$103,450	—$103,875 . .	$29,850.26 plus 35%	—$103,450	$105,025	—$118,363 . .	$27,830.95 plus 35%	—$105,025
$103,875	. . . .	$29,999.01 plus 39.6%	—$103,875	$118,363	. . . .	$32,499.25 plus 39.6%	—$118,363

TABLE 6—SEMIANNUAL Payroll Period

(a) SINGLE person (including head of household)—				(b) MARRIED person—			
If the amount of wages (after subtracting withholding allowances) is:		The amount of income tax to withhold is:		If the amount of wages (after subtracting withholding allowances) is:		The amount of income tax to withhold is:	
Not over $1,150		$0		Not over $4,300		$0	
Over—	But not over—		of excess over—	Over—	But not over—		of excess over—
$1,150	—$5,763 . .	$0.00 plus 10%	—$1,150	$4,300	—$13,525 . .	$0.00 plus 10%	—$4,300
$5,763	—$19,875 . .	$461.30 plus 15%	—$5,763	$13,525	—$41,750 . .	$922.50 plus 15%	—$13,525
$19,875	—$46,525 . .	$2,578.10 plus 25%	—$19,875	$41,750	—$79,900 . .	$5,156.25 plus 25%	—$41,750
$46,525	—$95,800 . .	$9,240.60 plus 28%	—$46,525	$79,900	—$119,525 . .	$14,693.75 plus 28%	—$79,900
$95,800	—$206,900 . .	$23,037.60 plus 33%	—$95,800	$119,525	—$210,050 . .	$25,788.75 plus 33%	—$119,525
$206,900	—$207,750 . .	$59,700.60 plus 35%	—$206,900	$210,050	—$236,725 . .	$55,662.00 plus 35%	—$210,050
$207,750	. . . .	$59,998.10 plus 39.6%	—$207,750	$236,725	. . . .	$64,998.25 plus 39.6%	—$236,725

TABLE 7—ANNUAL Payroll Period

(a) SINGLE person (including head of household)—				(b) MARRIED person—			
If the amount of wages (after subtracting withholding allowances) is:		The amount of income tax to withhold is:		If the amount of wages (after subtracting withholding allowances) is:		The amount of income tax to withhold is:	
Not over $2,300		$0		Not over $8,600		$0	
Over—	But not over—		of excess over—	Over—	But not over—		of excess over—
$2,300	—$11,525 . .	$0.00 plus 10%	—$2,300	$8,600	—$27,050 . .	$0.00 plus 10%	—$8,600
$11,525	—$39,750 . .	$922.50 plus 15%	—$11,525	$27,050	—$83,500 . .	$1,845.00 plus 15%	—$27,050
$39,750	—$93,050 . .	$5,156.25 plus 25%	—$39,750	$83,500	—$159,800 . .	$10,312.50 plus 25%	—$83,500
$93,050	—$191,600 . .	$18,481.25 plus 28%	—$93,050	$159,800	—$239,050 . .	$29,387.50 plus 28%	—$159,800
$191,600	—$413,800 . .	$46,075.25 plus 33%	—$191,600	$239,050	—$420,100 . .	$51,577.50 plus 33%	—$239,050
$413,800	—$415,500 . .	$119,401.25 plus 35%	—$413,800	$420,100	—$473,450 . .	$111,324.00 plus 35%	—$420,100
$415,500	. . . .	$119,996.25 plus 39.6%	—$415,500	$473,450	. . . .	$129,996.50 plus 39.6%	—$473,450

TABLE 8—DAILY or MISCELLANEOUS Payroll Period

(a) SINGLE person (including head of household)—				(b) MARRIED person—			
If the amount of wages (after subtracting withholding allowances) divided by the number of days in the payroll period is:		The amount of income tax to withhold per day is:		If the amount of wages (after subtracting withholding allowances) divided by the number of days in the payroll period is:		The amount of income tax to withhold per day is:	
Not over $8.80		$0		Not over $33.10		$0	
Over—	But not over—		of excess over—	Over—	But not over—		of excess over—
$8.80	—$44.30 . .	$0.00 plus 10%	—$8.80	$33.10	—$104.00 . .	$0.00 plus 10%	—$33.10
$44.30	—$152.90 . .	$3.55 plus 15%	—$44.30	$104.00	—$321.20 . .	$7.09 plus 15%	—$104.00
$152.90	—$357.90 . .	$19.84 plus 25%	—$152.90	$321.20	—$614.60 . .	$39.67 plus 25%	—$321.20
$357.90	—$736.90 . .	$71.09 plus 28%	—$357.90	$614.60	—$919.40 . .	$113.02 plus 28%	—$614.60
$736.90	—$1,591.50 . .	$177.21 plus 33%	—$736.90	$919.40	—$1,615.80 . .	$198.36 plus 33%	—$919.40
$1,591.50	—$1,598.10 . .	$459.23 plus 35%	—$1,591.50	$1,615.80	—$1,821.00 . .	$428.17 plus 35%	—$1,615.80
$1,598.10	. . . .	$461.54 plus 39.6%	—$1,598.10	$1,821.00	. . . .	$499.99 plus 39.6%	—$1,821.00

Wage Bracket Method Tables for Income Tax Withholding

SINGLE Persons—**WEEKLY** Payroll Period

(For Wages Paid through December 31, 2015)

And the wages are—		And the number of withholding allowances claimed is—										
At least	But less than	0	1	2	3	4	5	6	7	8	9	10
		The amount of income tax to be withheld is—										
$0	$55	$0	$0	$0	$0	$0	$0	$0	$0	$0	$0	$0
55	60	1	0	0	0	0	0	0	0	0	0	0
60	65	2	0	0	0	0	0	0	0	0	0	0
65	70	2	0	0	0	0	0	0	0	0	0	0
70	75	3	0	0	0	0	0	0	0	0	0	0
75	80	3	0	0	0	0	0	0	0	0	0	0
80	85	4	0	0	0	0	0	0	0	0	0	0
85	90	4	0	0	0	0	0	0	0	0	0	0
90	95	5	0	0	0	0	0	0	0	0	0	0
95	100	5	0	0	0	0	0	0	0	0	0	0
100	105	6	0	0	0	0	0	0	0	0	0	0
105	110	6	0	0	0	0	0	0	0	0	0	0
110	115	7	0	0	0	0	0	0	0	0	0	0
115	120	7	0	0	0	0	0	0	0	0	0	0
120	125	8	0	0	0	0	0	0	0	0	0	0
125	130	8	1	0	0	0	0	0	0	0	0	0
130	135	9	1	0	0	0	0	0	0	0	0	0
135	140	9	2	0	0	0	0	0	0	0	0	0
140	145	10	2	0	0	0	0	0	0	0	0	0
145	150	10	3	0	0	0	0	0	0	0	0	0
150	155	11	3	0	0	0	0	0	0	0	0	0
155	160	11	4	0	0	0	0	0	0	0	0	0
160	165	12	4	0	0	0	0	0	0	0	0	0
165	170	12	5	0	0	0	0	0	0	0	0	0
170	175	13	5	0	0	0	0	0	0	0	0	0
175	180	13	6	0	0	0	0	0	0	0	0	0
180	185	14	6	0	0	0	0	0	0	0	0	0
185	190	14	7	0	0	0	0	0	0	0	0	0
190	195	15	7	0	0	0	0	0	0	0	0	0
195	200	15	8	0	0	0	0	0	0	0	0	0
200	210	16	8	1	0	0	0	0	0	0	0	0
210	220	17	9	2	0	0	0	0	0	0	0	0
220	230	18	10	3	0	0	0	0	0	0	0	0
230	240	20	11	4	0	0	0	0	0	0	0	0
240	250	21	12	5	0	0	0	0	0	0	0	0
250	260	23	13	6	0	0	0	0	0	0	0	0
260	270	24	14	7	0	0	0	0	0	0	0	0
270	280	26	15	8	0	0	0	0	0	0	0	0
280	290	27	16	9	1	0	0	0	0	0	0	0
290	300	29	17	10	2	0	0	0	0	0	0	0
300	310	30	19	11	3	0	0	0	0	0	0	0
310	320	32	20	12	4	0	0	0	0	0	0	0
320	330	33	22	13	5	0	0	0	0	0	0	0
330	340	35	23	14	6	0	0	0	0	0	0	0
340	350	36	25	15	7	0	0	0	0	0	0	0
350	360	38	26	16	8	0	0	0	0	0	0	0
360	370	39	28	17	9	1	0	0	0	0	0	0
370	380	41	29	18	10	2	0	0	0	0	0	0
380	390	42	31	19	11	3	0	0	0	0	0	0
390	400	44	32	21	12	4	0	0	0	0	0	0
400	410	45	34	22	13	5	0	0	0	0	0	0
410	420	47	35	24	14	6	0	0	0	0	0	0
420	430	48	37	25	15	7	0	0	0	0	0	0
430	440	50	38	27	16	8	1	0	0	0	0	0
440	450	51	40	28	17	9	2	0	0	0	0	0
450	460	53	41	30	18	10	3	0	0	0	0	0
460	470	54	43	31	20	11	4	0	0	0	0	0
470	480	56	44	33	21	12	5	0	0	0	0	0
480	490	57	46	34	23	13	6	0	0	0	0	0
490	500	59	47	36	24	14	7	0	0	0	0	0
500	510	60	49	37	26	15	8	0	0	0	0	0
510	520	62	50	39	27	16	9	1	0	0	0	0
520	530	63	52	40	29	17	10	2	0	0	0	0
530	540	65	53	42	30	19	11	3	0	0	0	0
540	550	66	55	43	32	20	12	4	0	0	0	0
550	560	68	56	45	33	22	13	5	0	0	0	0
560	570	69	58	46	35	23	14	6	0	0	0	0
570	580	71	59	48	36	25	15	7	0	0	0	0
580	590	72	61	49	38	26	16	8	0	0	0	0
590	600	74	62	51	39	28	17	9	1	0	0	0

Wage Bracket Method Tables for Income Tax Withholding

SINGLE Persons—WEEKLY Payroll Period

(For Wages Paid through December 31, 2015)

And the wages are–		And the number of withholding allowances claimed is—										
At least	But less than	0	1	2	3	4	5	6	7	8	9	10
		The amount of income tax to be withheld is—										
$600	$610	$75	$64	$52	$41	$29	$18	$10	$2	$0	$0	$0
610	620	77	65	54	42	31	19	11	3	0	0	0
620	630	78	67	55	44	32	21	12	4	0	0	0
630	640	80	68	57	45	34	22	13	5	0	0	0
640	650	81	70	58	47	35	24	14	6	0	0	0
650	660	83	71	60	48	37	25	15	7	0	0	0
660	670	84	73	61	50	38	27	16	8	1	0	0
670	680	86	74	63	51	40	28	17	9	2	0	0
680	690	87	76	64	53	41	30	18	10	3	0	0
690	700	89	77	66	54	43	31	20	11	4	0	0
700	710	90	79	67	56	44	33	21	12	5	0	0
710	720	92	80	69	57	46	34	23	13	6	0	0
720	730	93	82	70	59	47	36	24	14	7	0	0
730	740	95	83	72	60	49	37	26	15	8	0	0
740	750	96	85	73	62	50	39	27	16	9	1	0
750	760	98	86	75	63	52	40	29	17	10	2	0
760	770	99	88	76	65	53	42	30	18	11	3	0
770	780	102	89	78	66	55	43	32	20	12	4	0
780	790	104	91	79	68	56	45	33	21	13	5	0
790	800	107	92	81	69	58	46	35	23	14	6	0
800	810	109	94	82	71	59	48	36	24	15	7	0
810	820	112	95	84	72	61	49	38	26	16	8	0
820	830	114	97	85	74	62	51	39	27	17	9	1
830	840	117	98	87	75	64	52	41	29	18	10	2
840	850	119	100	88	77	65	54	42	30	19	11	3
850	860	122	103	90	78	67	55	44	32	20	12	4
860	870	124	105	91	80	68	57	45	33	22	13	5
870	880	127	108	93	81	70	58	47	35	23	14	6
880	890	129	110	94	83	71	60	48	36	25	15	7
890	900	132	113	96	84	73	61	50	38	26	16	8
900	910	134	115	97	86	74	63	51	39	28	17	9
910	920	137	118	99	87	76	64	53	41	29	18	10
920	930	139	120	101	89	77	66	54	42	31	19	11
930	940	142	123	103	90	79	67	56	44	32	21	12
940	950	144	125	106	92	80	69	57	45	34	22	13
950	960	147	128	108	93	82	70	59	47	35	24	14
960	970	149	130	111	95	83	72	60	48	37	25	15
970	980	152	133	113	96	85	73	62	50	38	27	16
980	990	154	135	116	98	86	75	63	51	40	28	17
990	1,000	157	138	118	99	88	76	65	53	41	30	18
1,000	1,010	159	140	121	102	89	78	66	54	43	31	20
1,010	1,020	162	143	123	104	91	79	68	56	44	33	21
1,020	1,030	164	145	126	107	92	81	69	57	46	34	23
1,030	1,040	167	148	128	109	94	82	71	59	47	36	24
1,040	1,050	169	150	131	112	95	84	72	60	49	37	26
1,050	1,060	172	153	133	114	97	85	74	62	50	39	27
1,060	1,070	174	155	136	117	98	87	75	63	52	40	29
1,070	1,080	177	158	138	119	100	88	77	65	53	42	30
1,080	1,090	179	160	141	122	102	90	78	66	55	43	32
1,090	1,100	182	163	143	124	105	91	80	68	56	45	33
1,100	1,110	184	165	146	127	107	93	81	69	58	46	35
1,110	1,120	187	168	148	129	110	94	83	71	59	48	36
1,120	1,130	189	170	151	132	112	96	84	72	61	49	38
1,130	1,140	192	173	153	134	115	97	86	74	62	51	39
1,140	1,150	194	175	156	137	117	99	87	75	64	52	41
1,150	1,160	197	178	158	139	120	101	89	77	65	54	42
1,160	1,170	199	180	161	142	122	103	90	78	67	55	44
1,170	1,180	202	183	163	144	125	106	92	80	68	57	45
1,180	1,190	204	185	166	147	127	108	93	81	70	58	47
1,190	1,200	207	188	168	149	130	111	95	83	71	60	48
1,200	1,210	209	190	171	152	132	113	96	84	73	61	50
1,210	1,220	212	193	173	154	135	116	98	86	74	63	51
1,220	1,230	214	195	176	157	137	118	99	87	76	64	53
1,230	1,240	217	198	178	159	140	121	101	89	77	66	54
1,240	1,250	219	200	181	162	142	123	104	90	79	67	56

$1,250 and over   Use Table 1(a) for a **SINGLE person** on page 45. Also see the instructions on page 43.

Wage Bracket Method Tables for Income Tax Withholding

MARRIED Persons—WEEKLY Payroll Period

(For Wages Paid through December 31, 2015)

And the wages are–		And the number of withholding allowances claimed is—										
At least	But less than	0	1	2	3	4	5	6	7	8	9	10
		The amount of income tax to be withheld is—										
$ 0	$170	$0	$0	$0	$0	$0	$0	$0	$0	$0	$0	$0
170	175	1	0	0	0	0	0	0	0	0	0	0
175	180	1	0	0	0	0	0	0	0	0	0	0
180	185	2	0	0	0	0	0	0	0	0	0	0
185	190	2	0	0	0	0	0	0	0	0	0	0
190	195	3	0	0	0	0	0	0	0	0	0	0
195	200	3	0	0	0	0	0	0	0	0	0	0
200	210	4	0	0	0	0	0	0	0	0	0	0
210	220	5	0	0	0	0	0	0	0	0	0	0
220	230	6	0	0	0	0	0	0	0	0	0	0
230	240	7	0	0	0	0	0	0	0	0	0	0
240	250	8	0	0	0	0	0	0	0	0	0	0
250	260	9	1	0	0	0	0	0	0	0	0	0
260	270	10	2	0	0	0	0	0	0	0	0	0
270	280	11	3	0	0	0	0	0	0	0	0	0
280	290	12	4	0	0	0	0	0	0	0	0	0
290	300	13	5	0	0	0	0	0	0	0	0	0
300	310	14	6	0	0	0	0	0	0	0	0	0
310	320	15	7	0	0	0	0	0	0	0	0	0
320	330	16	8	1	0	0	0	0	0	0	0	0
330	340	17	9	2	0	0	0	0	0	0	0	0
340	350	18	10	3	0	0	0	0	0	0	0	0
350	360	19	11	4	0	0	0	0	0	0	0	0
360	370	20	12	5	0	0	0	0	0	0	0	0
370	380	21	13	6	0	0	0	0	0	0	0	0
380	390	22	14	7	0	0	0	0	0	0	0	0
390	400	23	15	8	0	0	0	0	0	0	0	0
400	410	24	16	9	1	0	0	0	0	0	0	0
410	420	25	17	10	2	0	0	0	0	0	0	0
420	430	26	18	11	3	0	0	0	0	0	0	0
430	440	27	19	12	4	0	0	0	0	0	0	0
440	450	28	20	13	5	0	0	0	0	0	0	0
450	460	29	21	14	6	0	0	0	0	0	0	0
460	470	30	22	15	7	0	0	0	0	0	0	0
470	480	31	23	16	8	0	0	0	0	0	0	0
480	490	32	24	17	9	1	0	0	0	0	0	0
490	500	33	25	18	10	2	0	0	0	0	0	0
500	510	34	26	19	11	3	0	0	0	0	0	0
510	520	35	27	20	12	4	0	0	0	0	0	0
520	530	36	28	21	13	5	0	0	0	0	0	0
530	540	38	29	22	14	6	0	0	0	0	0	0
540	550	39	30	23	15	7	0	0	0	0	0	0
550	560	41	31	24	16	8	1	0	0	0	0	0
560	570	42	32	25	17	9	2	0	0	0	0	0
570	580	44	33	26	18	10	3	0	0	0	0	0
580	590	45	34	27	19	11	4	0	0	0	0	0
590	600	47	35	28	20	12	5	0	0	0	0	0
600	610	48	37	29	21	13	6	0	0	0	0	0
610	620	50	38	30	22	14	7	0	0	0	0	0
620	630	51	40	31	23	15	8	0	0	0	0	0
630	640	53	41	32	24	16	9	1	0	0	0	0
640	650	54	43	33	25	17	10	2	0	0	0	0
650	660	56	44	34	26	18	11	3	0	0	0	0
660	670	57	46	35	27	19	12	4	0	0	0	0
670	680	59	47	36	28	20	13	5	0	0	0	0
680	690	60	49	37	29	21	14	6	0	0	0	0
690	700	62	50	39	30	22	15	7	0	0	0	0
700	710	63	52	40	31	23	16	8	0	0	0	0
710	720	65	53	42	32	24	17	9	1	0	0	0
720	730	66	55	43	33	25	18	10	2	0	0	0
730	740	68	56	45	34	26	19	11	3	0	0	0
740	750	69	58	46	35	27	20	12	4	0	0	0
750	760	71	59	48	36	28	21	13	5	0	0	0
760	770	72	61	49	38	29	22	14	6	0	0	0
770	780	74	62	51	39	30	23	15	7	0	0	0
780	790	75	64	52	41	31	24	16	8	0	0	0
790	800	77	65	54	42	32	25	17	9	1	0	0

Wage Bracket Method Tables for Income Tax Withholding

MARRIED Persons—WEEKLY Payroll Period

(For Wages Paid through December 31, 2015)

And the wages are–		And the number of withholding allowances claimed is—										
At least	But less than	0	1	2	3	4	5	6	7	8	9	10
		The amount of income tax to be withheld is—										
$800	$810	$78	$67	$55	$44	$33	$26	$18	$10	$2	$0	$0
810	820	80	68	57	45	34	27	19	11	3	0	0
820	830	81	70	58	47	35	28	20	12	4	0	0
830	840	83	71	60	48	37	29	21	13	5	0	0
840	850	84	73	61	50	38	30	22	14	6	0	0
850	860	86	74	63	51	40	31	23	15	7	0	0
860	870	87	76	64	53	41	32	24	16	8	1	0
870	880	89	77	66	54	43	33	25	17	9	2	0
880	890	90	79	67	56	44	34	26	18	10	3	0
890	900	92	80	69	57	46	35	27	19	11	4	0
900	910	93	82	70	59	47	36	28	20	12	5	0
910	920	95	83	72	60	49	37	29	21	13	6	0
920	930	96	85	73	62	50	39	30	22	14	7	0
930	940	98	86	75	63	52	40	31	23	15	8	0
940	950	99	88	76	65	53	42	32	24	16	9	1
950	960	101	89	78	66	55	43	33	25	17	10	2
960	970	102	91	79	68	56	45	34	26	18	11	3
970	980	104	92	81	69	58	46	35	27	19	12	4
980	990	105	94	82	71	59	48	36	28	20	13	5
990	1,000	107	95	84	72	61	49	37	29	21	14	6
1,000	1,010	108	97	85	74	62	51	39	30	22	15	7
1,010	1,020	110	98	87	75	64	52	40	31	23	16	8
1,020	1,030	111	100	88	77	65	54	42	32	24	17	9
1,030	1,040	113	101	90	78	67	55	43	33	25	18	10
1,040	1,050	114	103	91	80	68	57	45	34	26	19	11
1,050	1,060	116	104	93	81	70	58	46	35	27	20	12
1,060	1,070	117	106	94	83	71	60	48	36	28	21	13
1,070	1,080	119	107	96	84	73	61	49	38	29	22	14
1,080	1,090	120	109	97	86	74	63	51	39	30	23	15
1,090	1,100	122	110	99	87	76	64	52	41	31	24	16
1,100	1,110	123	112	100	89	77	66	54	42	32	25	17
1,110	1,120	125	113	102	90	79	67	55	44	33	26	18
1,120	1,130	126	115	103	92	80	69	57	45	34	27	19
1,130	1,140	128	116	105	93	82	70	58	47	35	28	20
1,140	1,150	129	118	106	95	83	72	60	48	37	29	21
1,150	1,160	131	119	108	96	85	73	61	50	38	30	22
1,160	1,170	132	121	109	98	86	75	63	51	40	31	23
1,170	1,180	134	122	111	99	88	76	64	53	41	32	24
1,180	1,190	135	124	112	101	89	78	66	54	43	33	25
1,190	1,200	137	125	114	102	91	79	67	56	44	34	26
1,200	1,210	138	127	115	104	92	81	69	57	46	35	27
1,210	1,220	140	128	117	105	94	82	70	59	47	36	28
1,220	1,230	141	130	118	107	95	84	72	60	49	37	29
1,230	1,240	143	131	120	108	97	85	73	62	50	39	30
1,240	1,250	144	133	121	110	98	87	75	63	52	40	31
1,250	1,260	146	134	123	111	100	88	76	65	53	42	32
1,260	1,270	147	136	124	113	101	90	78	66	55	43	33
1,270	1,280	149	137	126	114	103	91	79	68	56	45	34
1,280	1,290	150	139	127	116	104	93	81	69	58	46	35
1,290	1,300	152	140	129	117	106	94	82	71	59	48	36
1,300	1,310	153	142	130	119	107	96	84	72	61	49	38
1,310	1,320	155	143	132	120	109	97	85	74	62	51	39
1,320	1,330	156	145	133	122	110	99	87	75	64	52	41
1,330	1,340	158	146	135	123	112	100	88	77	65	54	42
1,340	1,350	159	148	136	125	113	102	90	78	67	55	44
1,350	1,360	161	149	138	126	115	103	91	80	68	57	45
1,360	1,370	162	151	139	128	116	105	93	81	70	58	47
1,370	1,380	164	152	141	129	118	106	94	83	71	60	48
1,380	1,390	165	154	142	131	119	108	96	84	73	61	50
1,390	1,400	167	155	144	132	121	109	97	86	74	63	51
1,400	1,410	168	157	145	134	122	111	99	87	76	64	53
1,410	1,420	170	158	147	135	124	112	100	89	77	66	54
1,420	1,430	171	160	148	137	125	114	102	90	79	67	56
1,430	1,440	173	161	150	138	127	115	103	92	80	69	57
1,440	1,450	174	163	151	140	128	117	105	93	82	70	59
1,450	1,460	176	164	153	141	130	118	106	95	83	72	60
1,460	1,470	177	166	154	143	131	120	108	96	85	73	62
1,470	1,480	179	167	156	144	133	121	109	98	86	75	63
1,480	1,490	180	169	157	146	134	123	111	99	88	76	65

| $1,490 and over | | Use Table 1(b) for a **MARRIED person** on page 45. Also see the instructions on page 43. |

Wage Bracket Method Tables for Income Tax Withholding

SINGLE Persons—BIWEEKLY Payroll Period

(For Wages Paid through December 31, 2015)

And the wages are—		And the number of withholding allowances claimed is—										
At least	But less than	0	1	2	3	4	5	6	7	8	9	10
		The amount of income tax to be withheld is—										
$ 0	$105	$0	$0	$0	$0	$0	$0	$0	$0	$0	$0	$0
105	110	2	0	0	0	0	0	0	0	0	0	0
110	115	2	0	0	0	0	0	0	0	0	0	0
115	120	3	0	0	0	0	0	0	0	0	0	0
120	125	3	0	0	0	0	0	0	0	0	0	0
125	130	4	0	0	0	0	0	0	0	0	0	0
130	135	4	0	0	0	0	0	0	0	0	0	0
135	140	5	0	0	0	0	0	0	0	0	0	0
140	145	5	0	0	0	0	0	0	0	0	0	0
145	150	6	0	0	0	0	0	0	0	0	0	0
150	155	6	0	0	0	0	0	0	0	0	0	0
155	160	7	0	0	0	0	0	0	0	0	0	0
160	165	7	0	0	0	0	0	0	0	0	0	0
165	170	8	0	0	0	0	0	0	0	0	0	0
170	175	8	0	0	0	0	0	0	0	0	0	0
175	180	9	0	0	0	0	0	0	0	0	0	0
180	185	9	0	0	0	0	0	0	0	0	0	0
185	190	10	0	0	0	0	0	0	0	0	0	0
190	195	10	0	0	0	0	0	0	0	0	0	0
195	200	11	0	0	0	0	0	0	0	0	0	0
200	205	11	0	0	0	0	0	0	0	0	0	0
205	210	12	0	0	0	0	0	0	0	0	0	0
210	215	12	0	0	0	0	0	0	0	0	0	0
215	220	13	0	0	0	0	0	0	0	0	0	0
220	225	13	0	0	0	0	0	0	0	0	0	0
225	230	14	0	0	0	0	0	0	0	0	0	0
230	235	14	0	0	0	0	0	0	0	0	0	0
235	240	15	0	0	0	0	0	0	0	0	0	0
240	245	15	0	0	0	0	0	0	0	0	0	0
245	250	16	1	0	0	0	0	0	0	0	0	0
250	260	17	1	0	0	0	0	0	0	0	0	0
260	270	18	2	0	0	0	0	0	0	0	0	0
270	280	19	3	0	0	0	0	0	0	0	0	0
280	290	20	4	0	0	0	0	0	0	0	0	0
290	300	21	5	0	0	0	0	0	0	0	0	0
300	310	22	6	0	0	0	0	0	0	0	0	0
310	320	23	7	0	0	0	0	0	0	0	0	0
320	330	24	8	0	0	0	0	0	0	0	0	0
330	340	25	9	0	0	0	0	0	0	0	0	0
340	350	26	10	0	0	0	0	0	0	0	0	0
350	360	27	11	0	0	0	0	0	0	0	0	0
360	370	28	12	0	0	0	0	0	0	0	0	0
370	380	29	13	0	0	0	0	0	0	0	0	0
380	390	30	14	0	0	0	0	0	0	0	0	0
390	400	31	15	0	0	0	0	0	0	0	0	0
400	410	32	16	1	0	0	0	0	0	0	0	0
410	420	33	17	2	0	0	0	0	0	0	0	0
420	430	34	18	3	0	0	0	0	0	0	0	0
430	440	35	19	4	0	0	0	0	0	0	0	0
440	450	36	20	5	0	0	0	0	0	0	0	0
450	460	37	21	6	0	0	0	0	0	0	0	0
460	470	39	22	7	0	0	0	0	0	0	0	0
470	480	40	23	8	0	0	0	0	0	0	0	0
480	490	42	24	9	0	0	0	0	0	0	0	0
490	500	43	25	10	0	0	0	0	0	0	0	0
500	520	45	27	11	0	0	0	0	0	0	0	0
520	540	48	29	13	0	0	0	0	0	0	0	0
540	560	51	31	15	0	0	0	0	0	0	0	0
560	580	54	33	17	2	0	0	0	0	0	0	0
580	600	57	35	19	4	0	0	0	0	0	0	0
600	620	60	37	21	6	0	0	0	0	0	0	0
620	640	63	40	23	8	0	0	0	0	0	0	0
640	660	66	43	25	10	0	0	0	0	0	0	0
660	680	69	46	27	12	0	0	0	0	0	0	0
680	700	72	49	29	14	0	0	0	0	0	0	0
700	720	75	52	31	16	1	0	0	0	0	0	0
720	740	78	55	33	18	3	0	0	0	0	0	0
740	760	81	58	35	20	5	0	0	0	0	0	0
760	780	84	61	38	22	7	0	0	0	0	0	0
780	800	87	64	41	24	9	0	0	0	0	0	0

Wage Bracket Method Tables for Income Tax Withholding

SINGLE Persons—BIWEEKLY Payroll Period

(For Wages Paid through December 31, 2015)

And the wages are—		And the number of withholding allowances claimed is—										
At least	But less than	0	1	2	3	4	5	6	7	8	9	10
		The amount of income tax to be withheld is—										
$800	$820	$90	$67	$44	$26	$11	$0	$0	$0	$0	$0	$0
820	840	93	70	47	28	13	0	0	0	0	0	0
840	860	96	73	50	30	15	0	0	0	0	0	0
860	880	99	76	53	32	17	1	0	0	0	0	0
880	900	102	79	56	34	19	3	0	0	0	0	0
900	920	105	82	59	36	21	5	0	0	0	0	0
920	940	108	85	62	39	23	7	0	0	0	0	0
940	960	111	88	65	42	25	9	0	0	0	0	0
960	980	114	91	68	45	27	11	0	0	0	0	0
980	1,000	117	94	71	48	29	13	0	0	0	0	0
1,000	1,020	120	97	74	51	31	15	0	0	0	0	0
1,020	1,040	123	100	77	54	33	17	2	0	0	0	0
1,040	1,060	126	103	80	57	35	19	4	0	0	0	0
1,060	1,080	129	106	83	60	37	21	6	0	0	0	0
1,080	1,100	132	109	86	63	40	23	8	0	0	0	0
1,100	1,120	135	112	89	66	43	25	10	0	0	0	0
1,120	1,140	138	115	92	69	46	27	12	0	0	0	0
1,140	1,160	141	118	95	72	49	29	14	0	0	0	0
1,160	1,180	144	121	98	75	52	31	16	0	0	0	0
1,180	1,200	147	124	101	78	55	33	18	2	0	0	0
1,200	1,220	150	127	104	81	58	35	20	4	0	0	0
1,220	1,240	153	130	107	84	61	38	22	6	0	0	0
1,240	1,260	156	133	110	87	64	41	24	8	0	0	0
1,260	1,280	159	136	113	90	67	44	26	10	0	0	0
1,280	1,300	162	139	116	93	70	47	28	12	0	0	0
1,300	1,320	165	142	119	96	73	50	30	14	0	0	0
1,320	1,340	168	145	122	99	76	53	32	16	1	0	0
1,340	1,360	171	148	125	102	79	56	34	18	3	0	0
1,360	1,380	174	151	128	105	82	59	36	20	5	0	0
1,380	1,400	177	154	131	108	85	62	39	22	7	0	0
1,400	1,420	180	157	134	111	88	65	42	24	9	0	0
1,420	1,440	183	160	137	114	91	68	45	26	11	0	0
1,440	1,460	186	163	140	117	94	71	48	28	13	0	0
1,460	1,480	189	166	143	120	97	74	51	30	15	0	0
1,480	1,500	192	169	146	123	100	77	54	32	17	2	0
1,500	1,520	195	172	149	126	103	80	57	34	19	4	0
1,520	1,540	199	175	152	129	106	83	60	37	21	6	0
1,540	1,560	204	178	155	132	109	86	63	40	23	8	0
1,560	1,580	209	181	158	135	112	89	66	43	25	10	0
1,580	1,600	214	184	161	138	115	92	69	46	27	12	0
1,600	1,620	219	187	164	141	118	95	72	49	29	14	0
1,620	1,640	224	190	167	144	121	98	75	52	31	16	0
1,640	1,660	229	193	170	147	124	101	78	55	33	18	2
1,660	1,680	234	196	173	150	127	104	81	58	35	20	4
1,680	1,700	239	200	176	153	130	107	84	61	38	22	6
1,700	1,720	244	205	179	156	133	110	87	64	41	24	8
1,720	1,740	249	210	182	159	136	113	90	67	44	26	10
1,740	1,760	254	215	185	162	139	116	93	70	47	28	12
1,760	1,780	259	220	188	165	142	119	96	73	50	30	14
1,780	1,800	264	225	191	168	145	122	99	76	53	32	16
1,800	1,820	269	230	194	171	148	125	102	79	56	34	18
1,820	1,840	274	235	197	174	151	128	105	82	59	36	20
1,840	1,860	279	240	202	177	154	131	108	85	62	39	22
1,860	1,880	284	245	207	180	157	134	111	88	65	42	24
1,880	1,900	289	250	212	183	160	137	114	91	68	45	26
1,900	1,920	294	255	217	186	163	140	117	94	71	48	28
1,920	1,940	299	260	222	189	166	143	120	97	74	51	30
1,940	1,960	304	265	227	192	169	146	123	100	77	54	32
1,960	1,980	309	270	232	195	172	149	126	103	80	57	34
1,980	2,000	314	275	237	198	175	152	129	106	83	60	37
2,000	2,020	319	280	242	203	178	155	132	109	86	63	40
2,020	2,040	324	285	247	208	181	158	135	112	89	66	43
2,040	2,060	329	290	252	213	184	161	138	115	92	69	46
2,060	2,080	334	295	257	218	187	164	141	118	95	72	49
2,080	2,100	339	300	262	223	190	167	144	121	98	75	52

$2,100 and over		Use Table 2(a) for a **SINGLE person** on page 45. Also see the instructions on page 43.

Wage Bracket Method Tables for Income Tax Withholding

MARRIED Persons—BIWEEKLY Payroll Period

(For Wages Paid through December 31, 2015)

And the wages are–		And the number of withholding allowances claimed is—										
At least	But less than	0	1	2	3	4	5	6	7	8	9	10
		The amount of income tax to be withheld is—										
$ 0	$340	$0	$0	$0	$0	$0	$0	$0	$0	$0	$0	$0
340	350	1	0	0	0	0	0	0	0	0	0	0
350	360	2	0	0	0	0	0	0	0	0	0	0
360	370	3	0	0	0	0	0	0	0	0	0	0
370	380	4	0	0	0	0	0	0	0	0	0	0
380	390	5	0	0	0	0	0	0	0	0	0	0
390	400	6	0	0	0	0	0	0	0	0	0	0
400	410	7	0	0	0	0	0	0	0	0	0	0
410	420	8	0	0	0	0	0	0	0	0	0	0
420	430	9	0	0	0	0	0	0	0	0	0	0
430	440	10	0	0	0	0	0	0	0	0	0	0
440	450	11	0	0	0	0	0	0	0	0	0	0
450	460	12	0	0	0	0	0	0	0	0	0	0
460	470	13	0	0	0	0	0	0	0	0	0	0
470	480	14	0	0	0	0	0	0	0	0	0	0
480	490	15	0	0	0	0	0	0	0	0	0	0
490	500	16	1	0	0	0	0	0	0	0	0	0
500	520	18	3	0	0	0	0	0	0	0	0	0
520	540	20	5	0	0	0	0	0	0	0	0	0
540	560	22	7	0	0	0	0	0	0	0	0	0
560	580	24	9	0	0	0	0	0	0	0	0	0
580	600	26	11	0	0	0	0	0	0	0	0	0
600	620	28	13	0	0	0	0	0	0	0	0	0
620	640	30	15	0	0	0	0	0	0	0	0	0
640	660	32	17	1	0	0	0	0	0	0	0	0
660	680	34	19	3	0	0	0	0	0	0	0	0
680	700	36	21	5	0	0	0	0	0	0	0	0
700	720	38	23	7	0	0	0	0	0	0	0	0
720	740	40	25	9	0	0	0	0	0	0	0	0
740	760	42	27	11	0	0	0	0	0	0	0	0
760	780	44	29	13	0	0	0	0	0	0	0	0
780	800	46	31	15	0	0	0	0	0	0	0	0
800	820	48	33	17	2	0	0	0	0	0	0	0
820	840	50	35	19	4	0	0	0	0	0	0	0
840	860	52	37	21	6	0	0	0	0	0	0	0
860	880	54	39	23	8	0	0	0	0	0	0	0
880	900	56	41	25	10	0	0	0	0	0	0	0
900	920	58	43	27	12	0	0	0	0	0	0	0
920	940	60	45	29	14	0	0	0	0	0	0	0
940	960	62	47	31	16	0	0	0	0	0	0	0
960	980	64	49	33	18	2	0	0	0	0	0	0
980	1,000	66	51	35	20	4	0	0	0	0	0	0
1,000	1,020	68	53	37	22	6	0	0	0	0	0	0
1,020	1,040	70	55	39	24	8	0	0	0	0	0	0
1,040	1,060	72	57	41	26	10	0	0	0	0	0	0
1,060	1,080	75	59	43	28	12	0	0	0	0	0	0
1,080	1,100	78	61	45	30	14	0	0	0	0	0	0
1,100	1,120	81	63	47	32	16	1	0	0	0	0	0
1,120	1,140	84	65	49	34	18	3	0	0	0	0	0
1,140	1,160	87	67	51	36	20	5	0	0	0	0	0
1,160	1,180	90	69	53	38	22	7	0	0	0	0	0
1,180	1,200	93	71	55	40	24	9	0	0	0	0	0
1,200	1,220	96	73	57	42	26	11	0	0	0	0	0
1,220	1,240	99	76	59	44	28	13	0	0	0	0	0
1,240	1,260	102	79	61	46	30	15	0	0	0	0	0
1,260	1,280	105	82	63	48	32	17	2	0	0	0	0
1,280	1,300	108	85	65	50	34	19	4	0	0	0	0
1,300	1,320	111	88	67	52	36	21	6	0	0	0	0
1,320	1,340	114	91	69	54	38	23	8	0	0	0	0
1,340	1,360	117	94	71	56	40	25	10	0	0	0	0
1,360	1,380	120	97	74	58	42	27	12	0	0	0	0
1,380	1,400	123	100	77	60	44	29	14	0	0	0	0
1,400	1,420	126	103	80	62	46	31	16	0	0	0	0
1,420	1,440	129	106	83	64	48	33	18	2	0	0	0
1,440	1,460	132	109	86	66	50	35	20	4	0	0	0
1,460	1,480	135	112	89	68	52	37	22	6	0	0	0
1,480	1,500	138	115	92	70	54	39	24	8	0	0	0

Wage Bracket Method Tables for Income Tax Withholding

MARRIED Persons—BIWEEKLY Payroll Period

(For Wages Paid through December 31, 2015)

And the wages are–		And the number of withholding allowances claimed is—										
At least	But less than	0	1	2	3	4	5	6	7	8	9	10
		The amount of income tax to be withheld is—										
$1,500	$1,520	$141	$118	$95	$72	$56	$41	$26	$10	$0	$0	$0
1,520	1,540	144	121	98	75	58	43	28	12	0	0	0
1,540	1,560	147	124	101	78	60	45	30	14	0	0	0
1,560	1,580	150	127	104	81	62	47	32	16	1	0	0
1,580	1,600	153	130	107	84	64	49	34	18	3	0	0
1,600	1,620	156	133	110	87	66	51	36	20	5	0	0
1,620	1,640	159	136	113	90	68	53	38	22	7	0	0
1,640	1,660	162	139	116	93	70	55	40	24	9	0	0
1,660	1,680	165	142	119	96	73	57	42	26	11	0	0
1,680	1,700	168	145	122	99	76	59	44	28	13	0	0
1,700	1,720	171	148	125	102	79	61	46	30	15	0	0
1,720	1,740	174	151	128	105	82	63	48	32	17	1	0
1,740	1,760	177	154	131	108	85	65	50	34	19	3	0
1,760	1,780	180	157	134	111	88	67	52	36	21	5	0
1,780	1,800	183	160	137	114	91	69	54	38	23	7	0
1,800	1,820	186	163	140	117	94	71	56	40	25	9	0
1,820	1,840	189	166	143	120	97	74	58	42	27	11	0
1,840	1,860	192	169	146	123	100	77	60	44	29	13	0
1,860	1,880	195	172	149	126	103	80	62	46	31	15	0
1,880	1,900	198	175	152	129	106	83	64	48	33	17	2
1,900	1,920	201	178	155	132	109	86	66	50	35	19	4
1,920	1,940	204	181	158	135	112	89	68	52	37	21	6
1,940	1,960	207	184	161	138	115	92	70	54	39	23	8
1,960	1,980	210	187	164	141	118	95	72	56	41	25	10
1,980	2,000	213	190	167	144	121	98	75	58	43	27	12
2,000	2,020	216	193	170	147	124	101	78	60	45	29	14
2,020	2,040	219	196	173	150	127	104	81	62	47	31	16
2,040	2,060	222	199	176	153	130	107	84	64	49	33	18
2,060	2,080	225	202	179	156	133	110	87	66	51	35	20
2,080	2,100	228	205	182	159	136	113	90	68	53	37	22
2,100	2,120	231	208	185	162	139	116	93	70	55	39	24
2,120	2,140	234	211	188	165	142	119	96	73	57	41	26
2,140	2,160	237	214	191	168	145	122	99	76	59	43	28
2,160	2,180	240	217	194	171	148	125	102	79	61	45	30
2,180	2,200	243	220	197	174	151	128	105	82	63	47	32
2,200	2,220	246	223	200	177	154	131	108	85	65	49	34
2,220	2,240	249	226	203	180	157	134	111	88	67	51	36
2,240	2,260	252	229	206	183	160	137	114	91	69	53	38
2,260	2,280	255	232	209	186	163	140	117	94	71	55	40
2,280	2,300	258	235	212	189	166	143	120	97	74	57	42
2,300	2,320	261	238	215	192	169	146	123	100	77	59	44
2,320	2,340	264	241	218	195	172	149	126	103	80	61	46
2,340	2,360	267	244	221	198	175	152	129	106	83	63	48
2,360	2,380	270	247	224	201	178	155	132	109	86	65	50
2,380	2,400	273	250	227	204	181	158	135	112	89	67	52
2,400	2,420	276	253	230	207	184	161	138	115	92	69	54
2,420	2,440	279	256	233	210	187	164	141	118	95	72	56
2,440	2,460	282	259	236	213	190	167	144	121	98	75	58
2,460	2,480	285	262	239	216	193	170	147	124	101	78	60
2,480	2,500	288	265	242	219	196	173	150	127	104	81	62
2,500	2,520	291	268	245	222	199	176	153	130	107	84	64
2,520	2,540	294	271	248	225	202	179	156	133	110	87	66
2,540	2,560	297	274	251	228	205	182	159	136	113	90	68
2,560	2,580	300	277	254	231	208	185	162	139	116	93	70
2,580	2,600	303	280	257	234	211	188	165	142	119	96	73
2,600	2,620	306	283	260	237	214	191	168	145	122	99	76
2,620	2,640	309	286	263	240	217	194	171	148	125	102	79
2,640	2,660	312	289	266	243	220	197	174	151	128	105	82
2,660	2,680	315	292	269	246	223	200	177	154	131	108	85
2,680	2,700	318	295	272	249	226	203	180	157	134	111	88
2,700	2,720	321	298	275	252	229	206	183	160	137	114	91
2,720	2,740	324	301	278	255	232	209	186	163	140	117	94
2,740	2,760	327	304	281	258	235	212	189	166	143	120	97
2,760	2,780	330	307	284	261	238	215	192	169	146	123	100
2,780	2,800	333	310	287	264	241	218	195	172	149	126	103
2,800	2,820	336	313	290	267	244	221	198	175	152	129	106
2,820	2,840	339	316	293	270	247	224	201	178	155	132	109
2,840	2,860	342	319	296	273	250	227	204	181	158	135	112
2,860	2,880	345	322	299	276	253	230	207	184	161	138	115

$2,880 and over   Use Table 2(b) for a **MARRIED person** on page 45. Also see the instructions on page 43.

Wage Bracket Method Tables for Income Tax Withholding

SINGLE Persons—SEMIMONTHLY Payroll Period

(For Wages Paid through December 31, 2015)

And the wages are—		And the number of withholding allowances claimed is—										
At least	But less than	0	1	2	3	4	5	6	7	8	9	10
		The amount of income tax to be withheld is—										
$ 0	$115	$0	$0	$0	$0	$0	$0	$0	$0	$0	$0	$0
115	120	2	0	0	0	0	0	0	0	0	0	0
120	125	3	0	0	0	0	0	0	0	0	0	0
125	130	3	0	0	0	0	0	0	0	0	0	0
130	135	4	0	0	0	0	0	0	0	0	0	0
135	140	4	0	0	0	0	0	0	0	0	0	0
140	145	5	0	0	0	0	0	0	0	0	0	0
145	150	5	0	0	0	0	0	0	0	0	0	0
150	155	6	0	0	0	0	0	0	0	0	0	0
155	160	6	0	0	0	0	0	0	0	0	0	0
160	165	7	0	0	0	0	0	0	0	0	0	0
165	170	7	0	0	0	0	0	0	0	0	0	0
170	175	8	0	0	0	0	0	0	0	0	0	0
175	180	8	0	0	0	0	0	0	0	0	0	0
180	185	9	0	0	0	0	0	0	0	0	0	0
185	190	9	0	0	0	0	0	0	0	0	0	0
190	195	10	0	0	0	0	0	0	0	0	0	0
195	200	10	0	0	0	0	0	0	0	0	0	0
200	205	11	0	0	0	0	0	0	0	0	0	0
205	210	11	0	0	0	0	0	0	0	0	0	0
210	215	12	0	0	0	0	0	0	0	0	0	0
215	220	12	0	0	0	0	0	0	0	0	0	0
220	225	13	0	0	0	0	0	0	0	0	0	0
225	230	13	0	0	0	0	0	0	0	0	0	0
230	235	14	0	0	0	0	0	0	0	0	0	0
235	240	14	0	0	0	0	0	0	0	0	0	0
240	245	15	0	0	0	0	0	0	0	0	0	0
245	250	15	0	0	0	0	0	0	0	0	0	0
250	260	16	0	0	0	0	0	0	0	0	0	0
260	270	17	0	0	0	0	0	0	0	0	0	0
270	280	18	1	0	0	0	0	0	0	0	0	0
280	290	19	2	0	0	0	0	0	0	0	0	0
290	300	20	3	0	0	0	0	0	0	0	0	0
300	310	21	4	0	0	0	0	0	0	0	0	0
310	320	22	5	0	0	0	0	0	0	0	0	0
320	330	23	6	0	0	0	0	0	0	0	0	0
330	340	24	7	0	0	0	0	0	0	0	0	0
340	350	25	8	0	0	0	0	0	0	0	0	0
350	360	26	9	0	0	0	0	0	0	0	0	0
360	370	27	10	0	0	0	0	0	0	0	0	0
370	380	28	11	0	0	0	0	0	0	0	0	0
380	390	29	12	0	0	0	0	0	0	0	0	0
390	400	30	13	0	0	0	0	0	0	0	0	0
400	410	31	14	0	0	0	0	0	0	0	0	0
410	420	32	15	0	0	0	0	0	0	0	0	0
420	430	33	16	0	0	0	0	0	0	0	0	0
430	440	34	17	1	0	0	0	0	0	0	0	0
440	450	35	18	2	0	0	0	0	0	0	0	0
450	460	36	19	3	0	0	0	0	0	0	0	0
460	470	37	20	4	0	0	0	0	0	0	0	0
470	480	38	21	5	0	0	0	0	0	0	0	0
480	490	39	22	6	0	0	0	0	0	0	0	0
490	500	41	23	7	0	0	0	0	0	0	0	0
500	520	43	25	8	0	0	0	0	0	0	0	0
520	540	46	27	10	0	0	0	0	0	0	0	0
540	560	49	29	12	0	0	0	0	0	0	0	0
560	580	52	31	14	0	0	0	0	0	0	0	0
580	600	55	33	16	0	0	0	0	0	0	0	0
600	620	58	35	18	1	0	0	0	0	0	0	0
620	640	61	37	20	3	0	0	0	0	0	0	0
640	660	64	39	22	5	0	0	0	0	0	0	0
660	680	67	42	24	7	0	0	0	0	0	0	0
680	700	70	45	26	9	0	0	0	0	0	0	0
700	720	73	48	28	11	0	0	0	0	0	0	0
720	740	76	51	30	13	0	0	0	0	0	0	0
740	760	79	54	32	15	0	0	0	0	0	0	0
760	780	82	57	34	17	1	0	0	0	0	0	0
780	800	85	60	36	19	3	0	0	0	0	0	0

Wage Bracket Method Tables for Income Tax Withholding

SINGLE Persons—SEMIMONTHLY Payroll Period

(For Wages Paid through December 31, 2015)

And the wages are–		And the number of withholding allowances claimed is—										
At least	But less than	0	1	2	3	4	5	6	7	8	9	10
		The amount of income tax to be withheld is—										
$800	$820	$88	$63	$38	$21	$5	$0	$0	$0	$0	$0	$0
820	840	91	66	41	23	7	0	0	0	0	0	0
840	860	94	69	44	25	9	0	0	0	0	0	0
860	880	97	72	47	27	11	0	0	0	0	0	0
880	900	100	75	50	29	13	0	0	0	0	0	0
900	920	103	78	53	31	15	0	0	0	0	0	0
920	940	106	81	56	33	17	0	0	0	0	0	0
940	960	109	84	59	35	19	2	0	0	0	0	0
960	980	112	87	62	37	21	4	0	0	0	0	0
980	1,000	115	90	65	40	23	6	0	0	0	0	0
1,000	1,020	118	93	68	43	25	8	0	0	0	0	0
1,020	1,040	121	96	71	46	27	10	0	0	0	0	0
1,040	1,060	124	99	74	49	29	12	0	0	0	0	0
1,060	1,080	127	102	77	52	31	14	0	0	0	0	0
1,080	1,100	130	105	80	55	33	16	0	0	0	0	0
1,100	1,120	133	108	83	58	35	18	1	0	0	0	0
1,120	1,140	136	111	86	61	37	20	3	0	0	0	0
1,140	1,160	139	114	89	64	39	22	5	0	0	0	0
1,160	1,180	142	117	92	67	42	24	7	0	0	0	0
1,180	1,200	145	120	95	70	45	26	9	0	0	0	0
1,200	1,220	148	123	98	73	48	28	11	0	0	0	0
1,220	1,240	151	126	101	76	51	30	13	0	0	0	0
1,240	1,260	154	129	104	79	54	32	15	0	0	0	0
1,260	1,280	157	132	107	82	57	34	17	1	0	0	0
1,280	1,300	160	135	110	85	60	36	19	3	0	0	0
1,300	1,320	163	138	113	88	63	38	21	5	0	0	0
1,320	1,340	166	141	116	91	66	41	23	7	0	0	0
1,340	1,360	169	144	119	94	69	44	25	9	0	0	0
1,360	1,380	172	147	122	97	72	47	27	11	0	0	0
1,380	1,400	175	150	125	100	75	50	29	13	0	0	0
1,400	1,420	178	153	128	103	78	53	31	15	0	0	0
1,420	1,440	181	156	131	106	81	56	33	17	0	0	0
1,440	1,460	184	159	134	109	84	59	35	19	2	0	0
1,460	1,480	187	162	137	112	87	62	37	21	4	0	0
1,480	1,500	190	165	140	115	90	65	40	23	6	0	0
1,500	1,520	193	168	143	118	93	68	43	25	8	0	0
1,520	1,540	196	171	146	121	96	71	46	27	10	0	0
1,540	1,560	199	174	149	124	99	74	49	29	12	0	0
1,560	1,580	202	177	152	127	102	77	52	31	14	0	0
1,580	1,600	205	180	155	130	105	80	55	33	16	0	0
1,600	1,620	208	183	158	133	108	83	58	35	18	1	0
1,620	1,640	211	186	161	136	111	86	61	37	20	3	0
1,640	1,660	214	189	164	139	114	89	64	39	22	5	0
1,660	1,680	218	192	167	142	117	92	67	42	24	7	0
1,680	1,700	223	195	170	145	120	95	70	45	26	9	0
1,700	1,720	228	198	173	148	123	98	73	48	28	11	0
1,720	1,740	233	201	176	151	126	101	76	51	30	13	0
1,740	1,760	238	204	179	154	129	104	79	54	32	15	0
1,760	1,780	243	207	182	157	132	107	82	57	34	17	1
1,780	1,800	248	210	185	160	135	110	85	60	36	19	3
1,800	1,820	253	213	188	163	138	113	88	63	38	21	5
1,820	1,840	258	217	191	166	141	116	91	66	41	23	7
1,840	1,860	263	222	194	169	144	119	94	69	44	25	9
1,860	1,880	268	227	197	172	147	122	97	72	47	27	11
1,880	1,900	273	232	200	175	150	125	100	75	50	29	13
1,900	1,920	278	237	203	178	153	128	103	78	53	31	15
1,920	1,940	283	242	206	181	156	131	106	81	56	33	17
1,940	1,960	288	247	209	184	159	134	109	84	59	35	19
1,960	1,980	293	252	212	187	162	137	112	87	62	37	21
1,980	2,000	298	257	215	190	165	140	115	90	65	40	23
2,000	2,020	303	262	220	193	168	143	118	93	68	43	25
2,020	2,040	308	267	225	196	171	146	121	96	71	46	27
2,040	2,060	313	272	230	199	174	149	124	99	74	49	29
2,060	2,080	318	277	235	202	177	152	127	102	77	52	31
2,080	2,100	323	282	240	205	180	155	130	105	80	55	33
2,100	2,120	328	287	245	208	183	158	133	108	83	58	35
2,120	2,140	333	292	250	211	186	161	136	111	86	61	37

$2,140 and over	Use Table 3(a) for a **SINGLE person** on page 45. Also see the instructions on page 43.

Wage Bracket Method Tables for Income Tax Withholding

MARRIED Persons—SEMIMONTHLY Payroll Period

(For Wages Paid through December 31, 2015)

And the wages are—		And the number of withholding allowances claimed is—										
At least	But less than	0	1	2	3	4	5	6	7	8	9	10
		The amount of income tax to be withheld is—										
$ 0	$360	$0	$0	$0	$0	$0	$0	$0	$0	$0	$0	$0
360	370	1	0	0	0	0	0	0	0	0	0	0
370	380	2	0	0	0	0	0	0	0	0	0	0
380	390	3	0	0	0	0	0	0	0	0	0	0
390	400	4	0	0	0	0	0	0	0	0	0	0
400	410	5	0	0	0	0	0	0	0	0	0	0
410	420	6	0	0	0	0	0	0	0	0	0	0
420	430	7	0	0	0	0	0	0	0	0	0	0
430	440	8	0	0	0	0	0	0	0	0	0	0
440	450	9	0	0	0	0	0	0	0	0	0	0
450	460	10	0	0	0	0	0	0	0	0	0	0
460	470	11	0	0	0	0	0	0	0	0	0	0
470	480	12	0	0	0	0	0	0	0	0	0	0
480	490	13	0	0	0	0	0	0	0	0	0	0
490	500	14	0	0	0	0	0	0	0	0	0	0
500	520	15	0	0	0	0	0	0	0	0	0	0
520	540	17	1	0	0	0	0	0	0	0	0	0
540	560	19	3	0	0	0	0	0	0	0	0	0
560	580	21	5	0	0	0	0	0	0	0	0	0
580	600	23	7	0	0	0	0	0	0	0	0	0
600	620	25	9	0	0	0	0	0	0	0	0	0
620	640	27	11	0	0	0	0	0	0	0	0	0
640	660	29	13	0	0	0	0	0	0	0	0	0
660	680	31	15	0	0	0	0	0	0	0	0	0
680	700	33	17	0	0	0	0	0	0	0	0	0
700	720	35	19	2	0	0	0	0	0	0	0	0
720	740	37	21	4	0	0	0	0	0	0	0	0
740	760	39	23	6	0	0	0	0	0	0	0	0
760	780	41	25	8	0	0	0	0	0	0	0	0
780	800	43	27	10	0	0	0	0	0	0	0	0
800	820	45	29	12	0	0	0	0	0	0	0	0
820	840	47	31	14	0	0	0	0	0	0	0	0
840	860	49	33	16	0	0	0	0	0	0	0	0
860	880	51	35	18	1	0	0	0	0	0	0	0
880	900	53	37	20	3	0	0	0	0	0	0	0
900	920	55	39	22	5	0	0	0	0	0	0	0
920	940	57	41	24	7	0	0	0	0	0	0	0
940	960	59	43	26	9	0	0	0	0	0	0	0
960	980	61	45	28	11	0	0	0	0	0	0	0
980	1,000	63	47	30	13	0	0	0	0	0	0	0
1,000	1,020	65	49	32	15	0	0	0	0	0	0	0
1,020	1,040	67	51	34	17	1	0	0	0	0	0	0
1,040	1,060	69	53	36	19	3	0	0	0	0	0	0
1,060	1,080	71	55	38	21	5	0	0	0	0	0	0
1,080	1,100	73	57	40	23	7	0	0	0	0	0	0
1,100	1,120	75	59	42	25	9	0	0	0	0	0	0
1,120	1,140	77	61	44	27	11	0	0	0	0	0	0
1,140	1,160	80	63	46	29	13	0	0	0	0	0	0
1,160	1,180	83	65	48	31	15	0	0	0	0	0	0
1,180	1,200	86	67	50	33	17	0	0	0	0	0	0
1,200	1,220	89	69	52	35	19	2	0	0	0	0	0
1,220	1,240	92	71	54	37	21	4	0	0	0	0	0
1,240	1,260	95	73	56	39	23	6	0	0	0	0	0
1,260	1,280	98	75	58	41	25	8	0	0	0	0	0
1,280	1,300	101	77	60	43	27	10	0	0	0	0	0
1,300	1,320	104	79	62	45	29	12	0	0	0	0	0
1,320	1,340	107	82	64	47	31	14	0	0	0	0	0
1,340	1,360	110	85	66	49	33	16	0	0	0	0	0
1,360	1,380	113	88	68	51	35	18	1	0	0	0	0
1,380	1,400	116	91	70	53	37	20	3	0	0	0	0
1,400	1,420	119	94	72	55	39	22	5	0	0	0	0
1,420	1,440	122	97	74	57	41	24	7	0	0	0	0
1,440	1,460	125	100	76	59	43	26	9	0	0	0	0
1,460	1,480	128	103	78	61	45	28	11	0	0	0	0
1,480	1,500	131	106	81	63	47	30	13	0	0	0	0
1,500	1,520	134	109	84	65	49	32	15	0	0	0	0
1,520	1,540	137	112	87	67	51	34	17	1	0	0	0
1,540	1,560	140	115	90	69	53	36	19	3	0	0	0
1,560	1,580	143	118	93	71	55	38	21	5	0	0	0
1,580	1,600	146	121	96	73	57	40	23	7	0	0	0

Wage Bracket Method Tables for Income Tax Withholding

MARRIED Persons—SEMIMONTHLY Payroll Period

(For Wages Paid through December 31, 2015)

And the wages are—		And the number of withholding allowances claimed is—										
At least	But less than	0	1	2	3	4	5	6	7	8	9	10
		The amount of income tax to be withheld is—										
$1,600	$1,620	$149	$124	$99	$75	$59	$42	$25	$9	$0	$0	$0
1,620	1,640	152	127	102	77	61	44	27	11	0	0	0
1,640	1,660	155	130	105	80	63	46	29	13	0	0	0
1,660	1,680	158	133	108	83	65	48	31	15	0	0	0
1,680	1,700	161	136	111	86	67	50	33	17	0	0	0
1,700	1,720	164	139	114	89	69	52	35	19	2	0	0
1,720	1,740	167	142	117	92	71	54	37	21	4	0	0
1,740	1,760	170	145	120	95	73	56	39	23	6	0	0
1,760	1,780	173	148	123	98	75	58	41	25	8	0	0
1,780	1,800	176	151	126	101	77	60	43	27	10	0	0
1,800	1,820	179	154	129	104	79	62	45	29	12	0	0
1,820	1,840	182	157	132	107	82	64	47	31	14	0	0
1,840	1,860	185	160	135	110	85	66	49	33	16	0	0
1,860	1,880	188	163	138	113	88	68	51	35	18	1	0
1,880	1,900	191	166	141	116	91	70	53	37	20	3	0
1,900	1,920	194	169	144	119	94	72	55	39	22	5	0
1,920	1,940	197	172	147	122	97	74	57	41	24	7	0
1,940	1,960	200	175	150	125	100	76	59	43	26	9	0
1,960	1,980	203	178	153	128	103	78	61	45	28	11	0
1,980	2,000	206	181	156	131	106	81	63	47	30	13	0
2,000	2,020	209	184	159	134	109	84	65	49	32	15	0
2,020	2,040	212	187	162	137	112	87	67	51	34	17	1
2,040	2,060	215	190	165	140	115	90	69	53	36	19	3
2,060	2,080	218	193	168	143	118	93	71	55	38	21	5
2,080	2,100	221	196	171	146	121	96	73	57	40	23	7
2,100	2,120	224	199	174	149	124	99	75	59	42	25	9
2,120	2,140	227	202	177	152	127	102	77	61	44	27	11
2,140	2,160	230	205	180	155	130	105	80	63	46	29	13
2,160	2,180	233	208	183	158	133	108	83	65	48	31	15
2,180	2,200	236	211	186	161	136	111	86	67	50	33	17
2,200	2,220	239	214	189	164	139	114	89	69	52	35	19
2,220	2,240	242	217	192	167	142	117	92	71	54	37	21
2,240	2,260	245	220	195	170	145	120	95	73	56	39	23
2,260	2,280	248	223	198	173	148	123	98	75	58	41	25
2,280	2,300	251	226	201	176	151	126	101	77	60	43	27
2,300	2,320	254	229	204	179	154	129	104	79	62	45	29
2,320	2,340	257	232	207	182	157	132	107	82	64	47	31
2,340	2,360	260	235	210	185	160	135	110	85	66	49	33
2,360	2,380	263	238	213	188	163	138	113	88	68	51	35
2,380	2,400	266	241	216	191	166	141	116	91	70	53	37
2,400	2,420	269	244	219	194	169	144	119	94	72	55	39
2,420	2,440	272	247	222	197	172	147	122	97	74	57	41
2,440	2,460	275	250	225	200	175	150	125	100	76	59	43
2,460	2,480	278	253	228	203	178	153	128	103	78	61	45
2,480	2,500	281	256	231	206	181	156	131	106	81	63	47
2,500	2,520	284	259	234	209	184	159	134	109	84	65	49
2,520	2,540	287	262	237	212	187	162	137	112	87	67	51
2,540	2,560	290	265	240	215	190	165	140	115	90	69	53
2,560	2,580	293	268	243	218	193	168	143	118	93	71	55
2,580	2,600	296	271	246	221	196	171	146	121	96	73	57
2,600	2,620	299	274	249	224	199	174	149	124	99	75	59
2,620	2,640	302	277	252	227	202	177	152	127	102	77	61
2,640	2,660	305	280	255	230	205	180	155	130	105	80	63
2,660	2,680	308	283	258	233	208	183	158	133	108	83	65
2,680	2,700	311	286	261	236	211	186	161	136	111	86	67
2,700	2,720	314	289	264	239	214	189	164	139	114	89	69
2,720	2,740	317	292	267	242	217	192	167	142	117	92	71
2,740	2,760	320	295	270	245	220	195	170	145	120	95	73
2,760	2,780	323	298	273	248	223	198	173	148	123	98	75
2,780	2,800	326	301	276	251	226	201	176	151	126	101	77
2,800	2,820	329	304	279	254	229	204	179	154	129	104	79
2,820	2,840	332	307	282	257	232	207	182	157	132	107	82
2,840	2,860	335	310	285	260	235	210	185	160	135	110	85
2,860	2,880	338	313	288	263	238	213	188	163	138	113	88
2,880	2,900	341	316	291	266	241	216	191	166	141	116	91
2,900	2,920	344	319	294	269	244	219	194	169	144	119	94

| $2,920 and over | Use Table 3(b) for a **MARRIED person** on page 45. Also see the instructions on page 43. |

Wage Bracket Method Tables for Income Tax Withholding

SINGLE Persons—**MONTHLY** Payroll Period

(For Wages Paid through December 31, 2015)

And the wages are—		And the number of withholding allowances claimed is—										
At least	But less than	0	1	2	3	4	5	6	7	8	9	10
		The amount of income tax to be withheld is—										
$ 0	$220	$0	$0	$0	$0	$0	$0	$0	$0	$0	$0	$0
220	230	3	0	0	0	0	0	0	0	0	0	0
230	240	4	0	0	0	0	0	0	0	0	0	0
240	250	5	0	0	0	0	0	0	0	0	0	0
250	260	6	0	0	0	0	0	0	0	0	0	0
260	270	7	0	0	0	0	0	0	0	0	0	0
270	280	8	0	0	0	0	0	0	0	0	0	0
280	290	9	0	0	0	0	0	0	0	0	0	0
290	300	10	0	0	0	0	0	0	0	0	0	0
300	320	12	0	0	0	0	0	0	0	0	0	0
320	340	14	0	0	0	0	0	0	0	0	0	0
340	360	16	0	0	0	0	0	0	0	0	0	0
360	380	18	0	0	0	0	0	0	0	0	0	0
380	400	20	0	0	0	0	0	0	0	0	0	0
400	420	22	0	0	0	0	0	0	0	0	0	0
420	440	24	0	0	0	0	0	0	0	0	0	0
440	460	26	0	0	0	0	0	0	0	0	0	0
460	480	28	0	0	0	0	0	0	0	0	0	0
480	500	30	0	0	0	0	0	0	0	0	0	0
500	520	32	0	0	0	0	0	0	0	0	0	0
520	540	34	1	0	0	0	0	0	0	0	0	0
540	560	36	3	0	0	0	0	0	0	0	0	0
560	580	38	5	0	0	0	0	0	0	0	0	0
580	600	40	7	0	0	0	0	0	0	0	0	0
600	640	43	10	0	0	0	0	0	0	0	0	0
640	680	47	14	0	0	0	0	0	0	0	0	0
680	720	51	18	0	0	0	0	0	0	0	0	0
720	760	55	22	0	0	0	0	0	0	0	0	0
760	800	59	26	0	0	0	0	0	0	0	0	0
800	840	63	30	0	0	0	0	0	0	0	0	0
840	880	67	34	0	0	0	0	0	0	0	0	0
880	920	71	38	4	0	0	0	0	0	0	0	0
920	960	75	42	8	0	0	0	0	0	0	0	0
960	1,000	80	46	12	0	0	0	0	0	0	0	0
1,000	1,040	86	50	16	0	0	0	0	0	0	0	0
1,040	1,080	92	54	20	0	0	0	0	0	0	0	0
1,080	1,120	98	58	24	0	0	0	0	0	0	0	0
1,120	1,160	104	62	28	0	0	0	0	0	0	0	0
1,160	1,200	110	66	32	0	0	0	0	0	0	0	0
1,200	1,240	116	70	36	3	0	0	0	0	0	0	0
1,240	1,280	122	74	40	7	0	0	0	0	0	0	0
1,280	1,320	128	78	44	11	0	0	0	0	0	0	0
1,320	1,360	134	84	48	15	0	0	0	0	0	0	0
1,360	1,400	140	90	52	19	0	0	0	0	0	0	0
1,400	1,440	146	96	56	23	0	0	0	0	0	0	0
1,440	1,480	152	102	60	27	0	0	0	0	0	0	0
1,480	1,520	158	108	64	31	0	0	0	0	0	0	0
1,520	1,560	164	114	68	35	2	0	0	0	0	0	0
1,560	1,600	170	120	72	39	6	0	0	0	0	0	0
1,600	1,640	176	126	76	43	10	0	0	0	0	0	0
1,640	1,680	182	132	82	47	14	0	0	0	0	0	0
1,680	1,720	188	138	88	51	18	0	0	0	0	0	0
1,720	1,760	194	144	94	55	22	0	0	0	0	0	0
1,760	1,800	200	150	100	59	26	0	0	0	0	0	0
1,800	1,840	206	156	106	63	30	0	0	0	0	0	0
1,840	1,880	212	162	112	67	34	0	0	0	0	0	0
1,880	1,920	218	168	118	71	38	4	0	0	0	0	0
1,920	1,960	224	174	124	75	42	8	0	0	0	0	0
1,960	2,000	230	180	130	80	46	12	0	0	0	0	0
2,000	2,040	236	186	136	86	50	16	0	0	0	0	0
2,040	2,080	242	192	142	92	54	20	0	0	0	0	0
2,080	2,120	248	198	148	98	58	24	0	0	0	0	0
2,120	2,160	254	204	154	104	62	28	0	0	0	0	0
2,160	2,200	260	210	160	110	66	32	0	0	0	0	0
2,200	2,240	266	216	166	116	70	36	3	0	0	0	0
2,240	2,280	272	222	172	122	74	40	7	0	0	0	0
2,280	2,320	278	228	178	128	78	44	11	0	0	0	0
2,320	2,360	284	234	184	134	84	48	15	0	0	0	0
2,360	2,400	290	240	190	140	90	52	19	0	0	0	0

Wage Bracket Method Tables for Income Tax Withholding

SINGLE Persons—**MONTHLY** Payroll Period

(For Wages Paid through December 31, 2015)

And the wages are—		And the number of withholding allowances claimed is—										
At least	But less than	0	1	2	3	4	5	6	7	8	9	10
		The amount of income tax to be withheld is—										
$2,400	$2,440	$296	$246	$196	$146	$96	$56	$23	$0	$0	$0	$0
2,440	2,480	302	252	202	152	102	60	27	0	0	0	0
2,480	2,520	308	258	208	158	108	64	31	0	0	0	0
2,520	2,560	314	264	214	164	114	68	35	2	0	0	0
2,560	2,600	320	270	220	170	120	72	39	6	0	0	0
2,600	2,640	326	276	226	176	126	76	43	10	0	0	0
2,640	2,680	332	282	232	182	132	82	47	14	0	0	0
2,680	2,720	338	288	238	188	138	88	51	18	0	0	0
2,720	2,760	344	294	244	194	144	94	55	22	0	0	0
2,760	2,800	350	300	250	200	150	100	59	26	0	0	0
2,800	2,840	356	306	256	206	156	106	63	30	0	0	0
2,840	2,880	362	312	262	212	162	112	67	34	0	0	0
2,880	2,920	368	318	268	218	168	118	71	38	4	0	0
2,920	2,960	374	324	274	224	174	124	75	42	8	0	0
2,960	3,000	380	330	280	230	180	130	80	46	12	0	0
3,000	3,040	386	336	286	236	186	136	86	50	16	0	0
3,040	3,080	392	342	292	242	192	142	92	54	20	0	0
3,080	3,120	398	348	298	248	198	148	98	58	24	0	0
3,120	3,160	404	354	304	254	204	154	104	62	28	0	0
3,160	3,200	410	360	310	260	210	160	110	66	32	0	0
3,200	3,240	416	366	316	266	216	166	116	70	36	3	0
3,240	3,280	422	372	322	272	222	172	122	74	40	7	0
3,280	3,320	428	378	328	278	228	178	128	78	44	11	0
3,320	3,360	437	384	334	284	234	184	134	84	48	15	0
3,360	3,400	447	390	340	290	240	190	140	90	52	19	0
3,400	3,440	457	396	346	296	246	196	146	96	56	23	0
3,440	3,480	467	402	352	302	252	202	152	102	60	27	0
3,480	3,520	477	408	358	308	258	208	158	108	64	31	0
3,520	3,560	487	414	364	314	264	214	164	114	68	35	2
3,560	3,600	497	420	370	320	270	220	170	120	72	39	6
3,600	3,640	507	426	376	326	276	226	176	126	76	43	10
3,640	3,680	517	433	382	332	282	232	182	132	82	47	14
3,680	3,720	527	443	388	338	288	238	188	138	88	51	18
3,720	3,760	537	453	394	344	294	244	194	144	94	55	22
3,760	3,800	547	463	400	350	300	250	200	150	100	59	26
3,800	3,840	557	473	406	356	306	256	206	156	106	63	30
3,840	3,880	567	483	412	362	312	262	212	162	112	67	34
3,880	3,920	577	493	418	368	318	268	218	168	118	71	38
3,920	3,960	587	503	424	374	324	274	224	174	124	75	42
3,960	4,000	597	513	430	380	330	280	230	180	130	80	46
4,000	4,040	607	523	440	386	336	286	236	186	136	86	50
4,040	4,080	617	533	450	392	342	292	242	192	142	92	54
4,080	4,120	627	543	460	398	348	298	248	198	148	98	58
4,120	4,160	637	553	470	404	354	304	254	204	154	104	62
4,160	4,200	647	563	480	410	360	310	260	210	160	110	66
4,200	4,240	657	573	490	416	366	316	266	216	166	116	70
4,240	4,280	667	583	500	422	372	322	272	222	172	122	74
4,280	4,320	677	593	510	428	378	328	278	228	178	128	78
4,320	4,360	687	603	520	437	384	334	284	234	184	134	84
4,360	4,400	697	613	530	447	390	340	290	240	190	140	90
4,400	4,440	707	623	540	457	396	346	296	246	196	146	96
4,440	4,480	717	633	550	467	402	352	302	252	202	152	102
4,480	4,520	727	643	560	477	408	358	308	258	208	158	108
4,520	4,560	737	653	570	487	414	364	314	264	214	164	114
4,560	4,600	747	663	580	497	420	370	320	270	220	170	120
4,600	4,640	757	673	590	507	426	376	326	276	226	176	126
4,640	4,680	767	683	600	517	433	382	332	282	232	182	132
4,680	4,720	777	693	610	527	443	388	338	288	238	188	138
4,720	4,760	787	703	620	537	453	394	344	294	244	194	144
4,760	4,800	797	713	630	547	463	400	350	300	250	200	150
4,800	4,840	807	723	640	557	473	406	356	306	256	206	156
4,840	4,880	817	733	650	567	483	412	362	312	262	212	162
4,880	4,920	827	743	660	577	493	418	368	318	268	218	168
4,920	4,960	837	753	670	587	503	424	374	324	274	224	174
4,960	5,000	847	763	680	597	513	430	380	330	280	230	180
5,000	5,040	857	773	690	607	523	440	386	336	286	236	186
5,040	5,080	867	783	700	617	533	450	392	342	292	242	192

$5,080 and over   Use Table 4(a) for a **SINGLE person** on page 45. Also see the instructions on page 43.

Wage Bracket Method Tables for Income Tax Withholding

MARRIED Persons—MONTHLY Payroll Period

(For Wages Paid through December 31, 2015)

And the wages are—		And the number of withholding allowances claimed is—										
At least	But less than	0	1	2	3	4	5	6	7	8	9	10
		The amount of income tax to be withheld is—										
$ 0	$720	$0	$0	$0	$0	$0	$0	$0	$0	$0	$0	$0
720	760	2	0	0	0	0	0	0	0	0	0	0
760	800	6	0	0	0	0	0	0	0	0	0	0
800	840	10	0	0	0	0	0	0	0	0	0	0
840	880	14	0	0	0	0	0	0	0	0	0	0
880	920	18	0	0	0	0	0	0	0	0	0	0
920	960	22	0	0	0	0	0	0	0	0	0	0
960	1,000	26	0	0	0	0	0	0	0	0	0	0
1,000	1,040	30	0	0	0	0	0	0	0	0	0	0
1,040	1,080	34	1	0	0	0	0	0	0	0	0	0
1,080	1,120	38	5	0	0	0	0	0	0	0	0	0
1,120	1,160	42	9	0	0	0	0	0	0	0	0	0
1,160	1,200	46	13	0	0	0	0	0	0	0	0	0
1,200	1,240	50	17	0	0	0	0	0	0	0	0	0
1,240	1,280	54	21	0	0	0	0	0	0	0	0	0
1,280	1,320	58	25	0	0	0	0	0	0	0	0	0
1,320	1,360	62	29	0	0	0	0	0	0	0	0	0
1,360	1,400	66	33	0	0	0	0	0	0	0	0	0
1,400	1,440	70	37	4	0	0	0	0	0	0	0	0
1,440	1,480	74	41	8	0	0	0	0	0	0	0	0
1,480	1,520	78	45	12	0	0	0	0	0	0	0	0
1,520	1,560	82	49	16	0	0	0	0	0	0	0	0
1,560	1,600	86	53	20	0	0	0	0	0	0	0	0
1,600	1,640	90	57	24	0	0	0	0	0	0	0	0
1,640	1,680	94	61	28	0	0	0	0	0	0	0	0
1,680	1,720	98	65	32	0	0	0	0	0	0	0	0
1,720	1,760	102	69	36	2	0	0	0	0	0	0	0
1,760	1,800	106	73	40	6	0	0	0	0	0	0	0
1,800	1,840	110	77	44	10	0	0	0	0	0	0	0
1,840	1,880	114	81	48	14	0	0	0	0	0	0	0
1,880	1,920	118	85	52	18	0	0	0	0	0	0	0
1,920	1,960	122	89	56	22	0	0	0	0	0	0	0
1,960	2,000	126	93	60	26	0	0	0	0	0	0	0
2,000	2,040	130	97	64	30	0	0	0	0	0	0	0
2,040	2,080	134	101	68	34	1	0	0	0	0	0	0
2,080	2,120	138	105	72	38	5	0	0	0	0	0	0
2,120	2,160	142	109	76	42	9	0	0	0	0	0	0
2,160	2,200	146	113	80	46	13	0	0	0	0	0	0
2,200	2,240	150	117	84	50	17	0	0	0	0	0	0
2,240	2,280	155	121	88	54	21	0	0	0	0	0	0
2,280	2,320	161	125	92	58	25	0	0	0	0	0	0
2,320	2,360	167	129	96	62	29	0	0	0	0	0	0
2,360	2,400	173	133	100	66	33	0	0	0	0	0	0
2,400	2,440	179	137	104	70	37	4	0	0	0	0	0
2,440	2,480	185	141	108	74	41	8	0	0	0	0	0
2,480	2,520	191	145	112	78	45	12	0	0	0	0	0
2,520	2,560	197	149	116	82	49	16	0	0	0	0	0
2,560	2,600	203	153	120	86	53	20	0	0	0	0	0
2,600	2,640	209	159	124	90	57	24	0	0	0	0	0
2,640	2,680	215	165	128	94	61	28	0	0	0	0	0
2,680	2,720	221	171	132	98	65	32	0	0	0	0	0
2,720	2,760	227	177	136	102	69	36	2	0	0	0	0
2,760	2,800	233	183	140	106	73	40	6	0	0	0	0
2,800	2,840	239	189	144	110	77	44	10	0	0	0	0
2,840	2,880	245	195	148	114	81	48	14	0	0	0	0
2,880	2,920	251	201	152	118	85	52	18	0	0	0	0
2,920	2,960	257	207	157	122	89	56	22	0	0	0	0
2,960	3,000	263	213	163	126	93	60	26	0	0	0	0
3,000	3,040	269	219	169	130	97	64	30	0	0	0	0
3,040	3,080	275	225	175	134	101	68	34	1	0	0	0
3,080	3,120	281	231	181	138	105	72	38	5	0	0	0
3,120	3,160	287	237	187	142	109	76	42	9	0	0	0
3,160	3,200	293	243	193	146	113	80	46	13	0	0	0
3,200	3,240	299	249	199	150	117	84	50	17	0	0	0
3,240	3,280	305	255	205	155	121	88	54	21	0	0	0
3,280	3,320	311	261	211	161	125	92	58	25	0	0	0
3,320	3,360	317	267	217	167	129	96	62	29	0	0	0
3,360	3,400	323	273	223	173	133	100	66	33	0	0	0

Wage Bracket Method Tables for Income Tax Withholding

MARRIED Persons—**MONTHLY** Payroll Period

(For Wages Paid through December 31, 2015)

And the wages are—		And the number of withholding allowances claimed is—										
At least	But less than	0	1	2	3	4	5	6	7	8	9	10
		The amount of income tax to be withheld is—										
$3,400	$3,440	$329	$279	$229	$179	$137	$104	$70	$37	$4	$0	$0
3,440	3,480	335	285	235	185	141	108	74	41	8	0	0
3,480	3,520	341	291	241	191	145	112	78	45	12	0	0
3,520	3,560	347	297	247	197	149	116	82	49	16	0	0
3,560	3,600	353	303	253	203	153	120	86	53	20	0	0
3,600	3,640	359	309	259	209	159	124	90	57	24	0	0
3,640	3,680	365	315	265	215	165	128	94	61	28	0	0
3,680	3,720	371	321	271	221	171	132	98	65	32	0	0
3,720	3,760	377	327	277	227	177	136	102	69	36	2	0
3,760	3,800	383	333	283	233	183	140	106	73	40	6	0
3,800	3,840	389	339	289	239	189	144	110	77	44	10	0
3,840	3,880	395	345	295	245	195	148	114	81	48	14	0
3,880	3,920	401	351	301	251	201	152	118	85	52	18	0
3,920	3,960	407	357	307	257	207	157	122	89	56	22	0
3,960	4,000	413	363	313	263	213	163	126	93	60	26	0
4,000	4,040	419	369	319	269	219	169	130	97	64	30	0
4,040	4,080	425	375	325	275	225	175	134	101	68	34	1
4,080	4,120	431	381	331	281	231	181	138	105	72	38	5
4,120	4,160	437	387	337	287	237	187	142	109	76	42	9
4,160	4,200	443	393	343	293	243	193	146	113	80	46	13
4,200	4,240	449	399	349	299	249	199	150	117	84	50	17
4,240	4,280	455	405	355	305	255	205	155	121	88	54	21
4,280	4,320	461	411	361	311	261	211	161	125	92	58	25
4,320	4,360	467	417	367	317	267	217	167	129	96	62	29
4,360	4,400	473	423	373	323	273	223	173	133	100	66	33
4,400	4,440	479	429	379	329	279	229	179	137	104	70	37
4,440	4,480	485	435	385	335	285	235	185	141	108	74	41
4,480	4,520	491	441	391	341	291	241	191	145	112	78	45
4,520	4,560	497	447	397	347	297	247	197	149	116	82	49
4,560	4,600	503	453	403	353	303	253	203	153	120	86	53
4,600	4,640	509	459	409	359	309	259	209	159	124	90	57
4,640	4,680	515	465	415	365	315	265	215	165	128	94	61
4,680	4,720	521	471	421	371	321	271	221	171	132	98	65
4,720	4,760	527	477	427	377	327	277	227	177	136	102	69
4,760	4,800	533	483	433	383	333	283	233	183	140	106	73
4,800	4,840	539	489	439	389	339	289	239	189	144	110	77
4,840	4,880	545	495	445	395	345	295	245	195	148	114	81
4,880	4,920	551	501	451	401	351	301	251	201	152	118	85
4,920	4,960	557	507	457	407	357	307	257	207	157	122	89
4,960	5,000	563	513	463	413	363	313	263	213	163	126	93
5,000	5,040	569	519	469	419	369	319	269	219	169	130	97
5,040	5,080	575	525	475	425	375	325	275	225	175	134	101
5,080	5,120	581	531	481	431	381	331	281	231	181	138	105
5,120	5,160	587	537	487	437	387	337	287	237	187	142	109
5,160	5,200	593	543	493	443	393	343	293	243	193	146	113
5,200	5,240	599	549	499	449	399	349	299	249	199	150	117
5,240	5,280	605	555	505	455	405	355	305	255	205	155	121
5,280	5,320	611	561	511	461	411	361	311	261	211	161	125
5,320	5,360	617	567	517	467	417	367	317	267	217	167	129
5,360	5,400	623	573	523	473	423	373	323	273	223	173	133
5,400	5,440	629	579	529	479	429	379	329	279	229	179	137
5,440	5,480	635	585	535	485	435	385	335	285	235	185	141
5,480	5,520	641	591	541	491	441	391	341	291	241	191	145
5,520	5,560	647	597	547	497	447	397	347	297	247	197	149
5,560	5,600	653	603	553	503	453	403	353	303	253	203	153
5,600	5,640	659	609	559	509	459	409	359	309	259	209	159
5,640	5,680	665	615	565	515	465	415	365	315	265	215	165
5,680	5,720	671	621	571	521	471	421	371	321	271	221	171
5,720	5,760	677	627	577	527	477	427	377	327	277	227	177
5,760	5,800	683	633	583	533	483	433	383	333	283	233	183
5,800	5,840	689	639	589	539	489	439	389	339	289	239	189
5,840	5,880	695	645	595	545	495	445	395	345	295	245	195
5,880	5,920	701	651	601	551	501	451	401	351	301	251	201
5,920	5,960	707	657	607	557	507	457	407	357	307	257	207
5,960	6,000	713	663	613	563	513	463	413	363	313	263	213
6,000	6,040	719	669	619	569	519	469	419	369	319	269	219
6,040	6,080	725	675	625	575	525	475	425	375	325	275	225
6,080	6,120	731	681	631	581	531	481	431	381	331	281	231

| $6,120 and over | Use Table 4(b) for a **MARRIED person** on page 45. Also see the instructions on page 43. |

Wage Bracket Method Tables for Income Tax Withholding

SINGLE Persons—DAILY Payroll Period

(For Wages Paid through December 31, 2015)

And the wages are—		And the number of withholding allowances claimed is—										
At least	But less than	0	1	2	3	4	5	6	7	8	9	10
		The amount of income tax to be withheld is—										
$0	$15	$0	$0	$0	$0	$0	$0	$0	$0	$0	$0	$0
15	18	1	0	0	0	0	0	0	0	0	0	0
18	21	1	0	0	0	0	0	0	0	0	0	0
21	24	1	0	0	0	0	0	0	0	0	0	0
24	27	2	0	0	0	0	0	0	0	0	0	0
27	30	2	0	0	0	0	0	0	0	0	0	0
30	33	2	1	0	0	0	0	0	0	0	0	0
33	36	3	1	0	0	0	0	0	0	0	0	0
36	39	3	1	0	0	0	0	0	0	0	0	0
39	42	3	2	0	0	0	0	0	0	0	0	0
42	45	3	2	0	0	0	0	0	0	0	0	0
45	48	4	2	1	0	0	0	0	0	0	0	0
48	51	4	3	1	0	0	0	0	0	0	0	0
51	54	5	3	1	0	0	0	0	0	0	0	0
54	57	5	3	2	0	0	0	0	0	0	0	0
57	60	6	3	2	0	0	0	0	0	0	0	0
60	63	6	4	2	1	0	0	0	0	0	0	0
63	66	7	4	2	1	0	0	0	0	0	0	0
66	69	7	5	3	1	0	0	0	0	0	0	0
69	72	7	5	3	2	0	0	0	0	0	0	0
72	75	8	6	3	2	0	0	0	0	0	0	0
75	78	8	6	4	2	1	0	0	0	0	0	0
78	81	9	7	4	2	1	0	0	0	0	0	0
81	84	9	7	5	3	1	0	0	0	0	0	0
84	87	10	7	5	3	2	0	0	0	0	0	0
87	90	10	8	6	3	2	0	0	0	0	0	0
90	93	11	8	6	4	2	1	0	0	0	0	0
93	96	11	9	6	4	2	1	0	0	0	0	0
96	99	12	9	7	5	3	1	0	0	0	0	0
99	102	12	10	7	5	3	1	0	0	0	0	0
102	105	12	10	8	6	3	2	0	0	0	0	0
105	108	13	11	8	6	4	2	1	0	0	0	0
108	111	13	11	9	6	4	2	1	0	0	0	0
111	114	14	11	9	7	5	3	1	0	0	0	0
114	117	14	12	10	7	5	3	1	0	0	0	0
117	120	15	12	10	8	5	3	2	0	0	0	0
120	123	15	13	11	8	6	4	2	0	0	0	0
123	126	16	13	11	9	6	4	2	1	0	0	0
126	129	16	14	11	9	7	4	3	1	0	0	0
129	132	16	14	12	10	7	5	3	1	0	0	0
132	135	17	15	12	10	8	5	3	2	0	0	0
135	138	17	15	13	10	8	6	4	2	0	0	0
138	141	18	16	13	11	9	6	4	2	1	0	0
141	144	18	16	14	11	9	7	4	3	1	0	0
144	147	19	16	14	12	9	7	5	3	1	0	0
147	150	19	17	15	12	10	8	5	3	2	0	0
150	153	20	17	15	13	10	8	6	3	2	0	0
153	156	20	18	15	13	11	9	6	4	2	1	0
156	159	21	18	16	14	11	9	7	4	3	1	0
159	162	22	19	16	14	12	9	7	5	3	1	0
162	165	22	19	17	15	12	10	8	5	3	2	0
165	168	23	20	17	15	13	10	8	6	3	2	0
168	171	24	20	18	15	13	11	8	6	4	2	1
171	174	25	21	18	16	14	11	9	7	4	3	1
174	177	25	22	19	16	14	12	9	7	5	3	1
177	180	26	22	19	17	14	12	10	8	5	3	2
180	183	27	23	20	17	15	13	10	8	6	3	2
183	186	28	24	20	18	15	13	11	8	6	4	2
186	189	28	25	21	18	16	13	11	9	7	4	2
189	192	29	25	22	19	16	14	12	9	7	5	3
192	195	30	26	22	19	17	14	12	10	7	5	3
195	198	31	27	23	19	17	15	13	10	8	6	3
198	201	31	28	24	20	18	15	13	11	8	6	4
201	204	32	28	25	21	18	16	13	11	9	7	4
204	207	33	29	25	21	18	16	14	12	9	7	5
207	210	34	30	26	22	19	17	14	12	10	7	5
210	213	34	31	27	23	19	17	15	12	10	8	6
213	216	35	31	28	24	20	18	15	13	11	8	6
216	219	36	32	28	24	21	18	16	13	11	9	6
219	222	37	33	29	25	21	18	16	14	12	9	7
222	225	37	34	30	26	22	19	17	14	12	10	7

Wage Bracket Method Tables for Income Tax Withholding

SINGLE Persons—**DAILY** Payroll Period

(For Wages Paid through December 31, 2015)

And the wages are—		And the number of withholding allowances claimed is—										
At least	But less than	0	1	2	3	4	5	6	7	8	9	10
		The amount of income tax to be withheld is—										
$225	$228	$38	$34	$31	$27	$23	$19	$17	$15	$12	$10	$8
228	231	39	35	31	27	24	20	17	15	13	11	8
231	234	40	36	32	28	24	21	18	16	13	11	9
234	237	40	37	33	29	25	21	18	16	14	11	9
237	240	41	37	34	30	26	22	19	17	14	12	10
240	243	42	38	34	30	27	23	19	17	15	12	10
243	246	43	39	35	31	27	24	20	17	15	13	10
246	249	43	40	36	32	28	24	20	18	16	13	11
249	252	44	40	37	33	29	25	21	18	16	14	11
252	255	45	41	37	33	30	26	22	19	16	14	12
255	258	46	42	38	34	30	27	23	19	17	15	12
258	261	46	43	39	35	31	27	23	20	17	15	13
261	264	47	43	40	36	32	28	24	20	18	16	13
264	267	48	44	40	36	33	29	25	21	18	16	14
267	270	49	45	41	37	33	30	26	22	19	16	14
270	273	49	46	42	38	34	30	26	23	19	17	15
273	276	50	46	43	39	35	31	27	23	20	17	15
276	279	51	47	43	39	36	32	28	24	20	18	15
279	282	52	48	44	40	36	33	29	25	21	18	16
282	285	52	49	45	41	37	33	29	26	22	19	16
285	288	53	49	46	42	38	34	30	26	22	19	17
288	291	54	50	46	42	39	35	31	27	23	20	17
291	294	55	51	47	43	39	36	32	28	24	20	18
294	297	55	52	48	44	40	36	32	29	25	21	18
297	300	56	52	49	45	41	37	33	29	25	22	19
300	303	57	53	49	45	42	38	34	30	26	22	19
303	306	58	54	50	46	42	39	35	31	27	23	19
306	309	58	55	51	47	43	39	35	32	28	24	20
309	312	59	55	52	48	44	40	36	32	28	25	21
312	315	60	56	52	48	45	41	37	33	29	25	22
315	318	61	57	53	49	45	42	38	34	30	26	22
318	321	61	58	54	50	46	42	38	35	31	27	23
321	324	62	58	55	51	47	43	39	35	31	28	24
324	327	63	59	55	51	48	44	40	36	32	28	25
327	330	64	60	56	52	48	45	41	37	33	29	25
330	333	64	61	57	53	49	45	41	38	34	30	26
333	336	65	61	58	54	50	46	42	38	34	31	27
336	339	66	62	58	54	51	47	43	39	35	31	28
339	341	67	63	59	55	51	47	44	40	36	32	28
341	343	67	63	59	56	52	48	44	40	36	32	29
343	345	68	64	60	56	52	48	45	41	37	33	29
345	347	68	64	60	57	53	49	45	41	37	33	30
347	349	69	65	61	57	53	49	46	42	38	34	30
349	351	69	65	61	58	54	50	46	42	38	34	31
351	353	70	66	62	58	54	50	47	43	39	35	31
353	355	70	66	62	59	55	51	47	43	39	35	32
355	357	71	67	63	59	55	51	48	44	40	36	32
357	359	71	67	63	60	56	52	48	44	40	36	33
359	361	72	68	64	60	56	52	49	45	41	37	33
361	363	72	68	64	61	57	53	49	45	41	37	34
363	365	73	69	65	61	57	53	50	46	42	38	34
365	367	73	69	65	62	58	54	50	46	42	38	35
367	369	74	70	66	62	58	54	51	47	43	39	35
369	371	74	70	66	63	59	55	51	47	43	39	36
371	373	75	71	67	63	59	55	52	48	44	40	36
373	375	76	71	67	64	60	56	52	48	44	40	37
375	377	76	72	68	64	60	56	53	49	45	41	37
377	379	77	72	68	65	61	57	53	49	45	41	38
379	381	77	73	69	65	61	57	54	50	46	42	38
381	383	78	74	69	66	62	58	54	50	46	42	39
383	385	78	74	70	66	62	58	55	51	47	43	39
385	387	79	75	70	67	63	59	55	51	47	43	40
387	389	80	75	71	67	63	59	56	52	48	44	40
389	391	80	76	71	68	64	60	56	52	48	44	41
391	393	81	76	72	68	64	60	57	53	49	45	41

$393 and over	Use Table 8(a) for a **SINGLE person** on page 46. Also see the instructions on page 43.

Wage Bracket Method Tables for Income Tax Withholding

MARRIED Persons—DAILY Payroll Period

(For Wages Paid through December 31, 2015)

And the wages are—		And the number of withholding allowances claimed is—										
At least	But less than	0	1	2	3	4	5	6	7	8	9	10
		The amount of income tax to be withheld is—										
$0	$39	$0	$0	$0	$0	$0	$0	$0	$0	$0	$0	$0
39	42	1	0	0	0	0	0	0	0	0	0	0
42	45	1	0	0	0	0	0	0	0	0	0	0
45	48	1	0	0	0	0	0	0	0	0	0	0
48	51	2	0	0	0	0	0	0	0	0	0	0
51	54	2	0	0	0	0	0	0	0	0	0	0
54	57	2	1	0	0	0	0	0	0	0	0	0
57	60	3	1	0	0	0	0	0	0	0	0	0
60	63	3	1	0	0	0	0	0	0	0	0	0
63	66	3	2	0	0	0	0	0	0	0	0	0
66	69	3	2	0	0	0	0	0	0	0	0	0
69	72	4	2	1	0	0	0	0	0	0	0	0
72	75	4	3	1	0	0	0	0	0	0	0	0
75	78	4	3	1	0	0	0	0	0	0	0	0
78	81	5	3	2	0	0	0	0	0	0	0	0
81	84	5	3	2	0	0	0	0	0	0	0	0
84	87	5	4	2	1	0	0	0	0	0	0	0
87	90	6	4	2	1	0	0	0	0	0	0	0
90	93	6	4	3	1	0	0	0	0	0	0	0
93	96	6	5	3	2	0	0	0	0	0	0	0
96	99	6	5	3	2	0	0	0	0	0	0	0
99	102	7	5	4	2	1	0	0	0	0	0	0
102	105	7	6	4	2	1	0	0	0	0	0	0
105	108	7	6	4	3	1	0	0	0	0	0	0
108	111	8	6	5	3	1	0	0	0	0	0	0
111	114	8	6	5	3	2	0	0	0	0	0	0
114	117	9	7	5	4	2	1	0	0	0	0	0
117	120	9	7	5	4	2	1	0	0	0	0	0
120	123	10	7	6	4	3	1	0	0	0	0	0
123	126	10	8	6	5	3	1	0	0	0	0	0
126	129	11	8	6	5	3	2	0	0	0	0	0
129	132	11	9	7	5	4	2	1	0	0	0	0
132	135	12	9	7	5	4	2	1	0	0	0	0
135	138	12	10	7	6	4	3	1	0	0	0	0
138	141	12	10	8	6	4	3	1	0	0	0	0
141	144	13	11	8	6	5	3	2	0	0	0	0
144	147	13	11	9	7	5	4	2	0	0	0	0
147	150	14	11	9	7	5	4	2	1	0	0	0
150	153	14	12	10	7	6	4	3	1	0	0	0
153	156	15	12	10	8	6	4	3	1	0	0	0
156	159	15	13	11	8	6	5	3	2	0	0	0
159	162	16	13	11	9	7	5	4	2	0	0	0
162	165	16	14	11	9	7	5	4	2	1	0	0
165	168	16	14	12	10	7	6	4	3	1	0	0
168	171	17	15	12	10	8	6	4	3	1	0	0
171	174	17	15	13	10	8	6	5	3	2	0	0
174	177	18	16	13	11	9	7	5	3	2	0	0
177	180	18	16	14	11	9	7	5	4	2	1	0
180	183	19	16	14	12	9	7	6	4	3	1	0
183	186	19	17	15	12	10	8	6	4	3	1	0
186	189	20	17	15	13	10	8	6	5	3	2	0
189	192	20	18	15	13	11	9	7	5	3	2	0
192	195	21	18	16	14	11	9	7	5	4	2	1
195	198	21	19	16	14	12	9	7	6	4	2	1
198	201	21	19	17	14	12	10	8	6	4	3	1
201	204	22	20	17	15	13	10	8	6	5	3	2
204	207	22	20	18	15	13	11	8	6	5	3	2
207	210	23	20	18	16	14	11	9	7	5	4	2
210	213	23	21	19	16	14	12	9	7	6	4	2
213	216	24	21	19	17	14	12	10	8	6	4	3
216	219	24	22	20	17	15	13	10	8	6	5	3
219	222	25	22	20	18	15	13	11	8	6	5	3
222	225	25	23	20	18	16	13	11	9	7	5	4
225	228	25	23	21	19	16	14	12	9	7	5	4
228	231	26	24	21	19	17	14	12	10	7	6	4
231	234	26	24	22	19	17	15	13	10	8	6	5
234	237	27	25	22	20	18	15	13	11	8	6	5
237	240	27	25	23	20	18	16	13	11	9	7	5
240	243	28	25	23	21	18	16	14	12	9	7	5
243	246	28	26	24	21	19	17	14	12	10	7	6
246	249	29	26	24	22	19	17	15	12	10	8	6

Wage Bracket Method Tables for Income Tax Withholding

MARRIED Persons—DAILY Payroll Period

(For Wages Paid through December 31, 2015)

And the wages are—		And the number of withholding allowances claimed is—										
At least	But less than	0	1	2	3	4	5	6	7	8	9	10
		The amount of income tax to be withheld is—										
$249	$252	$29	$27	$24	$22	$20	$18	$15	$13	$11	$8	$6
252	255	30	27	25	23	20	18	16	13	11	9	7
255	258	30	28	25	23	21	18	16	14	12	9	7
258	261	30	28	26	23	21	19	17	14	12	10	7
261	264	31	29	26	24	22	19	17	15	12	10	8
264	267	31	29	27	24	22	20	17	15	13	11	8
267	270	32	29	27	25	23	20	18	16	13	11	9
270	273	32	30	28	25	23	21	18	16	14	11	9
273	276	33	30	28	26	23	21	19	17	14	12	10
276	279	33	31	29	26	24	22	19	17	15	12	10
279	282	34	31	29	27	24	22	20	17	15	13	10
282	285	34	32	29	27	25	22	20	18	16	13	11
285	288	34	32	30	28	25	23	21	18	16	14	11
288	291	35	33	30	28	26	23	21	19	16	14	12
291	294	35	33	31	28	26	24	22	19	17	15	12
294	297	36	34	31	29	27	24	22	20	17	15	13
297	300	36	34	32	29	27	25	22	20	18	15	13
300	303	37	34	32	30	27	25	23	21	18	16	14
303	306	37	35	33	30	28	26	23	21	19	16	14
306	309	38	35	33	31	28	26	24	21	19	17	15
309	312	38	36	33	31	29	27	24	22	20	17	15
312	315	39	36	34	32	29	27	25	22	20	18	15
315	318	39	37	34	32	30	27	25	23	21	18	16
318	321	39	37	35	32	30	28	26	23	21	19	16
321	324	40	38	35	33	31	28	26	24	21	19	17
324	327	41	38	36	33	31	29	26	24	22	20	17
327	330	42	38	36	34	32	29	27	25	22	20	18
330	333	42	39	37	34	32	30	27	25	23	20	18
333	336	43	39	37	35	32	30	28	26	23	21	19
336	339	44	40	38	35	33	31	28	26	24	21	19
339	341	44	41	38	36	33	31	29	26	24	22	19
341	343	45	41	38	36	34	31	29	27	24	22	20
343	345	45	42	38	36	34	32	29	27	25	22	20
345	347	46	42	39	36	34	32	30	27	25	23	20
347	349	46	43	39	37	34	32	30	28	25	23	21
349	351	47	43	39	37	35	32	30	28	26	23	21
351	353	47	44	40	37	35	33	30	28	26	24	21
353	355	48	44	40	38	35	33	31	28	26	24	22
355	357	48	45	41	38	36	33	31	29	26	24	22
357	359	49	45	41	38	36	34	31	29	27	24	22
359	361	49	46	42	39	36	34	32	29	27	25	22
361	363	50	46	42	39	37	34	32	30	27	25	23
363	365	50	47	43	39	37	35	32	30	28	25	23
365	367	51	47	43	39	37	35	33	30	28	26	23
367	369	51	48	44	40	37	35	33	31	28	26	24
369	371	52	48	44	40	38	35	33	31	29	26	24
371	373	52	49	45	41	38	36	33	31	29	27	24
373	375	53	49	45	41	38	36	34	31	29	27	25
375	377	53	50	46	42	39	36	34	32	29	27	25
377	379	54	50	46	42	39	37	34	32	30	27	25
379	381	54	51	47	43	39	37	35	32	30	28	25
381	383	55	51	47	43	40	37	35	33	30	28	26
383	385	55	52	48	44	40	38	35	33	31	28	26
385	387	56	52	48	44	40	38	36	33	31	29	26
387	389	56	53	49	45	41	38	36	34	31	29	27
389	391	57	53	49	45	41	38	36	34	32	29	27
391	393	57	54	50	46	42	39	36	34	32	30	27
393	395	58	54	50	46	42	39	37	34	32	30	28
395	397	58	55	51	47	43	39	37	35	32	30	28
397	399	59	55	51	47	43	40	37	35	33	30	28
399	401	59	56	52	48	44	40	38	35	33	31	28
401	403	60	56	52	48	44	41	38	36	33	31	29
403	405	60	57	53	49	45	41	38	36	34	31	29
405	407	61	57	53	49	45	42	39	36	34	32	29
407	409	61	58	54	50	46	42	39	37	34	32	30

| **$409 and over** | Use Table 8(b) for a **MARRIED person** on page 46. Also see the instructions on page 43. |

Appendix  D

State Income Tax Information

The employee income tax rates for each state are presented below. *Tax Bracket* refers to the year-to-date earnings of the individual. *Marginal Tax Rate* refers to the amount of tax actually collected on each dollar the employee earns and is subject to change as the employee's earnings increase during the year. Note that the tax bracket, although generally pertaining to payroll-related income, also applies to other sources of personal revenue such as interest and dividends.

State	Tax Bracket (Single)	Tax Bracket (Married)	Marginal Tax Rate
Alabama	$0+	$0+	2%
	$500+	$100+	4%
	$3,000+	$6,000+	5%
Alaska	-0-	-0-	0%
Arizona	$0+	$0+	2.59%
	$10,000+	$20,000+	2.88%
	$25,000+	$50,000+	3.36%
	$50,000+	$100,000+	4.24%
	$150,000+	$300,000+	4.54%
California	$0+	$0+	1%
	$7,749+	$15,498+	2%
	$18,371+	$36,472+	4%
	$28,995+	$57,990+	6%
	$40,250+	$80,500+	8%
	$50,689+	$101,738+	9.3%
	$259,844+	$519,688+	10.3%
	$311,812+	$623,624+	11.3%
	$519,867+	$1,000,000+	12.3%
	$1,000,000+	$1,039,374+	13.3%
Colorado	$0+	$0+	4.63%
Connecticut	$0+	$0+	3.0%
	$10,000+	$20,000+	5.0%
	$50,000+	$100,000+	5.50%

State	Tax Bracket (Single)	Tax Bracket (Married)	Marginal Tax Rate
	$100,000+	$200,000+	6.0%
	$200,000+	$400,000+	6.50%
	$250,000+	$500,000+	6.70%
Delaware	$2,000+	$2,000+	2.20%
	$5,000+	$5,000+	3.90%
	$10,000+	$10,000+	4.80%
	$20,000+	$20,000+	5.20%
	$25,000+	$25,000+	5.55%
	$60,000+	$60,000+	6.60%
District of Columbia	$0+	$0+	4.0%
	$10,000+	$10,000+	6.0%
	$40,000+	$40,000+	7.0%
	$60,000+	$60,000+	8.50%
	$350,000+	$350,000+	8.95%
Florida	-0-	-0-	0%
Georgia	$0	$0	1.0%
	$750	$2,000	2.0%
	$2,250	$3,000	3.0%
	$3,750	$5,000	4.0%
	$5,250+	$7,000+	5.0%
	$7,000+	$10,000+	6.0%
Hawaii	$0+	$0+	1.40%
	$2,400+	$4,800+	3.20%
	$4,800+	$9,600+	5.50%
	$9,600+	$19,200+	6.40%
	$14,400+	$28,800+	6.80%
	$19,200+	$38,400+	7.20%
	$24,000+	$48,000+	7.60%
	$36,000+	$48,000+	7.90%
	$48,000+	$96,000+	8.25%
	$150,000+	$300,000+	9.0%
	$175,000+	$350,000+	10.0%
	$200,000+	$400,000+	11.0%
Idaho	$0+	$0+	1.60%
	$1,429+	$2,858+	3.60%
	$2,858+	$5,716+	4.10%
	$4,287+	$8,574+	5.10%
	$5,716+	$11,432+	6.10%
	$7,145+	$14,290+	7.10%
	$10,718+	$21,436+	7.40%
Illinois	$0+	$0+	3.75%
Indiana	$0+	$0+	3.30%

(continued)

State	Tax Bracket (Single)	Tax Bracket (Married)	Marginal Tax Rate
Iowa	$0+	$0+	0.36%
	$1,539+	$1,539+	0.72%
	$3,078+	$3,078+	2.43%
	$6,156+	$6,156+	4.50%
	$13,851	$13,851+	6.12%
	$23,085+	$23,085+	6.48%
	$30,780+	$30,780+	6.80%
	$46,710%+	$46,710%+	7.92%
	$69,255+	$69,255%	8.98%
Kansas	$0+	$0+	2.70%
	$15,000+	$30,000+	4.60%
Kentucky	$0+	$0+	2.0%
	$3,000+	$3,000+	3.0%
	$4,000+	$4,000+	4.0%
	$5,000+	$5,000+	5.0%
	$8,000+	$8,000+	5.8%
	$75,000+	$75,000+	6.0%
Louisiana	$0+	$0+	2.0%
	$12,500+	$12,500+	4.0%
	$50,000+	$100,000+	6.0%
Maine	$5,200+	$10,450+	6.50%
	$20,900+	$41,850+	7.95%
Maryland	$0+	$0+	2.0%
	$1,000+	$1,000+	3.0%
	$2,000+	$2,000+	4.0%
	$3,000+	$3,000+	4.75%
	$100,000+	$150,000+	5.0%
	$125,000+	$175,000+	5.25%
	$150,000+	$225,000+	5.50%
	$250,000+	$300,000+	5.75%
Massachusetts	$0+	$0+	5.20%
Michigan	$0+	$0+	4.25%
Minnesota	$0+	$0+	5.35%
	$25,070+	$36,651+	7.05%
	$82,360+	$145,621+	7.85%
	$154,950+	$258,261+	9.85%
Mississippi	$0+	$0+	3.0%
	$5,000+	$5,000+	4.0%
	$10,000+	$10,000+	5.0%
Missouri	$0+	$0+	1.50%
	$1,000+	$1,000+	2.0%
	$2,000+	$2,000+	2.5%
	$3,000	$3,000+	3.0%

State	Tax Bracket (Single)	Tax Bracket (Married)	Marginal Tax Rate
	$4,000+	$4,000+	3.5%
	$5,000+	$5,000+	4.0%
	$6,000+	$6,000+	4.5%
	$7,000+	$7,000+	5.0%
	$8,000+	$8,000+	5.5%
	$9,000+	$9,000+	6.0%
Montana	$0+	$0+	1.0%
	$2,800+	$2,800+	2.0%
	$5,000+	$5,000+	3.0%
	$7,600+	$7,600+	4.0%
	$10,300+	$10,300+	5.0%
	$13,300+	$13,300+	6.0%
	$17,000+	$17,000+	6.9%
Nebraska	$0+	$0+	2.46%
	$3,000+	$6,000+	3.51%
	$18,000+	$36,000+	5.01%
	$29,000+	$58,000+	6.84%
Nevada	-0-	-0-	0%
New Hampshire	-0-	-0-	0%
New Jersey	$0+	$0+	1.40%
	$20,000+	$20,000+	1.75%
	$35,000+	$50,000+	3.50%
	$40,000+	$70,000+	5.53%
	$75,000+	$80,000+	6.37%
	$100,000+	$150,000+	8.97%
New Mexico	$0+	$0+	1.70%
	$5,500+	$8,000+	3.20%
	$11,000+	$16,000+	4.70%
	$16,000+	$24,000+	4.90%
New York	$0+	$0+	4.00%
	$8,400+	$16,800+	4.50%
	$11,600+	$22,600+	5.25%
	$13,750+	$23,200+	5.90%
	$21,150+	$42,300+	6.45%
	$79,600+	$125,000+	6.65%
	$212,500+	$371,900+	6.85%
	$1,115,850+	$2,231,700+	8.82%
North Carolina	$0+	$0+	5.75%
North Dakota	$0+	$0+	1.22%
	$37,450+	$37,450+	2.27%
	$90,750+	$90,750+	2.52%
	$189,300+	$189,300+	2.93%
	$411,500+	$411,500+	3.22%

(continued)

State	Tax Bracket (Single)	Tax Bracket (Married)	Marginal Tax Rate
Ohio	$0+	$0+	0.53%
	$5,200+	$5,200+	1.06%
	$10,400+	$10,400+	2.11%
	$15,650+	$15,650+	2.64%
	$20,900+	$20,900+	3.17%
	$41,700+	$41,700+	3.70%
	$83,350+	$83,350+	4.23%
	$104,250+	$104,250+	4.91%
	$208,500+	$208,500+	5.33%
Oklahoma	$0+	$0+	0.5%
	$1,000+	$2,000+	1.0%
	$2,500+	$5,000+	2.0%
	$3,750+	$7,500+	3.0%
	$4,900+	$9,800+	4.0%
	$7,200+	$12,200+	5.0%
	$8,700+	$15,000+	5.25%
Oregon	$0+	$0+	5.0%
	$3,350+	$6,700+	7.0%
	$8,400+	$16,800+	9.0%
	$125,000+	$250,000+	9.90%
Pennsylvania	$0+	$0+	3.07%
Rhode Island	$0+	$0+	3.75%
	$60,550+	$60,550+	4.75%
	$137,650+	$137,650+	5.99%
South Carolina	$0+	$0+	0%
	$2,880+	$2,880+	3.0%
	$5,760+	$5,760+	4.0%
	$8,640+	$8,640+	5.0%
	$11,520+	$11,520+	6.0%
	$14,400+	$14,400+	7.0%
South Dakota	-0-	-0-	0%
Tennessee	-0-	-0-	0%
Texas	-0-	-0-	0%
Utah	$0+	$0+	5.0%
Vermont	$0+	$0+	3.55%
	$37,450+	$62,600+	6.80%
	$90,750+	$151,200+	7.80%
	$189,300+	$230,450+	8.80%
	$411,500+	$411,500+	8.95%
Virginia	$0+	$0+	2.0%
	$3,000+	$3,000+	3.0%
	$5,000+	$5,000+	5.0%
	$17,000+	$17,000+	5.75%

State	Tax Bracket (Single)	Tax Bracket (Married)	Marginal Tax Rate
Washington	-0-	-0-	0%
West Virginia	$0+	$0+	3.0%
	$10,000+	$10,000+	4.0%
	$25,000+	$25,000+	4.5%
	$40,000+	$40,000+	6.0%
	$60,000+	$60,000+	6.5%
Wisconsin	$0+	$0+	4.0%
	$11,090+	$14,790+	5.84%
	$22,190+	$29,580+	6.27%
	$244,270+	$325,700+	7.65%
Wyoming	-0-	-0-	0%

Appendix  E

State Revenue Department Information

Alabama

Alabama Department of Revenue
50 North Ripley Street
Montgomery, AL 36104
334-242-1300
www.revenue.alabama.gov

Alaska

Juneau Commissioner's Office
P.O. Box 110400
Juneau, AK 99811-0400
907-465-2300
www.revenue.state.ak.us

Arizona

Arizona Department of Revenue
P.O. Box 29009
Phoenix, AZ 85038-9009
602-255-2060
www.azdor.gov

Arkansas

Department of Finance and Administration
1509 West 7th Street
Little Rock, AR 72201
501-682-7290
www.dfa.arkansas.gov

California

Employment Development Department
P.O. Box 826880
Sacramento, CA 94280-0001
888-745-3886
www.edd.ca.gov

Colorado

Colorado Department of Revenue
1375 Sherman St.
Denver, CO 80261
(303) 238-7378
www.colorado.gov/revenue

Connecticut

Department of Revenue Services
25 Sigourney Street
Hartford, CT 06106
860-297-5962
www.ct.gov/drs

Delaware

Delaware Department of Revenue
Carvel State Office Building
820 North French Street
Wilmington, DE 19801
302-577-8200
www.revenue.delaware.gov

Florida

Florida Department of Revenue
5050 West Tennessee Street
Tallahassee, FL 32399
800-352-3671
dor.myflorida.com/dor

Georgia

Georgia Department of Revenue
1800 Century Blvd. NE, Suite 12000
Atlanta, GA 30345-3205
877-423-6711, option #1
dor.ga.gov/withholding-0

Hawaii

Department of Taxation (Oahu District)
Princess Ruth Keelikolani Building
830 Punchbowl Street
Honolulu, HI 96813-5094
808-587-4242
www.tax.hawaii.gov

Idaho

Idaho State Tax Commission
800 E. Park Blvd., Plaza IV
Boise, ID 83712-7742
(208) 334-7660
www.tax.idaho.gov

Illinois

Illinois Department of Revenue
James R. Thompson Center - Concourse Level

100 West Randolph Street
Chicago, IL 60601-3274
800-732-8866
www.revenue.state.il.us

Indiana

Indiana Department of Revenue
Indianapolis Taxpayer Services
100 N. Senate IGCN Rm N105
Indianapolis, IN 46206
317-233-4016
www.in.gov/dor

Iowa

Iowa Department of Revenue
Hoover State Office Building, 4th Floor
1305 E. Walnut
Des Moines, IA 50319
800-367-3388
www.iowa.gov/tax

Kansas

Kansas Department of Revenue
915 SW Harrison St.
Topeka, KS 66612-1588
785-368-8222
www.ksrevenue.org

Kentucky

Kentucky Department of Revenue
501 High Street
Frankfort, KY 40601-2103
502-564-4581
www.revenue.ky.gov/wht

Louisiana

Louisiana Department of Revenue
617 North Third Street
Baton Rouge, LA 70802
855-307-3893
www.rev.state.la.us

Maine

Maine Revenue Services
51 Commerce Drive
Augusta, ME 04330
207-626-8475
www.maine.gov/revenue

Maryland

Comptroller of Maryland
80 Calvert Street
P.O. Box 466
Annapolis, MD 21404-0466
800-638-2937
www.taxes.marylandtaxes.com

Massachusetts

Massachusetts Department of Revenue
P.O. Box 7010
Boston, MA 02204
800-392-6089
www.mass.gov/dor

Michigan

Michigan Department of Treasury
Lansing, MI 48922
517-373-3200
www.michigan.gov/treasury

Minnesota

Minnesota Department of Revenue
600 North Robert St.
St. Paul, MN 55101
651-556-3000
www.revenue.state.mn.us

Mississippi

Mississippi Department of Revenue
500 Clinton Center Drive
Clinton, MS 39056
601-923-7700
www.dor.ms.gov

Missouri

Missouri Department of Revenue
Harry S. Truman State Office Building
301 West High Street
Jefferson City, MO 65101
573-751-3505
www.dor.mo.gov

Montana

Montana Department of Revenue
Sam W. Mitchell Building
125 N. Roberts, 3rd Floor
Helena, MT 59601-4558
406-444-6900
www.revenue.mt.gov

Nebraska

Nebraska Department of Revenue
Nebraska State Office Building
301 Centennial Mall South
Lincoln, NE 68508
402-471-5729
www.revenue.nebraska.gov

Nevada

Nevada Department of Taxation
1550 College Parkway, Suite 115
Carson City, NV 89706
775-684-2000
www.tax.nv.gov

New Hampshire

New Hampshire Department of Revenue Administration
Governor Hugh Gallen State Office Park
109 Pleasant Street (Medical & Surgical Building)
Concord, NH 03301
603-230-5000
www.revenue.nh.gov

New Jersey

New Jersey Division of Taxation
Taxation Building
50 Barrack Street, 1st Floor Lobby
Trenton, NJ 08695
609-292-6400
www.nj.gov/treasury/taxation

New Mexico

Taxation & Revenue New Mexico
1100 South St. Francis Drive
Santa Fe, NM 87504
505-827-0700
www.tax.newmexico.gov

New York

New York State Department of Taxation and Finance
Building 9
W. A. Harriman Campus
Albany, NY 12227
518-485-6654
www.tax.ny.gov

North Carolina

North Carolina Department of Revenue
501 N. Wilmington St
Raleigh, NC 27604
877-252-3052
www.dornc.com

North Dakota

Office of State Tax Commissioner
600 E Boulevard Ave., Dept. 127
Bismarck, ND 58505-0599
701-328-1248
www.nd.gov/tax

Ohio

Ohio Department of Taxation
4485 Northland Ridge Blvd.
Columbus, OH 43229
888-405-4039
www.tax.ohio.gov

Oklahoma

Oklahoma Tax Commission
Connors Building, Capitol Complex
2501 North Lincoln Boulevard
Oklahoma City, OK 73194
405-521-3160
www.tax.ok.gov

Oregon

Oregon Department of Revenue
955 Center St. NE
Salem, OR 97301-2555
503-378-4988
www.oregon.gov/dor

Pennsylvania

Pennsylvania Department of Revenue
Strawberry Square Lobby, First Floor
Fourth and Walnut Streets
Harrisburg, PA 17128
717-783-1405
www.revenue.state.pa.us

Rhode Island

Rhode Island Division of Taxation
One Capitol Hill
Providence, RI 02908
401-574-8941
www.tax.ri.gov

South Carolina

South Carolina Department of Revenue
300A Outlet Pointe Blvd
Columbia, SC 29210
803-896-1450
www.sctax.org

South Dakota

South Dakota Department of Revenue
445 E Capitol Avenue
Pierre, SD 57501-3185
800-829-9188
dor.sd.gov

Tennessee

Tennessee Department of Revenue
Andrew Jackson Building
500 Deaderick Street
Nashville, TN 37242
615-253-0600
www.tn.gov/revenue

Texas

Texas Comptroller of Public Accounts
Lyndon B. Johnson State Office Building
111 East 17th Street
Austin, TX 78774
800-252-5555
www.window.state.tx.us

Utah

Utah State Tax Commission
210 North 1950 West
Salt Lake City, UT 84134
801-297-2200
www.tax.utah.gov

Vermont

Vermont Department of Taxes
133 State Street
Montpelier, VT 05633
802-828-2505
www.state.vt.us/tax

Virginia

Virginia Department of Taxation
1957 Westmoreland Street
Richmond, VA 23230
804-367-8037
www.tax.virginia.gov

Washington

Washington State Department of Revenue
Executive Office
P.O. Box 47450
Olympia, WA 98504-7450
800-647-7706
www.dor.wa.gov

West Virginia

West Virginia Department of Revenue
Taxpayer Services
1206 Quarrier Street
Charleston, WV 25301
800-982-8297
www.wva.state.wv.us/wvtax

Wisconsin

Wisconsin Department of Revenue
2135 Rimrock Road
Madison, WI 53713
608-266-2772
www.revenue.wi.gov

Wyoming

Wyoming Department of Revenue
122 West 25th Street, 2nd Floor West
Cheyenne, WY 82002-0110
307-777-5200
http://revenue.wyo.gov

Appendix F

Payroll Certification Information

Two levels of payroll certification are available from the American Payroll Association: Certified Payroll Professional (CPP) and Fundamental Payroll Certification (FPC). The following are the criteria for eligibility for each certification.

Certified Payroll Professional

The Certification Board of the American Payroll Association (APA) requires that payroll professionals fulfill **ONE** of the following criteria before they take the Certified Payroll Professional Examination.

Criteria 1

The payroll professional has been practicing a total of three (3) years out of the five (5) years preceding the date of the examination. The practice of payroll is defined as direct or related involvement in at least one of the following:

- Payroll Production, Payroll Reporting, Payroll Accounting
- Payroll Systems and Payroll Taxation
- Payroll Administration
- Payroll Education/Consulting

Criteria 2

Before a candidate takes the examination, the payroll professional has been employed in the practice of payroll as defined in Criteria 1 for at least the last 24 months, *and* has completed within the last 24 months, ALL of the following courses within **ONE** of the following three options offered by the APA:

Option 1

- Payroll Practice Essentials (three-day course: live or virtual) and
- Intermediate Payroll Concepts (two-day course: live or virtual) and
- Advanced Payroll Concepts (two-day course: live or virtual) and
- Strategic Payroll Practices (two-day course: live or virtual)

Option 2

- Payroll 101: Foundations of Payroll Certificate Program and
- Payroll 201: The Payroll Administration Certificate Program

Option 3

- Certified Payroll Professional Boot Camp

Criteria 3

Before a candidate takes the examination, the payroll professional has been employed in the practice of payroll as defined in Criteria 1, for at least the last 18 months, has **obtained the Fundamental Payroll Certification (FPC)** *and* has completed within the last 18 months ALL of the following courses within **ONE** of the following two options offered by the APA:

Option 1

- Intermediate Payroll Concepts (two-day course: live or virtual) and
- Advanced Payroll Concepts (two-day course: live or virtual) and
- Strategic Payroll Practices (two-day course: live or virtual)

Option 2

- Payroll 201: The Payroll Administration Certificate Program

Fundamental Payroll Certification (FPC)

The Fundamental Payroll Certification (FPC) is open to all those who wish to demonstrate a baseline of payroll competency. The FPC is designed for:

- Entry-Level Payroll Professionals
- Sales Professionals/Consultants serving the payroll industry
- Systems Analysts/Engineers writing payroll programs
- Payroll Service Bureau Client Representatives

APA membership is not required to take the FPC examination.

Contact Information

- APA's Certification Department
- 210-226-4600
- certification@americanpayroll.org

See website for examination handbook links, study group information, training resources, and other information.

- www.americanpayroll.org/certification

Glossary

401(k): A defined contribution plan in which employees may contribute either a specific amount or a percentage of their gross pay on a pre-tax or post-tax basis through payroll deductions.

403(b): A retirement plan designed for employees of certain nonprofit organizations.

A

Accrual: An accounting method in which revenues and expenses are recorded when they occur, not necessarily when any cash is exchanged.

ADA: The Americans with Disabilities Act of 1990.

Additional Medicare tax: An additional 0.9% Medicare tax levied upon employees who earn in excess of $200,000 per year, as mandated by the Affordable Care Act.

Adjusting entries: Journal entries created at the end of an accounting period to allocate income and expenses to the proper accounts.

Allocation: The storing of costs in one account and then dividing the costs based on a quantifiable activity.

Annual Total Compensation Report: A list of all compensation that an employee earns per year, including (but not limited to) salary, commissions, bonuses, and all fringe benefits; for example, health insurance, employer contributions to the employee's retirement plan, life insurance, and tuition reimbursement.

ARRA: The American Recovery and Reinvestment Act of 2009.

Asset: An item of value that a business uses in the course of its operations and from which it expects future economic benefit.

ATRA: The American Taxpayer Relief Act of 2012.

Automated Clearing House (ACH): The electronic network of financial institutions in the United States through which monetary transactions are transmitted in batches.

B

Balance sheet: A financial statement that lists the totals in the assets, liabilities, and owners' equity accounts of a firm for a specific date.

Benefit analysis: A calculation of the costs and benefits of a company, department, project, or employee.

Biweekly payroll: A pay frequency in which employees are paid 26 times per year.

C

Cafeteria plan: A benefit plan pursuant to Section 125 of the Internal Revenue Code that allows employees to designate specific amounts to be deducted from their payroll to pay for health and child-care expenses on a pre-tax basis.

Certified payroll: A report mandated for certain federal government contracts that verifies the accuracy of labor expenses incurred during completion of contract-related activities.

Charitable contributions: A payroll deduction in which an employee designates a specific amount of gross pay be paid to a community, religious, educational, or other IRS-designated charitable organization.

COBRA: The Consolidated Omnibus Budget Reconciliation Act of 1985.

Combination pay: Employee compensation that reflects two or more discrete pay bases during the same pay period.

Commission: Employee compensation paid upon completion of a task, often pertaining to sales-based activities.

Compensatory (comp) time: Paid time off granted to employees instead of paid overtime.

Consumer Credit Protection Act: Federal law that pertains to the percentage of wage garnishment that may be withheld from employee pay to satisfy legal obligations.

Copeland Anti-Kickback Act: Federal legislation enacted in 1934 that prohibits a federal contractor or subcontractor from inducing an employee to forego a portion of the wages guaranteed by the contract.

Credit: The right side of the T-account.

Current Tax Payment Act of 1943: Federal law enacted in 1943 that required employers to submit a timely remittance to the government of any taxes withheld from the employee pay.

D

Daily payroll: A pay frequency in which employees are paid each business day.

Davis-Bacon Act of 1931: Federal legislation enacted in 1931 that requires federal contractors to pay employees an amount commensurate with the prevailing local wage.

Debit: The left side of the T-account.

Defined benefit: A company-sponsored pension plan that uses the employee's salary and length of service to compute the amount of the benefit.

Defined contribution: A retirement plan to which the employee, and sometimes the employer, make a regular contribution.

Departmental classification: The division of payroll-related costs by employee function or organizational department.

Direct deposit: The electronic transmission of employee wages from the employer to the employee's account at a financial institution.

Disposable income: The amount of employee wages remaining after withholding federal, state, and local taxes.

Document destruction: The act of destroying documents that contain sensitive payroll and employee information.

DOMA: The Defense of Marriage Act of 1996, which was repealed in 2013.

Draw: A loan against future earnings that employees will repay from commissions.

Due care: The caution that a reasonable person would exercise to avoid being charged with negligence.

E

EEOC: The Equal Employment Opportunity Commission.

EFTPS: The Electronic Federal Tax Payment System.

ERISA: The Employee Retirement Income Security Act of 1974.

Escheatment: The transfer of personal property to the employee's state of residence when no legal owner claims the property.

ESOP: Employee Stock Ownership Plan.

Ethics: An individual's definition of right and wrong.

Exempt: An employee who is not subject to the overtime provisions of the Fair Labor Standards Act.

Expense: The cost of doing business, which may contain both cash and non-cash amounts.

F

FICA: The Federal Insurance Contributions Act of 1935.

File maintenance: The application of all transactions, including any necessary modifications, to an employee's file.

File security: The protection of sensitive payroll information by restricting access and securely storing files.

Firing: Involuntary termination of employment.

Flexible Spending Account: A tax-advantaged employee spending account as designated by Internal Revenue Code.

FLSA: The Fair Labor Standards Act of 1935.

FMLA: The Family Medical Leave Act.

Foreign Account Tax Compliance Act (FATCA):   Federal law that regulates the income tax withholdings of foreign employees.

Form 940:   The Employer's Annual Federal Unemployment Tax Return.

Form 941:   The Employer's Quarterly Federal Tax Return.

Form 944:   The Employer's Annual Federal Tax Return.

Form W-2:   Wage and Tax Statement.

Form W-3:   Transmittal of Wage and Tax Statements.

Fringe benefit: A company-sponsored benefit that supplements an employee's salary, usually on a non-cash basis.

FUTA: Federal Unemployment Tax Act of 1939.

FWH: Federal Withholding.

G

Garnishments: A legal procedure for the collection of money owed to a plaintiff through payroll deductions.

General Journal: A chronological record of a firm's financial transactions.

General Ledger: A record of a firm's financial transactions, grouped by account.

Gross pay: The amount of wages paid to an employee based on work performed, prior to any deductions for mandatory or voluntary deductions.

H

Health savings account (HSA):   A savings account that provides tax advantages for individuals with health plans that have high deductions via pre-tax payroll deductions.

HIPAA: The Health Insurance Portability and Accountability Act of 1996.

Hiring packet: A package of forms that a firm issues to new employees; for example, Form W-4, Form I-9, health insurance enrollment, etc.

Hourly: Wage determination based on the number of complete and partial hours during which an employee performs work-related tasks.

Hundredth-hour: The division of an hour into 100 increments used to compute employee wages as accurately as possible.

I

I-9:   The Employment Eligibility Verification.

Incentive stock options (ISOs):   A type of employee compensation in which the employee receives a firm's stock on a tax-advantaged basis.

Income statement: A financial report used to determine a firm's net income by computing the difference between revenues and expenses for a period; also known as the Profit and Loss statement.

Independent contractor: An individual who contracts to do work for a firm using his or her own tools and processes without being subject to direction by a firm's management.

Integrity: Possessing honesty and high moral principles.

Internal control: A firm's process of maintaining efficiency and effectiveness, work quality, accurate and reliable financial reports, and legal compliance.

IRA: Individual Retirement Account.

IRCA: Immigration Reform and Control Act of 1986.

ISO: Incentive Stock Options.

L

Labor distribution: The classification of a firm's labor by internally designated classifications.

Labor reports: A report that contains details about the number of hours worked and wages paid to employees.

Liability: A financial obligation of a firm arising from assets or revenues received in advance of future sale or service.

Local income taxes: Payroll taxes levied by a city or county government.

Local taxes: Payroll taxes levied by a city or county government.

Lookback period: The time frame used by the IRS to determine the payroll tax deposit schedule for a firm.

M

Mandated deductions: A post-tax payroll deduction that is ordered by a court of law or is otherwise nonvoluntary in nature.

Mandatory deductions: Payroll deductions over which the employee has no control; for example, taxes, garnishments, and certain retirement contributions.

Medicare tax: A payroll tax mandated to be paid by all employees of a firm to fund the Medicare program.

Minimum wage: The minimum hourly amount that employers may legally pay to employees.

Monthly depositor: A firm that must deposit its Federal Income Tax and FICA payroll withholdings and contributions on a monthly basis, based on the lookback period.

Monthly payroll: A pay frequency in which employees are paid 12 times per year.

N

Net pay: An employee's wages or salary less all mandatory and voluntary deductions.

New hire reporting: A process by which a firm notifies governmental authorities of any new hires shortly after the hire date.

Next business day depositor: A semi-weekly schedule depositor whose payroll tax liabilities exceed $100,000 for any pay period.

Nonexempt: An employee who is subject to all overtime provisions of the Fair Labor Standards Act; generally, an hourly employee.

O

Objectivity: Making decisions that are free from bias or subjectivity.

On-call time: The nonwork time that an employee is expected to be available for workplace-related emergencies.

OSHA: The Occupational Safety and Health Act of 1970.

Outsourced vendor: A party external to a firm that provides goods and/or services.

Overtime: Time that an employee works beyond his or her normal working hours.

Owner's equity: The financial investment and any accumulated profits or losses of the owner of a firm.

P

Pay advice: A document detailing employee pay and deductions that either accompanies the paycheck or notifies the employee of the direct deposit of net pay.

Paycard: A debit card issued to employees that contains electronically transmitted wages.

Pay period: The recurring period during which a firm collects employee labor data and pays employees in accordance with wage and/or salary agreements.

Payroll allocation: The total of all compensation that a firm pays its employees, divided into functional units or other internal designations.

Payroll audit: An examination of a firm's payroll records to determine legal compliance.

Payroll deposits: The firm's remittance of payroll taxes through the EFTPS or via check.

Payroll review: Verification of payroll accuracy for a period.

Payroll tax reports: Reports that an employer must file with governmental authorities that offer details of the period's tax liability.

Percentage method: A method used to compute an employee's income tax liability that involves computations based on the employee's wages, marital status, pay frequency, and number of withholdings claimed on Form W-4.

Period-end adjustments: General Journal entries used in accrual-based accounting to recognize appropriate costs and revenues during a period.

Piece rate: Employee compensation based on the production of a unit or completion of an action during a specified time period.

Posting: Transferring the details of Journal entries to the General Ledger accounts.

Privacy Act of 1974: Protected employees by removing personal identifiers from payroll records and restricting access to personnel records.

Prove: Ensuring that the sum of the rows of the payroll register equals the sum of the columns.

PRWOR: Personal Responsibility and Work Opportunity Reconciliation Act of 1996.

Public interest: A process reflecting the transparency and public accountability of accounting records.

Publication 15: The Employer's Tax Guide published by the Internal Revenue Service.

Q

Quarter-hour: The division of an hour into 15-minute increments as a means of computing hourly work.

R

Regulation E: Federal legislation protecting consumers who use electronic funds transfer to access their net pay.

Remit: To send money in payment of an obligation.

Resignation: Voluntary termination of employment.

Revenue: Money earned by a firm in the course of conducting its principal business operations.

Review process: Examination and analysis of accounting records to ensure accuracy and completeness.

Rule: The accounting practice in which the final totals of financial reports are double-underlined.

S

Salary: A fixed amount paid to an employee on a regular basis, often expressed in annual terms.

Schedule B: The Report of Tax Liability for Semi-weekly Depositors.

Semimonthly payroll: The payroll frequency in which employees are paid 24 times per year.

Semi-weekly depositor: A firm that must deposit its federal income tax and FICA payroll withholdings and contributions within three days of the pay date, based on the lookback period.

SEP: A Simplified Employee Pension individual retirement account.

Separation of duties: An internal control method in which payroll duties are spread among two or more employees.

SIMPLE: The Savings Incentive Match Plan for Employees.

SIMPLE 401(k):   A retirement plan for employees of companies that employ 100 or fewer workers. An annual investment limit of $11,500 exists for this type of retirement plan.

Sleep time: Time spent sleeping at an employee's premises as a part of an employee's work schedule.

Sleeping time: Employees that are required to be on duty for 24 hours or more may be allowed up to 5 hours of sleep without a reduction in pay.

Social Security tax: A tax paid by both employers and employees that is used to fund the Social Security program.

SOX: The Sarbanes–Oxley Act of 2002.

State income taxes: Income taxes levied by a state government on employee payroll.

State taxes: Income taxes levied by a state government on employee payroll.

Statute of limitations: The time limit attached to certain legal actions.

Statutory deductions: Payroll deductions mandated by law.

Statutory employee: A special class of employees who run their own business but must be treated as employees for tax reasons.

Supporting documents: Paperwork that supports the payroll calculations; for example, time sheets and the payroll register.

SUTA: The State Unemployment Tax Act of 1939.

T

Tax matching: The process in FICA taxes where the employer and employee pay the same amount of tax for the wages earned during a pay period.

Tax rate: The percentage to be used when computing certain types of taxes.

Tax remittance: The payment of a firm's payroll tax liability.

Tax table: A set of pre-calculated tables issued by federal and state governments to facilitate income tax computations for employee payroll.

Termination: Ceasing employment with a firm.

Time card: A record of the time worked during a period for an individual employee.

Tipped employees: An employee who engages in an occupation in which he or she customarily and regularly receives more than $30 per month in tips.

Tipped wage: The base wage paid to employees who earn the majority of their income through customer tips.

Total: Computing the sum of each row and each column of the payroll register.

Travel time: Time that an employee spends traveling for the employer's benefit.

Trial balance: An internal accounting statement in which the accountant determines that the debits equal the credits for the amounts in the General Ledger.

U

Union dues: Amounts paid on a regular basis by employees who are required to be part of a union as a condition of their employment.

USERRA: The Uniformed Services Employment and Reemployment Rights Act of 1994.

V

Voluntary deductions: Amounts that an employee elects to have deducted from his or her paycheck and remitted to a third party; for example, charitable contributions, savings bond purchases, and health club fees.

VPN: Virtual Private Network.

W

W-4:   The Employee Withholding Allowance Certificate.

Wage base: The maximum annual salary that is subject to tax liability, commonly used for Social Security, FUTA, and SUTA taxes.

Wage-bracket method: The use of tax tables located in federal and state publications that facilitate the determination of employee income tax deductions for payroll.

Wait time: The time that an employee is paid to wait on the employer's premises for the benefit of the employer.

Walsh–Healey Public Contracts Act: Legislation enacted in 1936 that required employers working on federal contracts in excess of $10,000 to pay employees the federal minimum wage and follow the overtime provisions of the Fair Labor Standards Act.

Weekly payroll: The payroll frequency in which employees are paid 52 times per year.

Workers' compensation: A mandatory insurance policy paid by employers that provides wage replacement and medical benefits to employees who are injured in the course of their employment.

Index